ve

UN S

Ben van Berkel

tudio

Caroline Bos

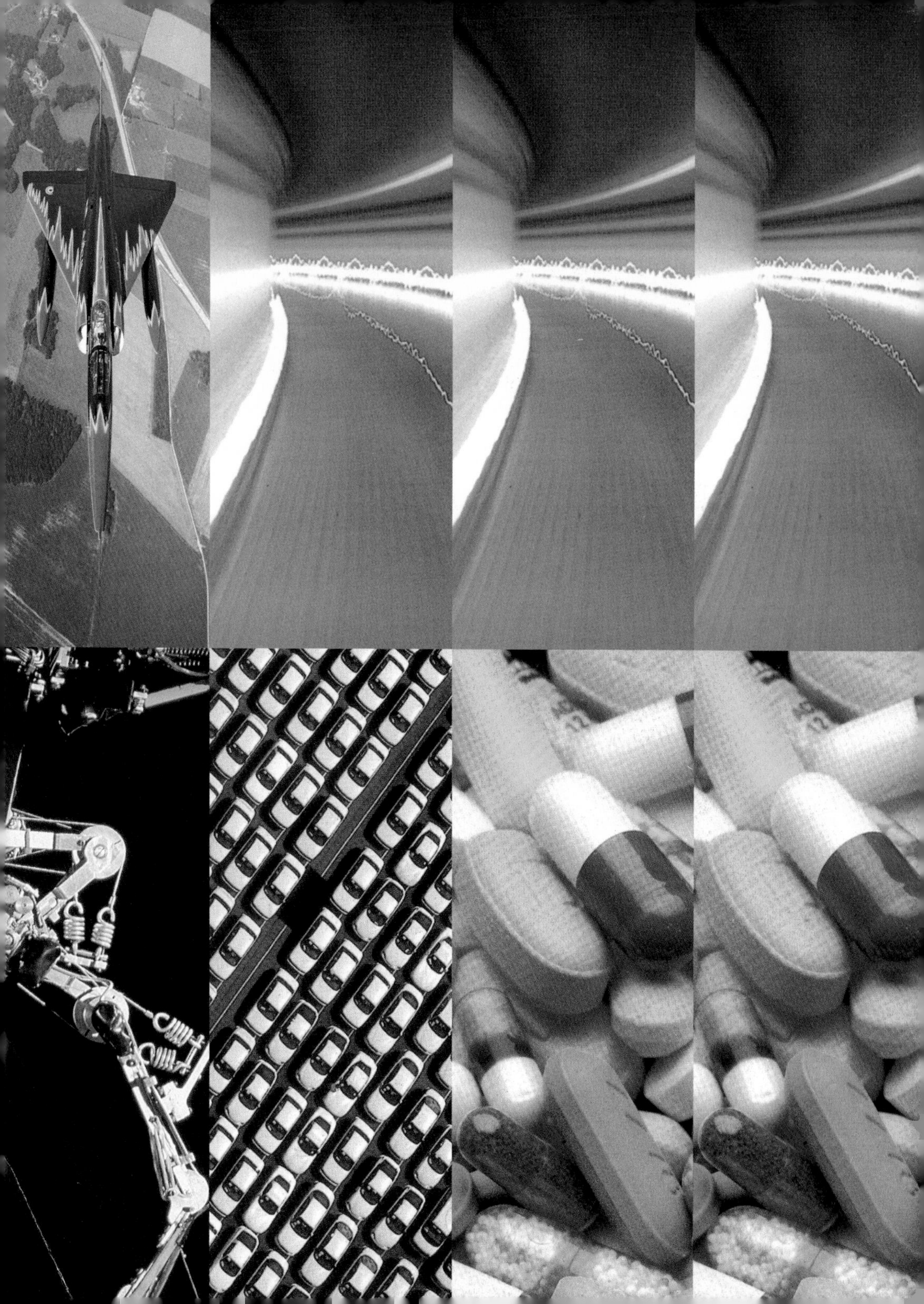

① Imag

ination

liquid politic

Sex Warhol Television
Disney Fellini Resonance
God Pornography Therapy
Tarkowski Politics XTC
Money Bergman Barbie
UFO Mao New Age Kinsey
Fashion Frank Zappa
Fear Megalomania Diana
Versace Le Corbusier
Totalitarianism Stalin
Inspiration New Age
Fundamentalism Global-
ism Hollywood Sign
Madonna Utopianis Drugs

Trance Drugs Space age Science fiction Black Holes Alienation Connectedness Complexity Funkadelic Riefenstahl Fractals Porsche Chaos Cyberpunk Dali Feminine Sony Individuality Medical science Therapy Fashion Oblivion End of world scenario Pippi Glamour Scandal Marilyn Monroe Celebrity Nietzsche Nintendo Serialism

CONTENTS

Move

Introduction

Move is about redefining organisational structures on all levels. Structures are no longer seen as the representation of homogeneous, linear systems, but as process fields of materialisation. Structures are scaleless, subject to evolution, expansion, inversion and other contortions and manipulations. Structures are free to assume different identities; they are becoming endless. Move introduces inclusiveness in the design approach; an integration of construction, circulation and programme. Inclusiveness allows fragmentation and difference to be absorbed into a coherent, continuous approach, abandoning the strategies of fragmentation and collage. A five-year long architectural production period has gone into this book. At the heart of this architectural production are two questions and three topics. The first question is: how can we instrumentalise the global imagination into contemporary organisational structures? The second question is: how can we instrumentalise the new public, mediated space into contemporary architectural effects? The three topics concern the ways in which the three enduring ingredients of architecture - the imagination, techniques and effects - are converted into architecture today. These three topics serve as the structuring element of Move.

Part 1 Imagination examines the new role of the architect in the context of changing patterns. How does the architectural imagination respond to these changes? The search for a new policy is a response to new circumstances. The subtitle of this book, Liquid Politic, indicates that diffuse and fluid processes have a political dimension that profoundly affects the making. The design and production of buildings results from dynamic, highly evolved, interactive processes. Architects have drifted into these new working models without articulating their own policy. Large public projects in which infrastructure and programmes come together to form a new kind of urban node demand an architectural approach which is radically different from the traditional method of urban planning that consisted of shifting about disjointed units. The new inclusive approach entails the comprehensive and seamless assemblage of construction, programme and circulation. ***Part 2 Techniques*** has as its subject the impact of new techniques on the design and production of architecture. During a long process, which began in the eighteenth century, traditional techniques have increasingly been transformed into machines and have thus lost their impact on the conceptualisation of architecture. As a result, the discipline is in danger of losing its specific knowledge, its own envisioning practices. We have catalogued three techniques that instrumentalise the contemporary phenomenon of mediation in an architectural manner. Underlying these three architectural techniques are the two meta-techniques dealing with mediation and communication: Network and Spin. Mediation breeds spin - the practice that enables the effective communication of complex policies to a mass audience. In an age in which politics are dissociated from fixed values, spin-doctors are becoming the real politicians. Who will be the real architects? New techniques must be invented to allow the architectural imagination to find relevance in contemporary circumstances - and to communicate its policy. ***Part 3 Effects*** addresses two effects of the combination of the contemporary imagination and contemporary techniques. The re-thinking of organisational structures is at issue. The objective of finding a model that embodies the inclusive approach in combination with the use of new computational techniques results in the manipulation of architectural ingredients as malleable, orientable and non-orientable structures. The surface as the object of transformative strategies is being replaced by three-dimensional, at times even four-dimensional, principles. The topological continuum is investigated with the aid of knotting concepts, spring structures, effects such as faciality and mathematical models such as the Klein Bottle. As the subtitle Radiant Synthetic suggests, these new effects share two characteristics with effects in other fields varying from natural phenomena to fashion: they are synthetically produced by the more or less violent interaction of elements and their fall-out is vast.

We would like to thank our Move co-workers: Sonja Cabalt, Machteld Kors, Francesca de Chatel, Kate Simms, Guus Kemme, John Simons, Cor Rosbeek and Remco Bruggink. Thanks also to the UN Studio (Van Berkel & Bos) staff members past and present for their talent and commitment; special thanks to the management, co-ordination and design teams. Thanks also to all those, friends and others, who have taken time to discuss ideas with us and who have shared (or challenged) our interests: Greg Lynn, Sylvia Lavin, Cynthia Davidson, Peter Eisenman, Phyllis Lambert, Ralph Lerner, Frank Gehry, Henry Cobb, Philip Johnson, Terence Riley, Sanford Kwinter, Jeffrey Kipnis, Stan Allen, Jesse Reiser, Elizabeth Diller, Riccardo Scofidio, Beatriz Colomina, Mark Wigley, Claudia Gould, Andrea Schwann, Kenneth Frampton, Aaron Betsky, Joseph Giovannini, Karl Chu, Robert Somol, Charles Jencks, Cecil Balmond, Daniel and Nina Libeskind, Sir Norman Foster, Mohson Mostafavi, Homa Fardjadi, Zaha Hadid,

Patrick Schumacher, Brett Steele, Michael Hensel, Johan Bettum, Kivi Sotamaa, Alejandro Zaera-Polo, Farshid Moussavi, Leon van Schaik, Zahava Elenberg, Peter Brew, Ross Benson, Kurt Forster, Pipilotti Rist, Harm Lux, Jaime Salazar, Manuel Gausa, Richard Levene, Fernando Màrquez Cecilia, Monica Gili, Bernard Cache, Marc Emery, Axel Sowa, Rowan Moore, Raymond Ryan, Lucy Bullivant, John Welsh, Toyo Ito, Kazuo Seijima, Arata Isozaki, Rumiko Ito, Nikolaus Kuhnert, Angelika Schnell, Dietmar Steiner, Hans Hollein, Wolf Prix, Günther Domenig, Kristin Feireiss, Hans Jürgen Commerell, Helge Achenbach, Christophe Egret, Bart Lootsma, Mariëtte van Stralen, Hans van Dijk, Pi de Bruijn, Rem Koolhaas, Matthijs Bouw, Joost Meuwissen, Petra Blaisse, Thomas van Leeuwen, Reyn van der Lugt, Wiel Arets, Vedran Mimica, Ole Bouman, Kees Christiaanse, Rudi Fuchs, Janny Rodermond, Wim and Hetty Laverman, Hans and Tonny Wilbrink, Michel and Greet Schoonderbeek, Fons and Vera Asselbergs, Martine de Maeseneer, Joop Linthorst, Riek Bakker, Michael van Gessel, Hans van der Ven, Wim Hartman, Tjerk Ruimschotel, Adriaan Geuze, Hans Reynders, Cor Maartense, Adri Duyvestein, Jan Doets, Jan Garvelink and many others.

Imagination

Liquid politic

The necessity to become a little mad is not part of an architectural education. To dare to put forward ideas, to offer up visions and to realise the unexpected requires pushing the imagination. But how crazy should we get? Not too much: people still have to use the costly stuff that we produce. Not too little: let's be less boring in the future. The architectural imagination is a combination of utility and philosophy. It responds to specific needs and situations, but keeps in mind that architecture is also a thought about how we want to live in our world. These two, utility and philosophy, should not drift apart. The secret is to unify them and to always let them be mutually enforcing. How do we reconcile deep thinking with utility? Be curious, always ask 'do you have an idea for us?' Be interested in other philosophies and in fantasy, play and experiment. Extend and deepen reality. Be prolific. Keep churning out the works so as to get better and so as to grow into your own thinking. Above all, know the world in which we are living and be skilful at developing combinatorial models to get the most out of every technique, effect and idea. Today, the architectural imagination is influenced by the dynamics of society and the simultaneity of local difference and global homogeneity, which have profoundly changed our thinking about structures. The ways in which the world is organised have liquefied on many levels. Systems comprising politics, economy, demographics and the natural sciences are increasingly thought of as amorphous and lawless assemblages of energetic principles lacking clearly delineated borders. The study of living organisms generates understandings that apply equally to economic regimes and to the development of urban settlements. The transformation of the democratic, western culture of nations into a system of denationalised processes is paralleled by a similar paradigm shift in the way we regard the body, where chemical processes take the place of organs as the prime constituent. As different thought systems infiltrate each other, presumed stratified orders disappear on many levels. Inherent energetic forces shape all organisa-

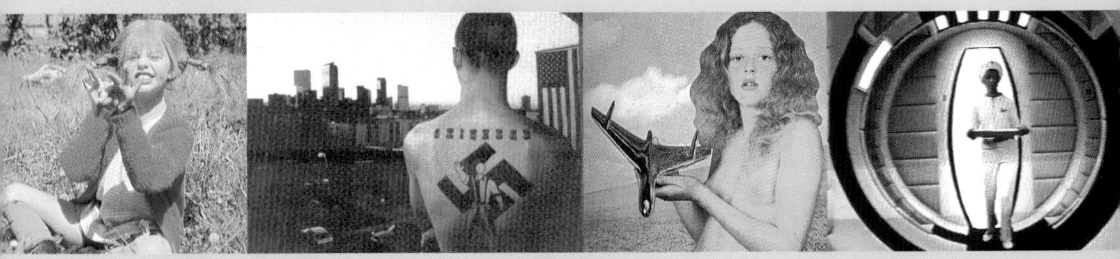

tional structures. Structures no longer represent homogeneous, linear systems, but process fields of materialisation. These are based on spatial and mate-

rial devices and their dissipative nature allows energies incorporating genetic, chemical, economic, cultural and political information to flow in and out.
In using liquidity in the architectural imagination, contemporary phenomena come to be treated as symptoms whose sense must be sought in the forces that produce them. These underlying forces modify the topology of organisational structures - the challenge for architecture is to define these forces in its own specific terms. Techniques are developed which help inventory, intuit and imagine the new liquid states as architectural entities. 'Liquid architecture' does not consist of mobilising the liquid; this is not about generating projects with fluent, melting shapes. The architecture of the liquid does not refer to the formal materialisation of a building, instrument, or fixed structure. It refers rather to triggering the imagination by pointing to something that is itself external to

architecture and works towards structures generated by a complex field of multiple forces. In the same way that a cosmologist uses his knowledge of the universe to visualise situations so far removed that they are beyond the reach of telescopes, as in the theories of the big bang and black holes, the architect can access remote and complex situations by combining specific knowledge and visualising techniques.

When used to organise contemporary structures, this process constitutes a policy. Policy today means a critically generated engagement with the situation in which the production of architecture takes place, with the architectural imagination and the collective imagination of public life, and with the techniques that make the interrelations between these categories visible.

Architects formulate their policy by activating the imagination and using new, enabling techniques. No capital is needed - only the will and the capacity for fabrication. Imagination is itself empowering. As in politics and economy, power in the building industry is operational and consensual. There are no predestined losers. So 'let's throw the dice'... Repetition and habitual activation turn imagination into belief. Not static per se and not identified with a solid goal, policy is the affirmation of choice and vision.

The new concept of the architect

The architect is going to be the fashion designer of the future. Learning from Calvin Klein, the architect will be concerned with dressing the future, speculating, anticipating coming events and holding up a mirror to the world. The architect's practice will be organised as a limitless virtual studio, like Andy Warhol's Factory scattered; a network of superstars. Network practice extends existing forms of co-operation with clients, investors, users and technical consultants to include design engineers, finance people, management gurus, process specialists, designers and stylists. The new architectural network studio is a hybrid mixture of club, atelier, laboratory and car plant, encouraging plug-in professionalism. As in contemporary manufacturing, efficiency and diversity, continuity and differentiation are inseparable, with customised Audis and Volkswagens rolling off the same production line. Making use of new technologies, the network architect benefits from the increased transferability of knowledge. The will to invent is fundamental, ensuring that the basic values of the discipline, ranging from geometry to materialisation, are always evolving. Because all experiments require proof of evidence, the experimental practice continually oscillates between the abstract world of ideas and the physical world. New procedures and new techniques are tested out in site-specific, project-based experiments.

The actual design process of architecture will be like making a film: invisible research and business culminating into a short time of intense action, when mixed teams decide how to fit out a new city, a new airport. Time is on the architect's side. The correlative approach to plan development makes use of the mapping of time to reveal relations in informational data and logistics. Developing specific visualising techniques, re-thinking virtual and material organisational structures, engaging public space, public forces and the public imagination, puts the architect once more at the centre of his own world. New concepts of control transform the untenable position of master builder into a public scientist. As an expert on everyday public information, the architect collects information that is potentially structuring, co-ordinates it, transforms it and offers ideas and images for the organisation of public life in an endless, seamless system.

Deep Plan

The new architect faces a new assignment. Increasingly involved as the architect is in the realisation of bridges, motorways and urban revitalisation plans, alongside houses, offices and public buildings, the traditional procedures of practice are becoming inadequate. Urban nodes and infrastructure are some of the most important questions facing architecture at the moment. In response, public network projects are developed using a strategy we call Deep Planning. Throughout history, urban strategies have been related to social-political strategies - from the Neo-Platonic Renaissance city, to the Haussmannisation of Paris, the equal-potential structure of the grid and Deconstructivist fragmentation.

Equally politic is the move from the traditional interpretation of the urban planning process as a shifting-around of volumes on a planar surface to a completely new approach based on new techniques and a new co-operative work strategy. Using combinations of digital techniques, an integral approach to projects combining infrastructure, urbanism and various programmes has been developed. This approach requires the extended overview of the network to detect correspondences and overlaps between the locations, parties and programmes involved. The procedure of the Deep

Plan involves generating a situation-specific, dynamic, organisational structure plan with the aid of parameter-based techniques. The in-depth, interactive nature of the Deep Plan means that it incorporates economics, infrastructure, programme and construction in time. The method demonstrates where different topographical areas produce shared values. As a result, relations instead of the optimisation of individual data form the parameters of the project, generating potentials that no single, individual interest could have engendered. This approach is utilitarian in that it deals with real economic and public conditions, but this is crucially an interactive, operational utility. Needs are not met in a reactive way, but are drawn together and transformed, leading to re-negotiations of the relations between the parties. This approach endorses a specific societal policy by centring on collective interests. A simple, opportunist response to what is being asked

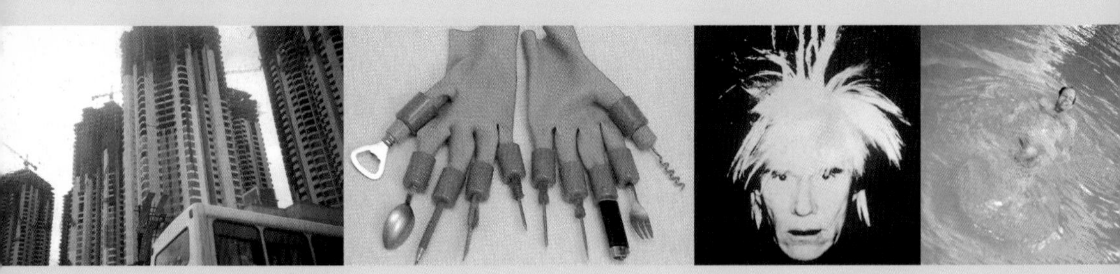

is impossible in a large-scale, multi-client project of considerable complexity. And a preconceived idea of urbanism preceding the specifics of location, programme or users has become redundant. Instead, the project emerges interactively. Structures emerging in this way operate through living forces at physical and public levels; they are performance envelopes. They are in motion as long as those forces are in motion and contain no hidden meaning independent of those forces.

Deep Planning also includes an emerging articulation of a policy of mobility and the incorporation into architecture of aspects of duration and time. This aspect is related to the decoding of public space caused by intensive cross-cultural rituals and communication systems. The combined use of automated design and animation techniques enables a working method that integrates questions of user movement, urban planning, construction and the potential for programme to develop at certain points in this web. New computational techniques make it possible to

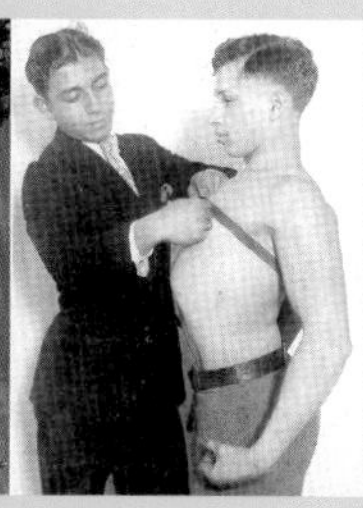

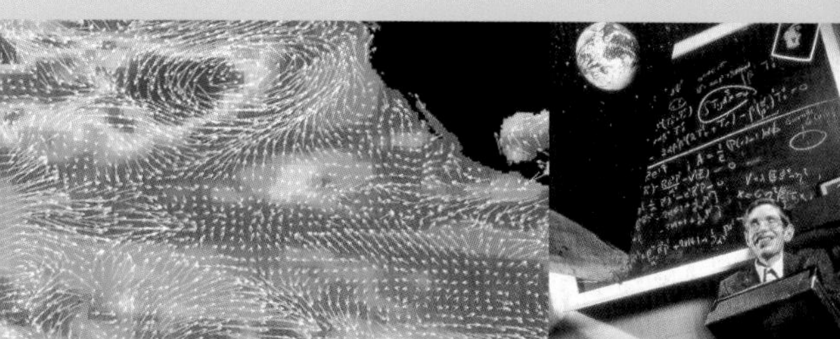

lay bare a multiplicity of experiences and activate this knowledge in new ways. When mapping movement patterns, the time-programme relationship is

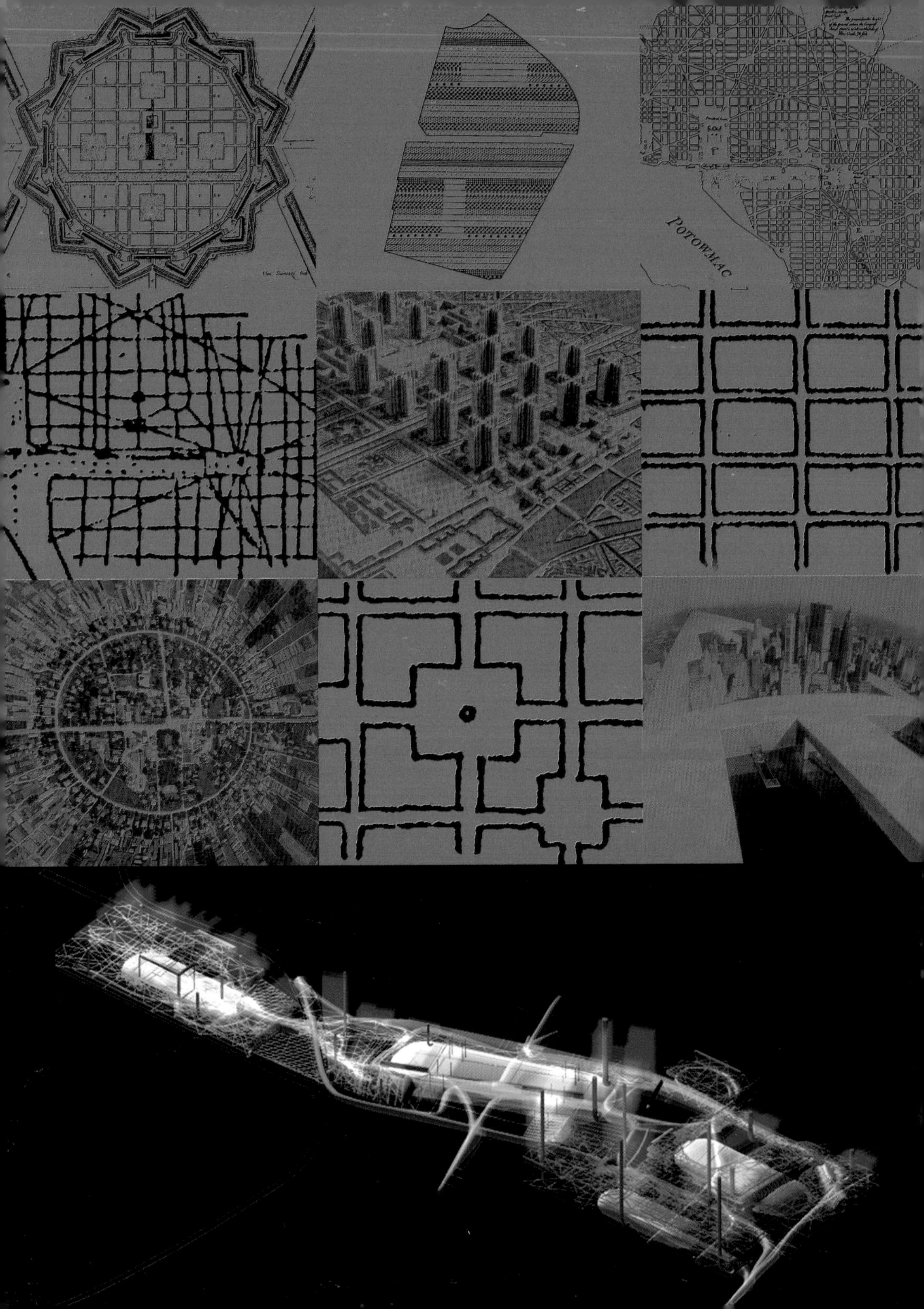
POTOWMAC

not compartmentalised, but reflects synchronous, continuous time. Temporal conditions are connected to programmatic themes in a simulation of the non-segmented manner in which time flows in a real situation. Separate infrastructure layers may be classified, calculated and tested individually, to be subsequently interwoven to achieve both effective flux and effective interaction. The Deep Plan offers a new abstraction, which, unlike the reductionism of an urbanism based on Euclidean geometry, is proliferating, unfolding and generative, re-activating public life in urban planning.

The scandal-filled life of the Erasmus Bridge has turned it into a typical late-twentieth century media star. Adoration, public humiliation, health problems, a spell in rehabilitation; the bridge has seen it all. Does it hurt to see architecture dragged down to this level? Or is it better that architecture be part of mass culture rather than stay in its ivory tower? Shouldn't architecture engage people?

Baby-blue monster

'Mobile Forces' was the accompanying battle cry, as the Erasmus Bridge was meant from its earliest, most sketchy beginnings to incorporate the multitude of changeable public, urban, economic, political and constructive considerations that direct all large-scale projects.

The bridge is the product of an integrated design approach. Construction, urbanism, infrastructure and public functions are given shape in one comprehensive gesture. To achieve fluent working relationships between the different parties involved, the whole design and building process took place in Auto-Cad, enhancing control on all levels and significantly deepening the insight of the architect in the technical design. During preliminary and definitive design phases, the design was continuously refined. The five differently

shaped concrete piers, the railings, the landings, the details of fixtures and joints and the maintenance equipment were all integrally designed.

Rising to a height of 139 metres and spanning a width of 800 metres, the bridge over the river Maas forms an orientation point within the city. The asymmetric pylon with its bracket construction in sky-coloured steel has 2000 different facades. The long, diagonal cables physically and metaphorically link Rotterdam South to the City Centre. Thirty-two stays attached to the top of the pylon and eight backstays keep the construction in balance. Five concrete piers carry the steel deck that is divided into different traffic lanes: two footpaths, two cycle tracks, tram rails and two carriageways for cars.

Sweeping concrete staircases lead up from the parking garage on the north side, extending the curve of the landing to pedestrian level and contributing to the public quality of the bridge as a square in the sky.

At night, when the bridge is reduced to a silhouette, a special light project emphasises the interior of the bridge, with its bundled cables rising high above the water as a dematerialised reflection of its daytime identity.

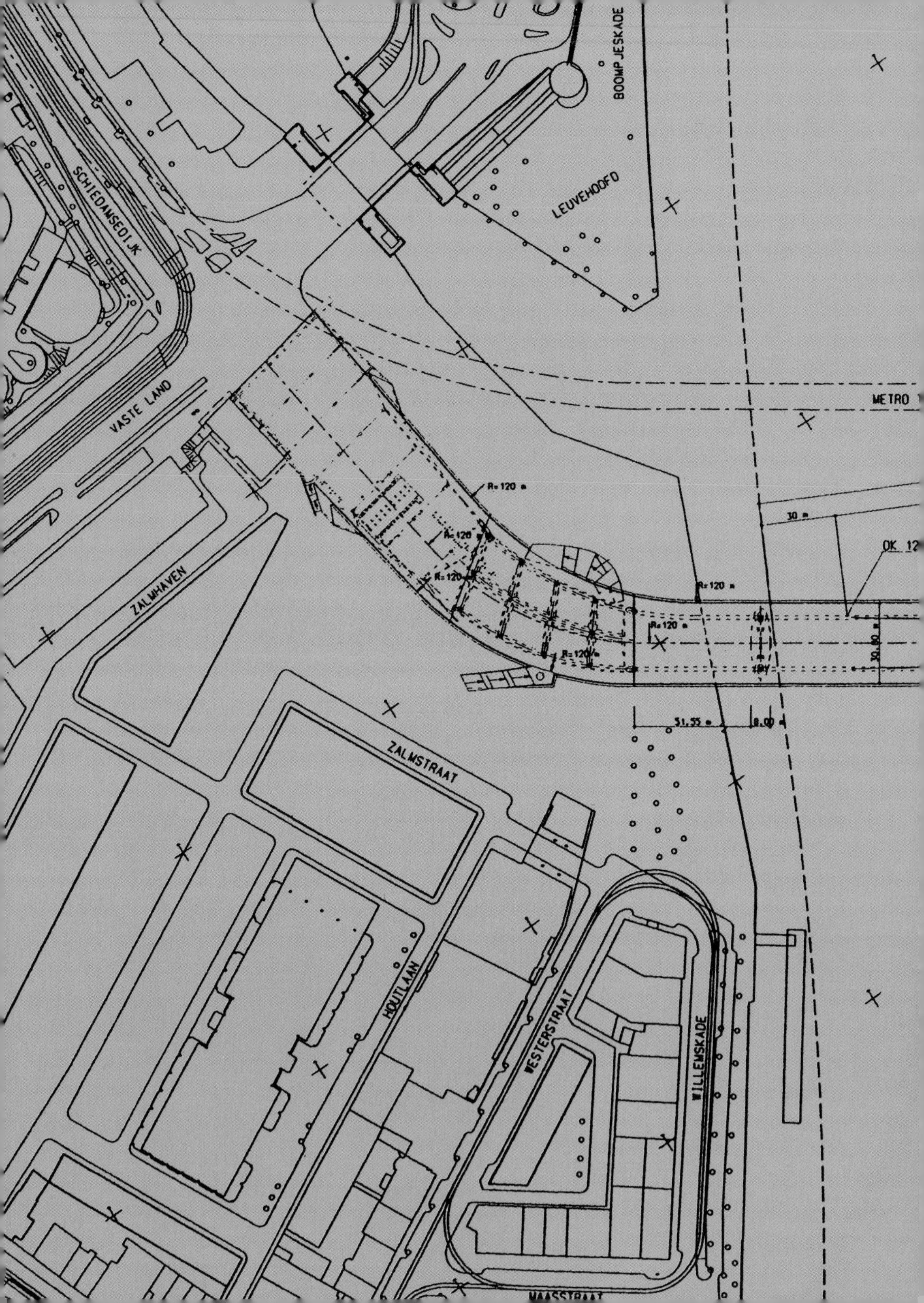
BOOMPJESKADE
LEUVEHOOFD
SCHIEDAMSEDIJK
VASTE LAND
METRO
R=120 m
30 m
ZALMHAVEN
ZALMSTRAAT
51,55 m
8,00 m
HOUTLAAN
WESTERSTRAAT
WILLEMSKADE

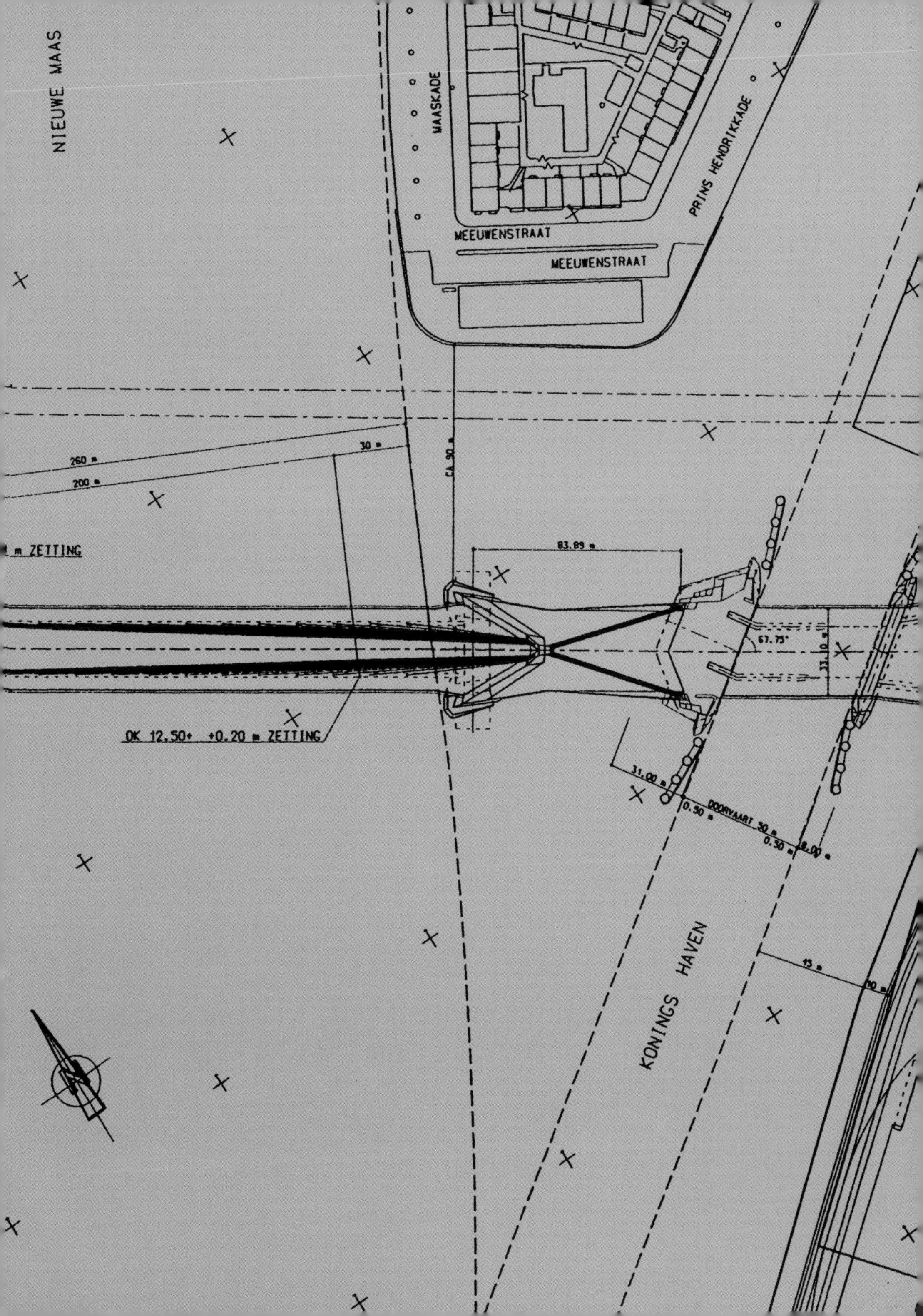
NIEUWE MAAS
MAASKADE
PRINS HENDRIKKADE
MEEUWENSTRAAT
MEEUWENSTRAAT
260 m
200 m
30 m
CA 90 m
m ZETTING
83.89 m
67.75°
33.10 m
OK 12.50+ +0.20 m ZETTING
31.00 m
0.50 m
DOORVAART 30 m
0.30 m
8.00 m
KONINGS HAVEN
45 m
10 m

St Paul's Cathedral at Abidjan,

Ivory Coast, 1983-1985

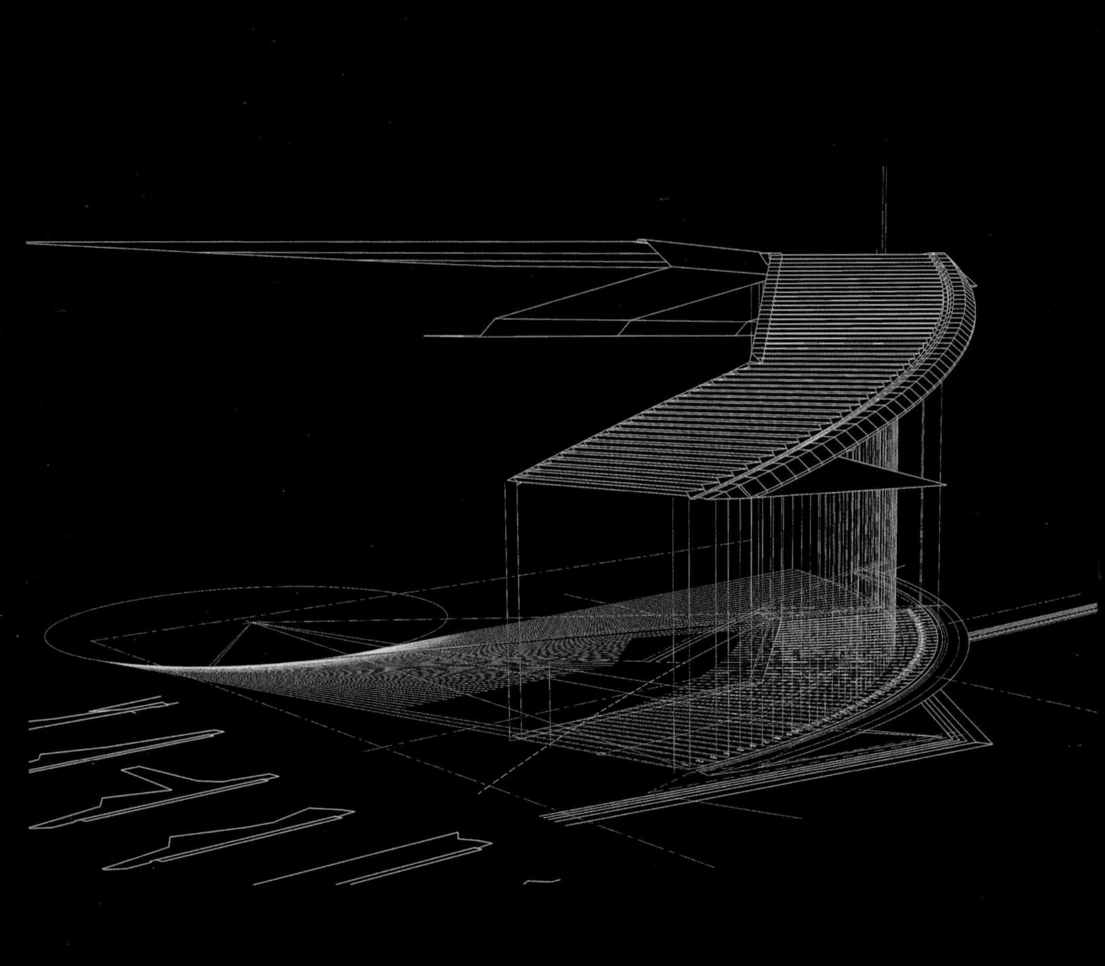

connection bridge deck to car par

Binnenstad
Maritiem

SPA

point of application

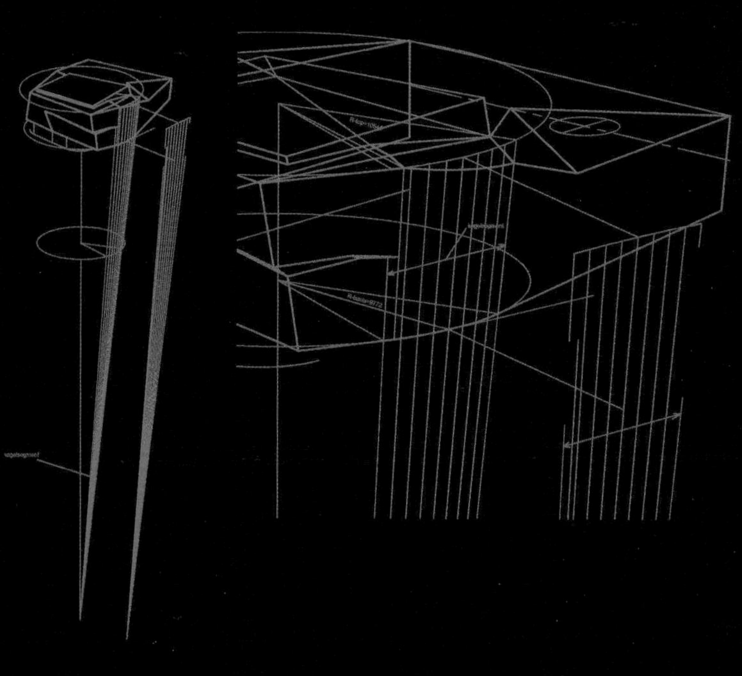

curvature of bridge deck modifies

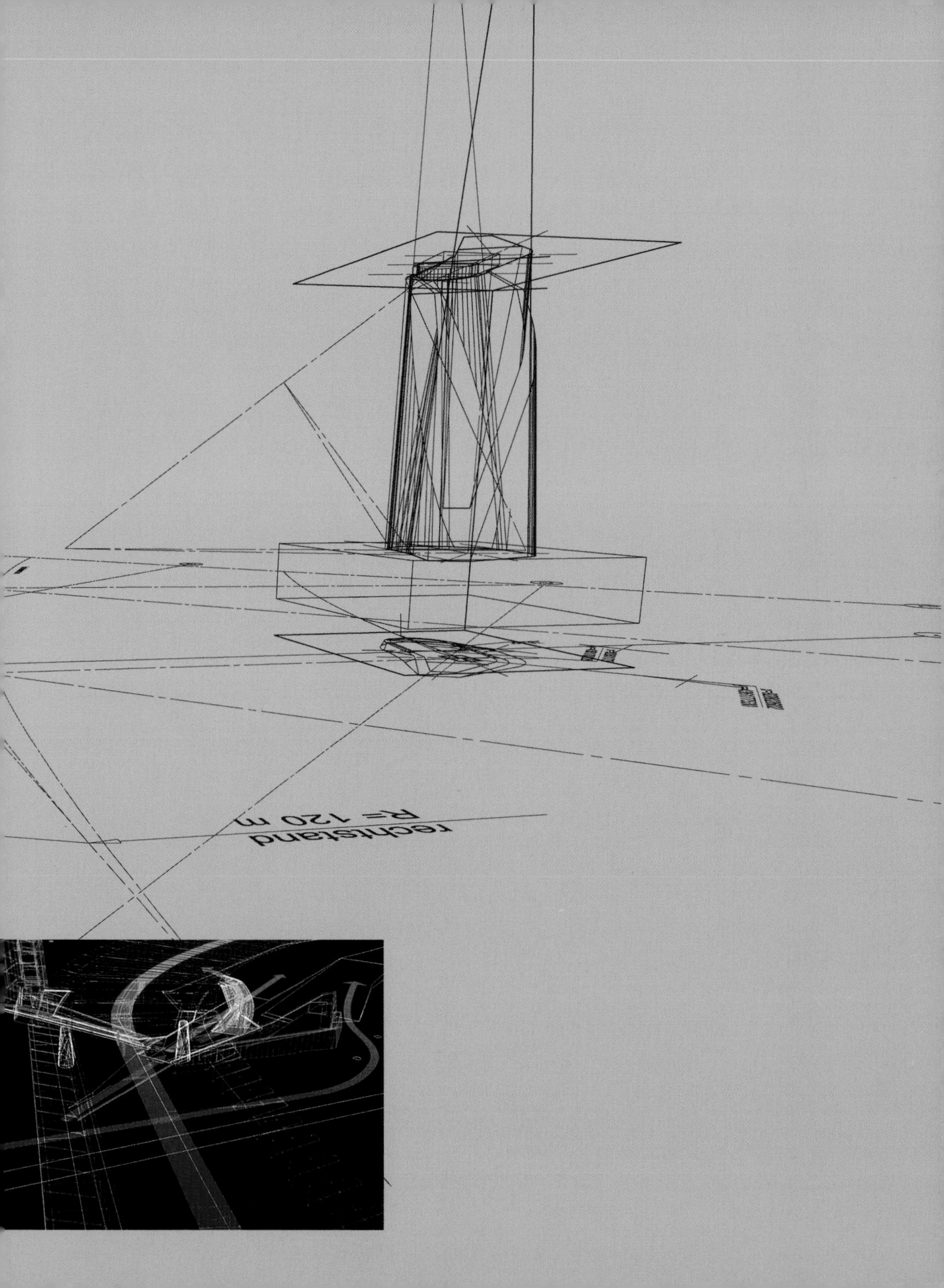
rechtstand
R= 120 m

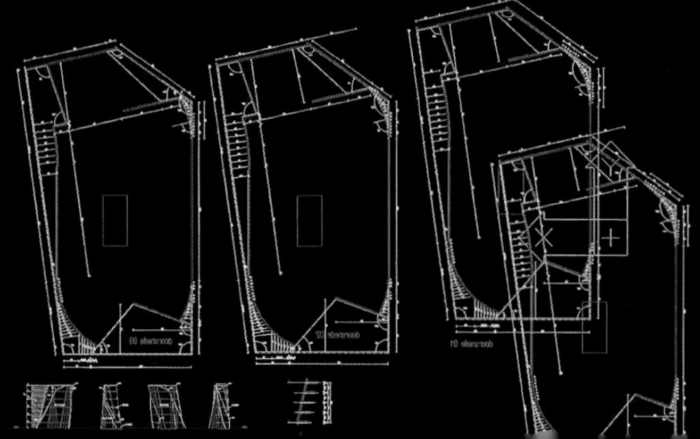

HEEREMA
GROOTINT
HEEREMA
GROOTINT

HEEREMA
GROOTINT
HEEREMAC
Derrick Barge - 102
Lift Cap. 2x 6000
HEEREMA
GROOTINT

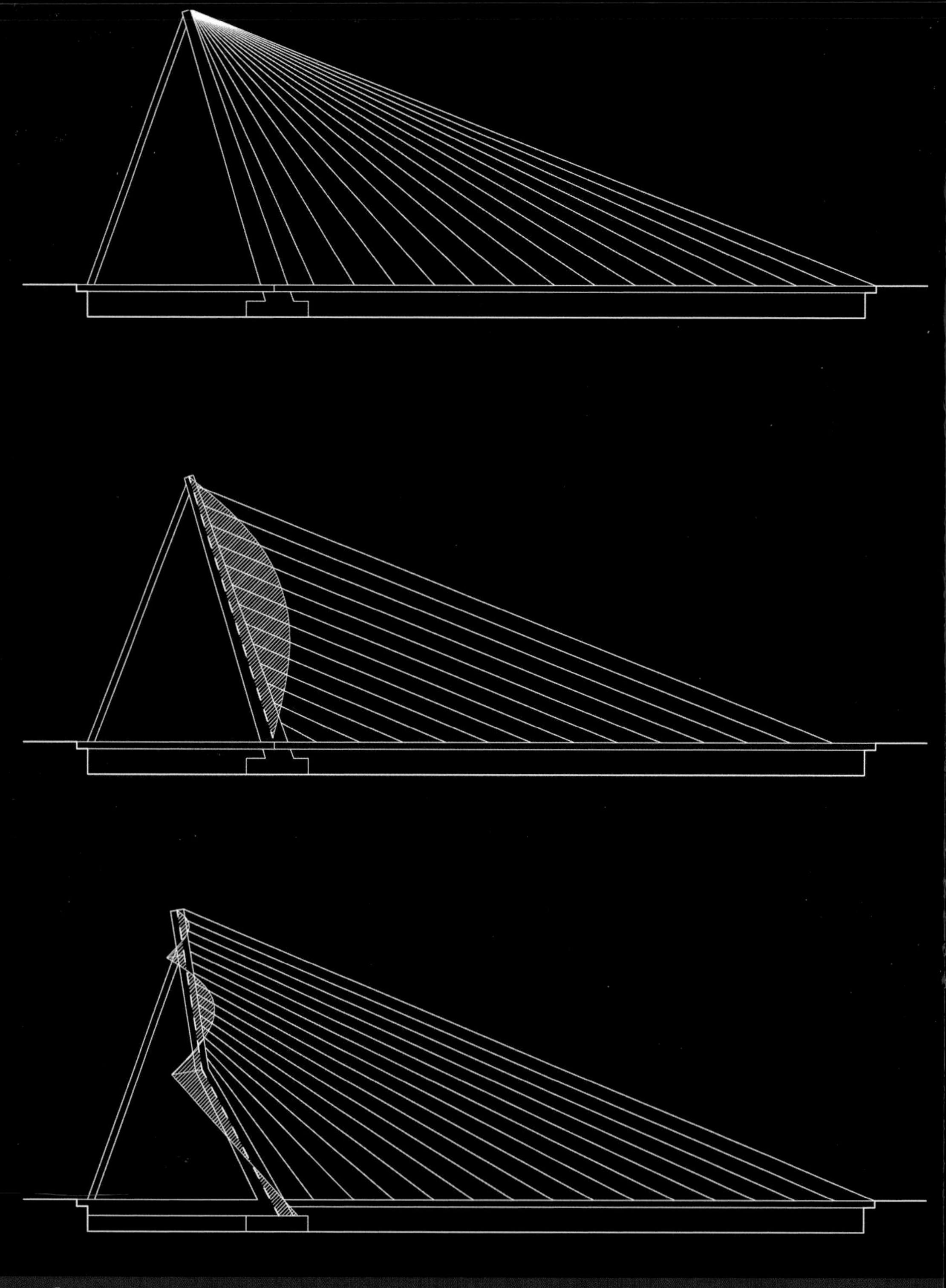

forces structuring pylon

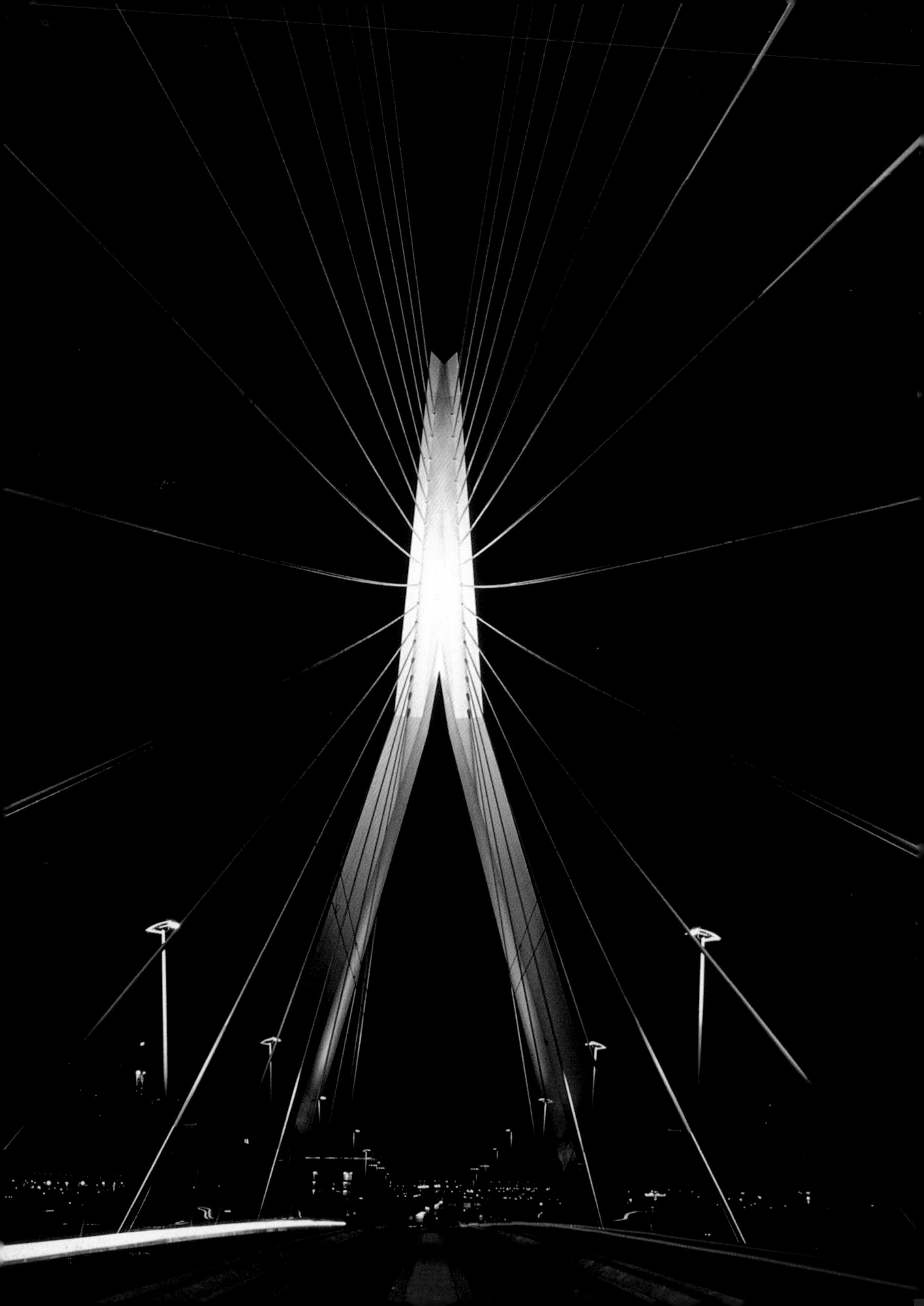

In the coming decades a new type of building will go up everywhere; a roofed-over amalgam of trains, busses, offices, parking garages and shops, situated on large plots in or very near historic town centres. This is a totally new typology for the disciplines of architecture, urbanism and infrastructure. The new building for the urban transportation area addresses all three of these fields and requires an integral approach. This is no time for laissez-faire urbanism; design a big, neutral space and within a few years, or even months, it will be going out of control with unplanned additional shops, pavilions and street furniture.

Intensification of movement patterns

The Mainport study is part of the Utrecht City Project, a long-term scheme for the modernisation and expansion of the town centre of Utrecht. Mainport studies the location of the railway and bus stations, which is situated like a large wedge between the old town and the 1970s shopping mall of Hoog Catherijne.

Mainport did not result in a design, nor was it intended to. The study provides icons and diagrams. The icons are visual and spatial interpretations of short, summarising, umbrella-notions, which can be carried through in later phases as

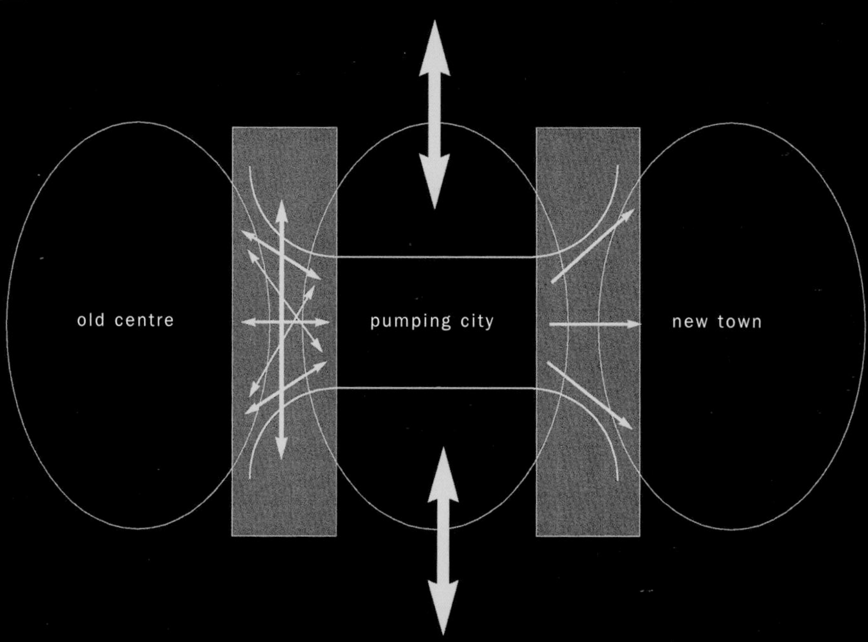

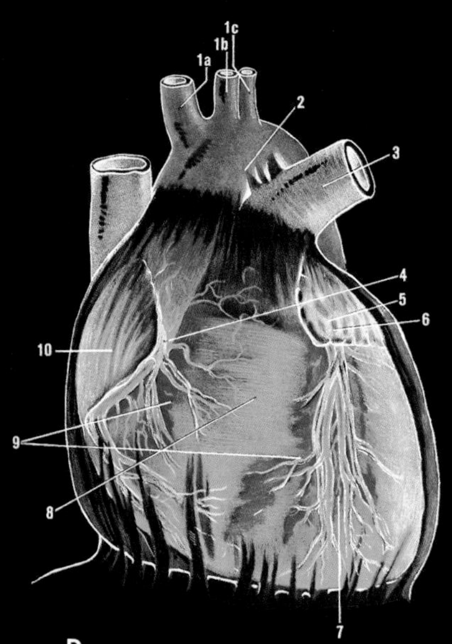

D

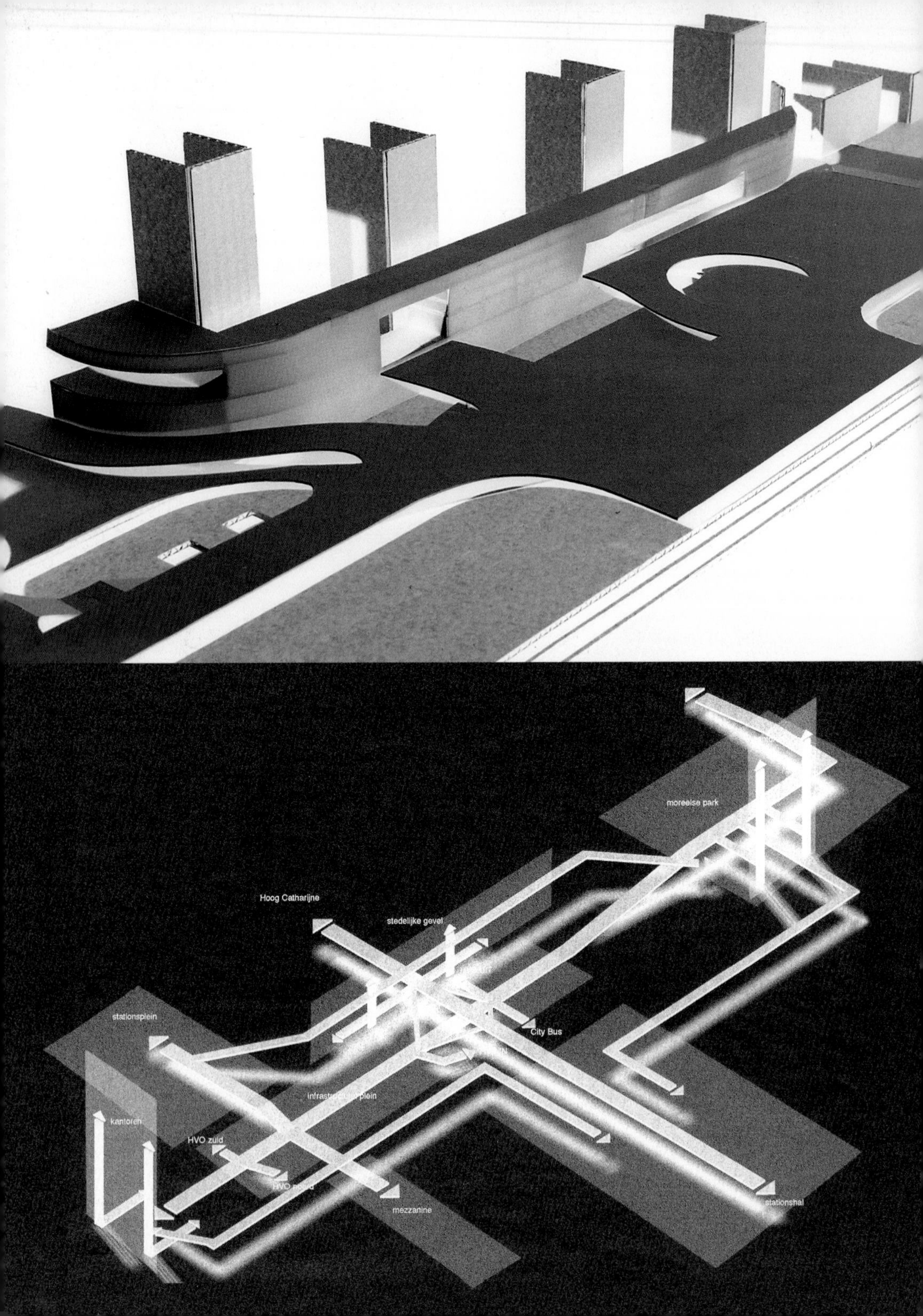
Hoog Catharijne
stedelijke gevel
moreelse park
stationsplein
City Bus
kantoren
HVO zuid
mezzanine
stationshal

gauges. The diagrams are abstract maps of relationships. There are several types of diagrams; some study the relationships between the planned office buildings and the cultural and shopping facilities. Movement flow diagrams examine pedestrian connections with the systems of infrastructure, projected up to the year 2010. These diagrams enable a quick, comprehensive insight into the layers of the location, resulting in shorter, more effective links between transport systems and other programmes. Extruding the diagrams to 3D renders visible the density of passenger flow. Also being studied are visual links, penetration of daylight, shadows cast by surrounding buildings, a new type of bus system and other pragmatic aspects. All of these ultimately lead to an idea about how the multitude of interconnected infrastructure and programme elements can become manifest as one working building.

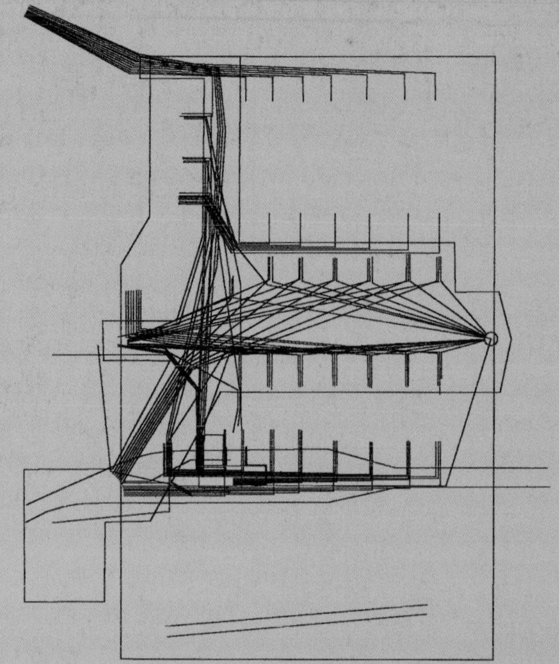

pedestrian connections

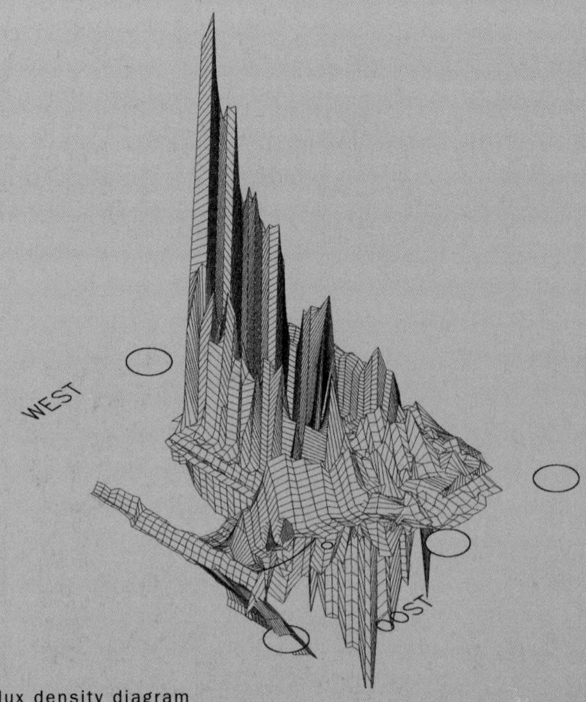

flux density diagram

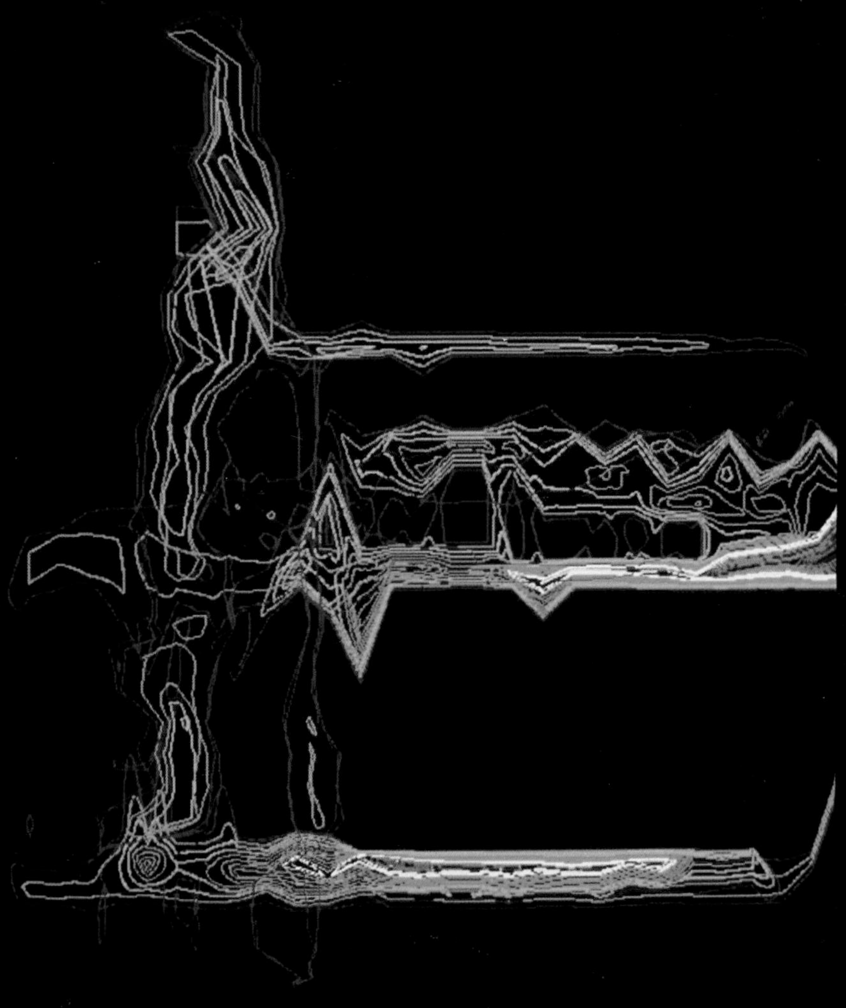

flow diagram including peak moments

DAK

LADDER

HVS

light/shadow effects

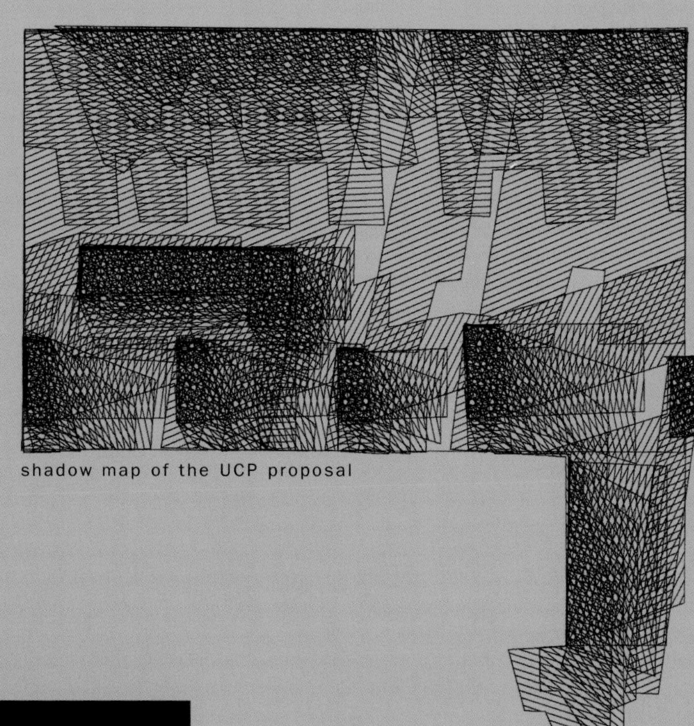
shadow map of the UCP proposal

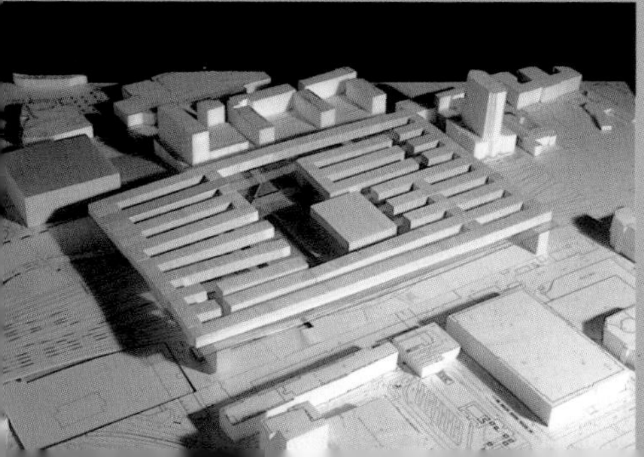

infrastructural loops

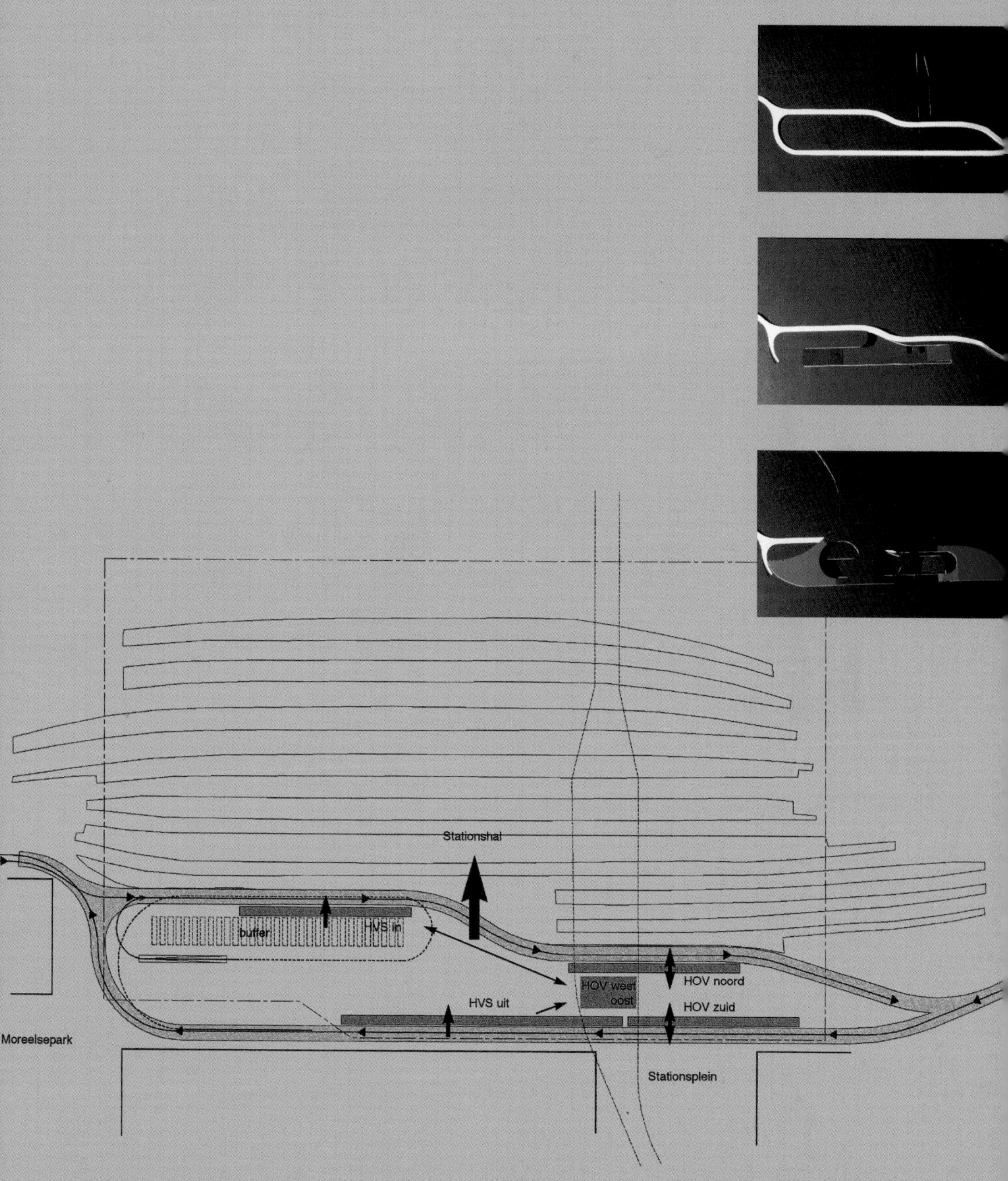

location development

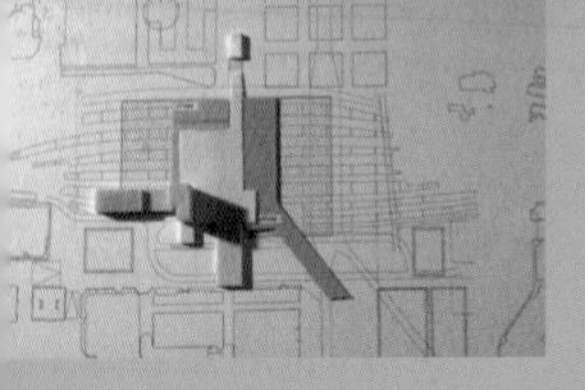

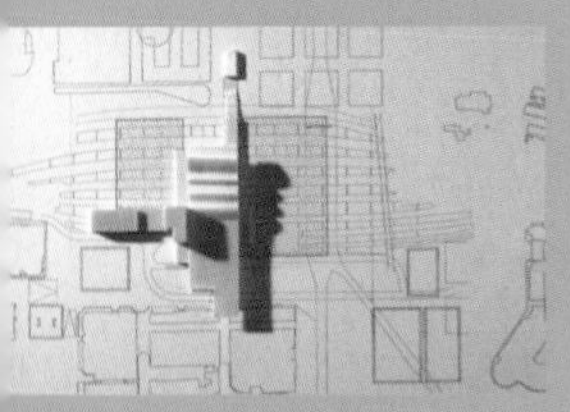

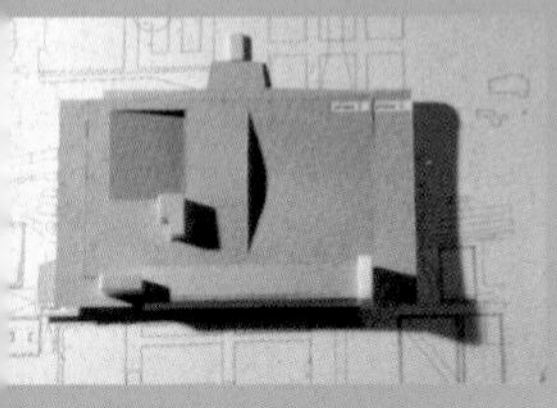

UCP Mainport

tation Balcony
Hoog Catharijne

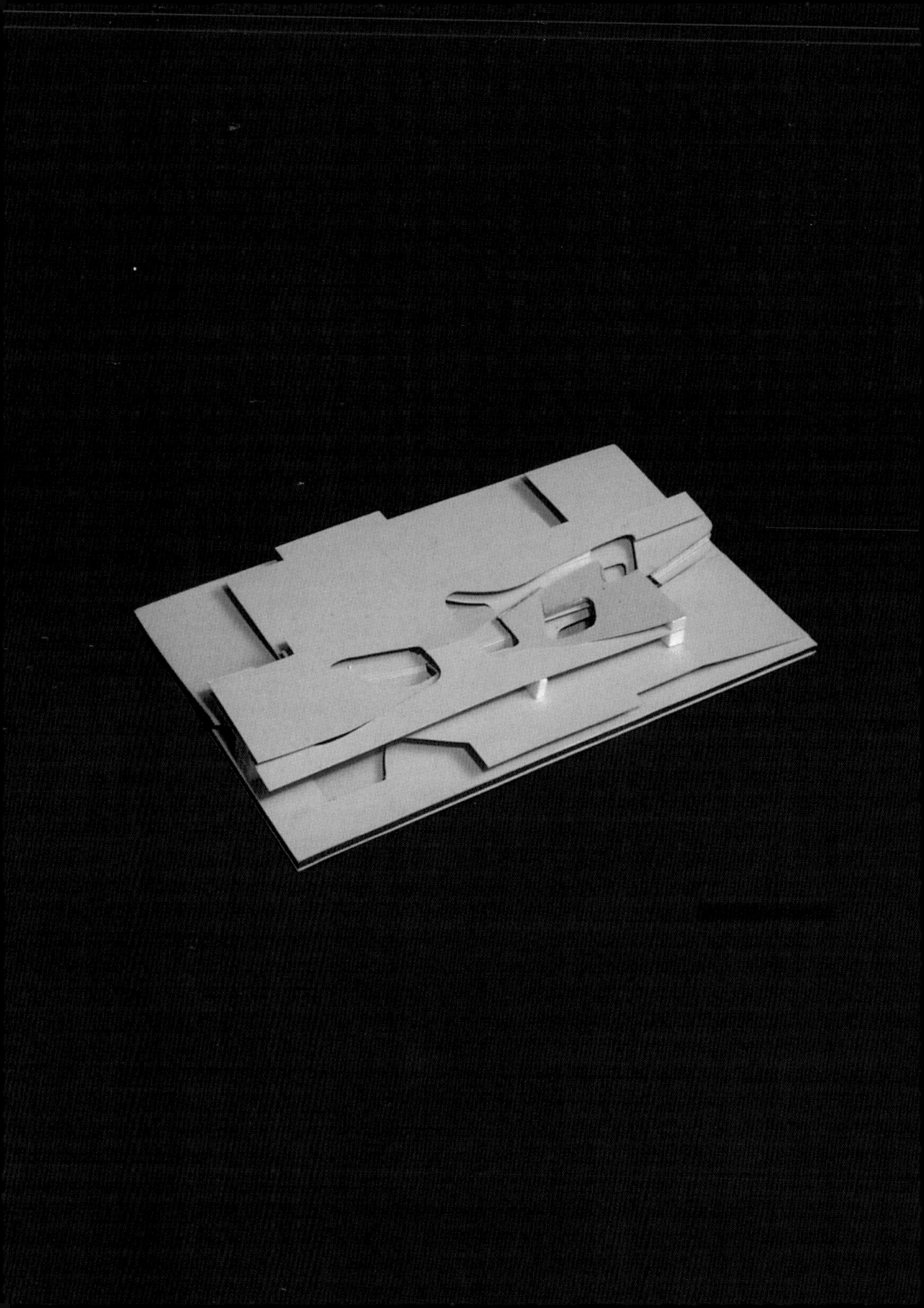

Station Balcony

In the second phase, a specific segment of a future extension of the Hoog Catherijne shopping centre was studied. Situated between station hall and city axis, this area was conceived as a mediator. Overlooking the railway tracks, the balcony zone mediates between different urban conditions and between the local programmes of offices, station, parking and shopping. It also mediates between different time-space relations, such as the 24-hour activity of the station versus the day-and-night pattern of the traditional town centre. Again studies, rather than schemes, are produced - this time investigating the relationships between pedestrian circulation patterns, shopper types, commercial zoning and time. The qualities of the traditional town centre cannot be duplicated in a contemporary shopping centre; these studies serve to investigate how alternative qualities can be broached to achieve a place in which people will be happy to spend their time.

balcony zone central hall

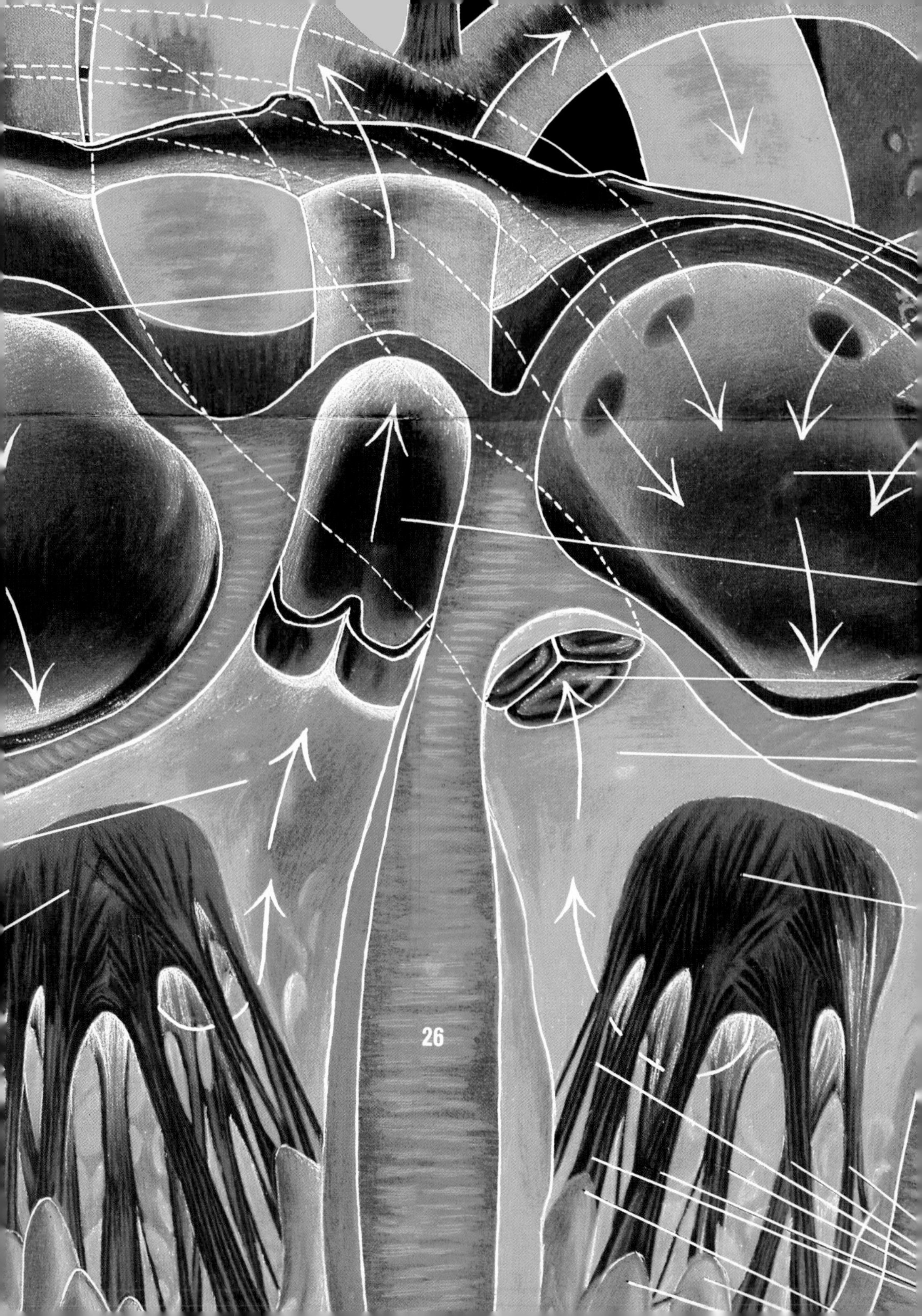
26

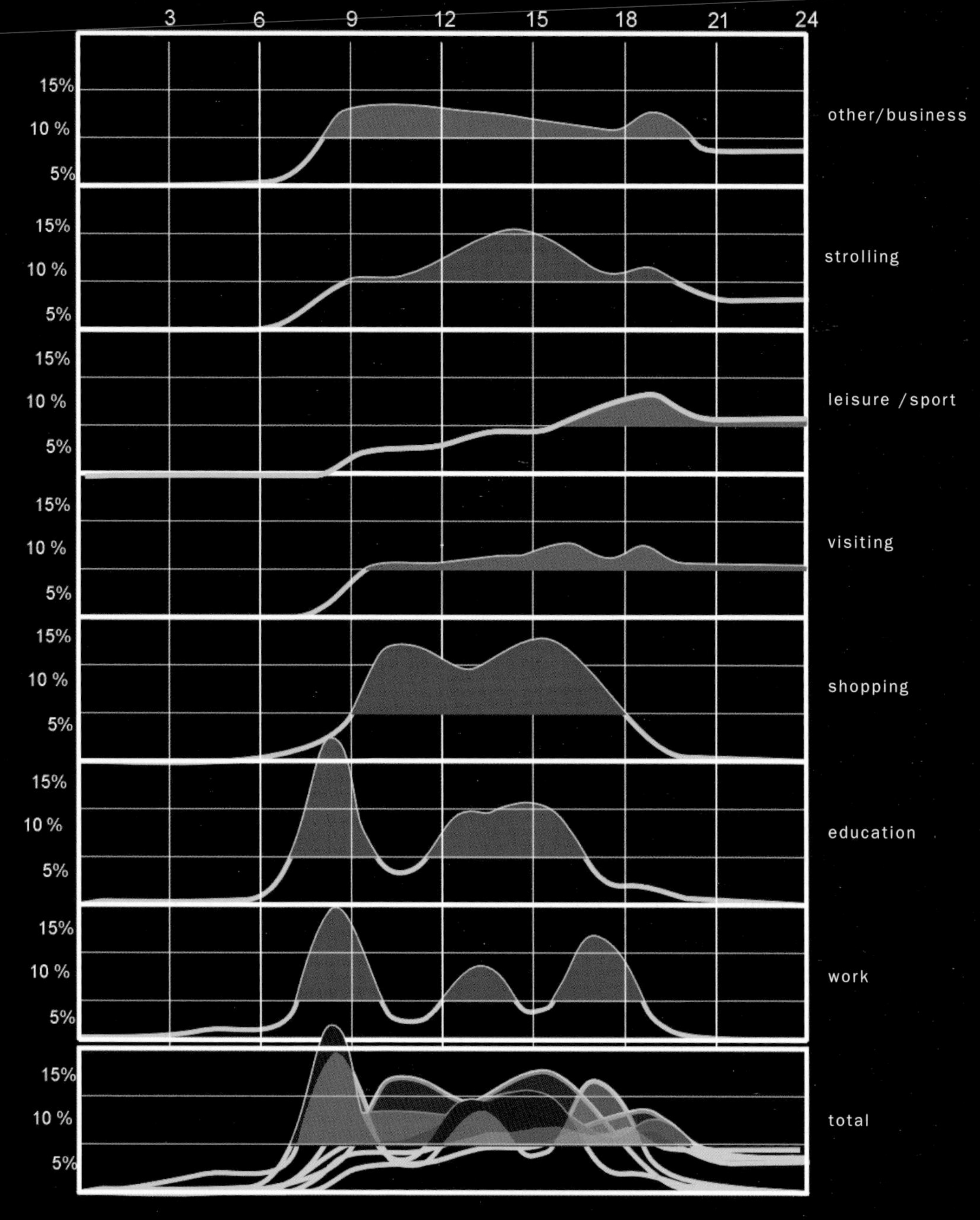

how the Dutch spend their time

Fun shopping

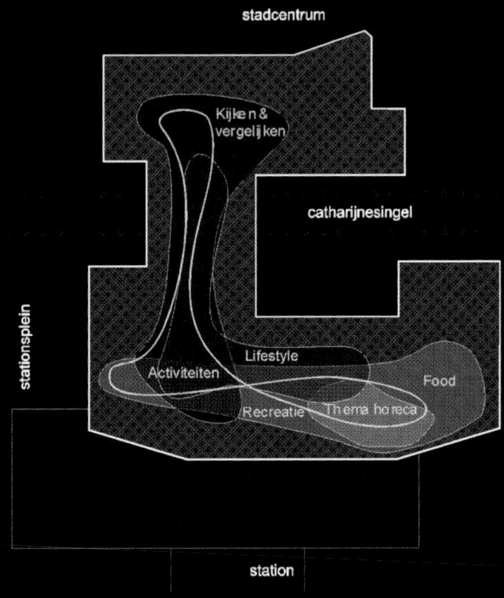

Run shopping

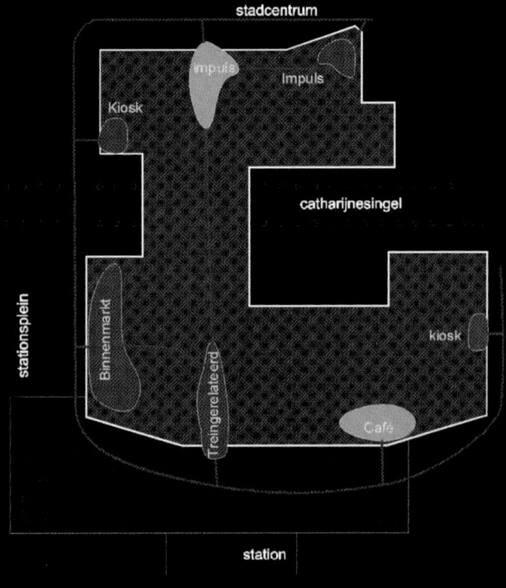

shopping patterns

Night shopping

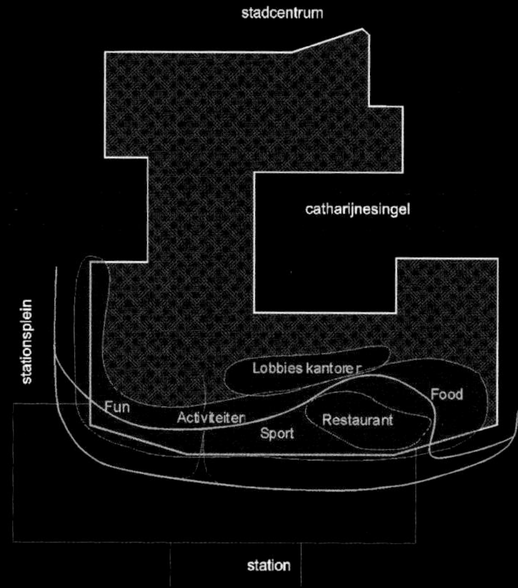

Daily shopping

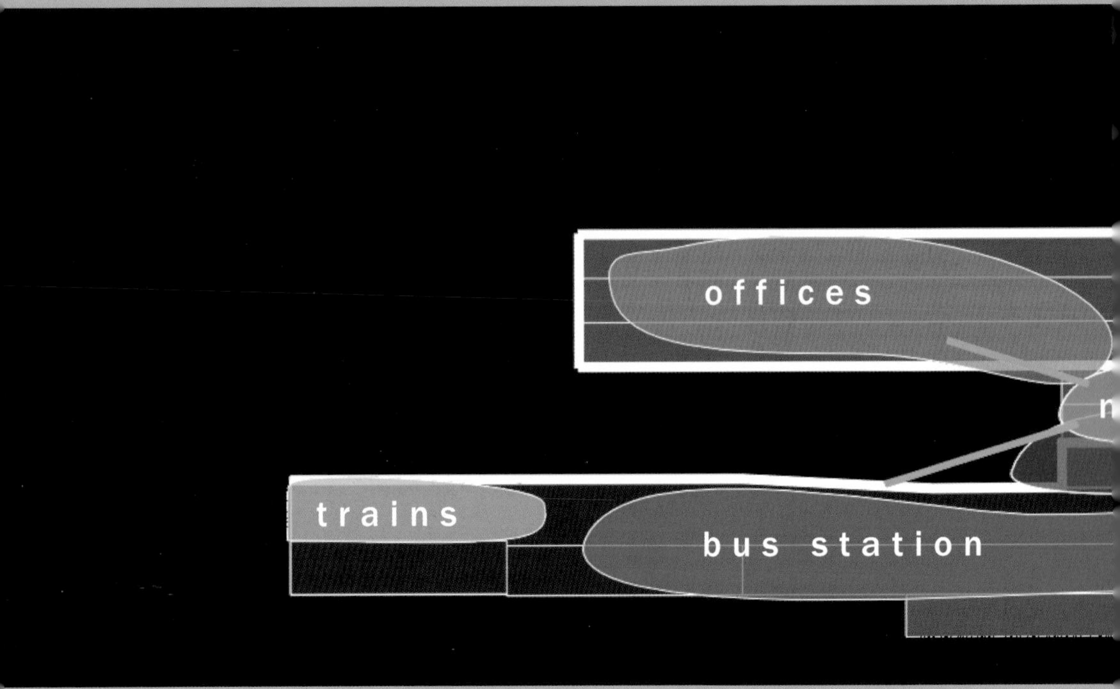

offices

trains

bus station

balcony zone mediator

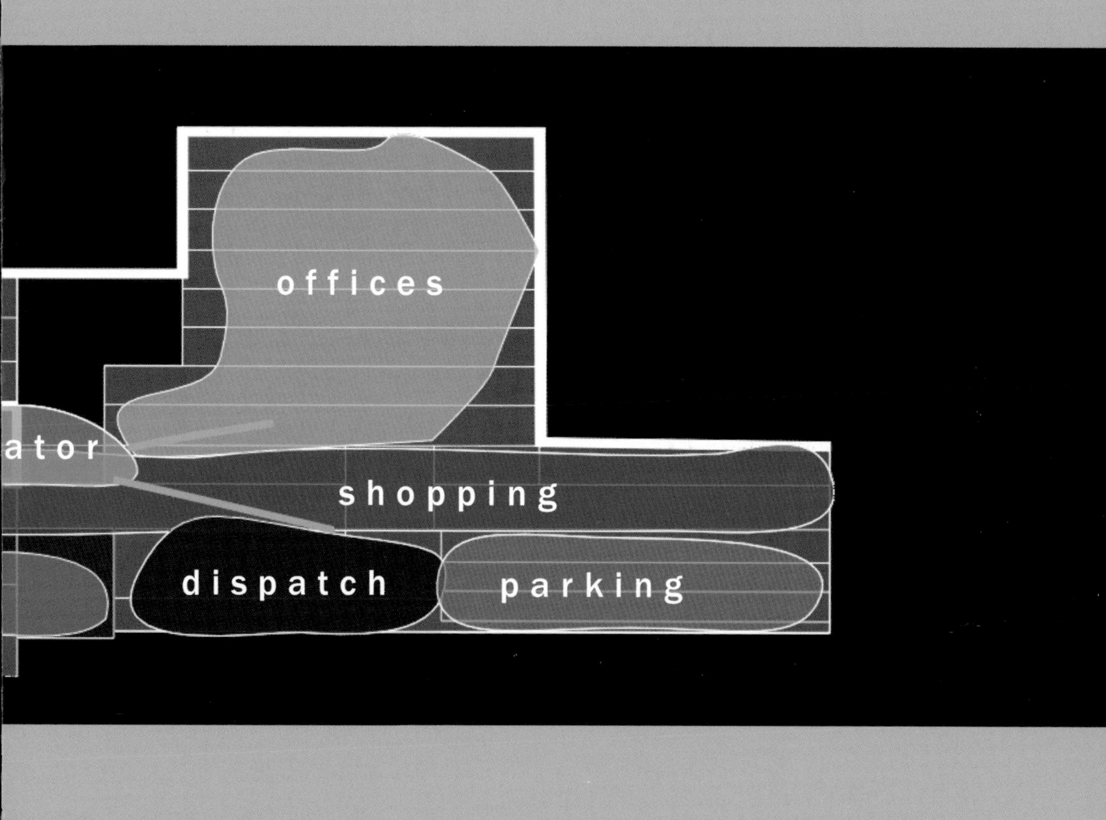
offices
ator
shopping
dispatch
parking

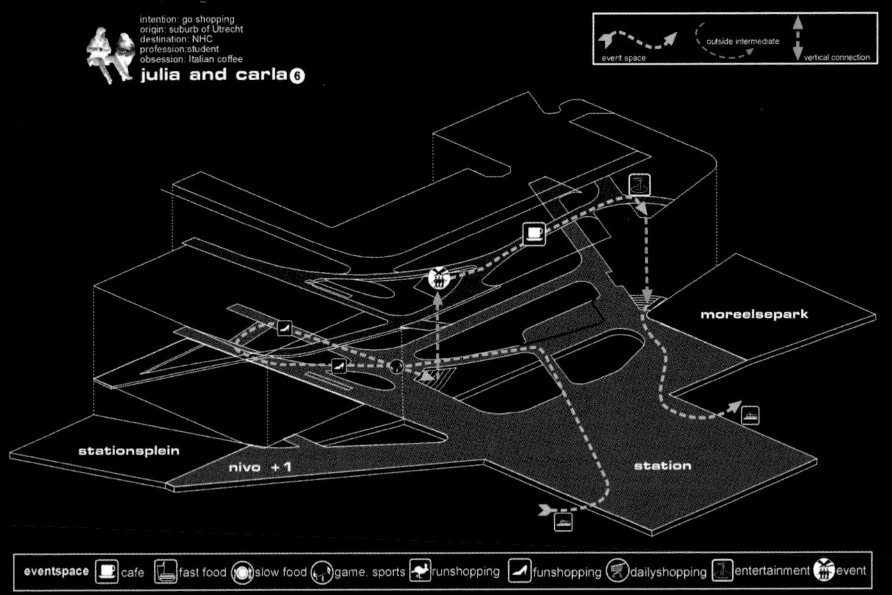

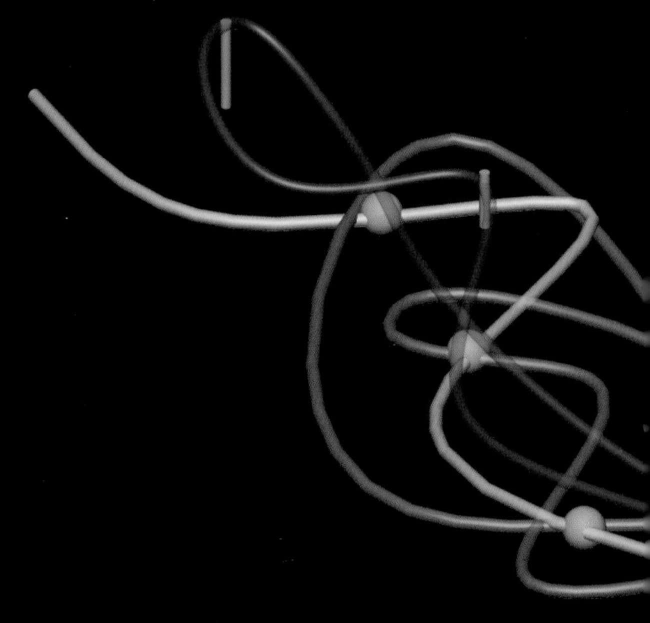

shopper type studies

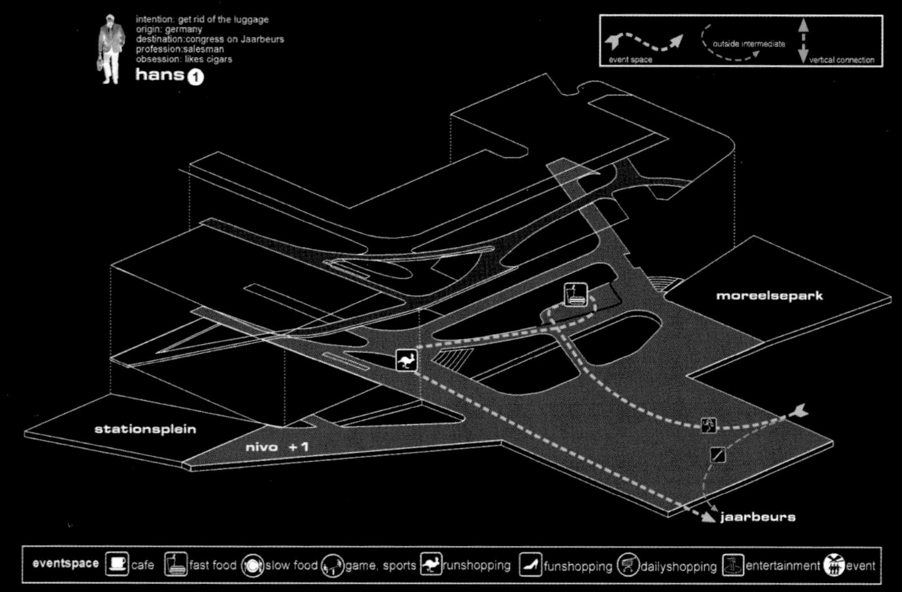
intention: get rid of the luggage
origin: germany
destination:congress on Jaarbeurs
profession:salesman
obsession: likes cigars
hans 1
event space
outside intermediate
vertical connection
moreelsepark
stationsplein
nivo +1
jaarbeurs
eventspace
cafe
fast food
slow food
game, sports
runshopping
funshopping
dailyshopping
entertainment
event

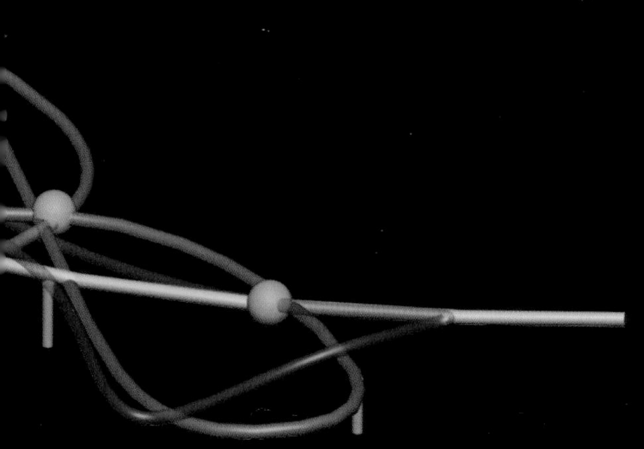

balcony zone, mediator

The A4 motorway between Amsterdam and Rotterdam vividly evokes the condition of Dutchness: it bisects three distinct landscapes over a 50 mile stretch; it is the economic lynchpin of the Randstad, connecting Schiphol Airport with the Rotterdam port; and it is jam-packed 24 hours per day. It can and will be widened, but extending the motorway gobbles up more precious space, which makes anxious administrators wonder how much non-infrastructural space will eventually be left over in this small country. So from time to time the possibility of stacking infrastructure is re-examined.

Fantasy 2000: Gotham city in the polder

This particular study concentrates on a section of the A4 situated south of Amsterdam. The setting: traditional ribbon development meets Kuala Lumpur - glittering company headquarters stand in serried ranks along a clogged motorway. Multiplying the strands is not the solution here; classical sci-fi and Situationists' work have to some extent shown us this vision already, without effect. We have focused on integrating the existing infrastructure into a new distribution system that services the region, accelerating transfer to and from the A4.

Adding new layers of infrastructure next to and

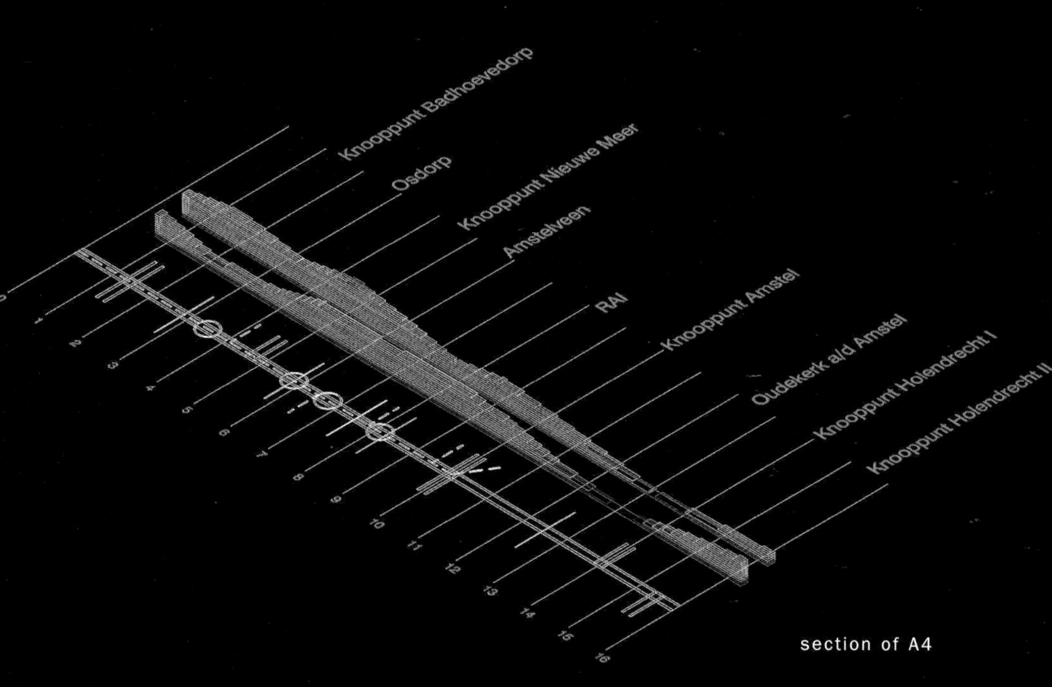

section of A4

on top of existing ones increases accessibility. The new decks are loops, which provide connections between the A4 and specific locations to stimulate flow. The study investigates the shape these infrastructural nodes may take, their interaction with public transport systems and their potential to become buildings.

  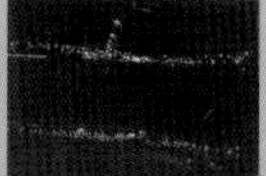 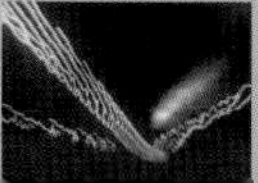  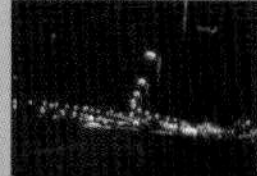 

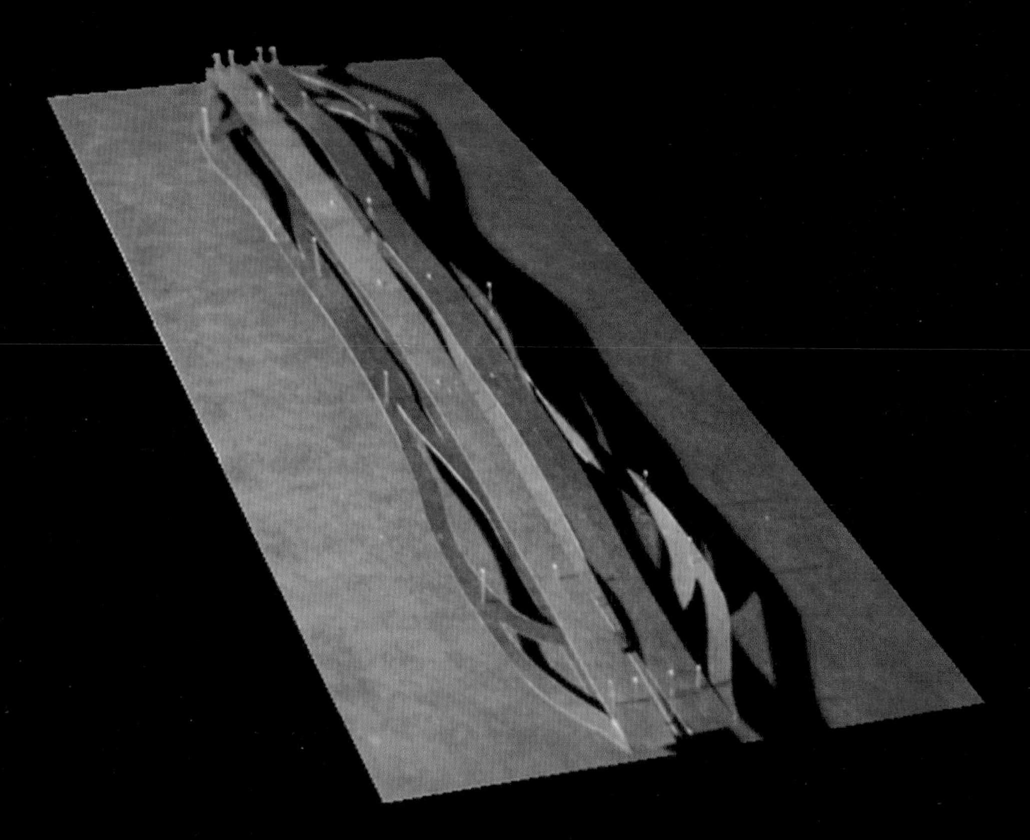

additional lanes optimise circulation

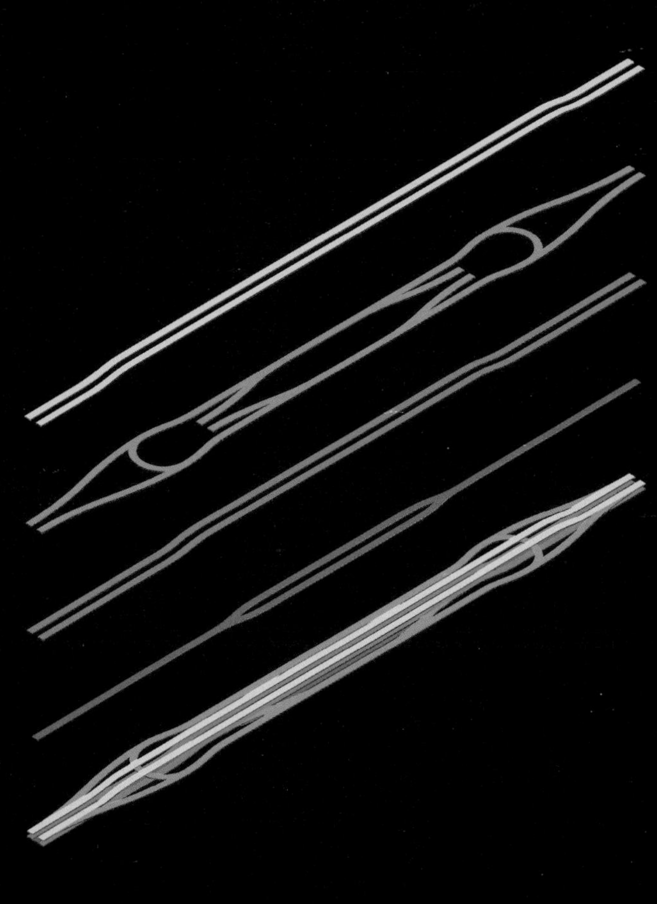

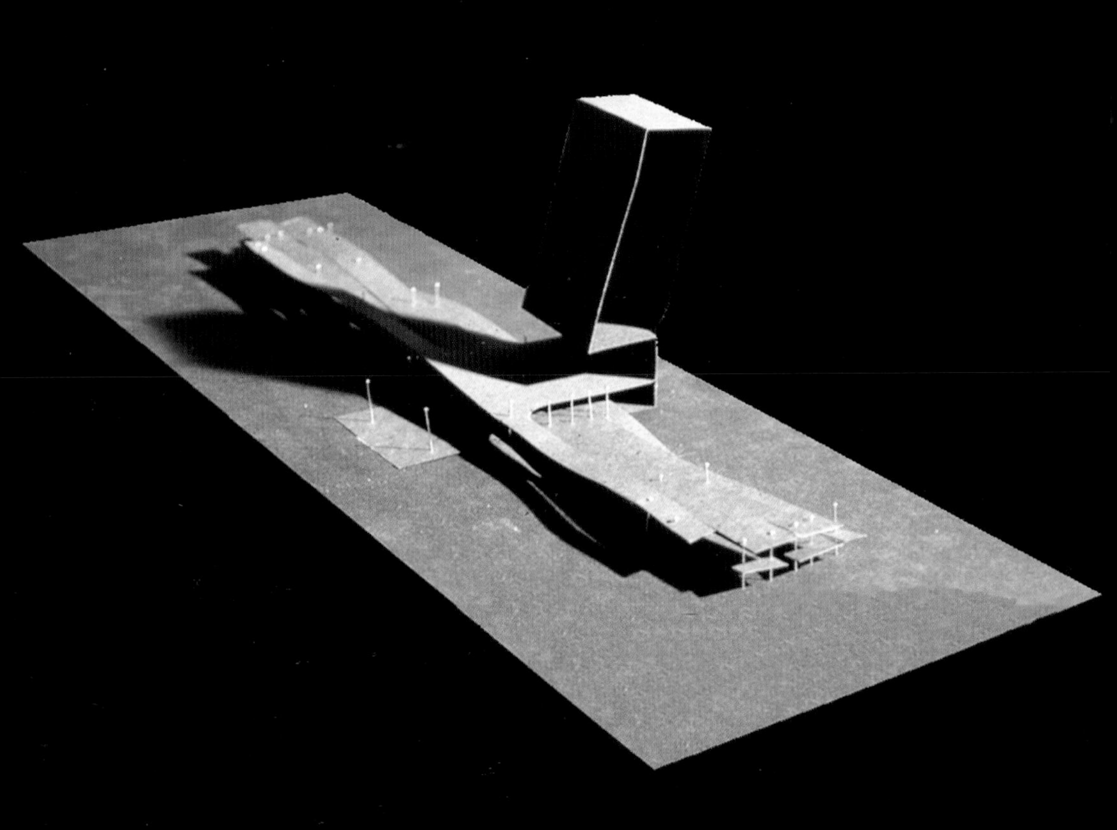

infrastructure transforming intc

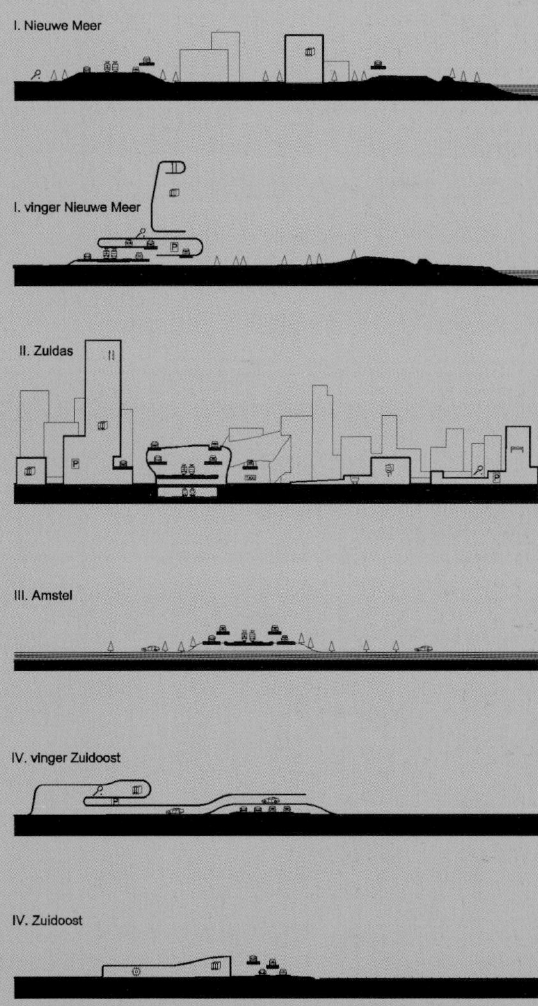
I. Nieuwe Meer
I. vinger Nieuwe Meer
II. Zuidas
III. Amstel
IV. vinger Zuidoost
IV. Zuidoost

Urbanism is shopping. All new urban plans today are engendered by the need for more retail outlets of better quality. Shopping is a science. Experts on shopping are presently counted as some of the best-qualified and most highly valued members of society. Shopping is a language. New words invented in relation to shopping are among the most imaginative and original architectural concepts of our time. But when shopping only means buying the same branded products everywhere, the bubble bursts. Inclusive shopping means integrating commercial functions with public life.

Satellite town: from suburb to total convenience assemblage

Nieuwegein could be a winner. The town is easily accessible and centrally located in the vicinity of Utrecht. Its covered shopping centre, which extends for 400 metres, is a raging success. But both the architecture and layout of this new town, with a population that has grown from 0 to 60,000 inhabitants within 15 years, are on the shabby side. Research is being conducted with an eye to revitalising its centre, anticipating a considerable expansion.

This research compares several base models of different dimensions and configurations, ranging

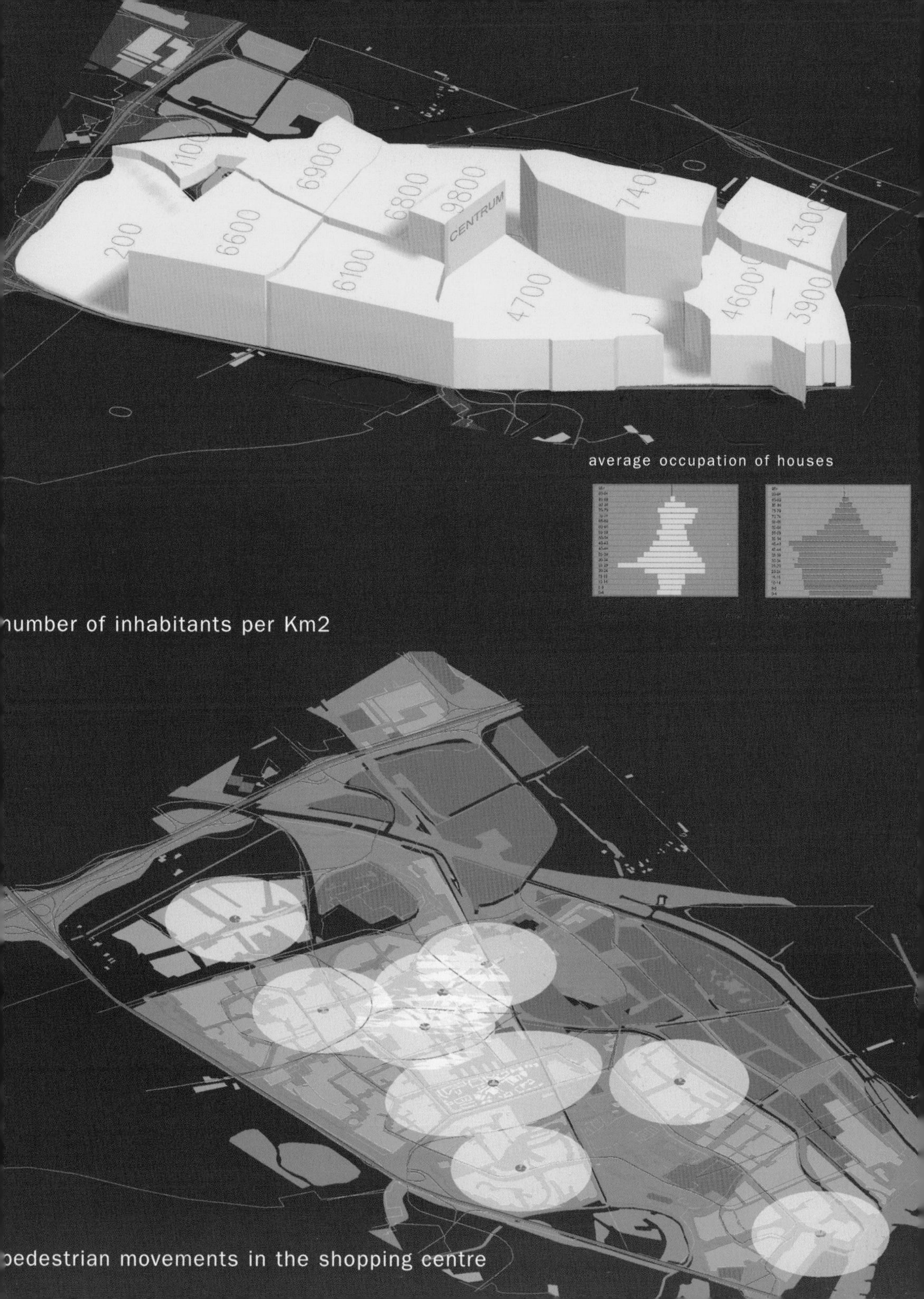
1100
6900
6800
9800
CENTRUM
740
4300
200
6600
6100
4700
4600
3900
average occupation of houses
number of inhabitants per Km2
pedestrian movements in the shopping centre

pedestrian and cycle movement directed towards the centre

number of visitors a week to City plaza Nieuwegein

from additions of 80,000 to 300,000 square metres of mixed-use space, with cultural, office and shopping programmes combined. A wide range of studies investigates ways in which the expansions could be realised within the existing town structure. These include grid structure analysis, volume studies, ground level studies, time-flux studies and referential studies, studies of the town centre and its architecture, parking options, studies of public space, the connections within the town and phasing.
The rectangular centre is divided into three horizontal strokes, relating to different densities and infrastructure connections with the hinterland. At first two, later more, multifunctional anchors are proposed which attract pedestrian movement into the centre. As these anchors fulfil their role, the movement generated between them will establish a pumping circulatory system. The ground level will become a public pedestrian zone, forming a coherent field running through the entire centre, alternately raised and undulating and lowered and flat. Underneath, extensive car parks are stituated, freeing the ground plane for pedestrian movement. Multiple connections to the upper levels enable quick, effective transitions from travel to work, from shopping to leisure modes.

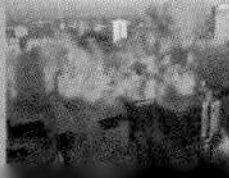

1981

1989

density studies

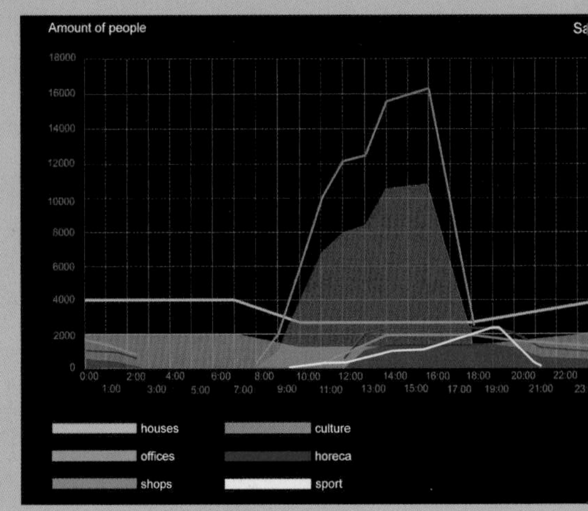

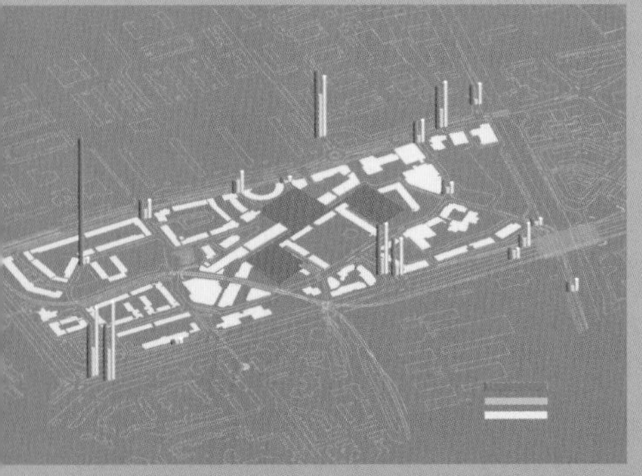

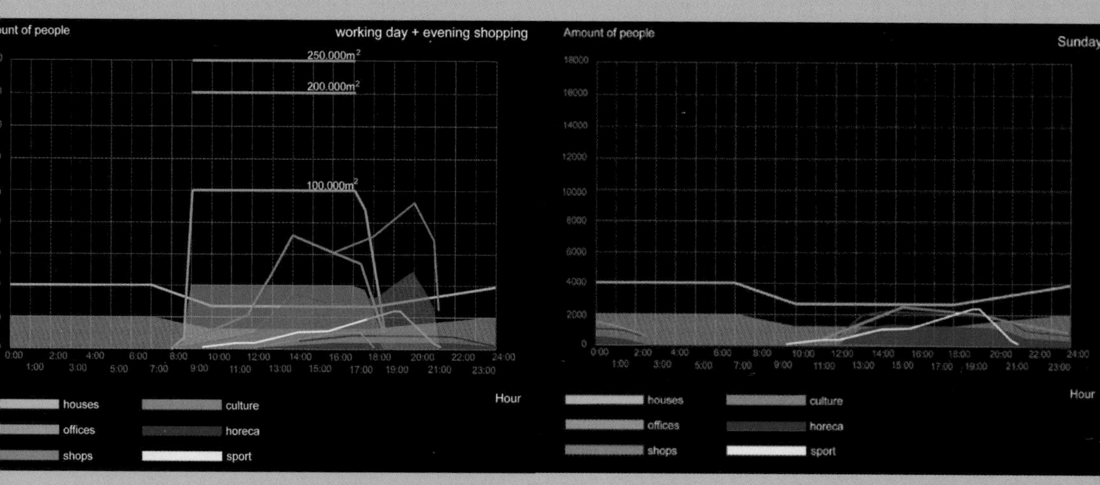

Amount of people
working day + evening shopping
250.000m²
200.000m²
100.000m²
0:00 2:00 4:00 6:00 8:00 10:00 12:00 14:00 16:00 18:00 20:00 22:00 24:00
1:00 3:00 5:00 7:00 9:00 11:00 13:00 15:00 17:00 19:00 21:00 23:00
Hour
houses
offices
shops
culture
horeca
sport
Amount of people
Sunday
18000
16000
14000
12000
10000
8000
6000
4000
2000
0
0:00 2:00 4:00 6:00 8:00 10:00 12:00 14:00 16:00 18:00 20:00 22:00 24:00
1:00 3:00 5:00 7:00 9:00 11:00 13:00 15:00 17:00 19:00 21:00 23:00
Hour
houses
offices
shops
culture
horeca
sport

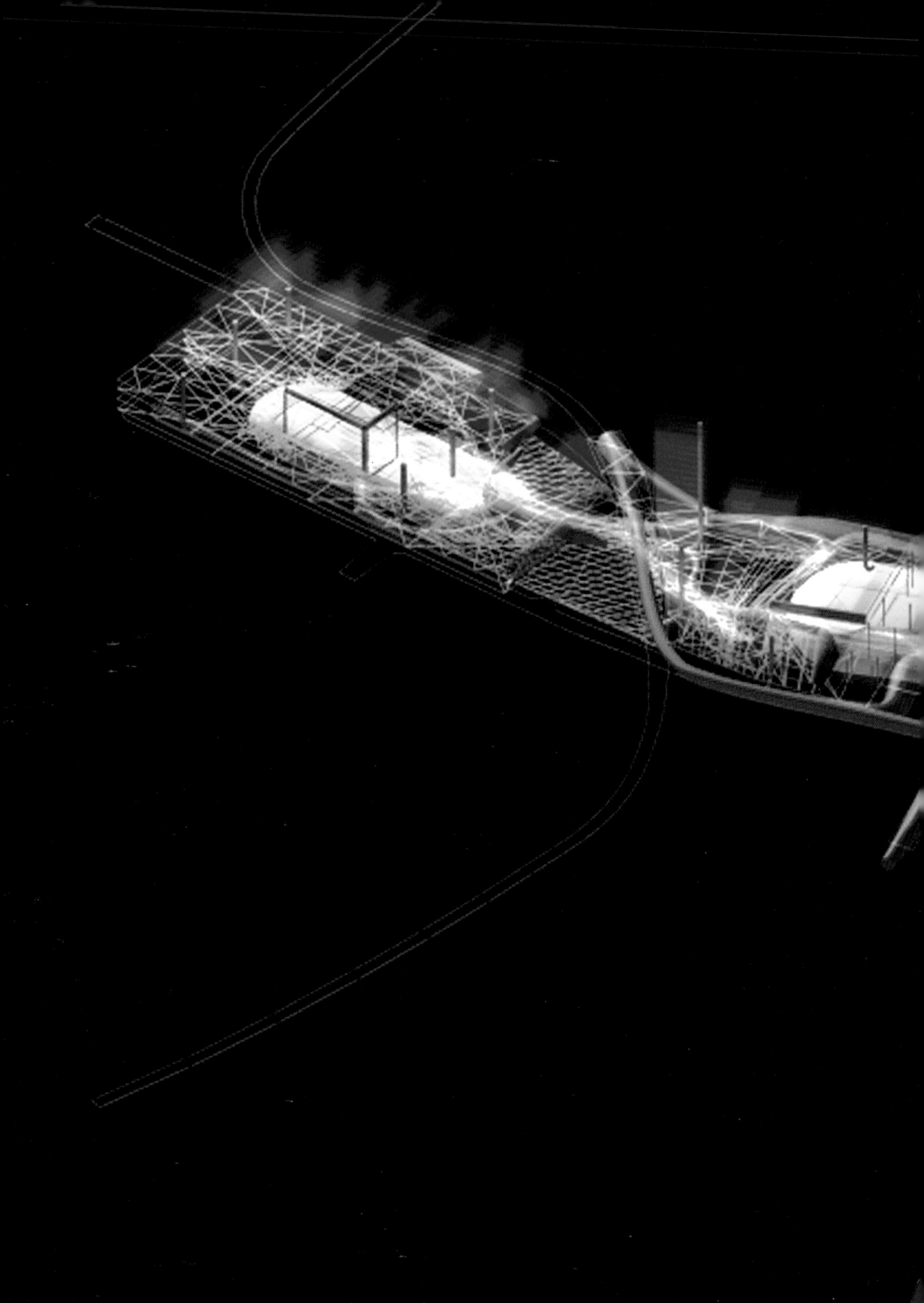

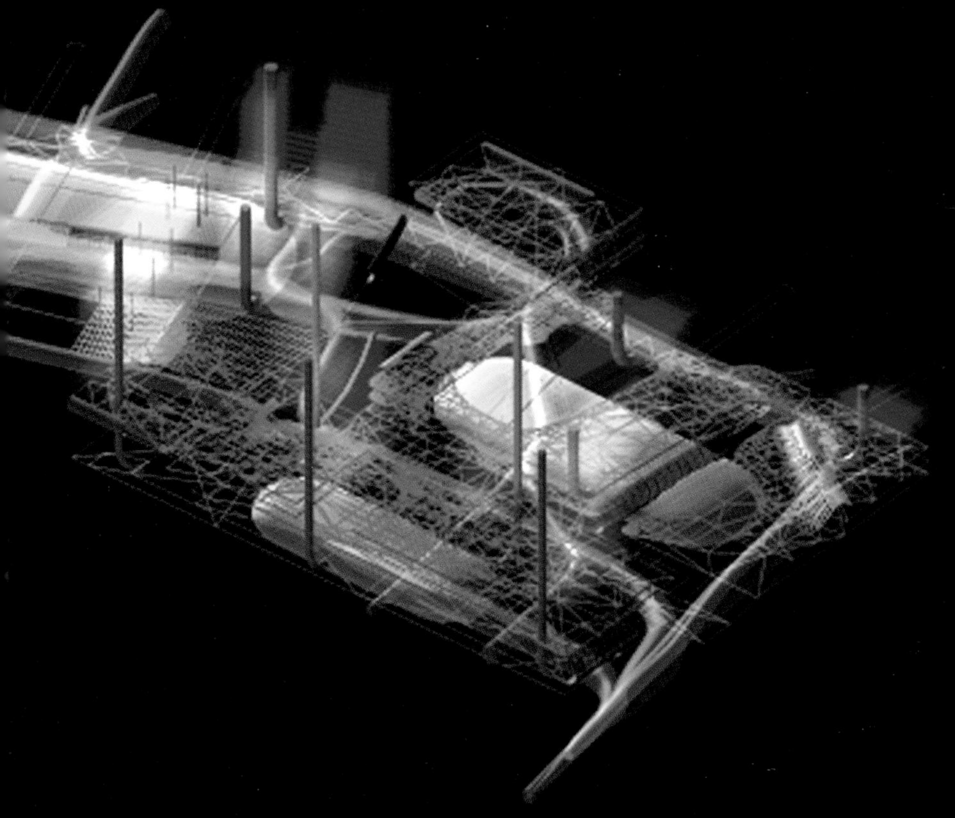

flux saturday 16h

programmatic time flux studies

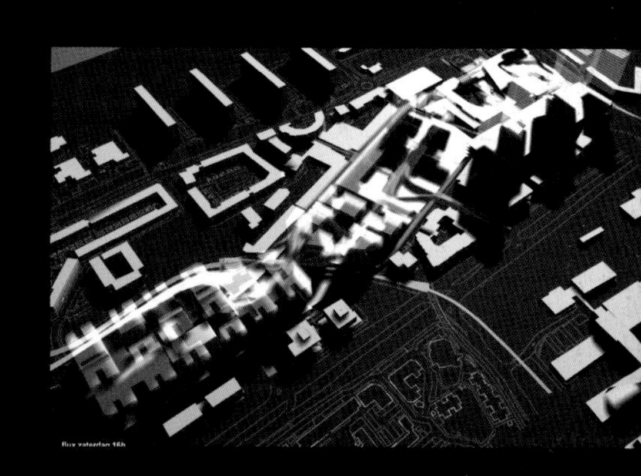
flux zaterdag 16h

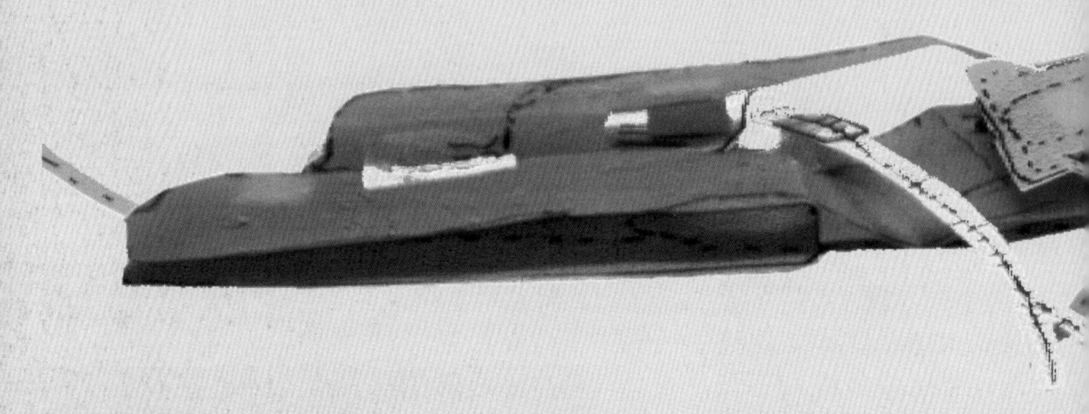

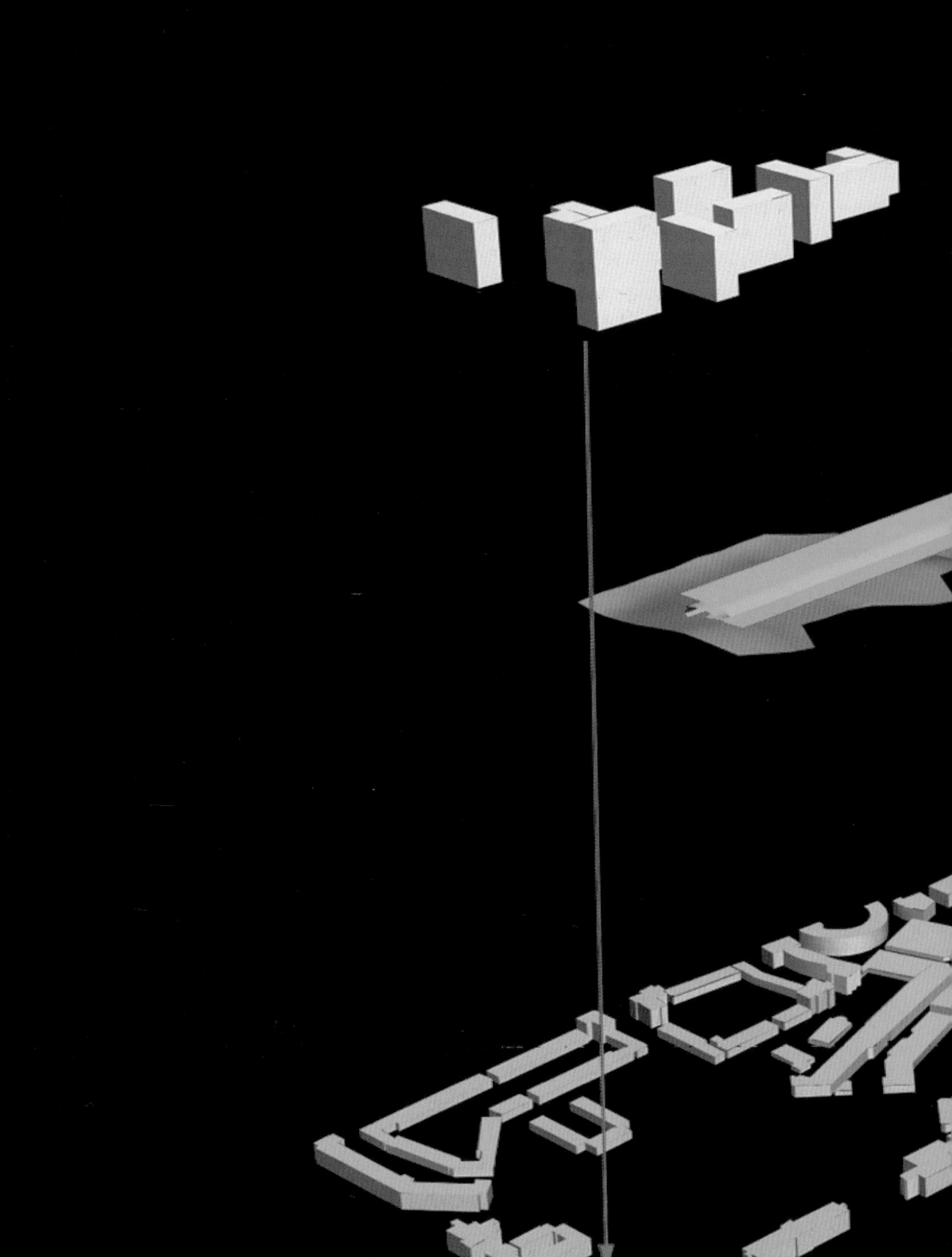

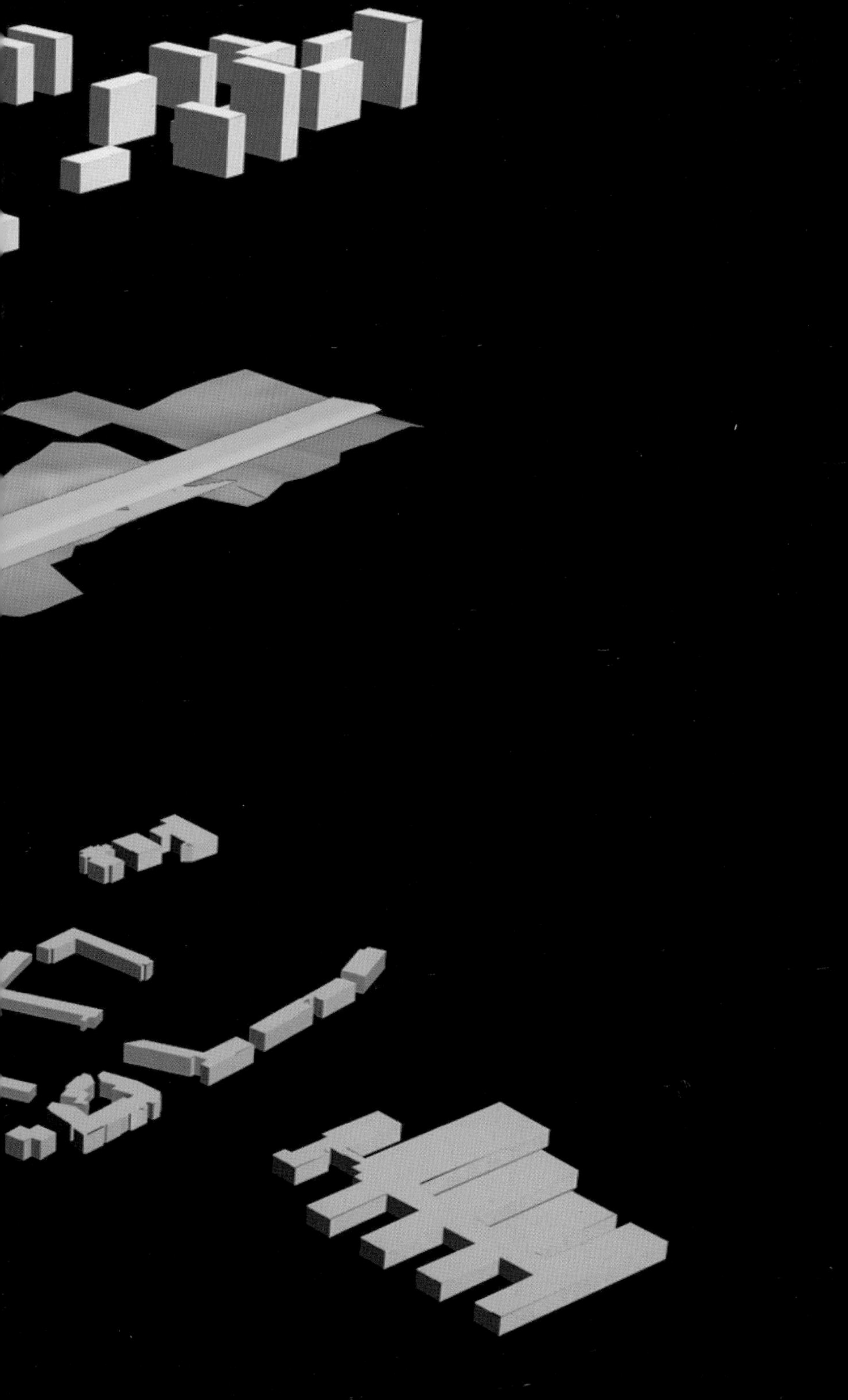

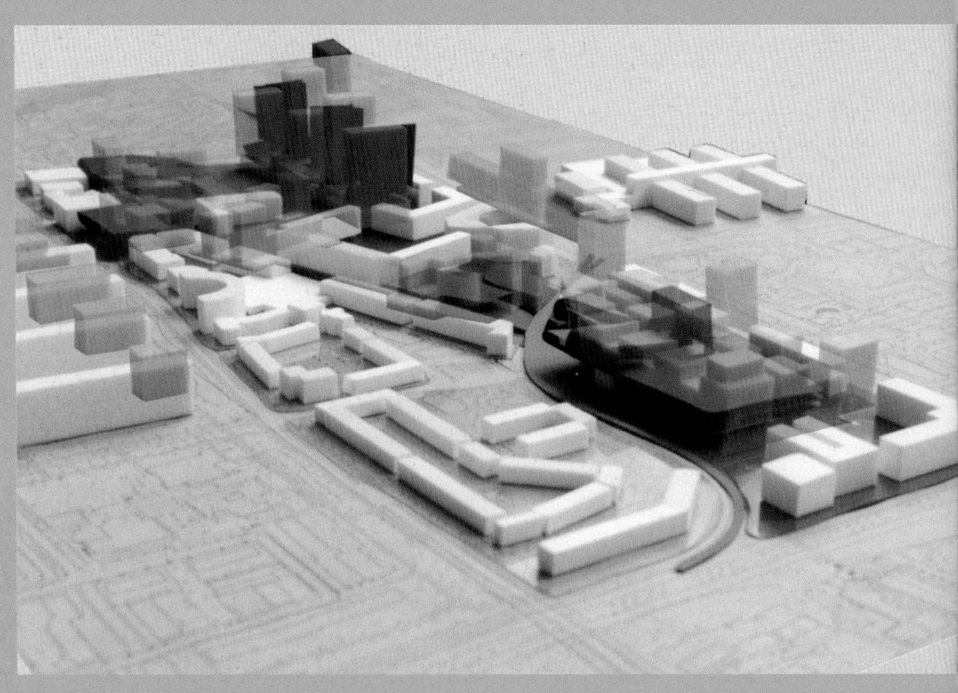

coherent ground level incorporates

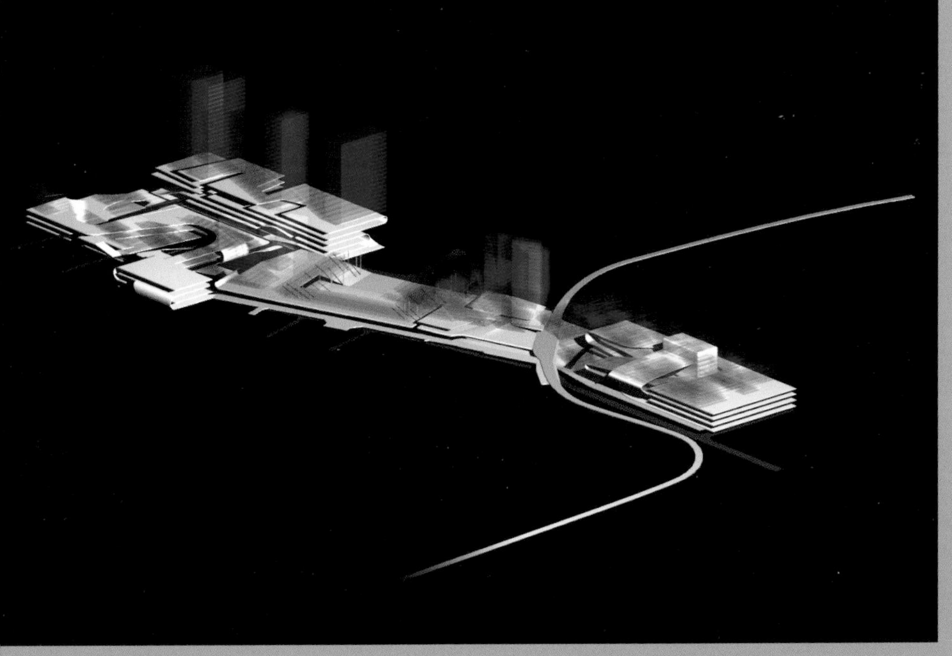

position of vertical connections

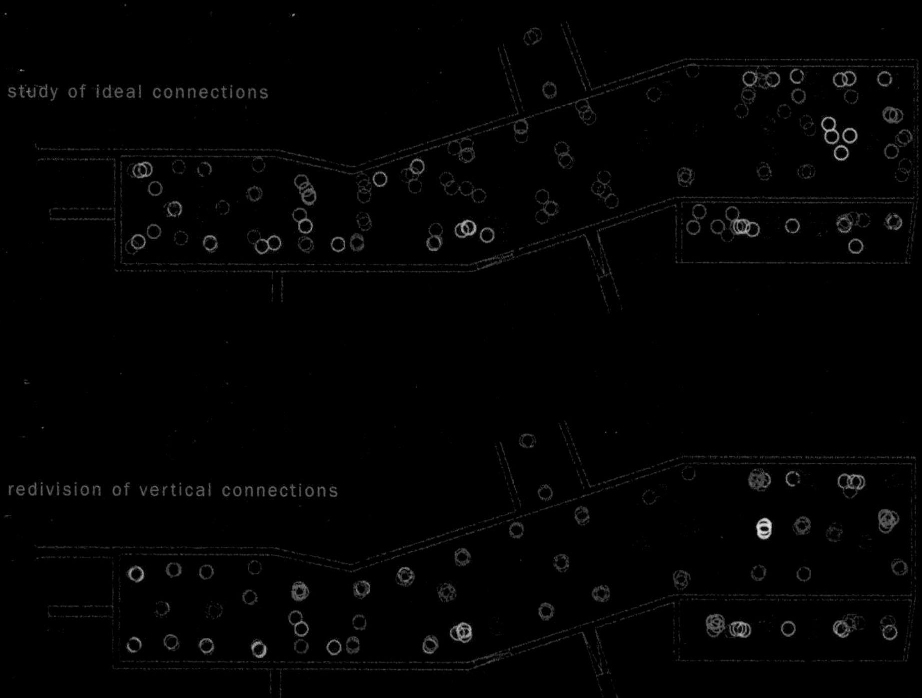

shops housing offices culture hotel restaurant cafe municipal hall library

MUSEUM

integrated spatial, constructive and programmatic models

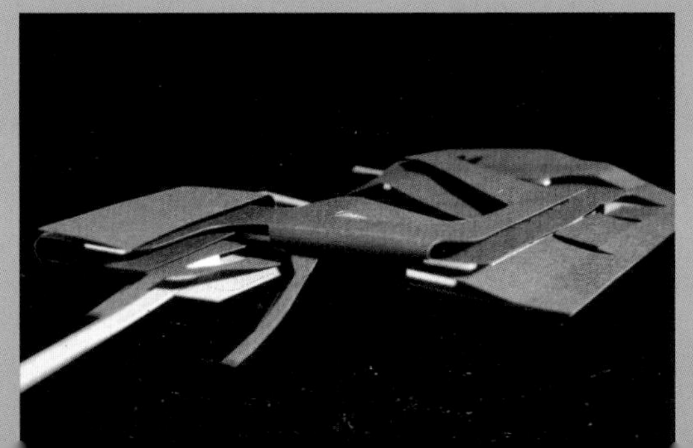

Putting the seduction back into bridge design; here is a recipe for shamelessness. The architectural imagination does not normally acknowledge sensuality, even though our culture is saturated with it. Architecture is supposed to be serious; money, sums and gravity are its ingredients, not glamour and sex. But it's all about ...

Sex and the single pylon

The two bridges were designed in a two-phase limited competition by a team of assistant designers, structural engineers and planning, financial and process management consultants. The Papendorpse Bridge connects two suburbs of Utrecht: the austere post-war neighbourhood of Kanaleneiland and the extensive new residential area of Leidsche Rijn, which is based on a contemporary, open and differentiated urban scheme. The bridge design was subject to a number of clearly formulated preconditions. The bridge deck needs to be raised high above the water to allow ships to pass underneath, which has consequences for landings and main structure. Noise control is especially important on the Kanaleneiland side and the bridge should provide a distinctive architectural evocation. The single-pylon bridge typology is chosen for site-specific reasons; it needs

only a small number of piers and so does not become an oppressive presence in residential areas. The torsional pylon is a clear visual announcement of the Leidsche Rijn development, and what's more, suits the moderate budget.
The long ramps of the bridge, which are separated by the grounded pylon, weave like ribbons through the surroundings. The separation of the bridge-deck into several lanes enhances traffic safety. Pedestrians and cyclists follow a low-slung trajectory, while motorised traffic climbs up to a higher level. By splitting up the various traffic streams, openings in the bridge-deck ensue, through which light reaches the ground level.

The second bridge, the HOV Bridge for pedestrians and cyclists has a curving deck, emanating from its topography. The pylon is placed to the side of the deck. As a result, the cables are attached to it in a semi-circular, dynamic arrangement.

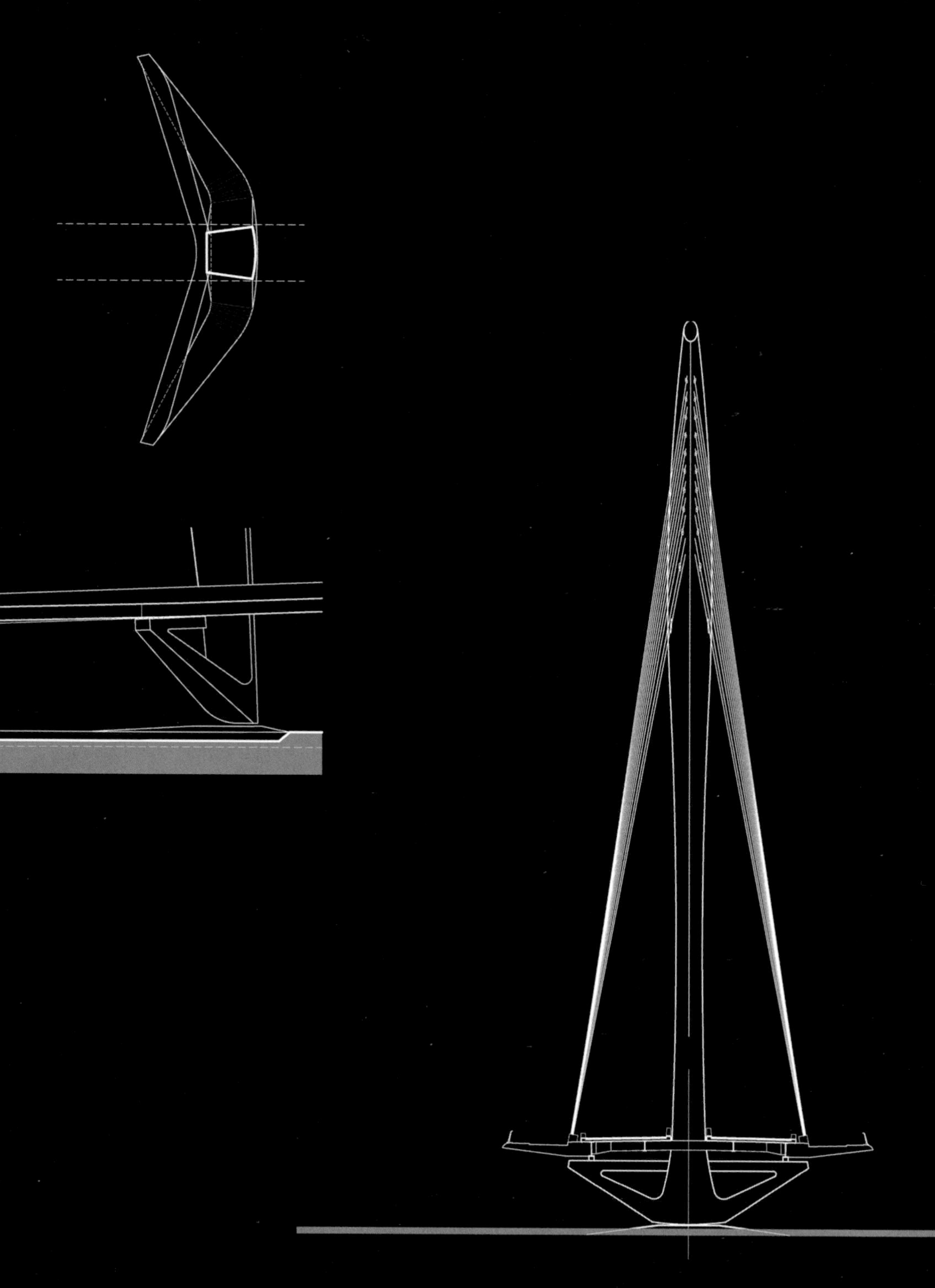

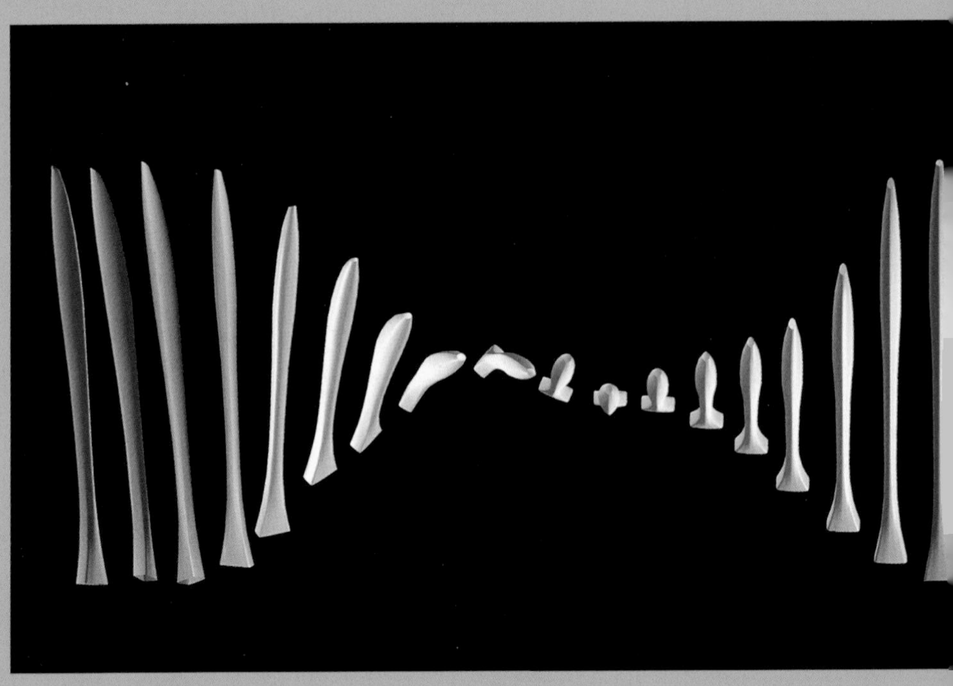

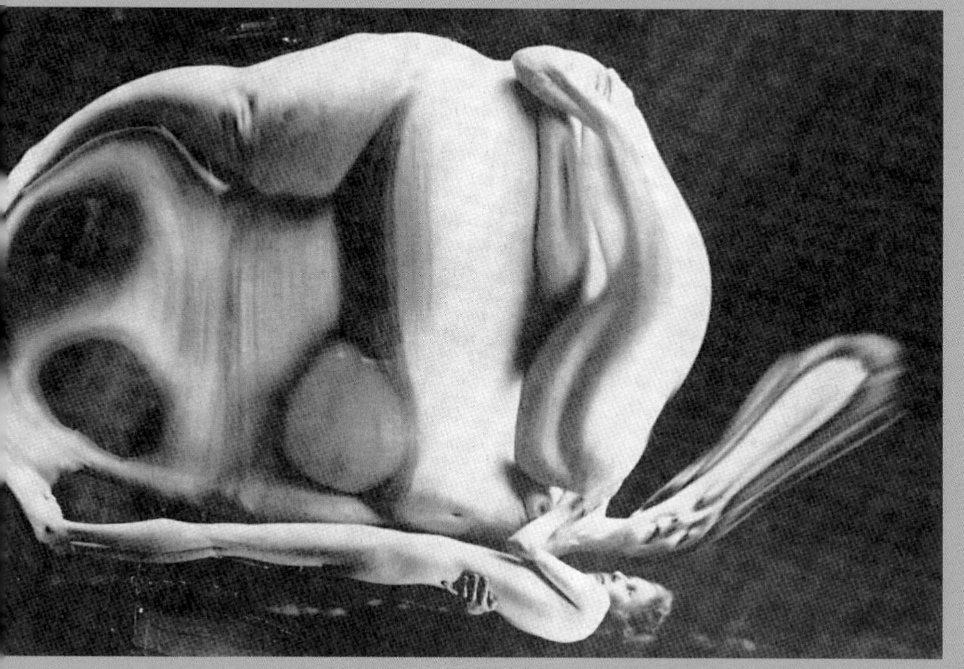

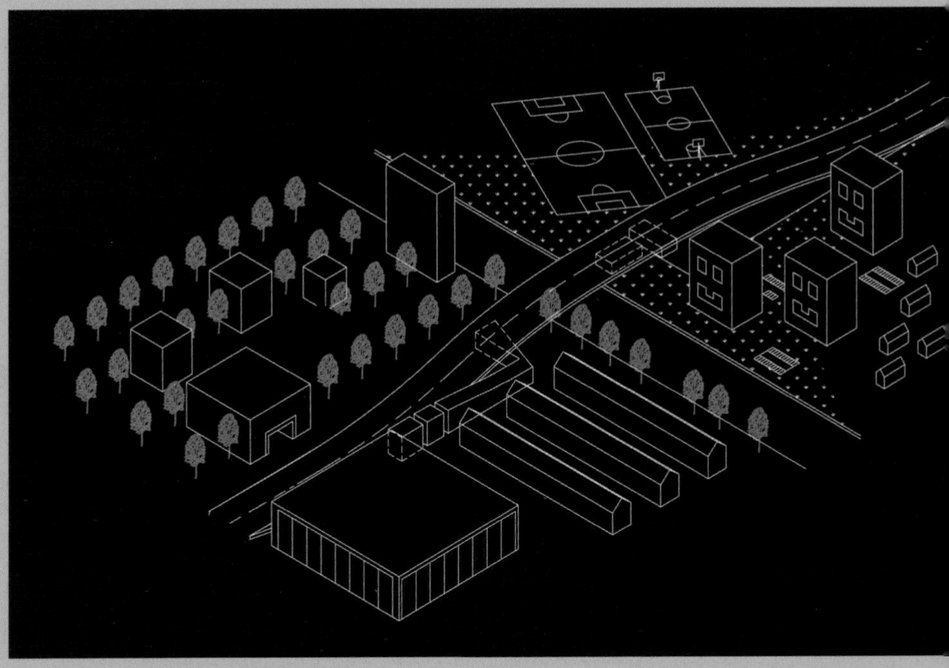

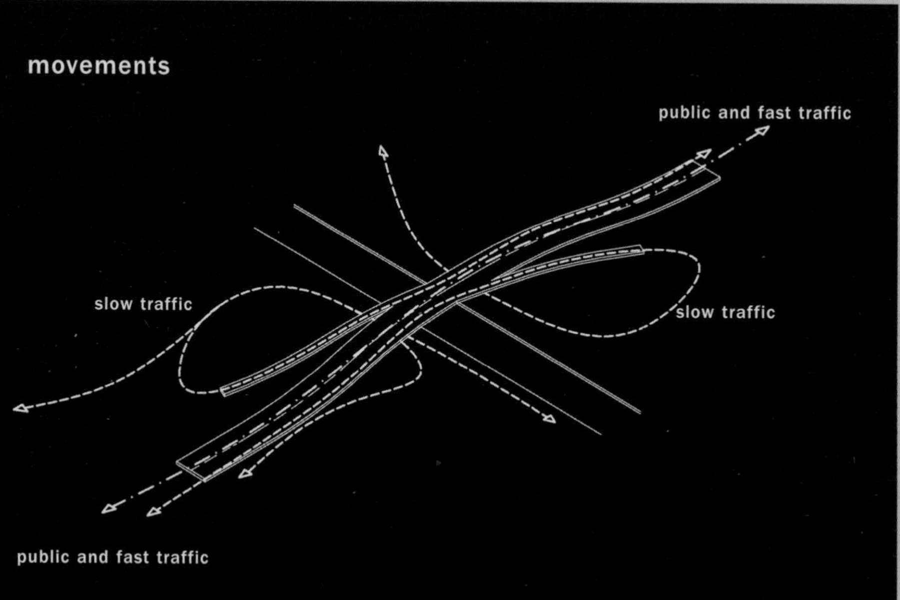
movements
public and fast traffic
slow traffic
slow traffic
public and fast traffic

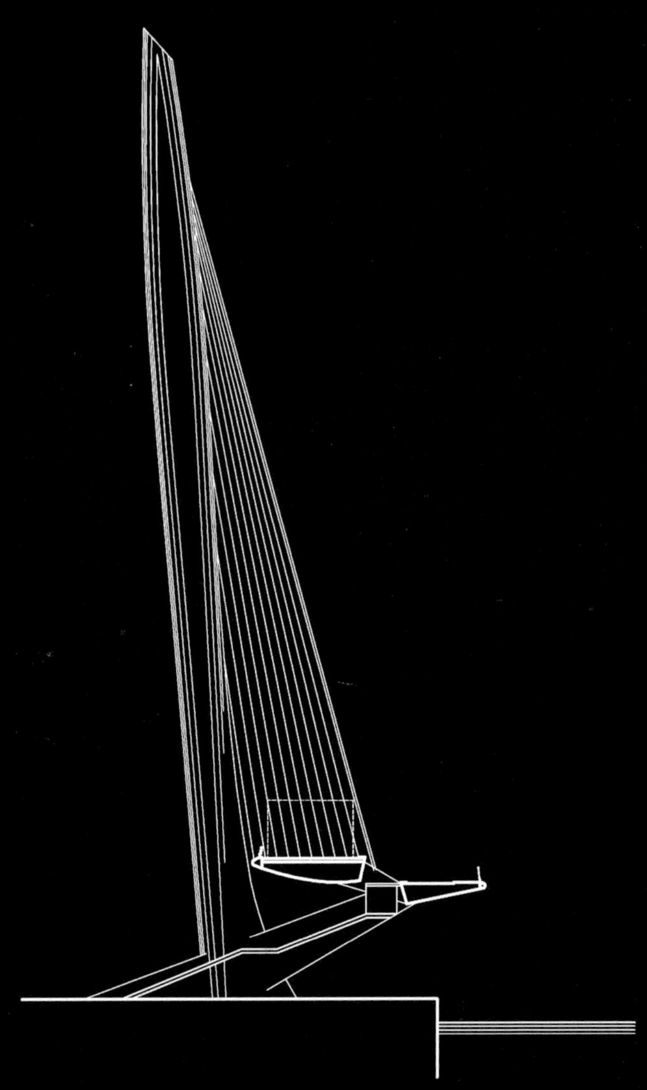

HOV Bridge

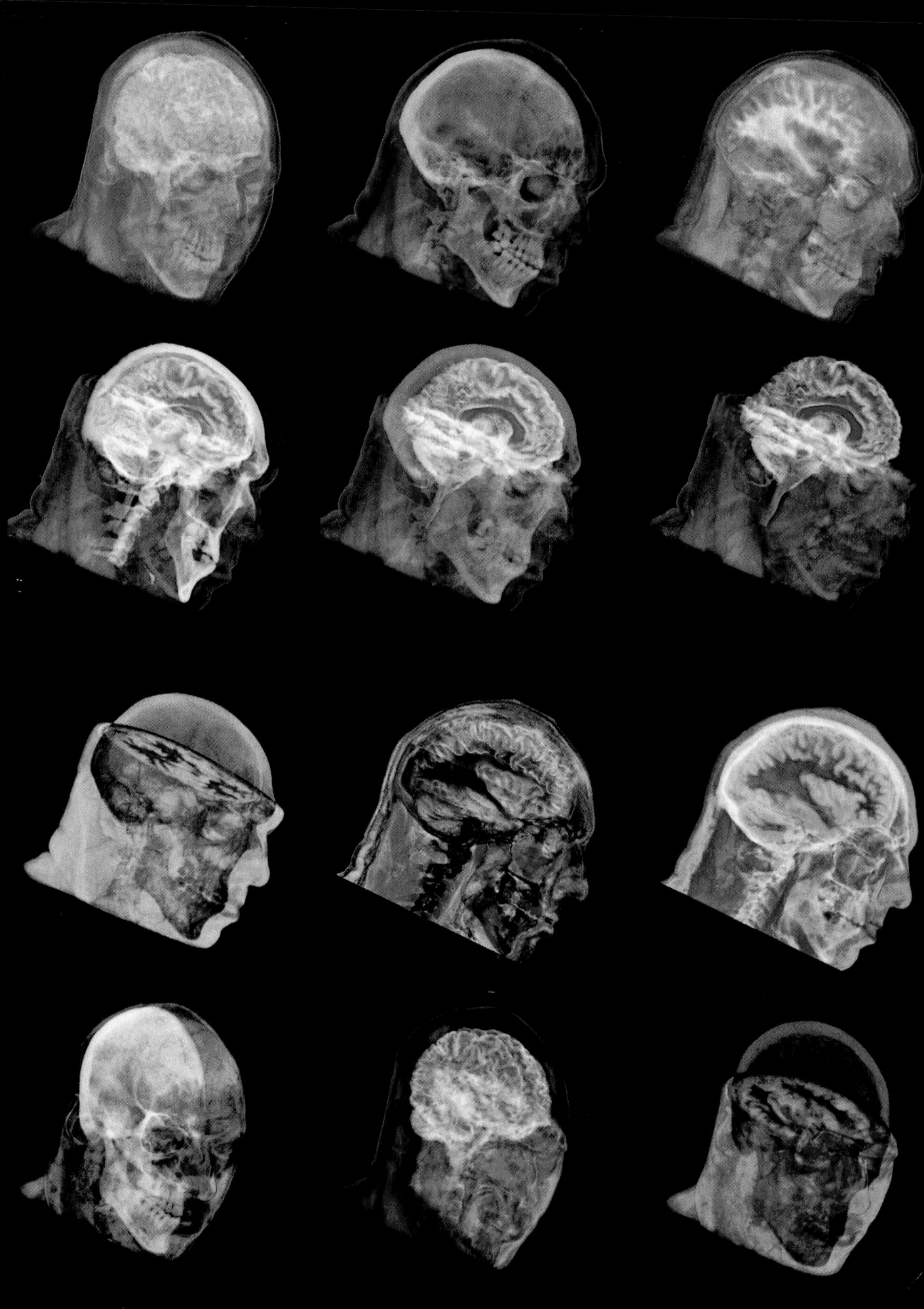

Material organisation

Architecture still articulates its concepts, design decisions and processes almost exclusively by means of a posteriori rationalisations. The compulsive force of legitimising arguments still dominates, even though it represents only a limited interpretation of the complex web of considerations that surrounds a project. Yet, for the most part, we cannot bear to analyse our own internal discourse for fear of disrupting the notion of the eminent utility of our projects and accordingly precipitating their disappearance. Strategies, formulations and the ways in which interests evolve are related to architecture's dependent position within the economic process. Frustratingly, because of this there is hardly any real architectural theory to be found, despite the diversity of the practices operational today and a hugely expanded volume of architectural publications. There is only after-theory.

Wrongly, theory and technique, just as theory and the material imagination, are disconnected from each other. The private imagination of architecture ostensibly disengages itself from the material and from the public imagination, which is in reality impossible. The architectural imagination is as much informed by material stuff as it is by the misty, semi-conscious preoccupations of the collective vision, such as magazine glamour, sex and celebrity. The contingent manifestations of the surrealism and the vast logistics of everyday life exert a concrete fascination, which architecture relies on for its own production of ideas. There are two types of considerations at the foundation of organising architectural structures: pre-physical and physical or material aspects. The search for new forms of ordering principles, different from Cartesian geometry, has resulted in far-reaching virtual organisations. Architects have studied flocking behaviour, swarm systems and similar self-organising systems to discover their ramifications for virtual concepts of control. But the implications of material organisational transformations have been less intensely investigated.

How can we approach materiality in a new way?

The current generation of architects is already free.

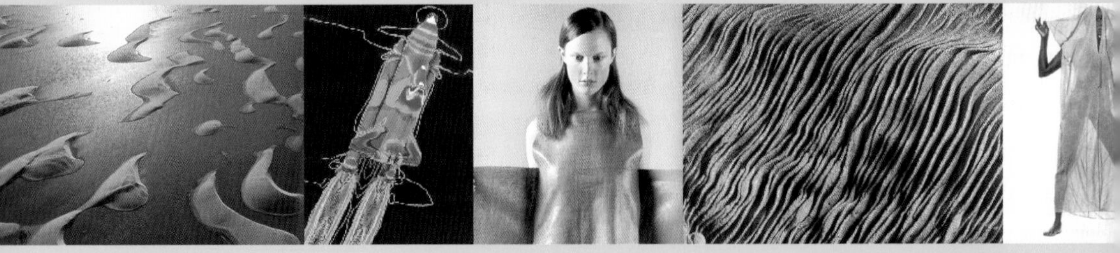

We have already forgotten history, shaken off the metaphors belonging to wood, bricks and steel. We have already seen emptiness. Now it is time redefine

materiality. Let's re-think materials in relation to organisational structures. The subject of material organisational research is not the chemical composition, the sensibility, or the invention of materials, but their performance in the emergence of the project. Unforeseeable effects appear when re-thinking organisational structures surpasses the virtual and takes materiality equally into account. A real exploitation of new techniques includes calculating the dimensions, thickness and tensile forces of materials used in specific works of architecture. The behaviour of materials in specific situations significantly contributes to the structural organisation of architecture.
Contemporary techniques enable new insights to be gained into this type of behaviour. Computer studies of the pylon of the Erasmus Bridge, which display different colours according to how the steel reacts to the structural forces at various points, are comparable to brain

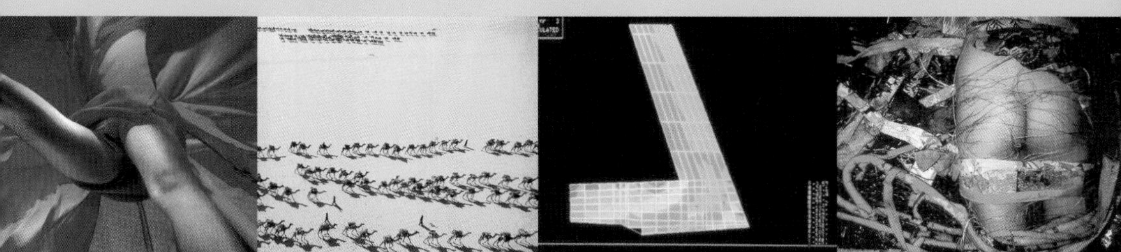

scans in which the part of the brain in use at a particular moment is shown in colour. More is revealed than structure alone: entire processes are made visible,

demonstrating how the material and the virtual are interwoven in topological geometries. The limits of possible organisations become manifest through the strengths and weaknesses of materials. The development of new design and building techniques pushes material theory forward. The bottom-up thinking of material organisation is combined with the top-down thinking of virtual organisation to achieve an architecture that is both topologically and materially rooted.

A key question for architecture is how to fit large-scale infrastructural projects in dense urban situations. In this project, material effects comply with the directness and fast action of everyday life. Movement, texture and light modify the emergence and disappearance of the tunnel and its two service buildings.

Speed

The tunnel is part of the continuing redevelopment of the old docks of Amsterdam and was developed in close collaboration with a syndicate of civil engineers and installation consultants. The architectural contribution to the project consists of the tunnel entrances and two service buildings. A criss-cross steel construction above the tunnel entrances provides a gradual transition from the outside to the interior of the tunnel. The small buildings contain the ventilators of the tunnel. As urban signposts, the service buildings marking the tunnel mouths have see-through geometrical planes that envelop their concrete cores. At night they are lit from within. The facades are more or less transparent depending on the time of day, the incidence of light and the position of the spectator. Their shape derives from their sideways positioning in relation to the tunnel entrances.

HET IJ
LOKATIE TIJDEL
TUNNELELEMENT
IJHAVEN
LOKATIE VERONDIEPING
PANAMAWEG
VERLENGDE

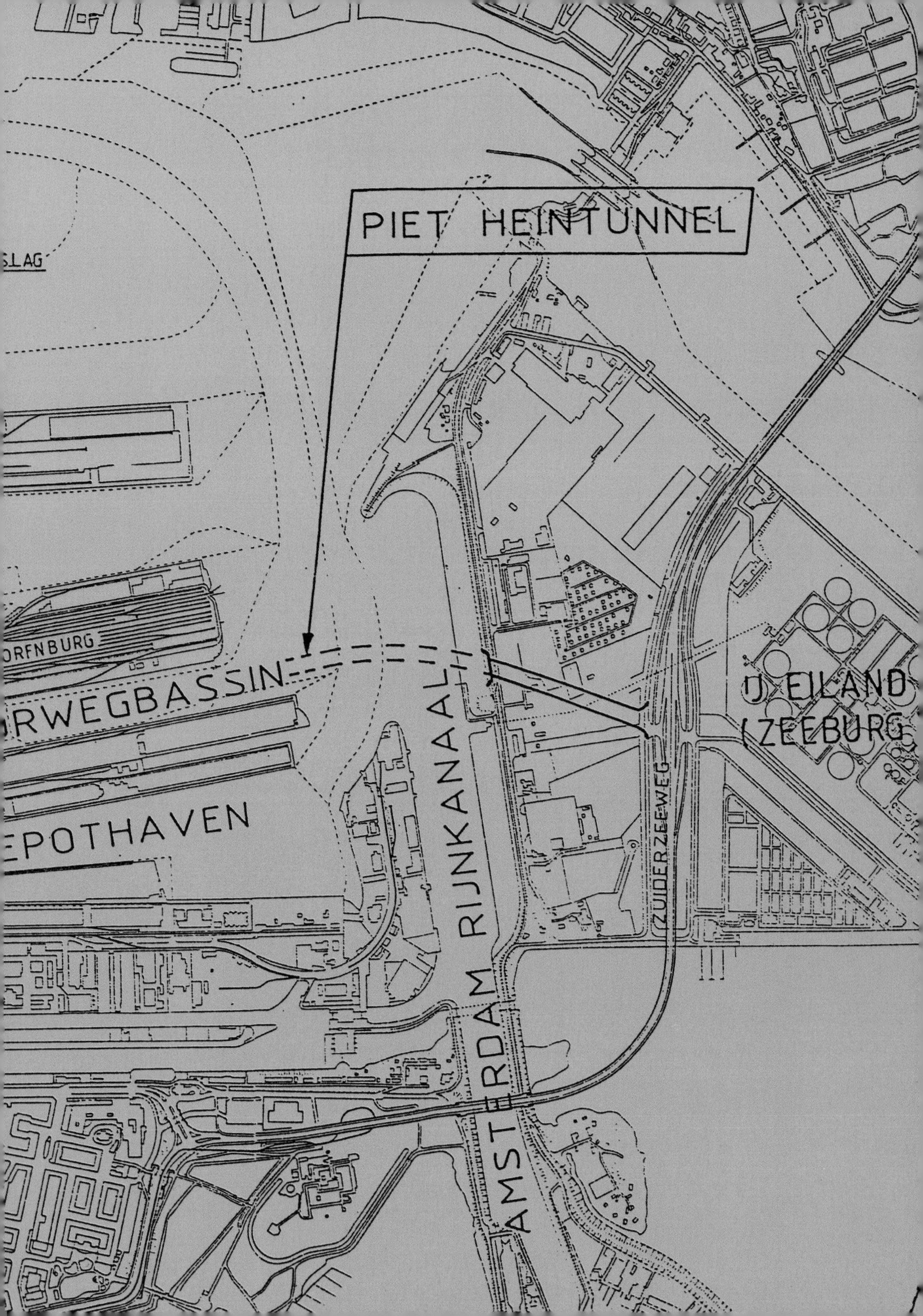
PIET HEINTUNNEL
SLAG
ORFNBURG
RWEGBASSIN
EPOTHAVEN
AMSTERDAM RIJNKANAAL
ZUIDERZEEWEG
IJ-EILAND
(ZEEBURG)

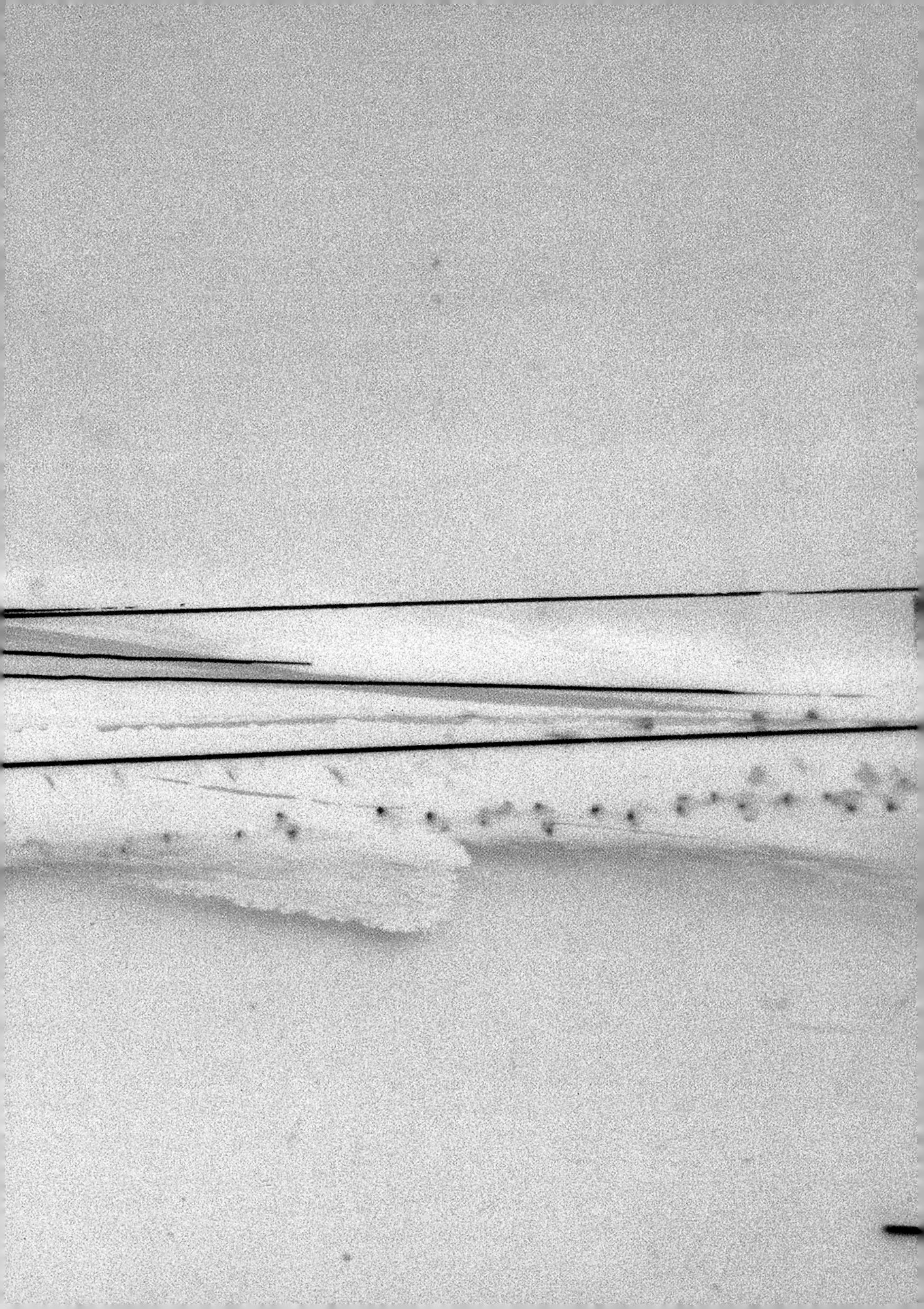

The exploration of the limits of materials is the structuring element of the objects that shape this interior. A bench of laminated wood pushes irregularity and indeterminacy - glued glass pushes adhesiveness.

Manipulation of materiality

Situated on the fourth floor of the building, the Directors room of the Netherlands Architecture Institute is part of the administrative department. A partially sandblasted glazed wall separates the room from the rest of the floor. On the Director's side, the glass wall is used as a screen for video and slide projection; a specially designed box housing the video and slide projector is suspended from the ceiling. The projected images can also be seen from the small waiting room on the other side of the glazed wall, be it in reverse.

The room is soberly furnished, in accordance with the rest of the building. The principal space-structuring element is a storage unit of stainless steel and sandblasted glass, containing show-cases and cupboards. Through the translucent glass, the skyline of Rotterdam can be seen. The hinges are glued to the glass doors - producing a 'look, no screws' effect.

detail storage unit

The waiting room contains a bench and small table of indeterminate scale-less character. These objects are made from thin slices of wood glued together. Exploiting the properties of this composite substance enables a complex shape, which is not derived from the plan analysis or the function analysis of the object but from its material potential.

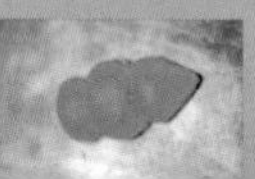

One material is used principally; horizontal concrete panels cover the interior walls, floors and ceilings, rendering the interior as uniform and continuous as a smooth, grey, cigar box.

Almost-nothingness

The gallery and café are situated in an Art Nouveau complex in the former East Berlin and the same materials and details are used for both. In the gallery, the sober interior provides a neutral background for the works being exhibited. The consistent use of concrete is like the lining of a box - or a skin covering the carcass of the old structure. In places, the skin swells up to form a piece of furniture, also made of concrete. Thin, pliant light fittings are the only objects to perforate the continuous concrete surface.

In the café, benches of laminated wood and glazed, silk-screened walls have been added as foils to the concrete. Benches, tables and cup-boards constructed of multiple layers of headers establish a new way of working with this material. Green glass, printed with an enlarged computer image of wood structure is applied in front of the concrete walls.

movable hanging system

Planning the wrong way around, starting with a detail or a material, which becomes a parameter for the development of the larger project, makes more sense than beginning with the formulation of a concept. Instead of trying to impose a simplistic standard pattern on an unpredictable and constantly changing world, we identify meaningful parameters within contemporary conditions. These parameters form the basis for the activities, directions and strategies underlying the organisation of urban plans. Such an approach, which is more experimental than conceptual, engenders specific and concrete research techniques and transformative design processes.

Retail therapy: cosmetic surgery for shops

The renovation of the V&D Department store in Emmen precedes the urban study of the same location by a year. This reversal of the usual order signifies a more generative understanding of local structures. The work on the department store provides material for the transformative processes of urbanism, as well as revealing qualities and potentials of the location.

The centre of Emmen is a Dutch-modern, basic 1960s low-rise, light-brick, concrete and tarmac constellation of minimal allure, of which the

M&S MODE

Generale Bank

department store is part. Its renovation and conversion include the reorganisation of the building and the addition of a gallery, apartments and smaller shop outlets, as well as a re-cladding of the external surfaces. New glazed facades have replaced heavy concrete plates. A range of facade types can be distinguished from a simple utilitarian skin to the rounded glazed facade of the gallery.
The urban proposal continues the strategy of engaging, extending and complicating the existing, uniform, architectural mass by selecting phased interventions at strategic points. Three significant nodes have been identified to function as entrance points to the area. New developments are to be specifically linked to the existing low-rise structure in a manner defined by the term 'square building'; this establishes a strong relation to the ground plane.

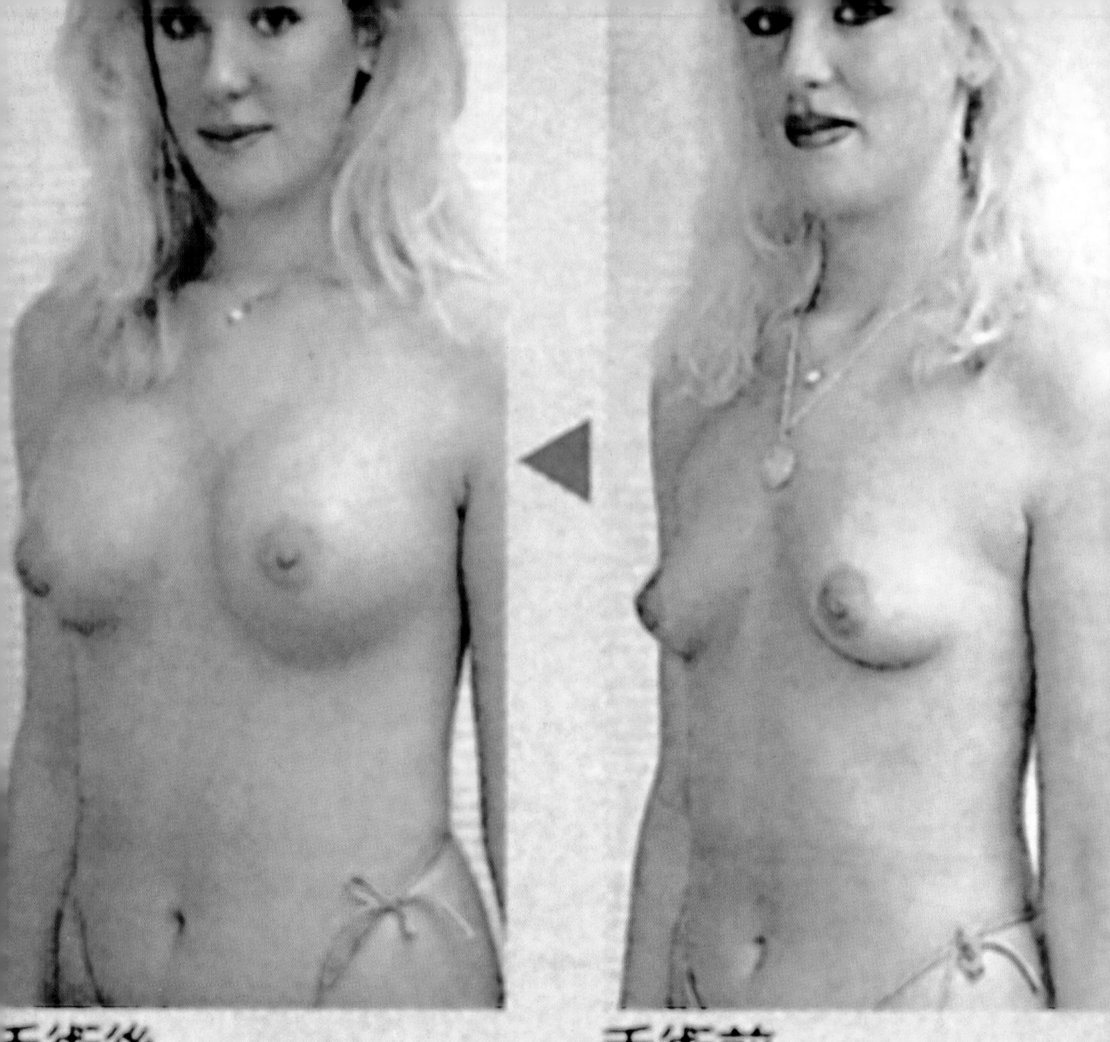

手術後　　　手術前

成功率99%以上

陥没乳頭

乳管を残したまま完治します。
当日からシャワー・ブラジャーOKです。

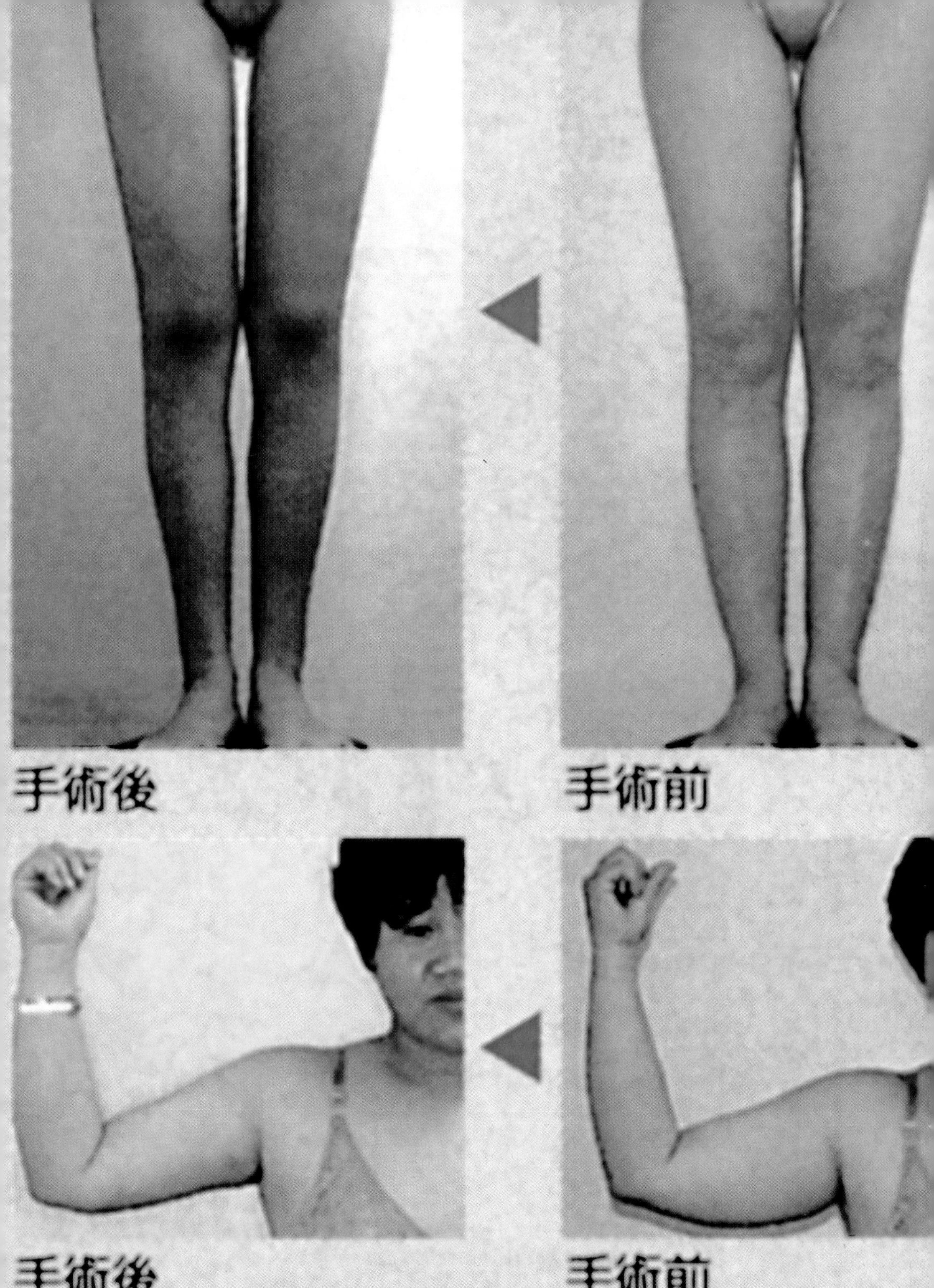
手術後
手術前
手術後
手術前

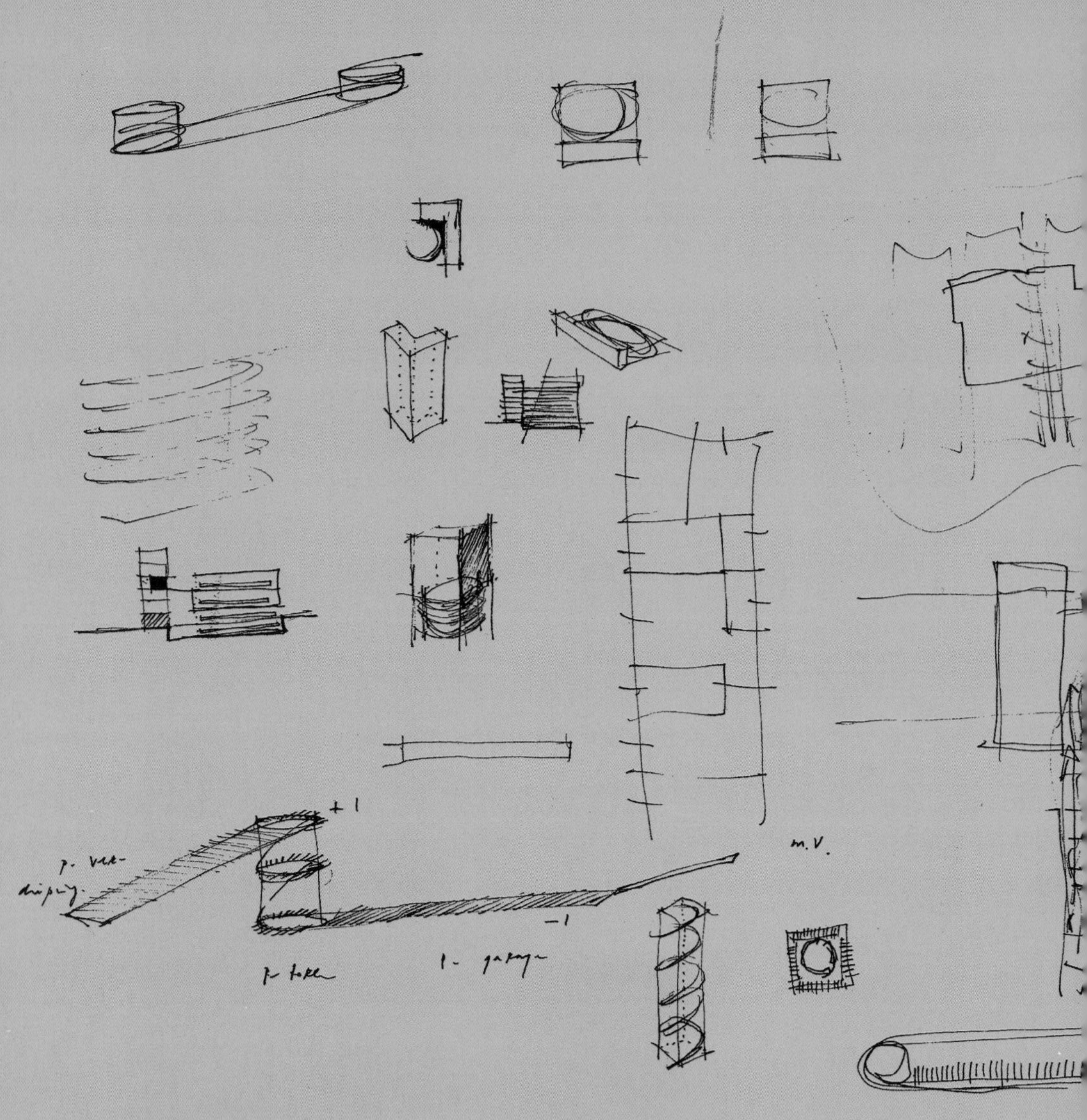
+1
−1
p. garage
m.V.

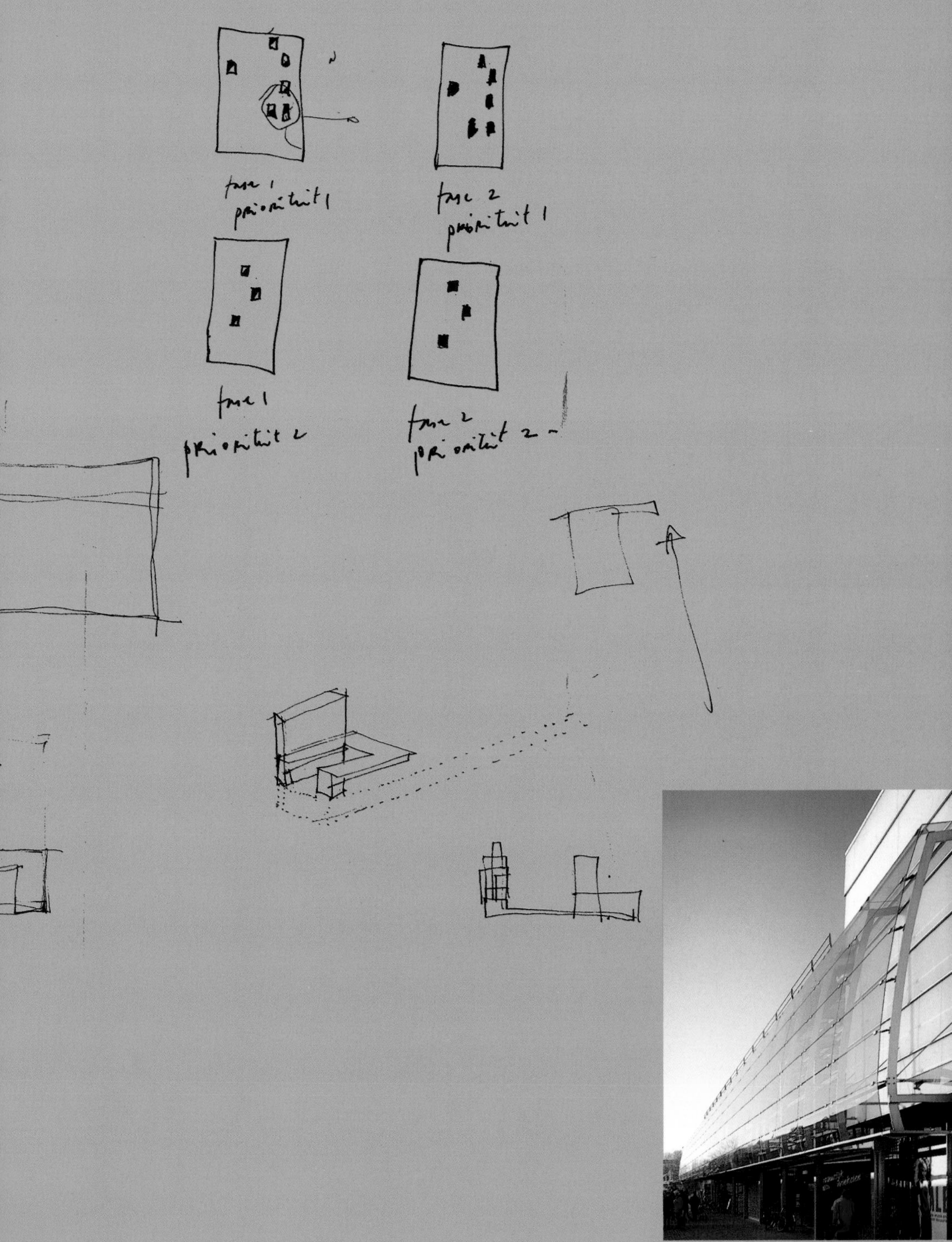
fase 1
prioriteit 1
fase 2
prioriteit 1
fase 1
prioriteit 2
fase 2
prioriteit 2

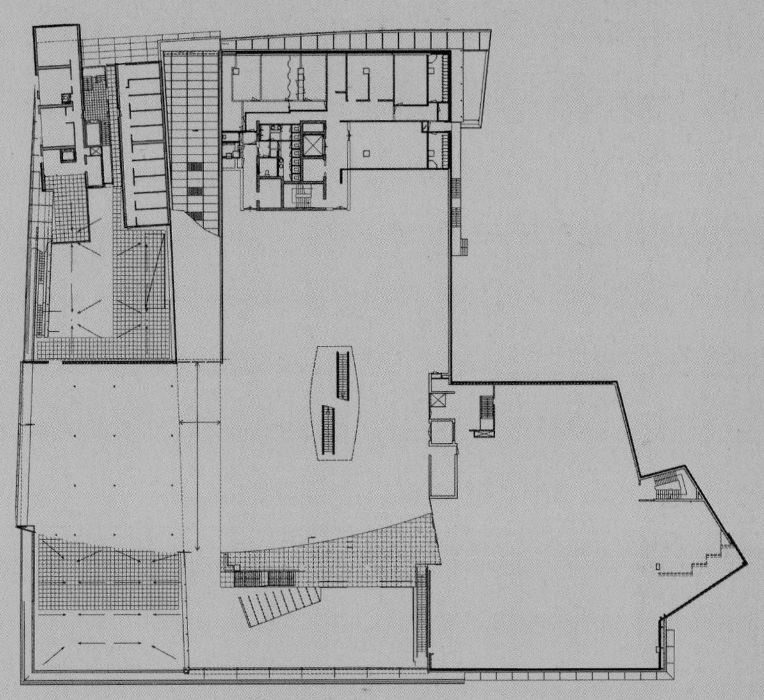

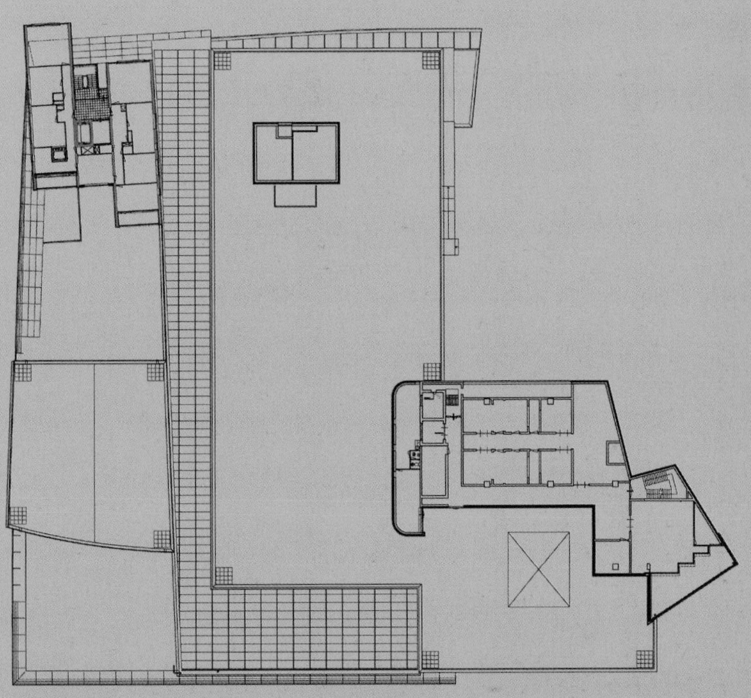

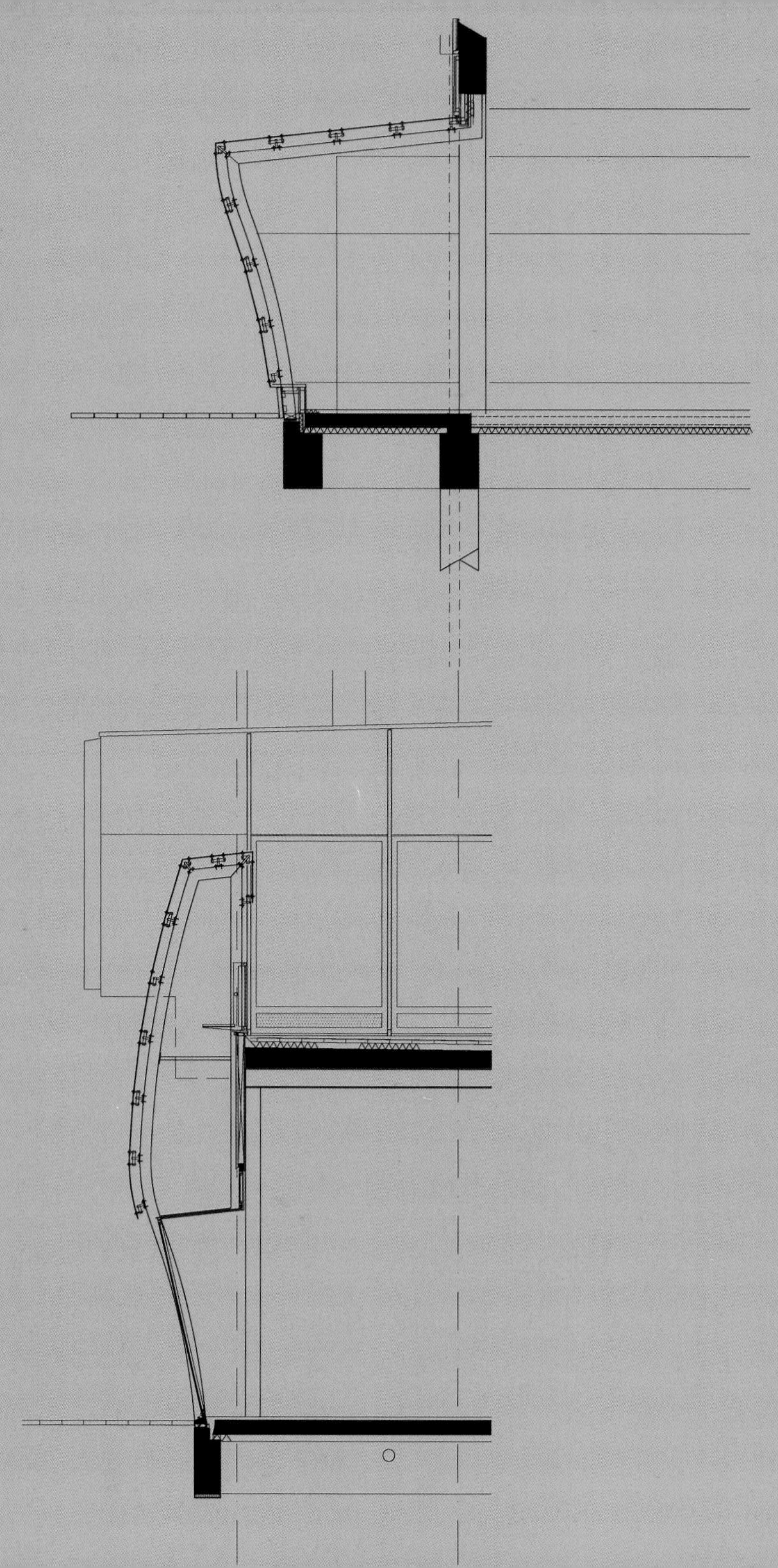

SALE
AFPRYZINGEN OP EEN GROOT
DEEL VAN DE COLLECTIE
SALE
AFPRYZINGEN OP EEN GROOT
DEEL VAN DE COLLECTIE

Technological objects and infrastructure are increasingly seen as an integral part of the environment. Designing them as such requires the involvement of architects in civil engineering projects. Architects and engineers have to learn to work together in a new, non-hierarchical relationship, in which their differing concerns and approaches are placed on an equal footing. The question is how to optimise this new connection, how to effectuate control and motivation in a new and better way of organising utilitarian structures.

Bascule Bridges

Bridge for an ordinary place

An intense mixture of technique and infrastructure has resulted in a bridge consisting of three individual decks, which open and close asynchronously, imitating the movement of playing fingers. In the flat polder landscape, the bridge links a new housing development to the main road. The longitudinal separation of the bridge deck into two pedestrian and cycle routes and one road for cars enhances traffic safety. The finger-like arrangement also results in extra mooring space for pleasure boats. A cycle path runs below the bridge, along the waterfront, contributing to the low key recreational value of this workaday location.

The bridge elements are controlled from the bridge master's house; a small edifice that is perched eight metres above the water level. The technical facilities are placed at ground level; the main programme is channelled upstairs, where the domestic spaces and workrooms of the bridge master are situated. Perforated steel plates, which are applied to the concrete core of the building, reveal the functions of the lower half from some angles. Depending on the viewpoint, the building is transparent, semi-transparent, or closed. Moiré effects are gleaned from certain perspectives. A concrete footbridge leads to the glazed entranceway.

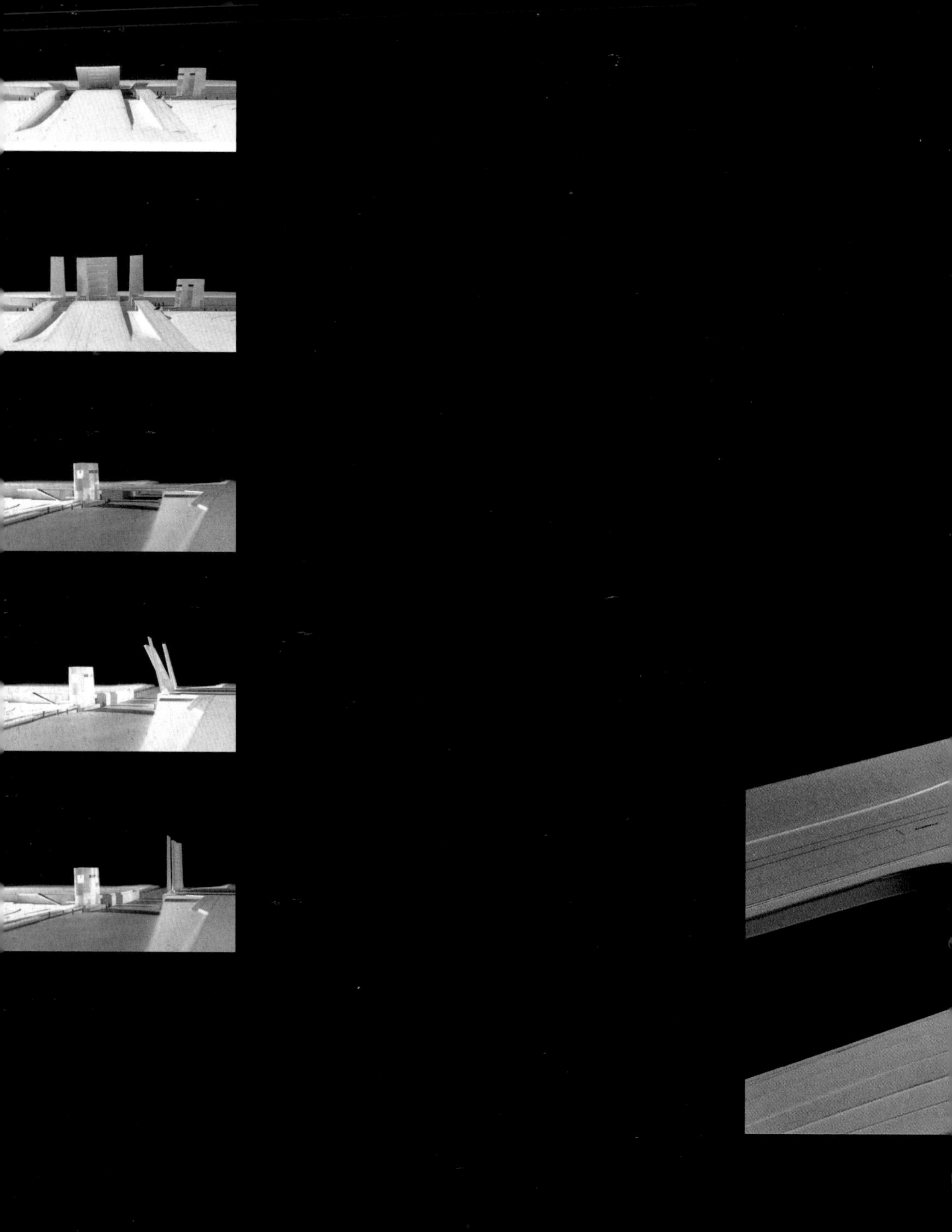

individual decks open and close

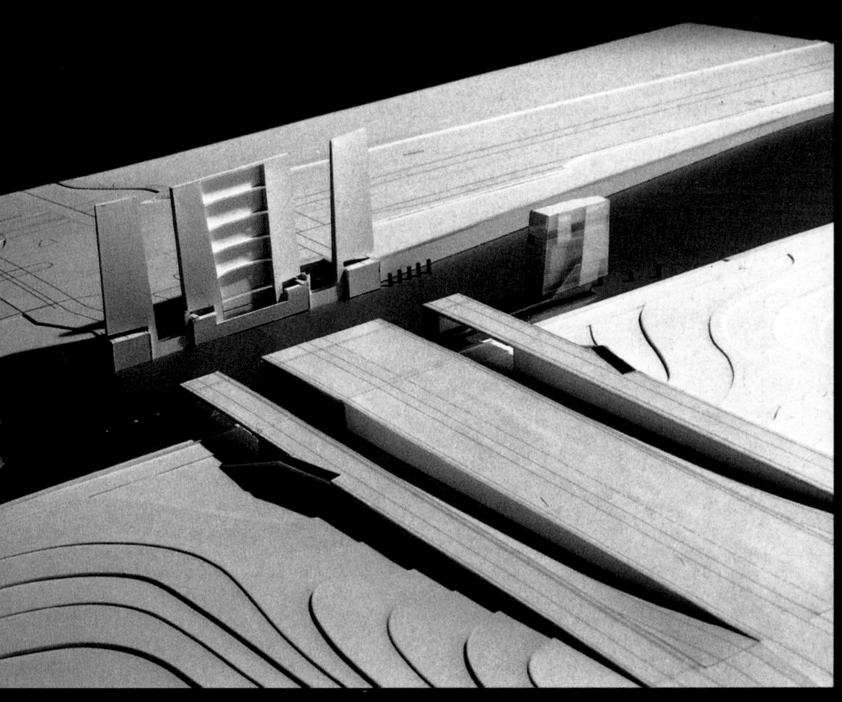

synchronously

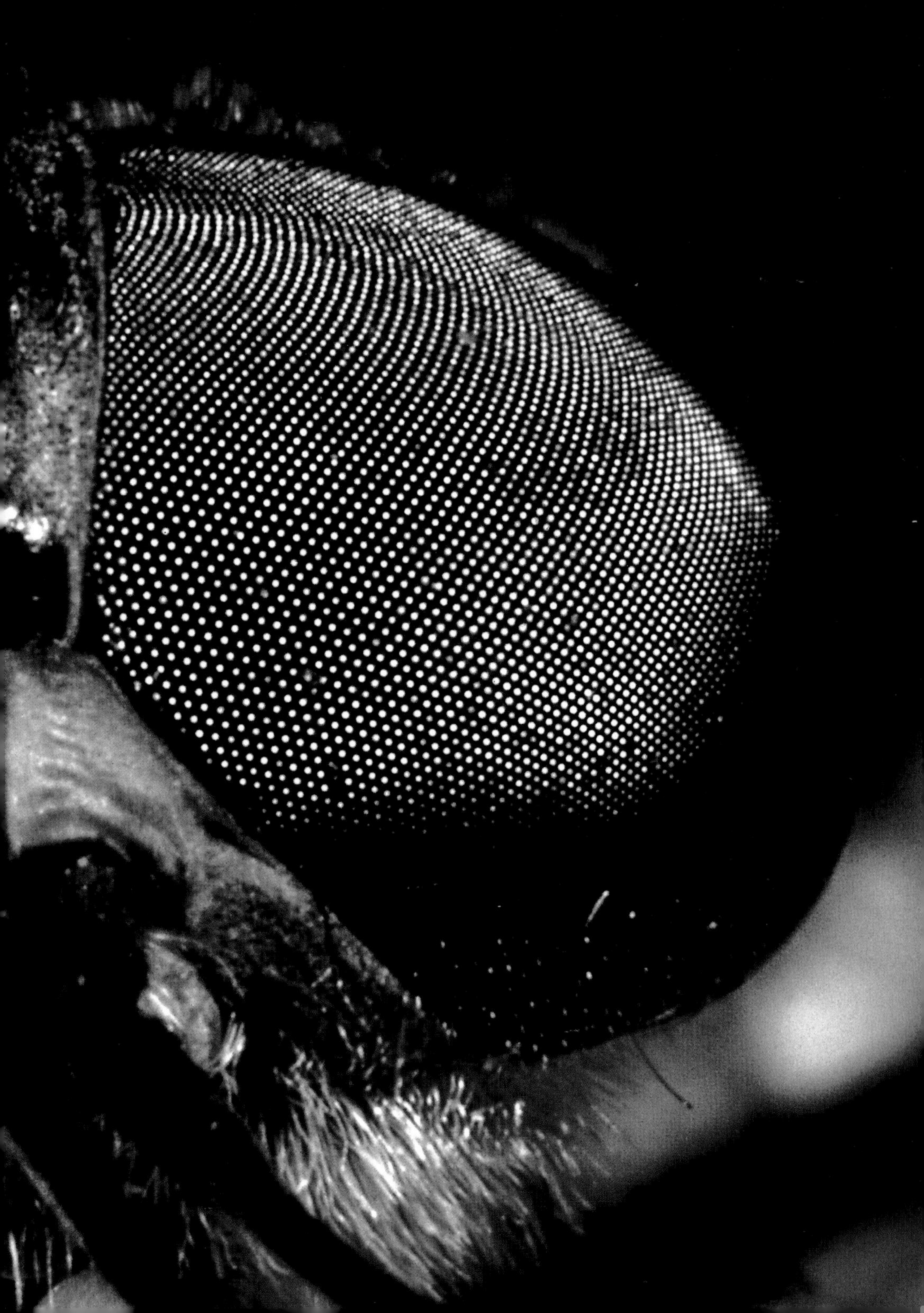

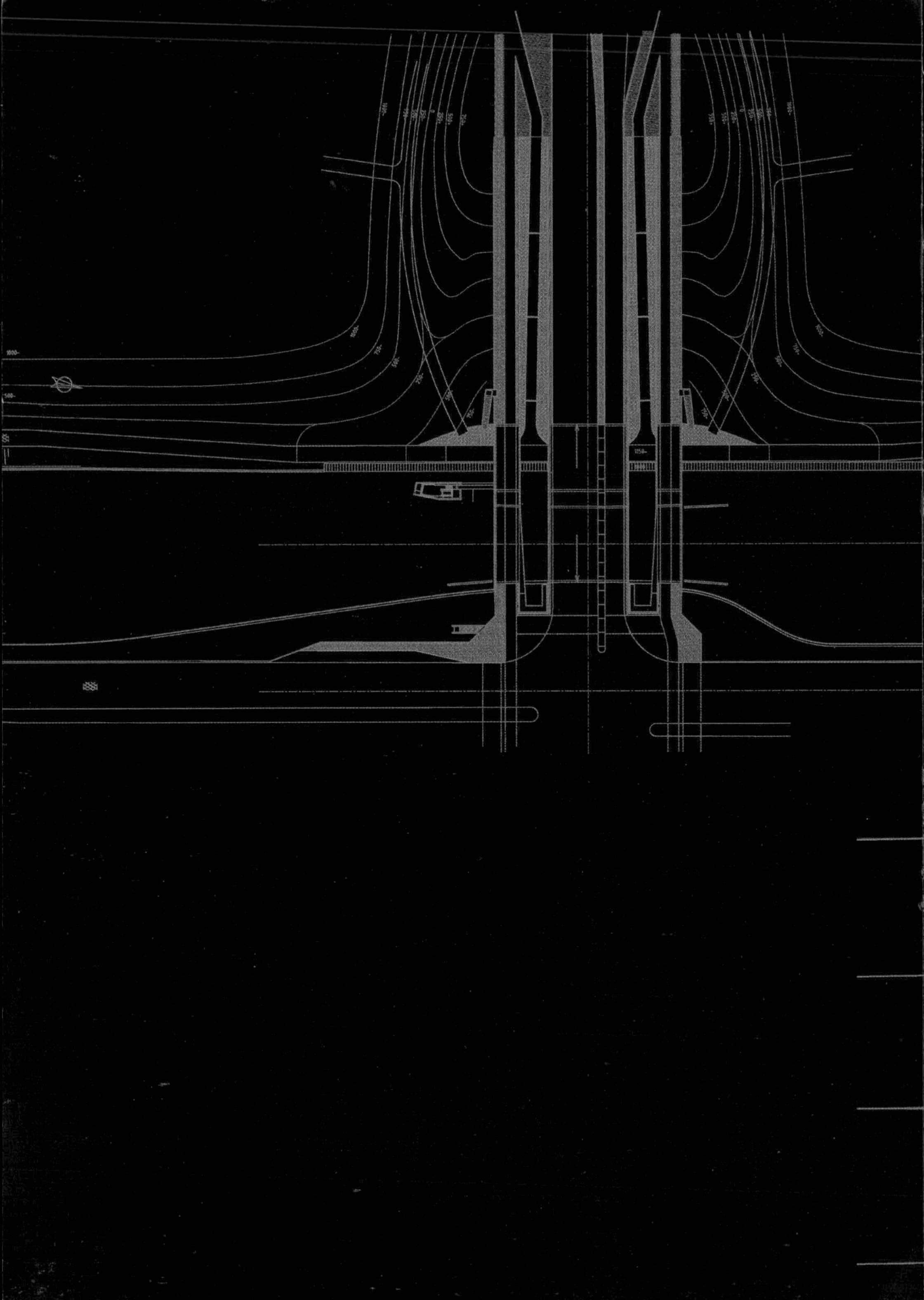

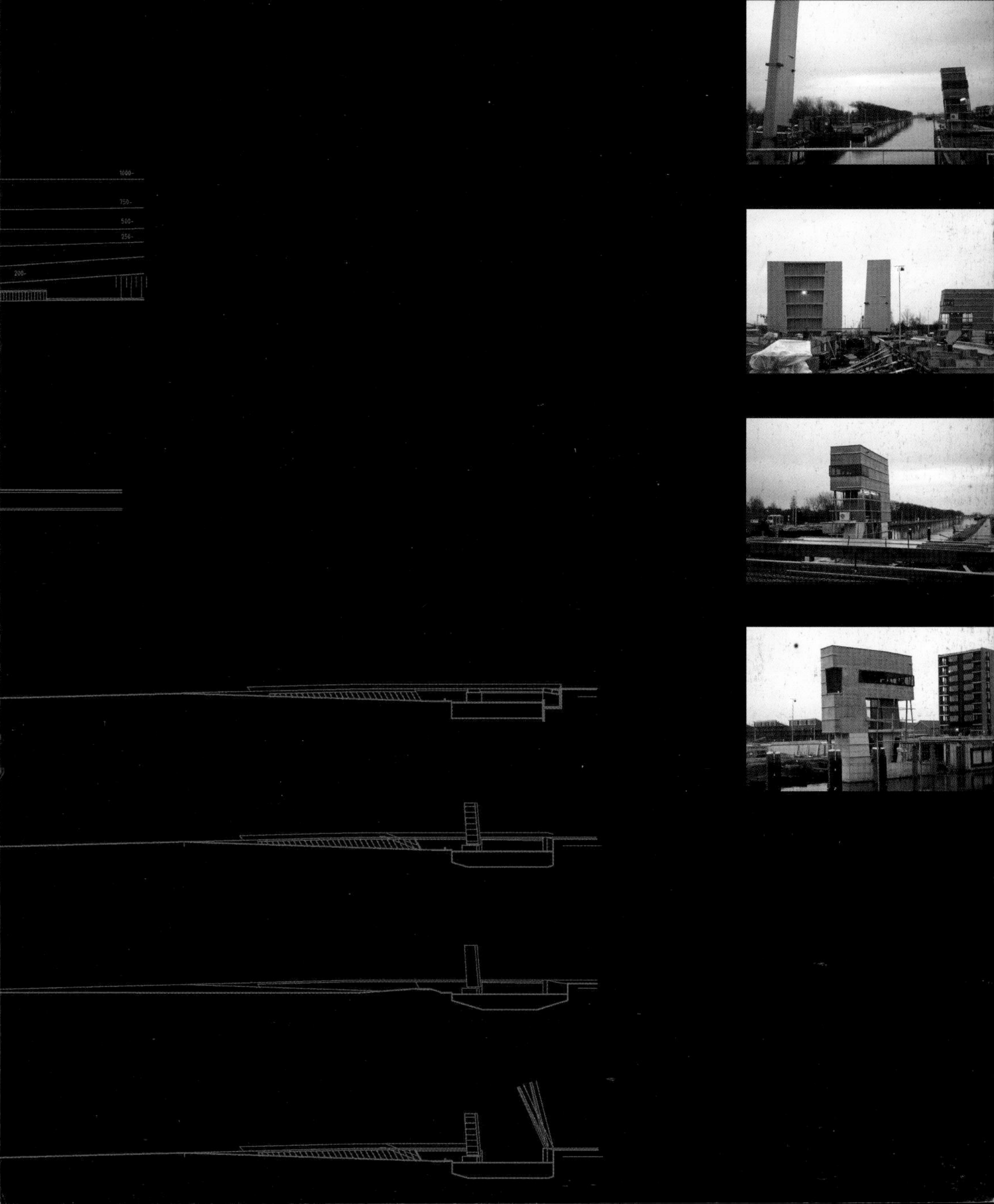
1000-
750-
500-
250-
200-

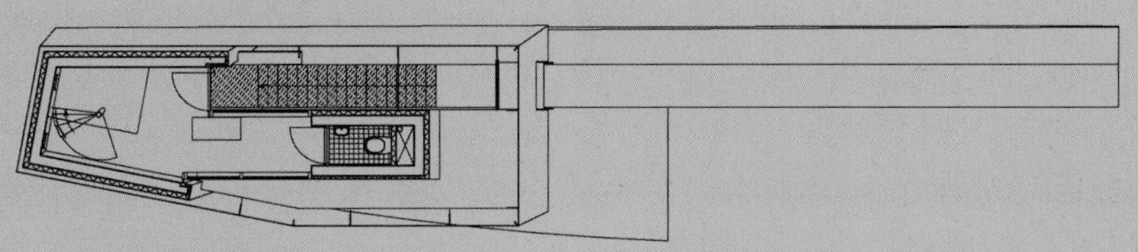

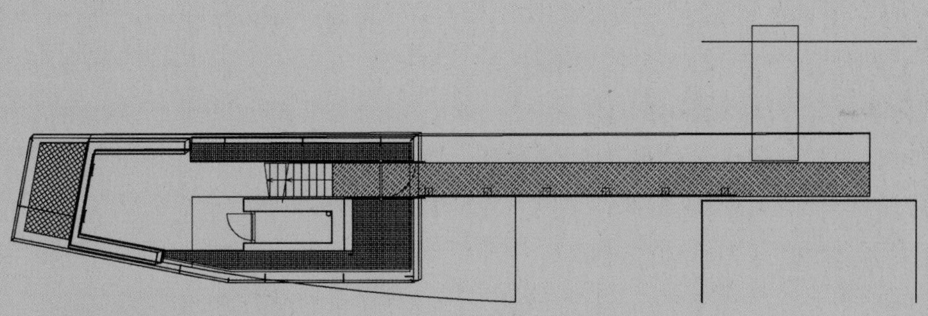

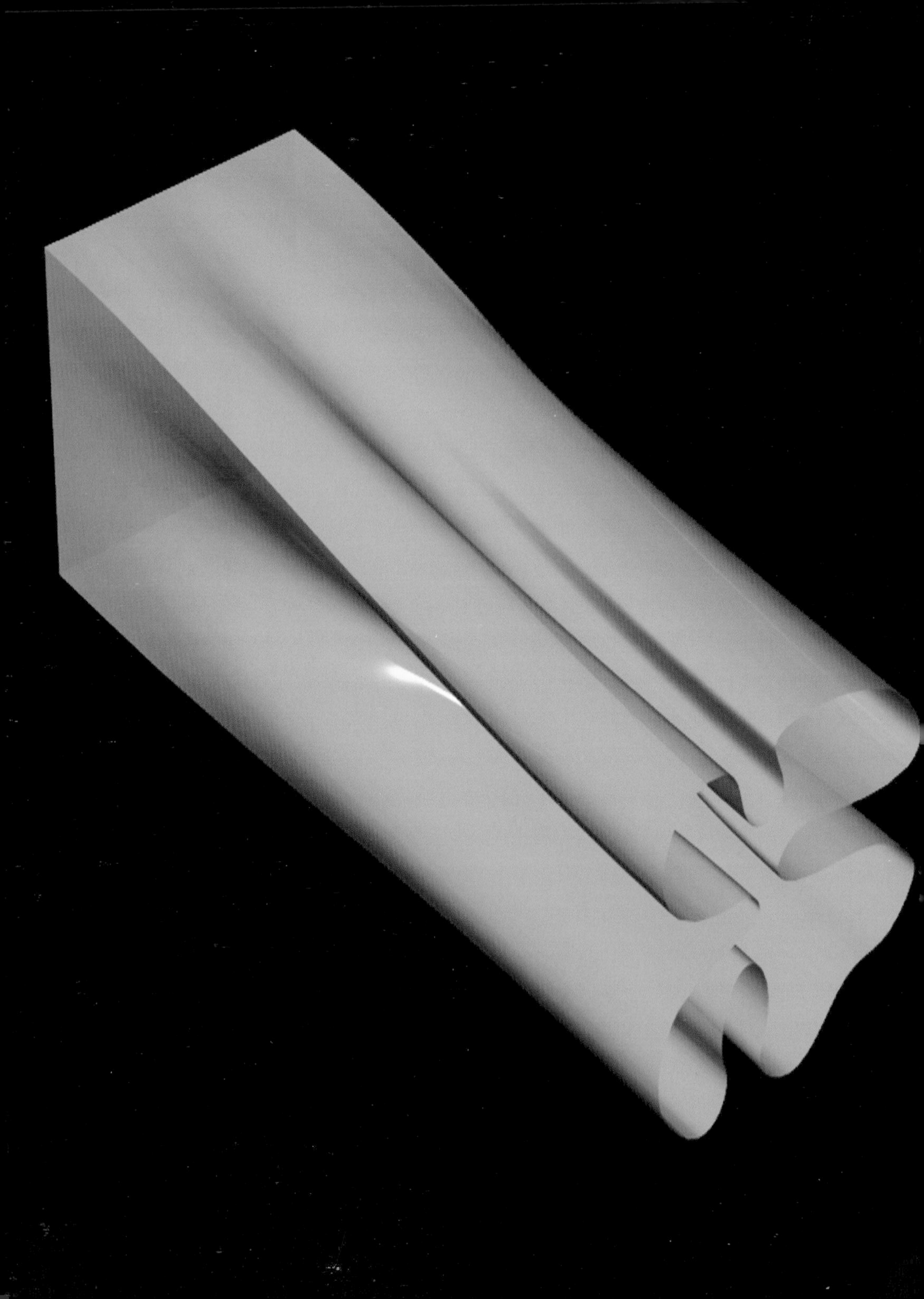

Inclusiveness

Blob or box - it doesn't matter anymore. To redefine organisational structures in an inclusive way means to proportion all information at the basis of the project in one, comprehensive system. Time and construction are compressed into one organisational structure. Rationality and fantasy coincide. The inclusive organisation absorbs all aspects of a project; its material and virtual systems and its underlying values are all taken into the equation. As values shift, the proportions change. If the resulting project possesses proportions that work and it sounds right, it can take any form. Just as any construction that holds up, is a good, or a good-enough, construction, the inclusive organisation is good, or good-enough, when it has fairly balanced out its inherent material and immaterial values.
Inclusiveness is about efficiency. The inclusive organisation tolerates any style, any concept. There is no wastage; all the fragmented analyses of the past can be recycled, connected and taken up in the line of continuity proposed by the inclusive model. The inclusive model is anti nothing. Do you like boxes? No problem, nowadays your shoes can be packed in a box or a bag; you can put the box in the bag too - it’s up to you.

We no longer think in terms of individual ingredients but instead base the organisation on one comprehensive gesture incorporating difference. All material and immaterial aspects of the project, the engineering and the substance of architecture result from a unifying approach of these points. In this way, the understanding and treatment of projects like the single-family house, the museum, music centre or library shifts from an iconic typology with its determinants in local conventions to a new, multi-facetted approach.

There is more to this than the understanding that complex geometries and simple geometries are part and parcel of the same system. The insight that a straight line is nothing more than a section out of a larger curve is an important one. Both the theoretical understanding and the production processes of architecture benefit from this breakdown of the opposition between orthogonal and formless configurations. But inclusiveness goes

beyond geometry, which is only one of the parameters with which architecture works.

Inclusiveness applies to the non-hierarchical, complex,

generative nature of an integral design process that takes on board all aspects of architecture. The shifting fields of engineering, urbanism and infrastructure form some of the most important parameters of architecture. These fields exist concurrently in one project. So why should we treat the project as fragmented during the design process? Having re-organised our profession to make better use of co-operative working methods, as well as computational and mediation techniques, we are now able to see all these layers of existence together - in one meeting or on one screen. On a computer station all facets of a project can be quickly and comprehensively examined, switching from wire-frame model to detail, from installations to surface renderings. Complex insights on many levels are presented in an accelerated and compressed way. With these new visualisations, a new form of control opens up. Inclusiveness means switching between four or five

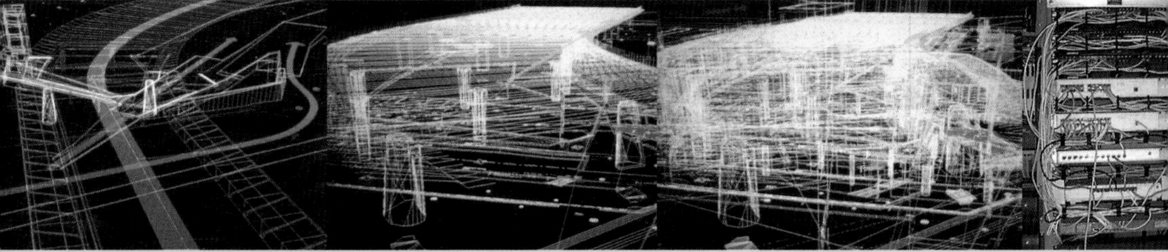

themes, in the way that computer software allows you to switch between layers of information. In the shifting between architecture, engineering, movement, public

life and private imagination it is not the material composition that matters, but the relational order between the components. The new integral visualisation of a project challenges the imagination to also make that switch from construction to spatial effect to organisation. Switching between layers of meaning also means that the inclusive model is the hybridization of multiplicitous sources; the project is not founded on isolated concepts being worked out in a linear process. In that sense inclusiveness implies anti-process thinking. The procedure of inclusive design involves a form of combinative analytical thinking. This entails the examination of the relevant elements of the project in relation to each other - putting pragmatic parameters such as economic values and differential densities on an equal footing with factors such as geometry and policy.
The inclusive project is about assembling and integrally organising layers of significance, both material and immaterial. Redefining organisational structures in this way, switching between themes, using the architectural imagination to proportion information and finally making it sound right, is unconnected to a particular form or geometry. The same information can be proportioned in numerous ways without altering any of the structuring parameters, in the same way that a donut can be twisted into a Möbius strip without

losing its original proportions. The geometry of the inclusive project is a topologically generated one; it is a textured field, a localised relief structure that is based on specific information and that can take on any form, any style, any look. In short, in the inclusive organisation blob and box are the same. Made of the same substance, mobilising ingredients on material, temporal, virtual and constructional levels, the distinction has become meaningless. But don't forget it has to sound right.

The introduction of climatic installations governs the extension and renovation of the museum. These machines organise the new interior arrangement, turning the museum into a breathing machine.

Breathing machine

Four basic needs are addressed in the restructuring of the museum and are intertwined and organised so as to overlap. The museum, which originally dates from 1928, is made to comply with contemporary climatic requirements. A new space to accommodate temporary exhibitions is obtained by roofing over one of the two courtyards. Aligning and enlarging the connections between the rooms improves the entire routing system. Finally, a pavilion, used as restaurant and small meeting hall, is added, situated in the newly landscaped second courtyard.

In the new room, the climatic installations are placed inside vertical elements that are positioned on top of the existing columns of the storage basement under the former courtyard. The elements consist of a steel column, covered on three sides with frosted glass and on the remaining side connected to a concrete wall. This wall serves as a hanging surface and hovers partially above the floor. Air, which is continually

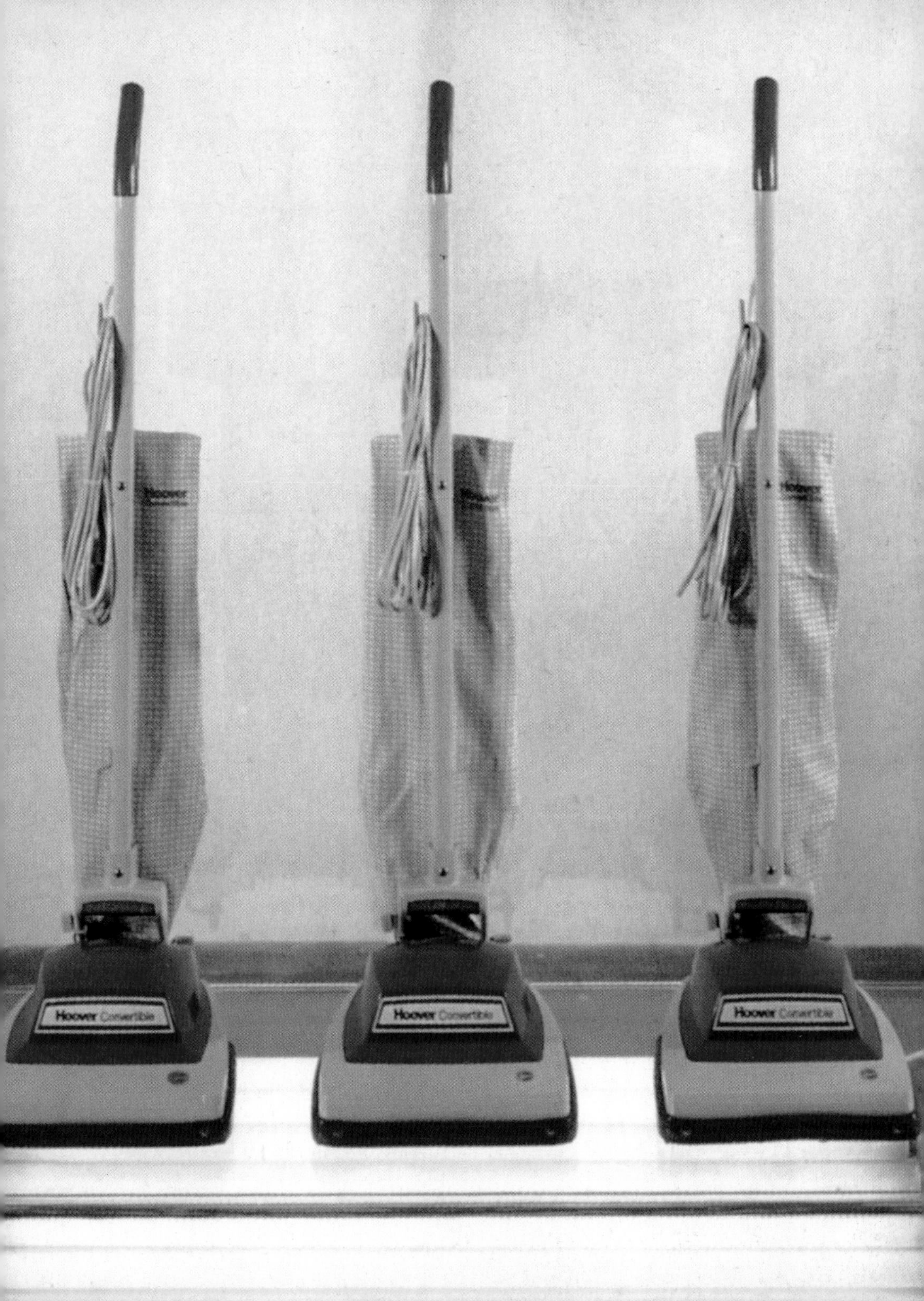
Hoover Convertible
Hoover Convertible
Hoover Convertible

inhaled through slits at the bottom of these walls, is filtered and exhaled at the top.

Frosted glass windows in the ceiling filter the daylight. Openings in the otherwise closed facades around the second courtyard provide visual and physical links between the old and new parts of the building.

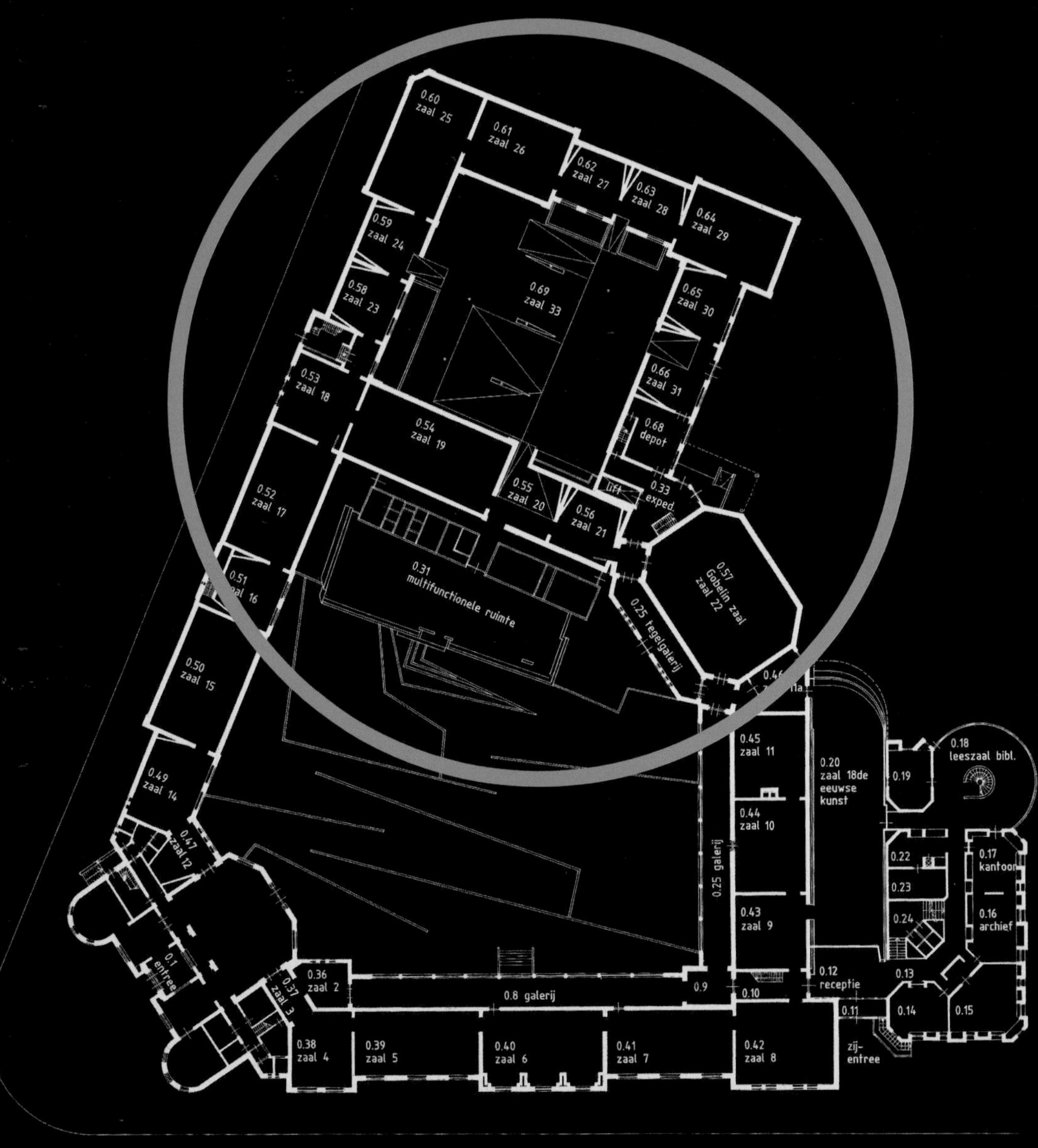

0.60 zaal 25
0.61 zaal 26
0.62 zaal 27
0.63 zaal 28
0.64 zaal 29
0.59 zaal 24
0.69 zaal 33
0.65 zaal 30
0.58 zaal 23
0.66 zaal 31
0.53 zaal 18
0.68 depot
0.54 zaal 19
0.55 zaal 20
lift
0.33 exped.
0.56 zaal 21
0.52 zaal 17
0.57 Gobelin zaal zaal 22
0.31 multifunctionele ruimte
0.51 zaal 16
0.25 tegelgalerij
0.50 zaal 15
0.45 zaal 11
0.20 zaal 18de eeuwse kunst
0.19
0.18 leeszaal bibl.
0.49 zaal 14
0.44 zaal 10
0.47 zaal 12
0.25 galerij
0.22
0.17 kantoor
0.23
0.16 archief
0.24
0.43 zaal 9
0.1 entree
0.36 zaal 2
0.37 zaal 3
0.8 galerij
0.9
0.10
0.12 receptie
0.13
0.11
0.14
0.15
0.38 zaal 4
0.39 zaal 5
0.40 zaal 6
0.41 zaal 7
0.42 zaal 8
zij-entree

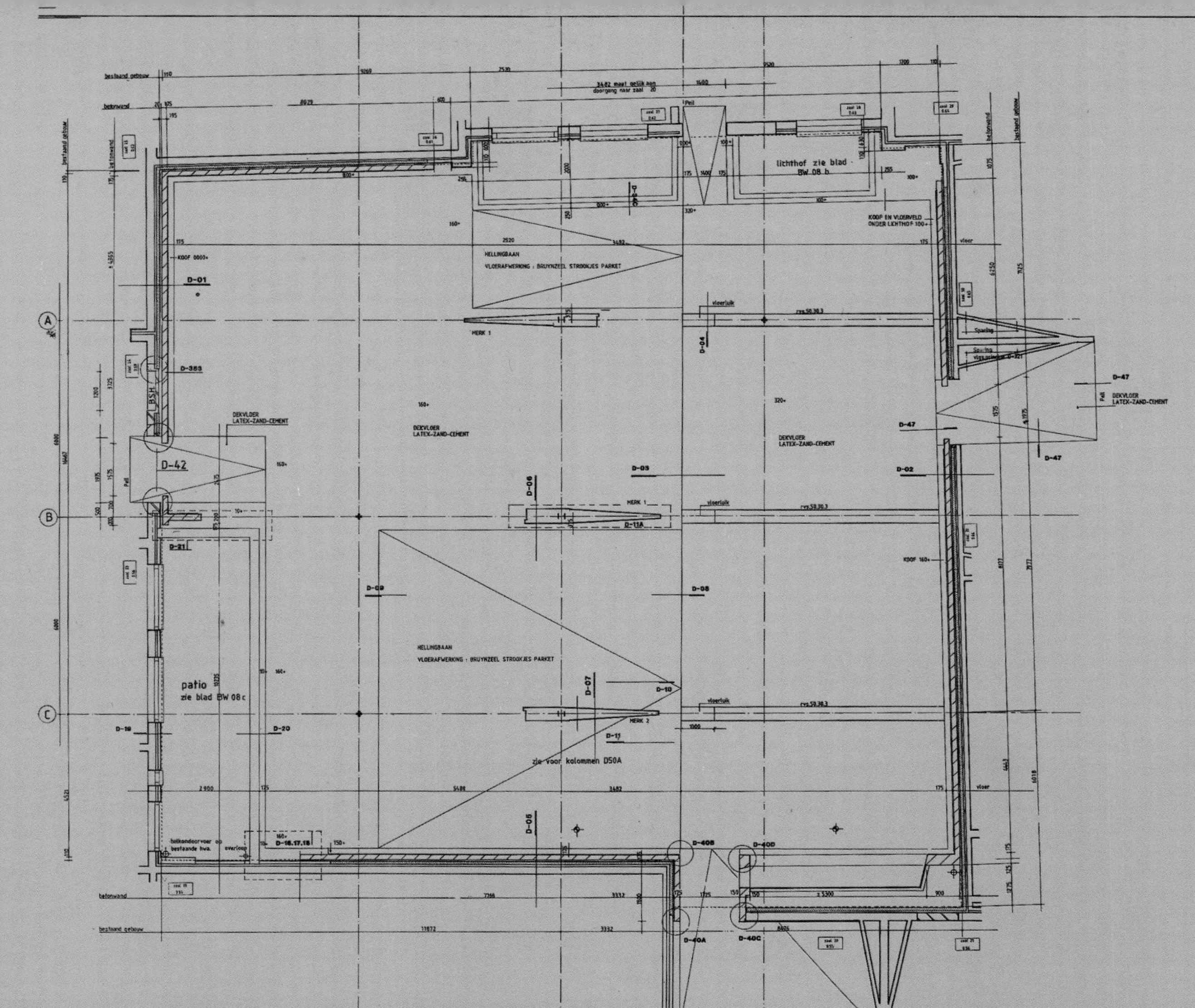

bestaand gebouw
betonwand
3482 maat gelijk aan
doorgang naar zaal 20
lichthof zie blad
BW 08 h
KOOP EN VLOERVELD
ONDER LICHTHOF 100+
HELLINGBAAN
VLOERAFWERKING : BRUYNZEEL STROOKJES PARKET
D-01
D-383
DEKVLOER
LATEX-ZAND-CEMENT
D-42
D-21
D-04
vloerluik
MERK 1
D-47
D-03
D-02
D-06
D-11A
D-09
D-08
D-07
D-10
MERK 2
D-11
zie voor kolommen D50A
patio
zie blad BW 08 c
D-19
D-20
D-16.17.18
D-05
D-40B
D-40D
D-40A
D-40C
vloer

Supermarket, temple and social meeting place; programmatically, the contemporary museum is a hybrid space. Technically and structurally, the museum is no less heterogeneous. As a fusion of routing, installations, blank walls, construction, rooms both dark and light, this museum project takes as its departure point the effective achievement of all-including structures to make these components gel.

Space age inspiration: *light and flow structure*

Two main structures organise the museum: the staircase, which starts on the square in front of the museum and continues to the balcony zone on the upper level and the ceiling, which follows the same route. Both elements serve several functions at once. The staircase forms the structural core of the building and is also a distributor in that its branches shoot off to the various programme parts, such as the café, library, museum and central hall. The ceiling, meanwhile, incorporates all the installations and lends coherence to the museum, which in its turn houses a great variety of miscellaneous objects and art works. The public, administrative and storage functions are housed on the ground floor, while the museum and exhibition spaces occupy the first floor. Divided lengthways into parallel streets with

central stair well is constructive and
organises programme distribution

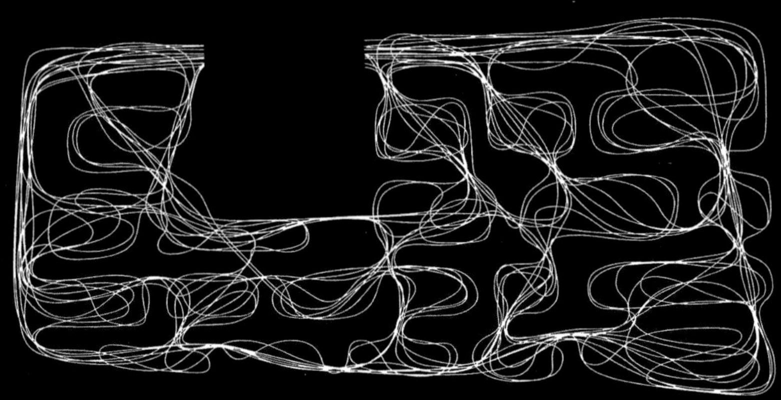

multiple lateral openings, the structure of the museum floor hybridizes the severely regulated with the informal. Attracted by light or by cross-views through the streets, visitors may follow their own individual routes. In this way, the equal-potential structure of the floor plan is challenged and deformed by more fluid and dynamic movement patterns, generating a new structure.

Like a luminous blanket, the ceiling covers, but does not conceal or disguise the multitude of installations for lighting and climate control, the fixings and fittings, the sprinklers and alarms. The undulating ceiling has a wave-like structure, which varies according to the expected movement of visitors. In spaces where most people converge, the waves in the ceiling are more frequent, while they are less frequent and shallower in spaces where less climate-controlling machinery needs to be housed. The ceiling slats are all removable for easy access and machinery maintenance.

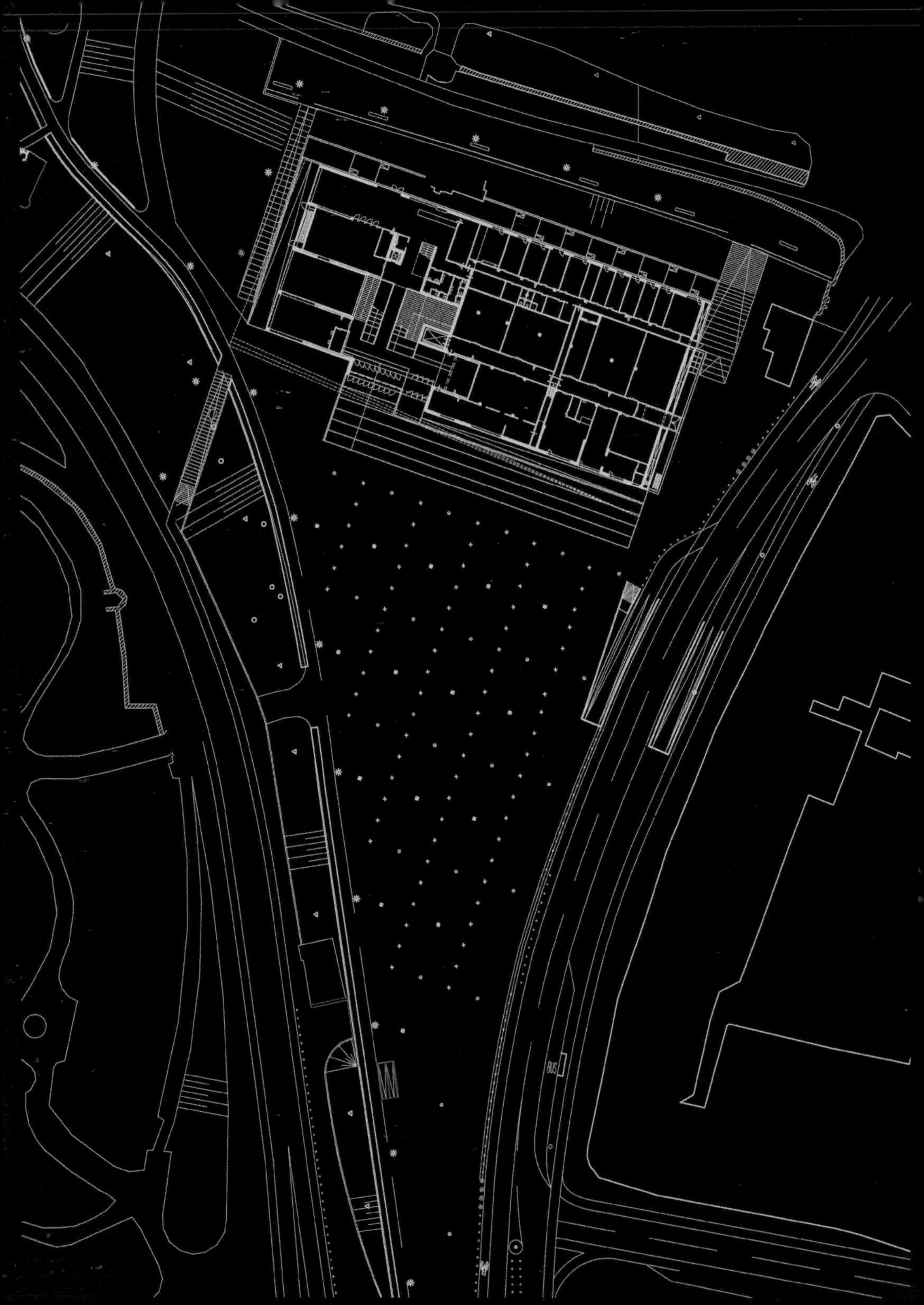
BUS

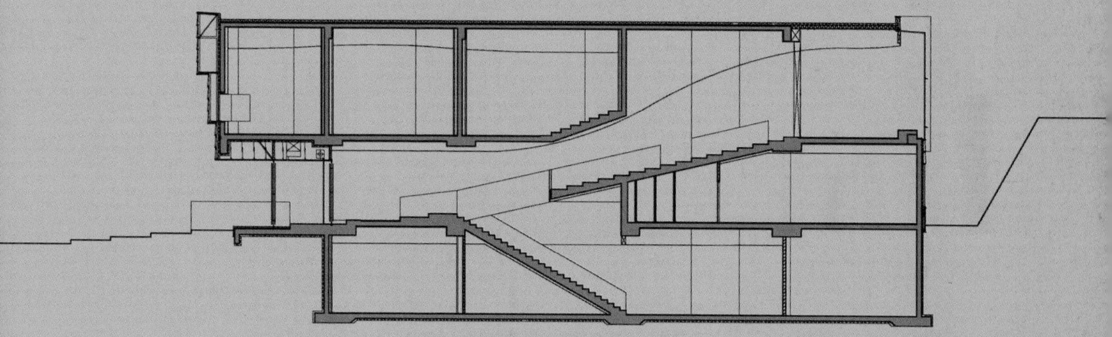

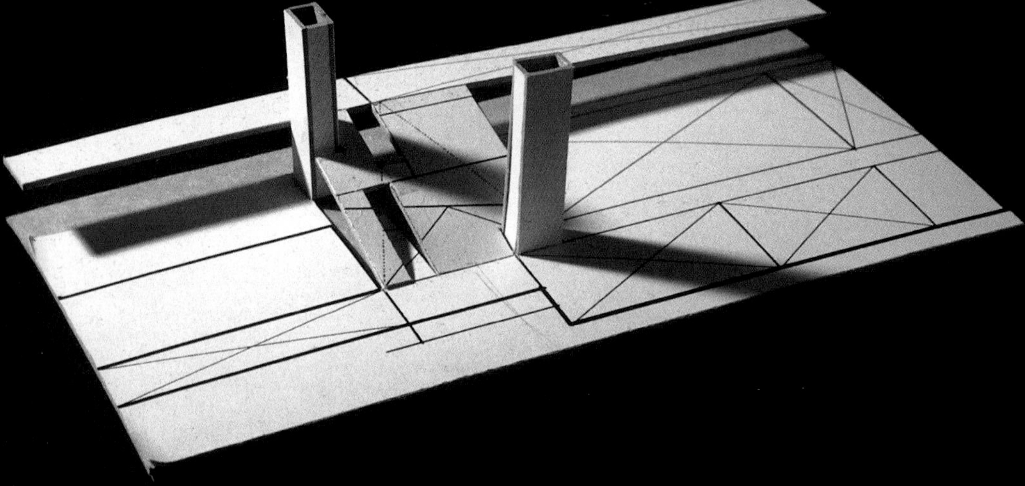

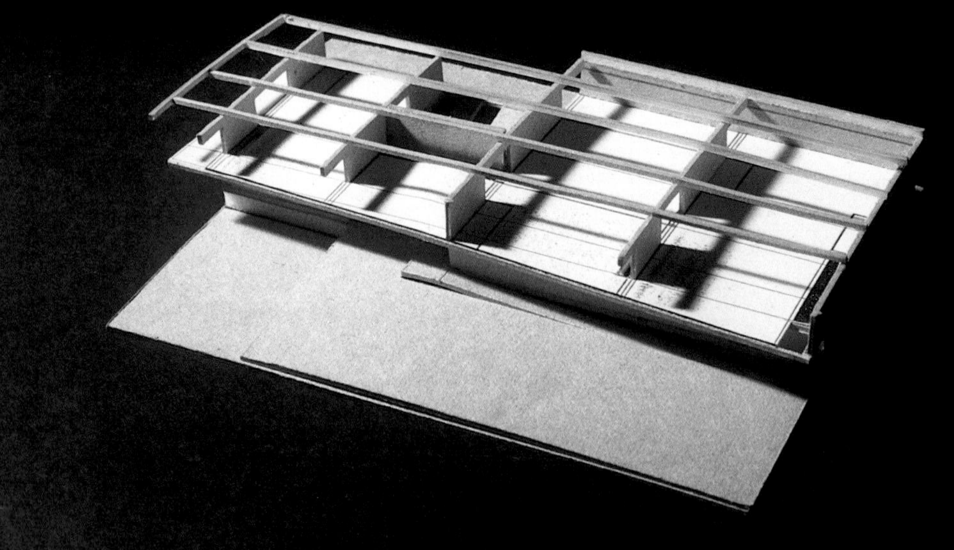

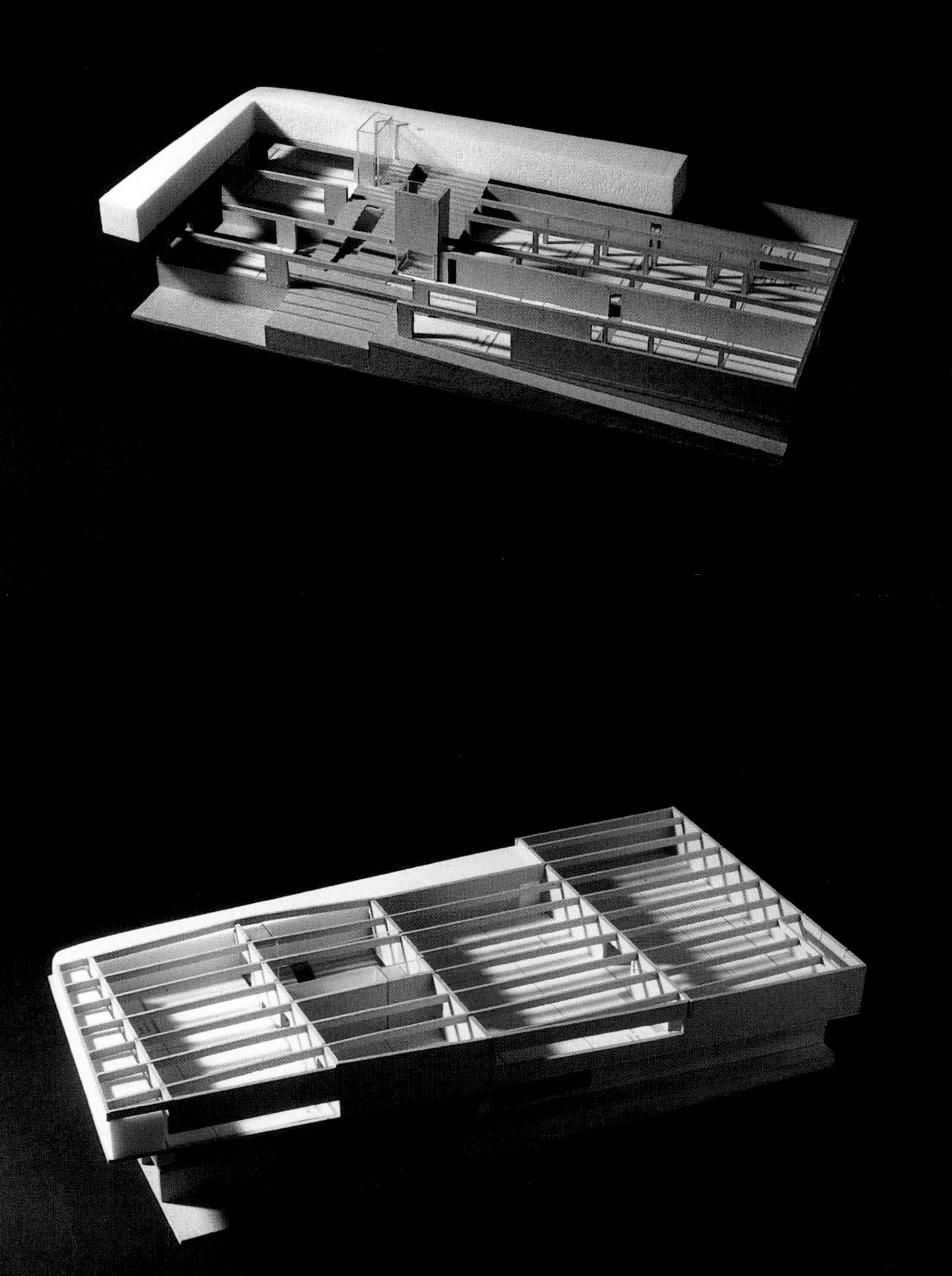

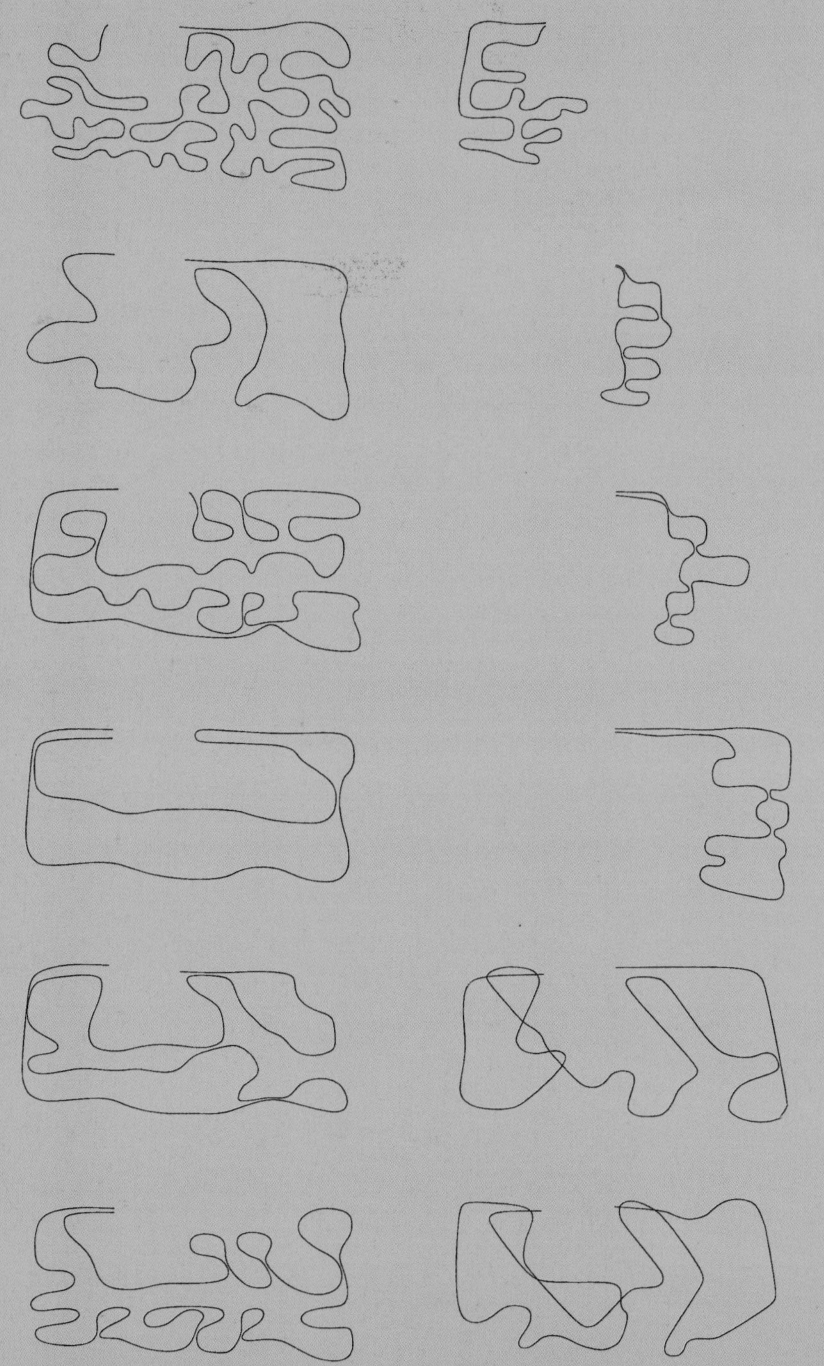

88 ways to view the collection

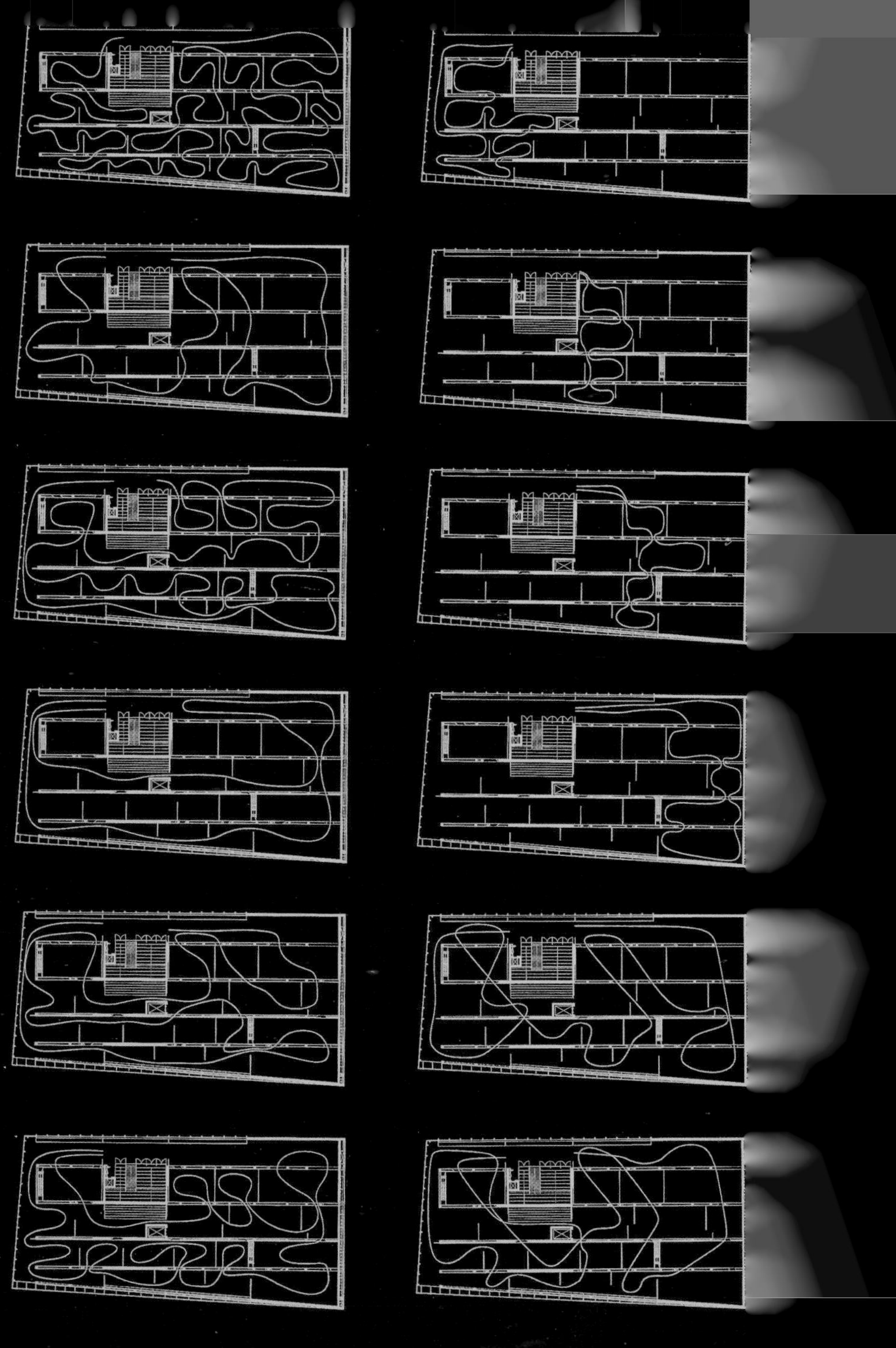

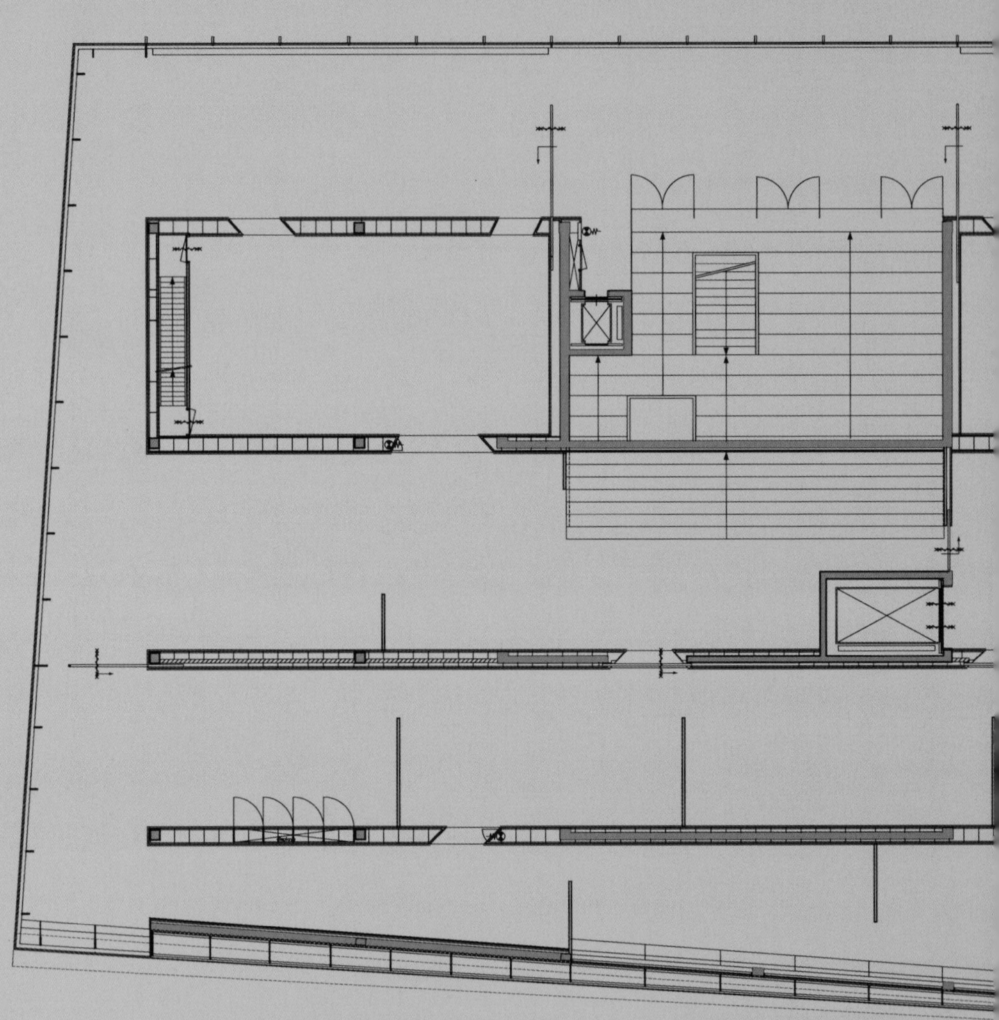

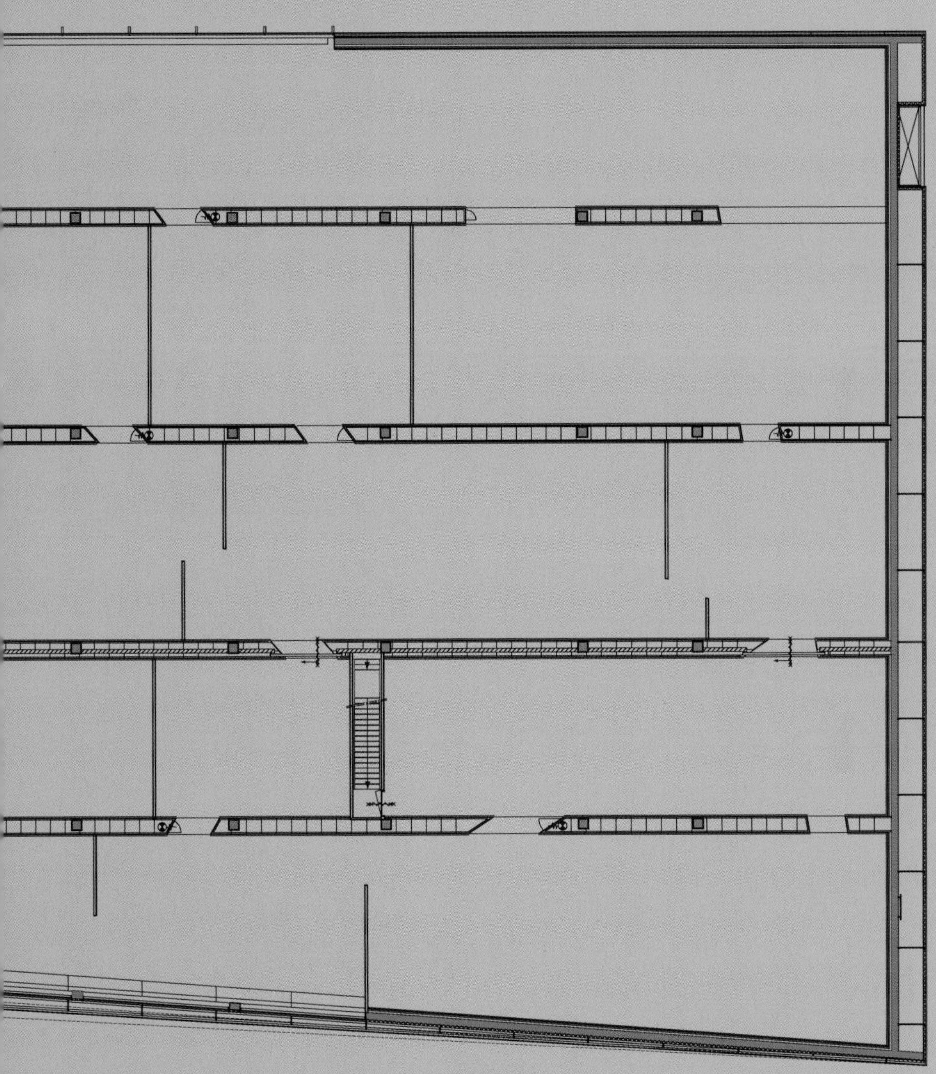

ceiling

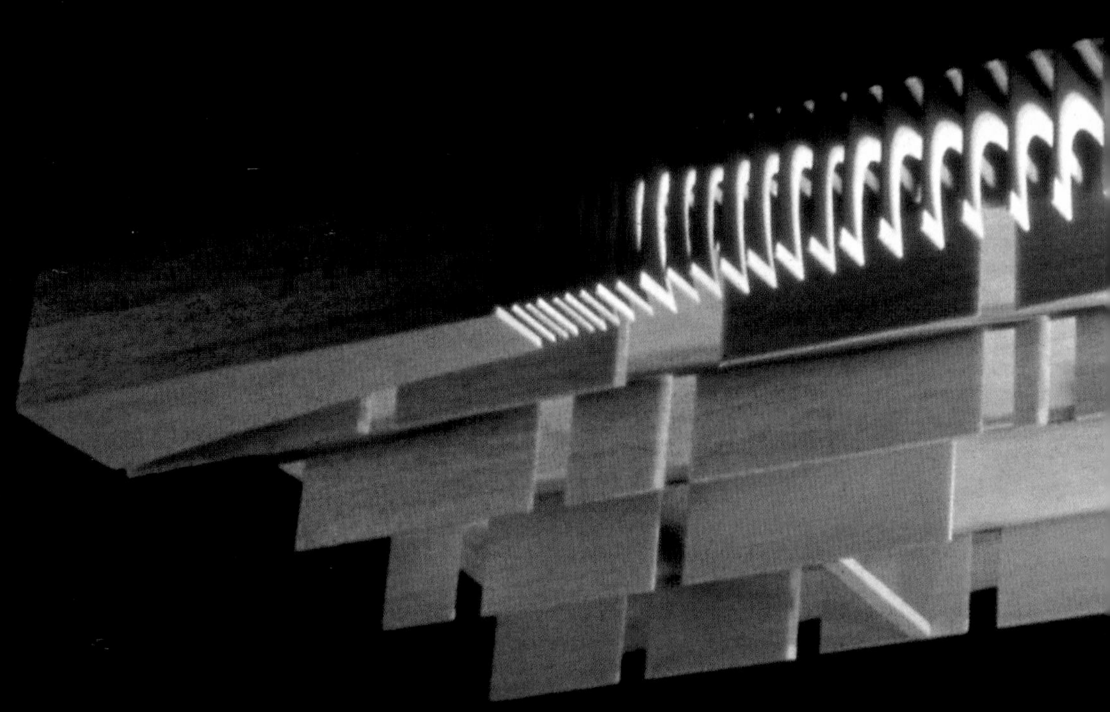

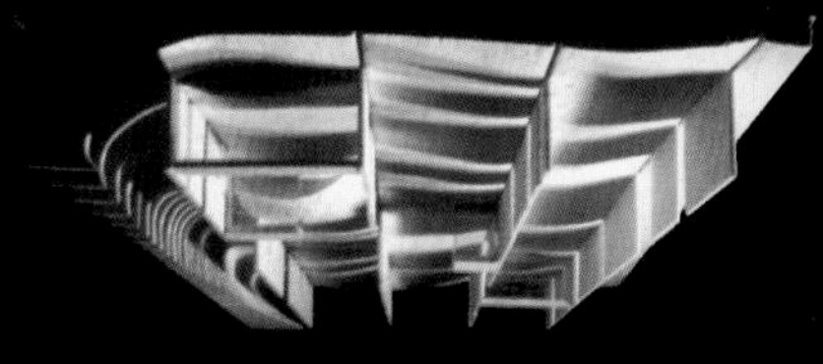

test-room researching effects o

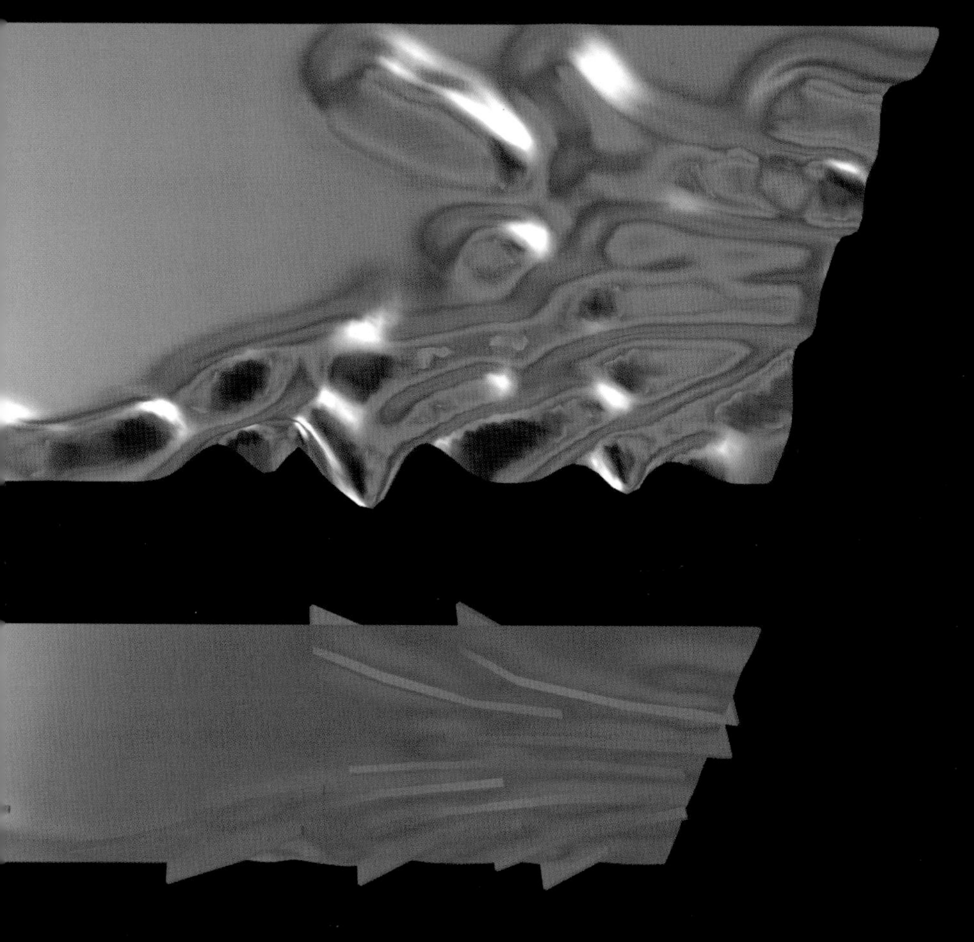

brightness and shadow of ceiling

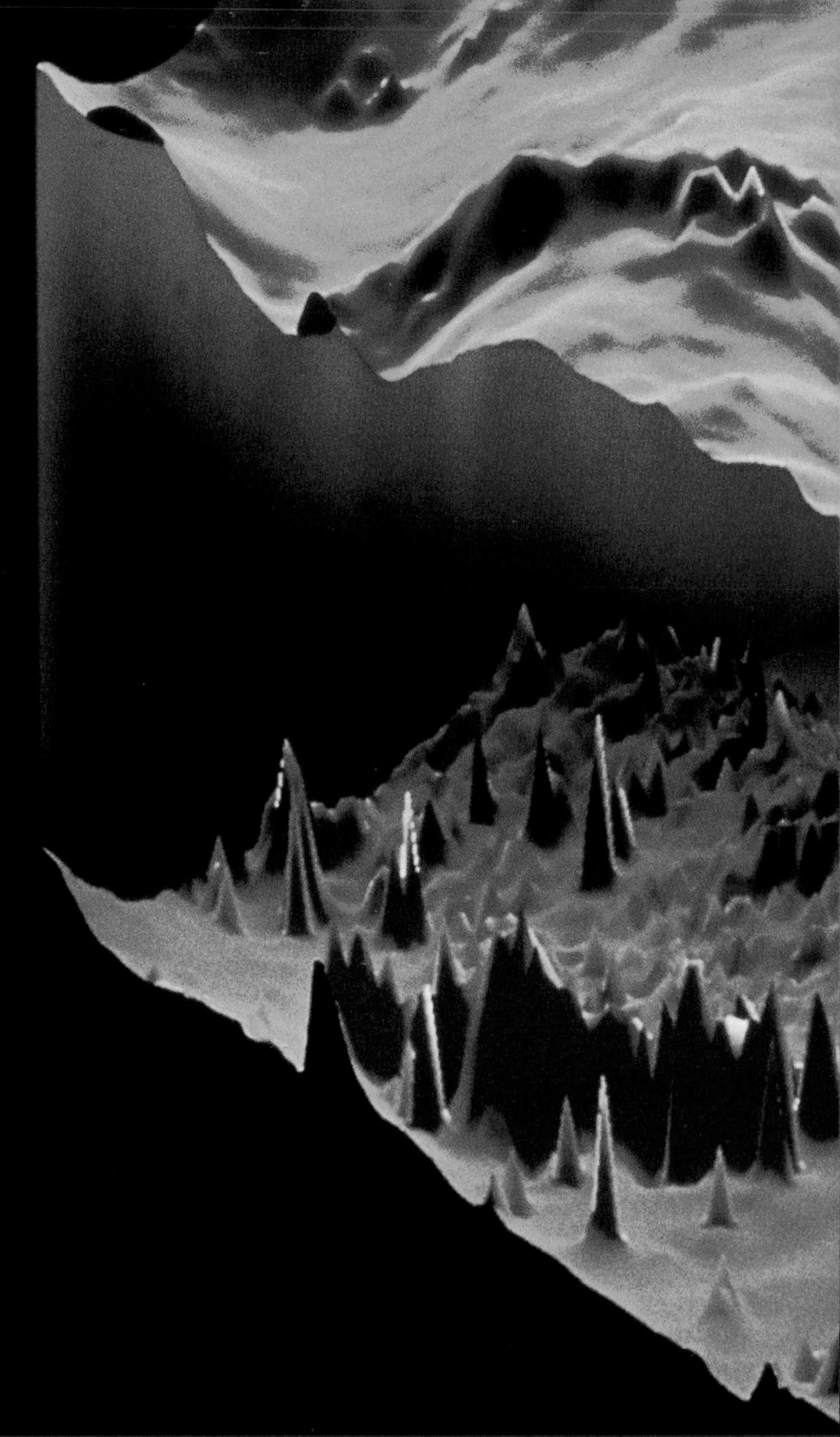

satellite recording of relation between

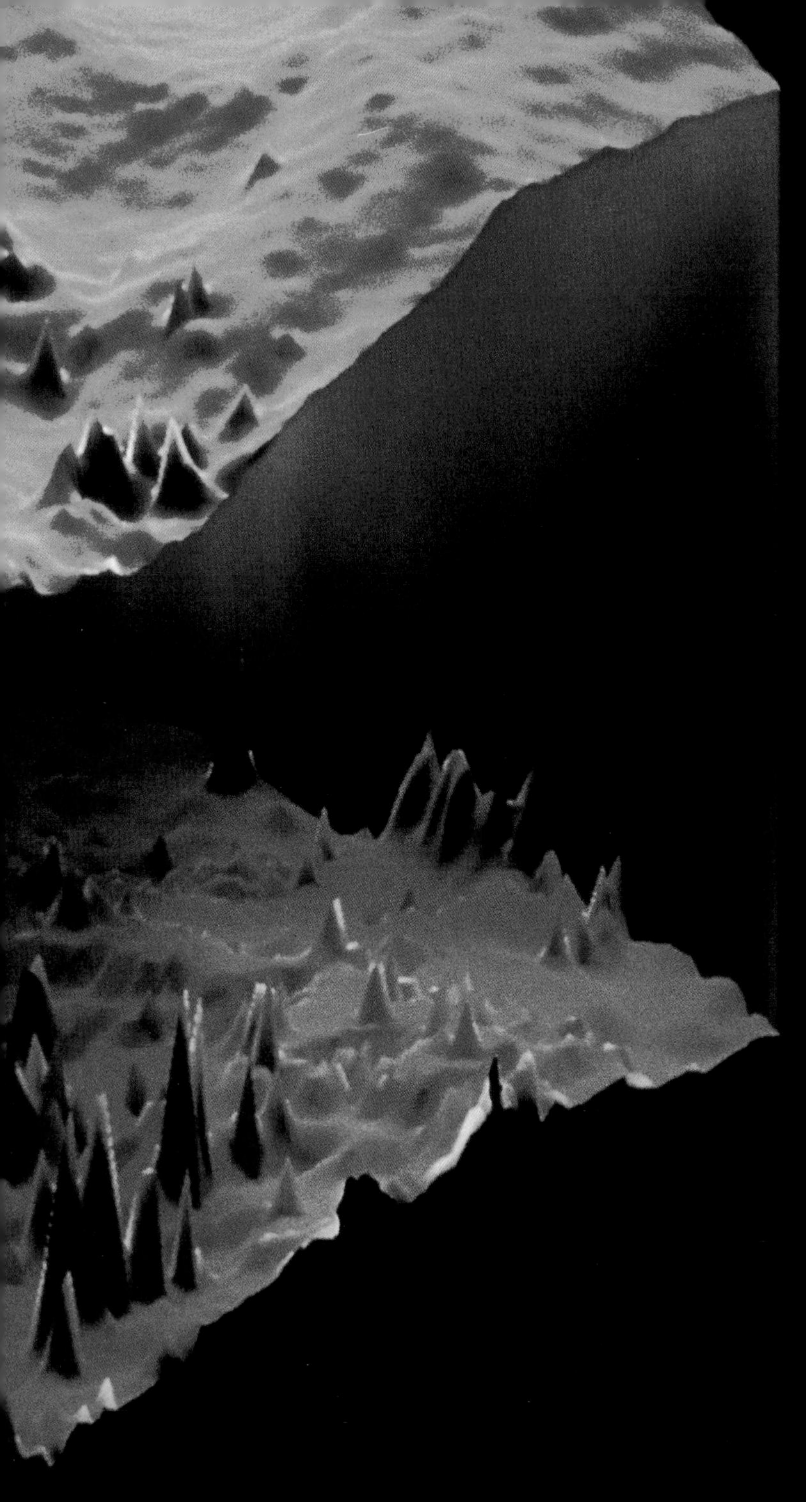

rocky ocean floor and wave patterns

balcony-zone overlooking roman

rampart

Materially and organisationally, the model for the museum is basalt lava that has solidified around pockets of air. The voids organise the field. In the history of the site a multi-layered pattern was recognised, which forms the basis for the new two-fold structure. The lava-like organisation is framed by a load-bearing superstructure, which has just four foundation points going down to the ground level. The museum space in between the four points is suspended from the structural roof, allowing for a free division of the mass between the ruins and the roof.

Porosity as strategy

The location for this limited competition for a new museum is a bombsite on which stood a Gothic cathedral until the Second World War. Its disappearance exposed layers of ruins dating back to romanesque times; church after church had been built and demolished on this spot between the sixth and the eleventh century AD. Our proposal suspends the building above these remains from a table-like structure which is rooted in the ruins. The new structure reflects and incorporates aspects of the patterns of the various temples and churches from the past.

The museum block that hangs from the table is riddled with holes. Light shafts descend from the

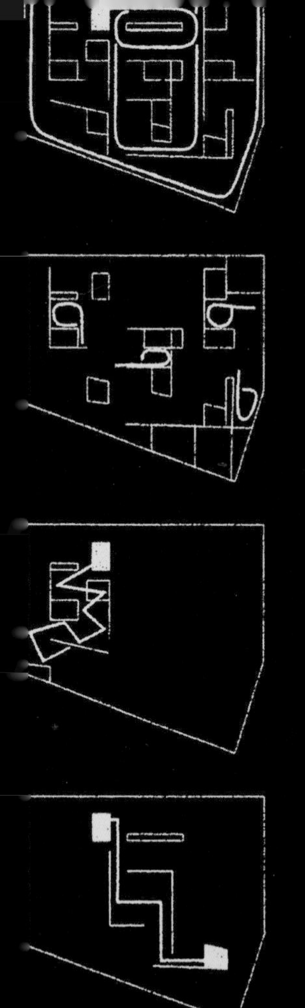

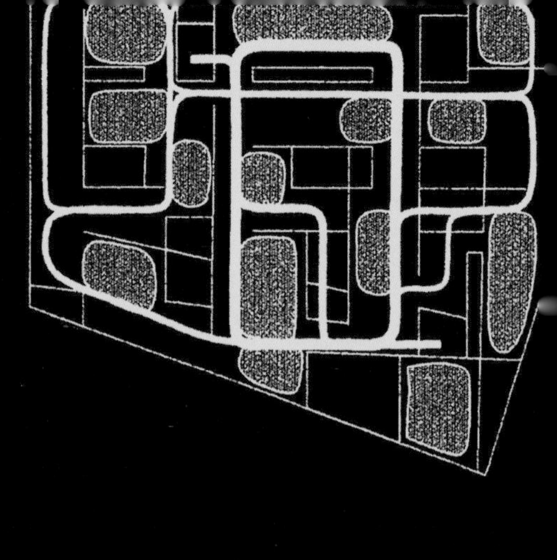

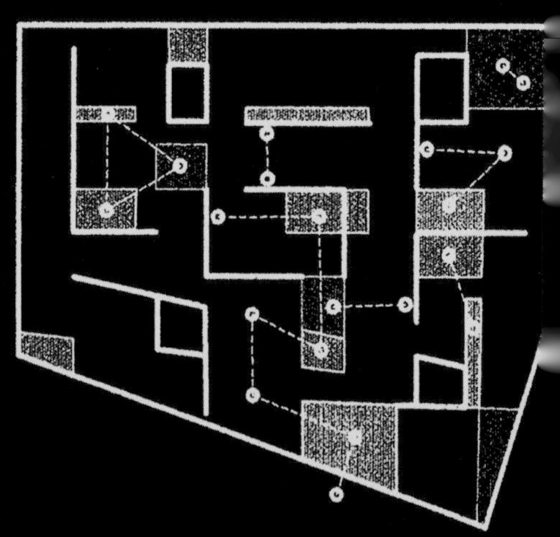

anisation of space structuring elements

roof and niches rise up from the ruins. The volumetric wrapping of the voids creates the museum envelope, which consists of tightly interwoven spaces with different light sources, heights, sizes and organisations.
Display case becomes wall, light shaft becomes floor - views, voids, outside and inside spaces tend toward ambiguity. The condition of overlapping qualities is intrinsic to the conception of the project as one, porous volume - differentiated yet homogeneous.

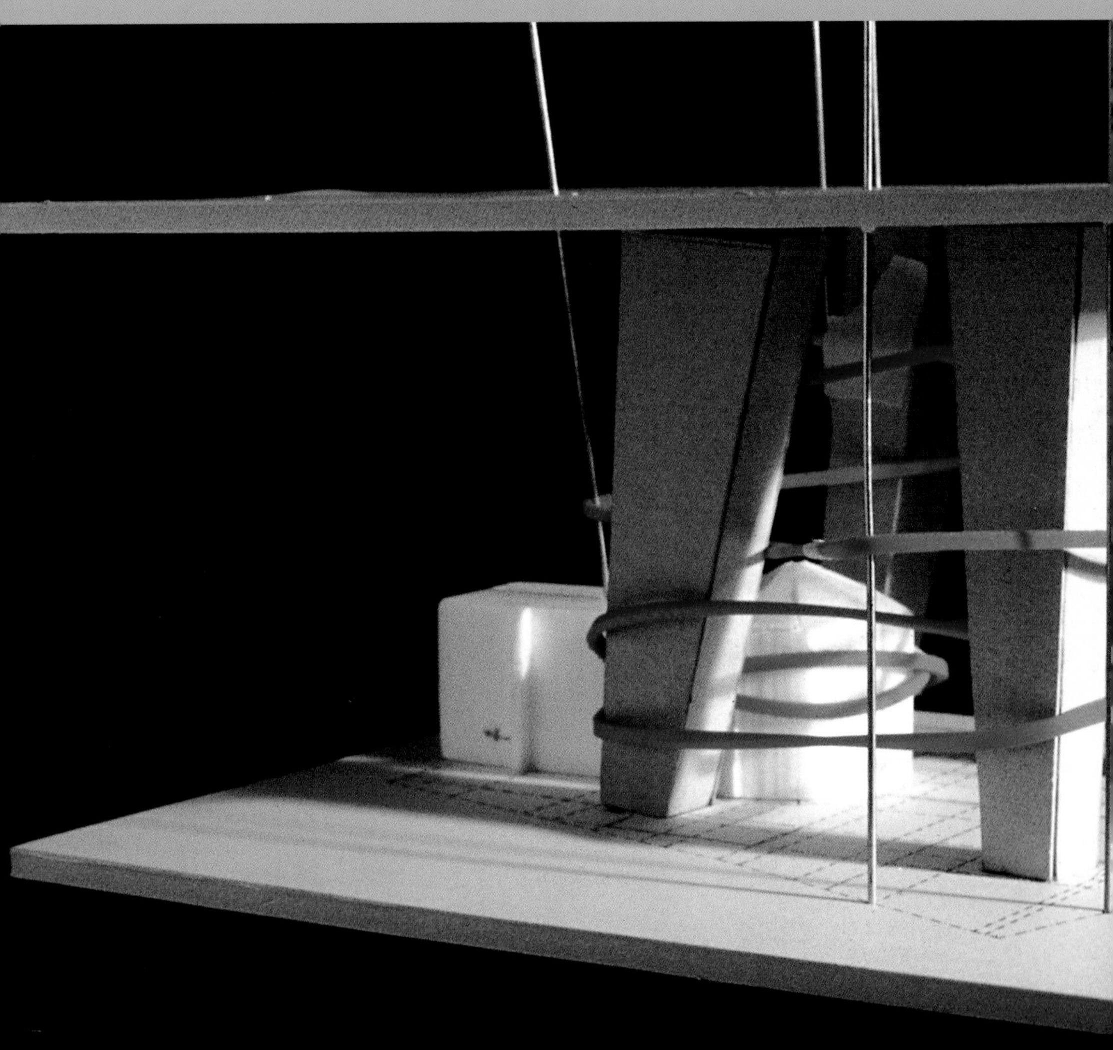

infrastructural towers support structure

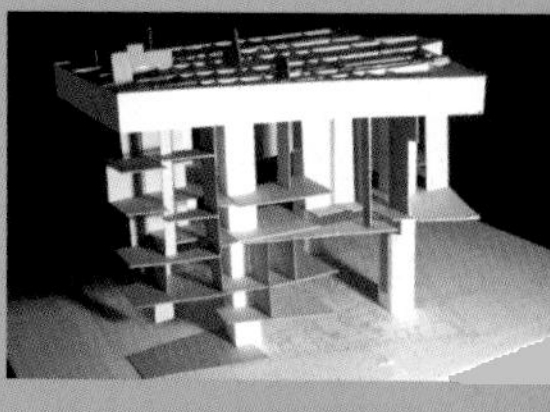

spatial continuity of the museum

structure

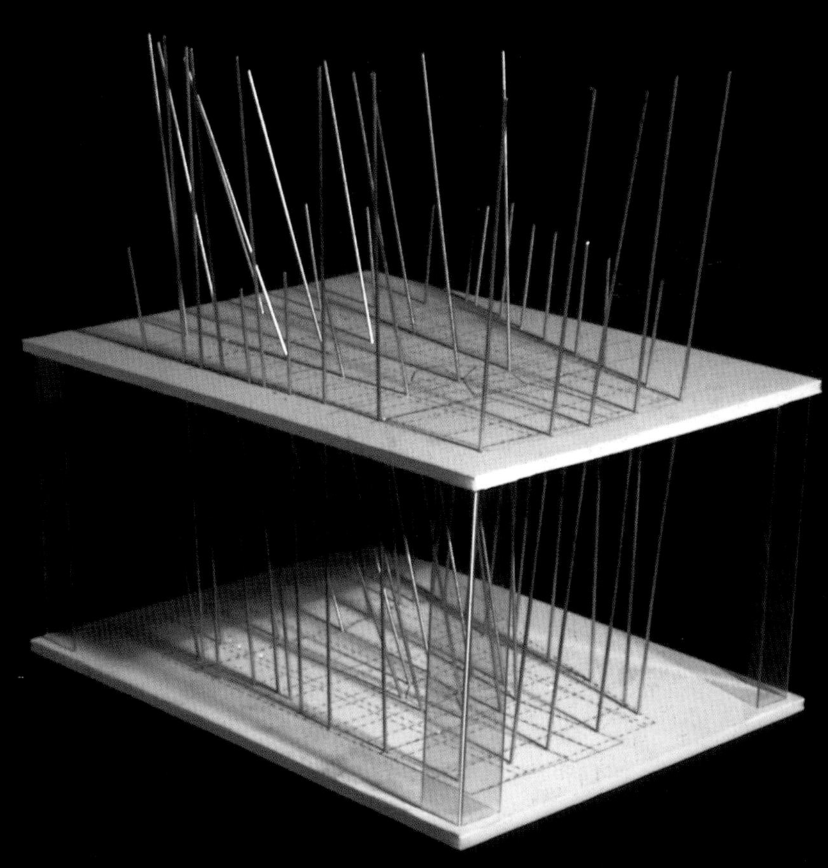

suspended structure

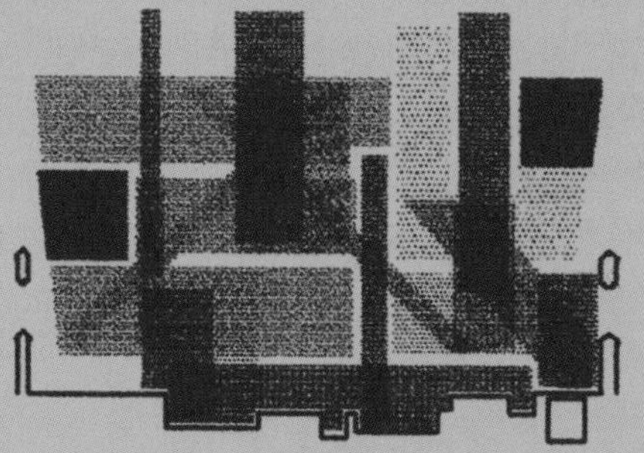

superimposition of inside and outside spaces

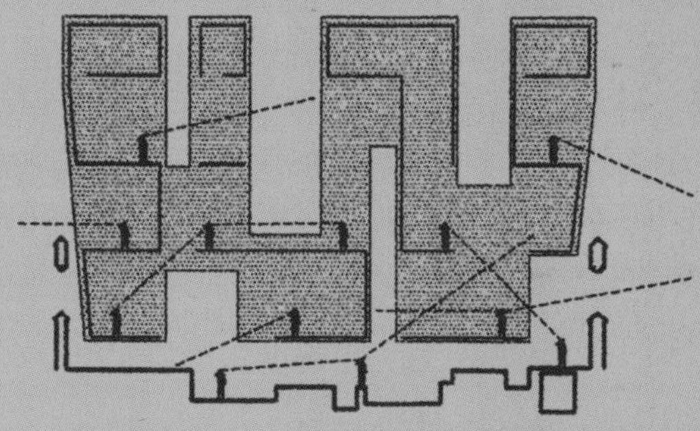

visual connections

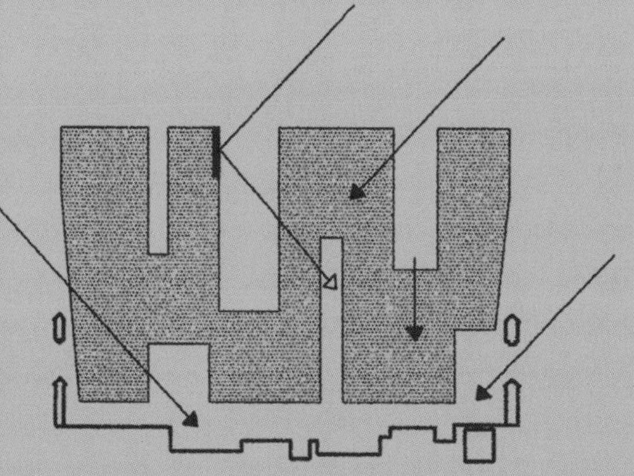

natural lighting

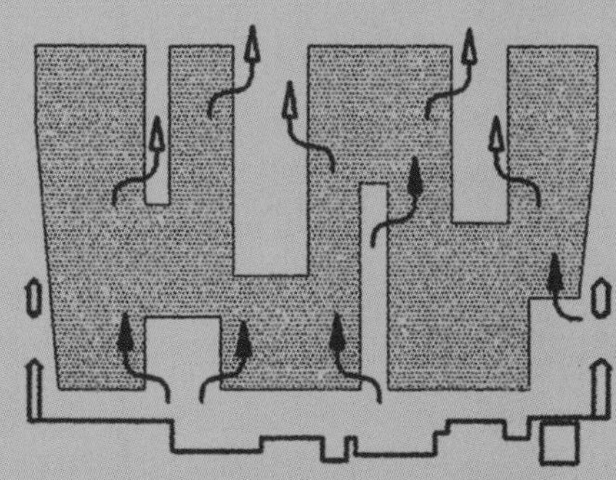

air conditioning by thermal air

exhibition space inside

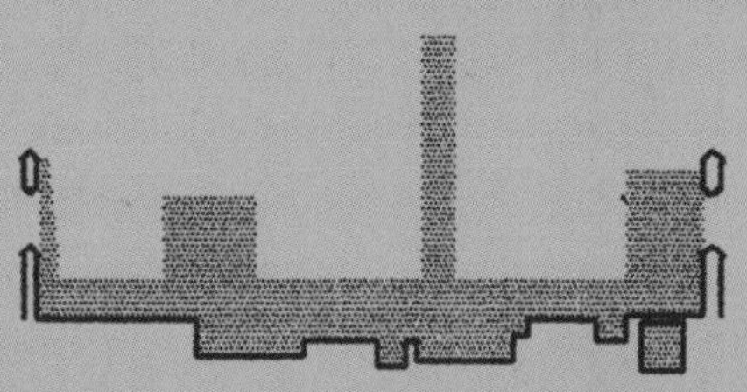

exhibition space outside

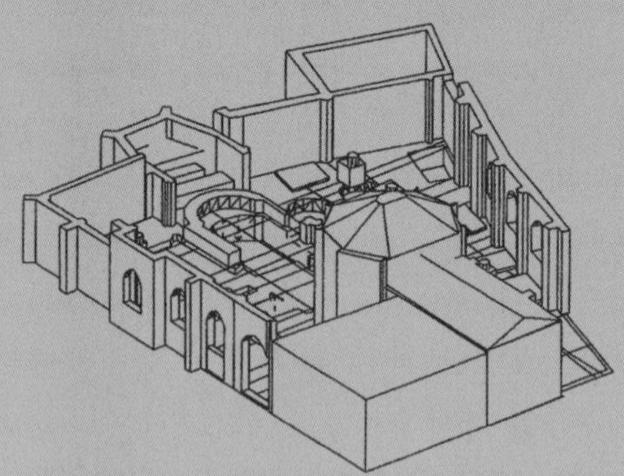

ruins

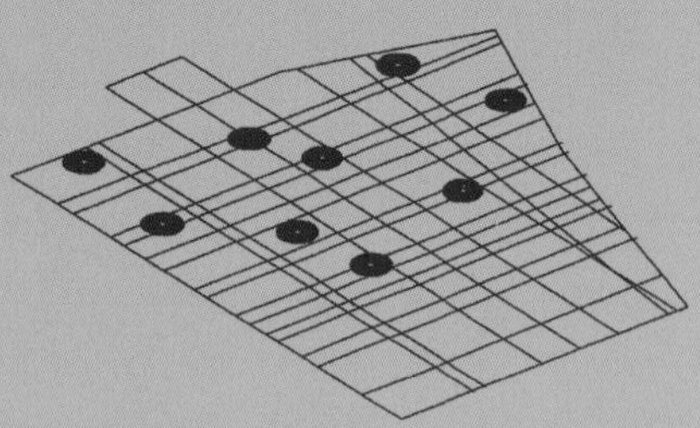

historical matrix

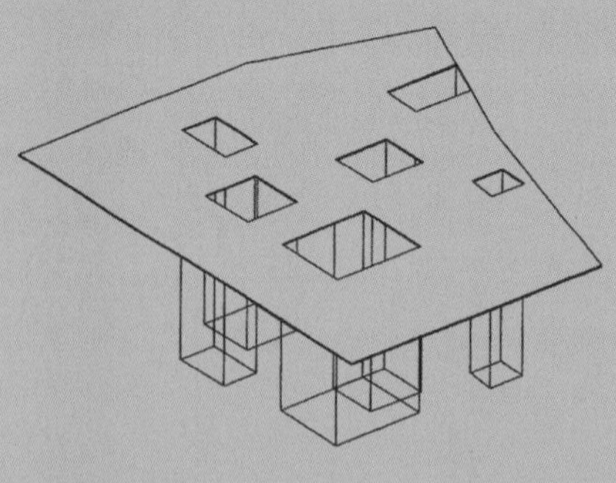

suspended light shaft

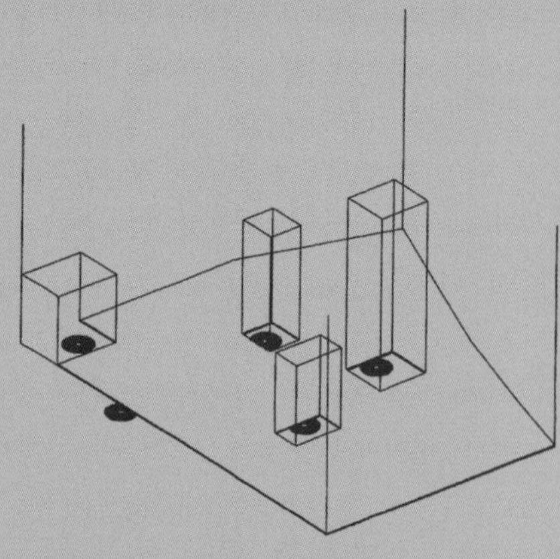

suspended showcases

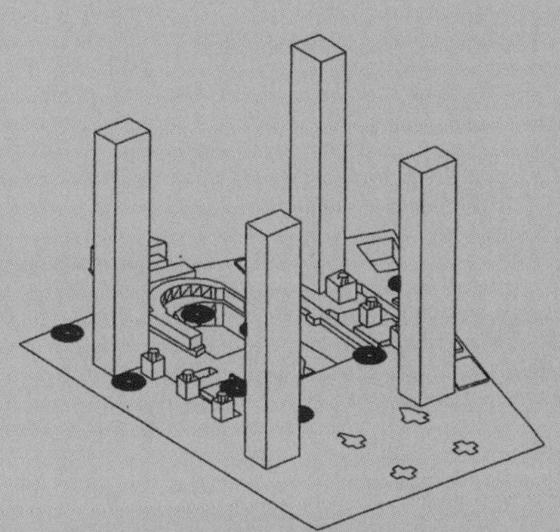

infrastructural towers

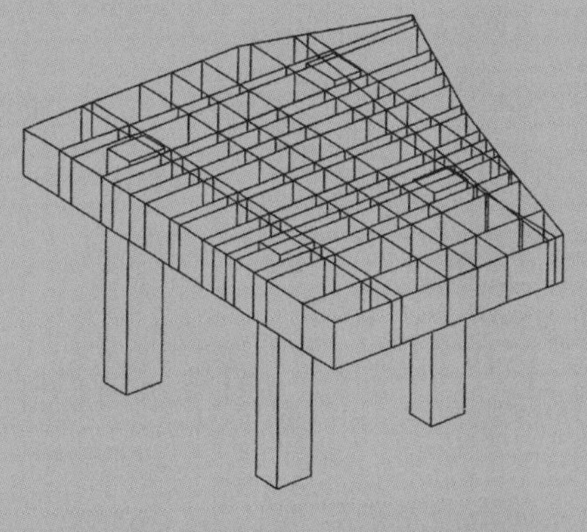

supporting grid for suspended construction

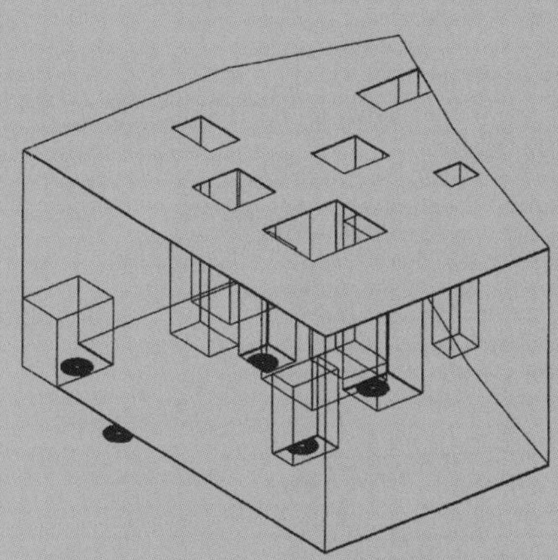

exhibition volume in between

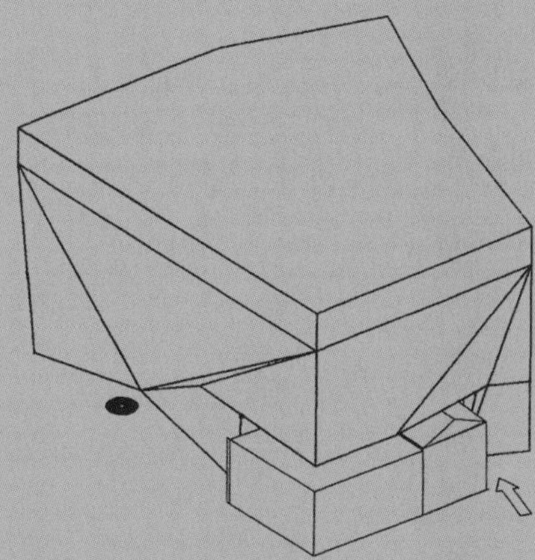

transformation of the skin

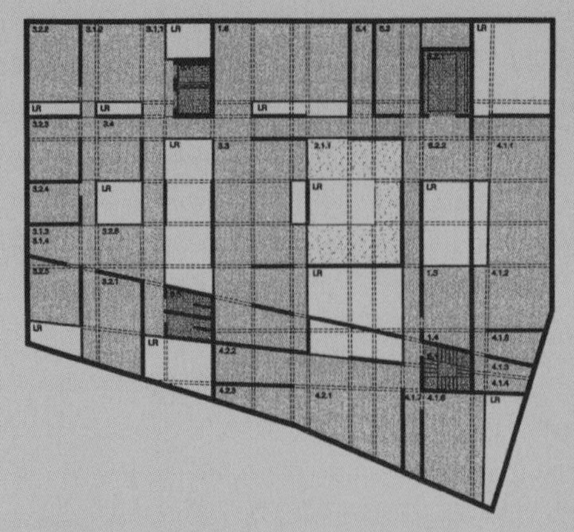

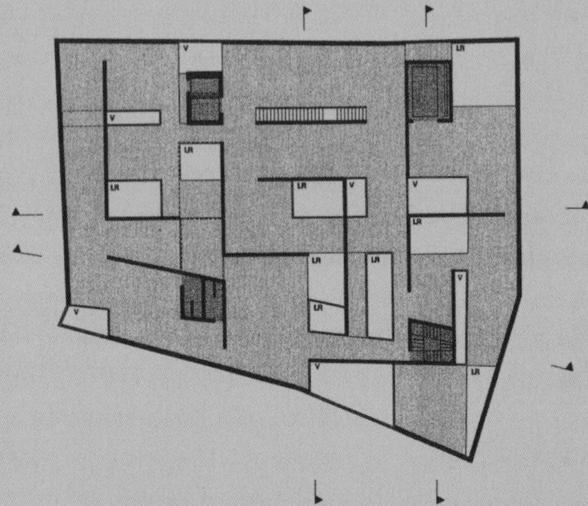

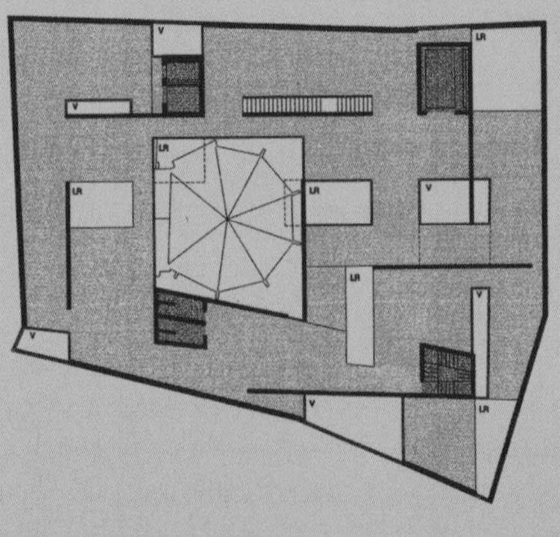

+71.2
+67.9
+62.6
+59.3
+54.0
+49.9
+46.6

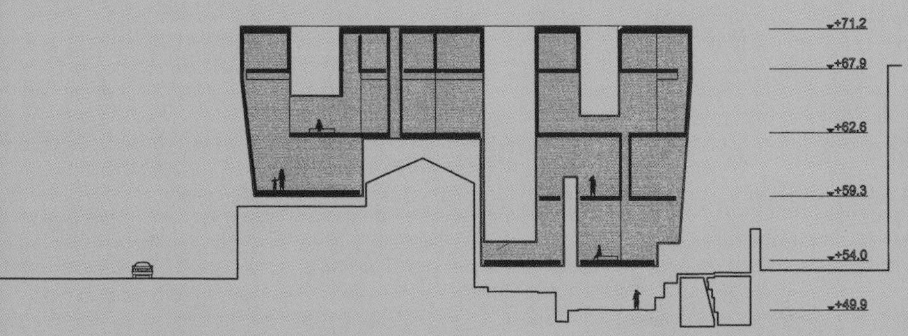
+71.2
+67.9
+62.6
+59.3
+54.0
+49.9

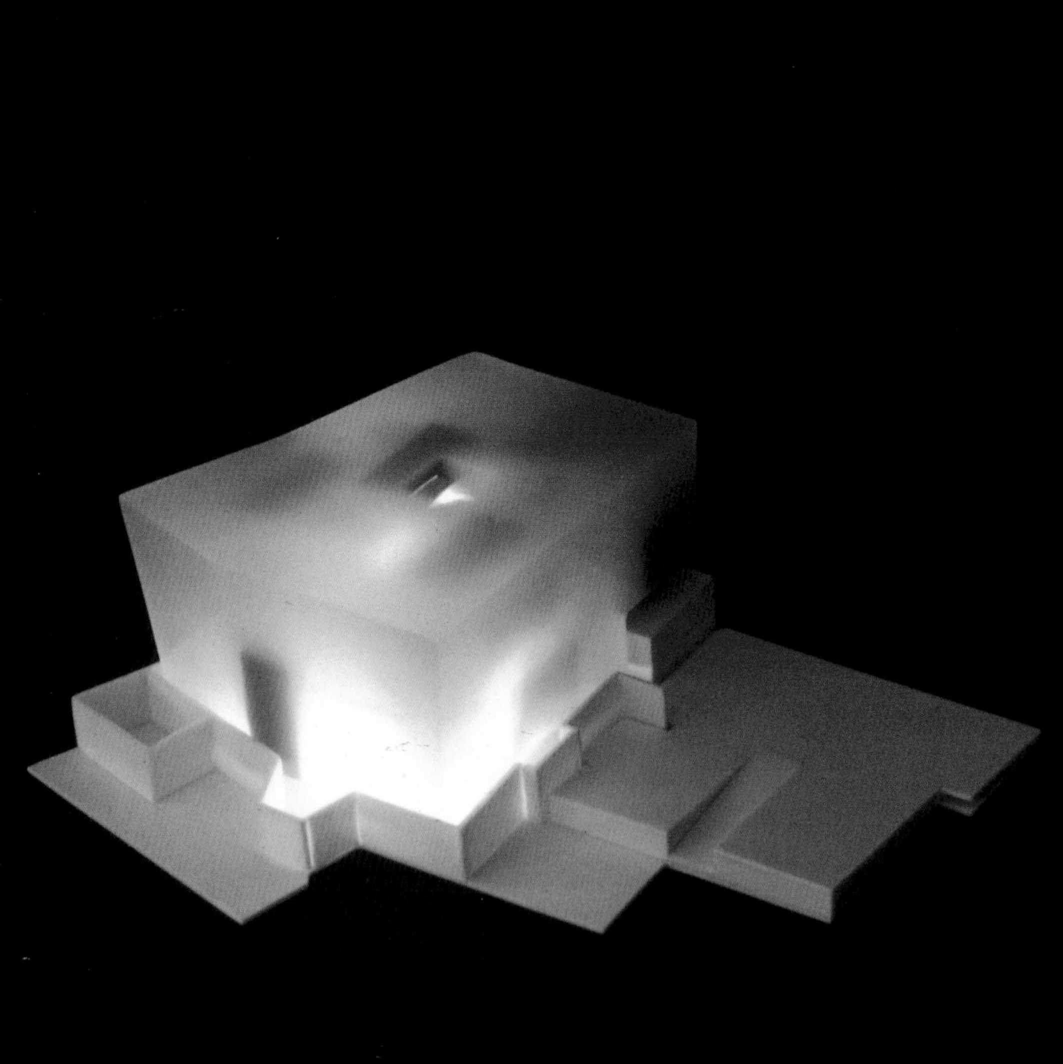

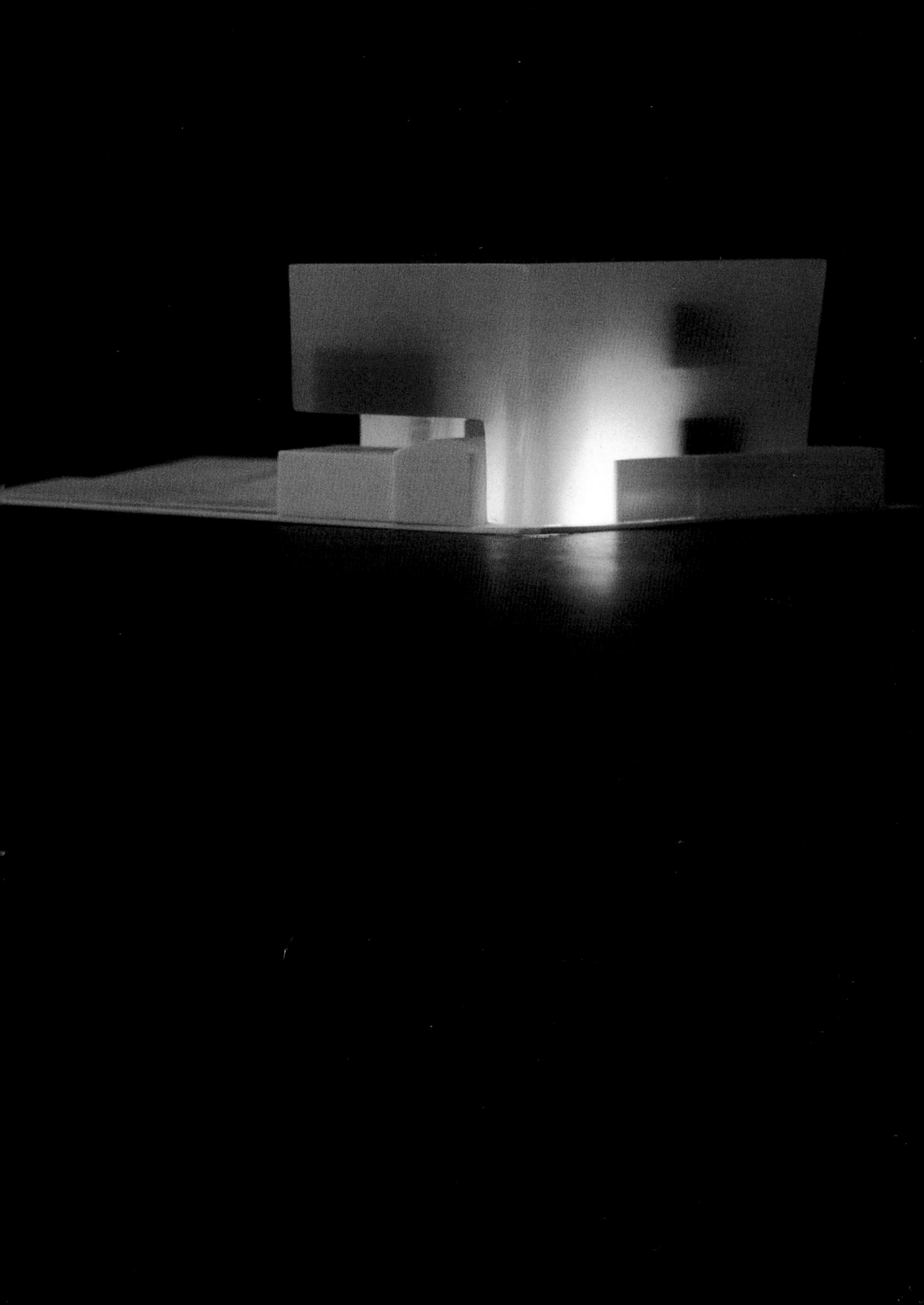

A consistent plane that contains future projections lends unity to the location and exerts an alternative form of control over potential developments. The foundation of a coherent surface that is capable of absorbing later pragmatic differentiation is a simpler and richer option than trying to govern future development of the site by spinning a web of anticipatory regulations.

Smart surface; towards material incorporation

The leftover plot bordering the crowded centre of Innsbruck is defined as a plateau made of one material that follows and incorporates the folds of the landscape like a flexible skin and even covers the electrical substation on the location. The plateau contains the potential for future development on this under-exploited site: lines of sight and directions of movement are traced in the ground plane, forming a virtual infrastructure. The electrical substation is smoothly incorporated into the plateau, like a hump in the landscape. Glass strips, which illuminate the building from within, contribute to the acceptability of the building. Instead of being an alien technical object that poses a threat to its surroundings, the switching substation is thus integrated, almost domesticated, in its placement within the town.

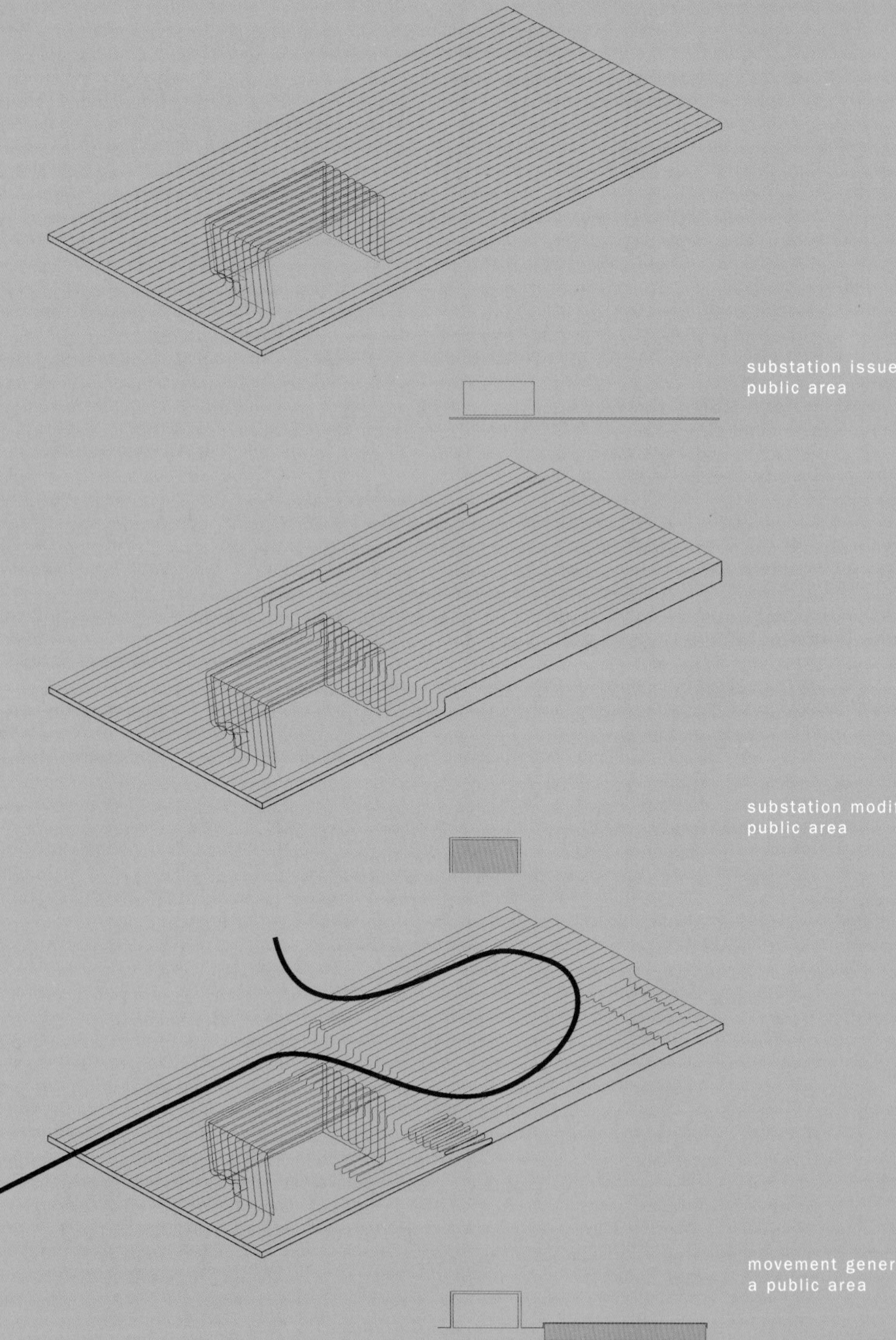
substation issues from
public area
substation modifies
public area
movement generates
a public area

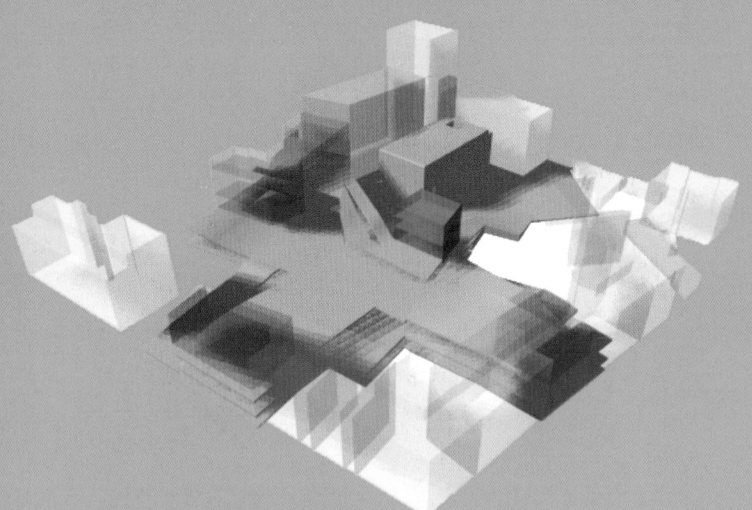

medium development mixed programme,equal density

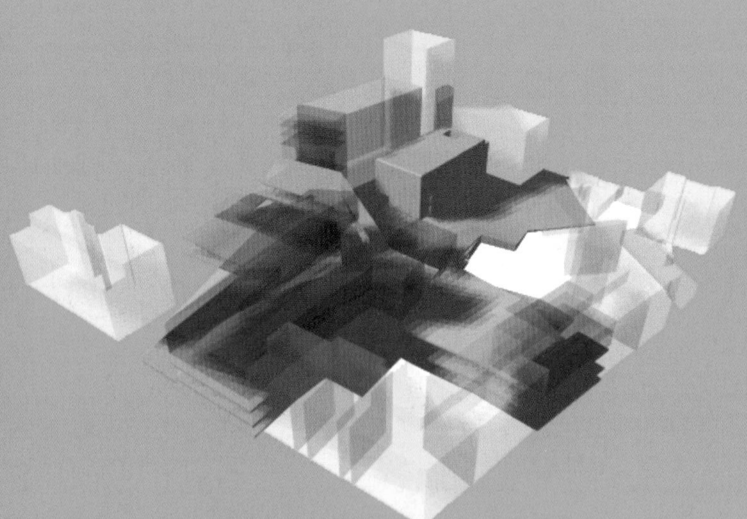

medium development mixed density,equal programme

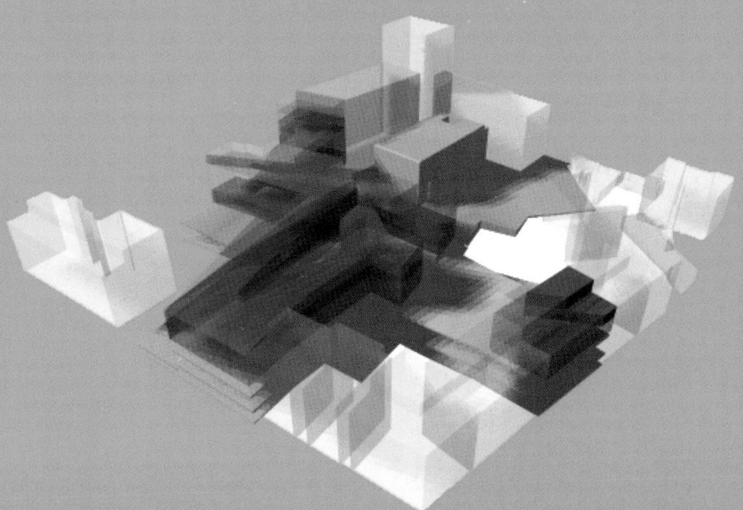

high development mixed programme,equal density

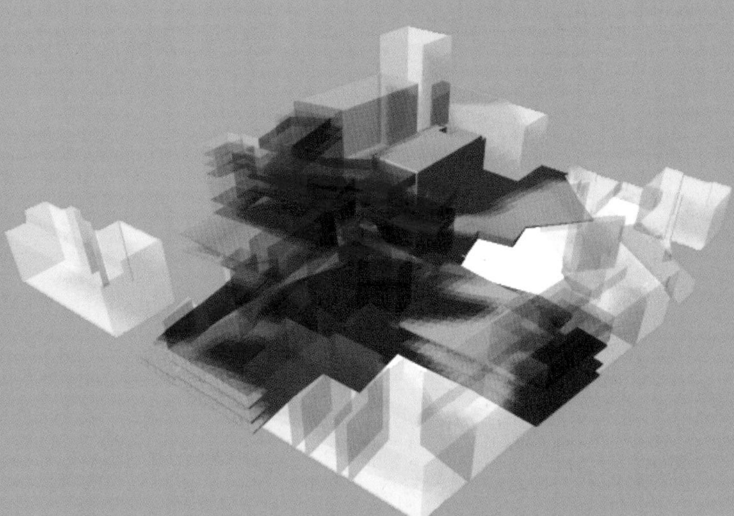

high development mixed density,equal programme

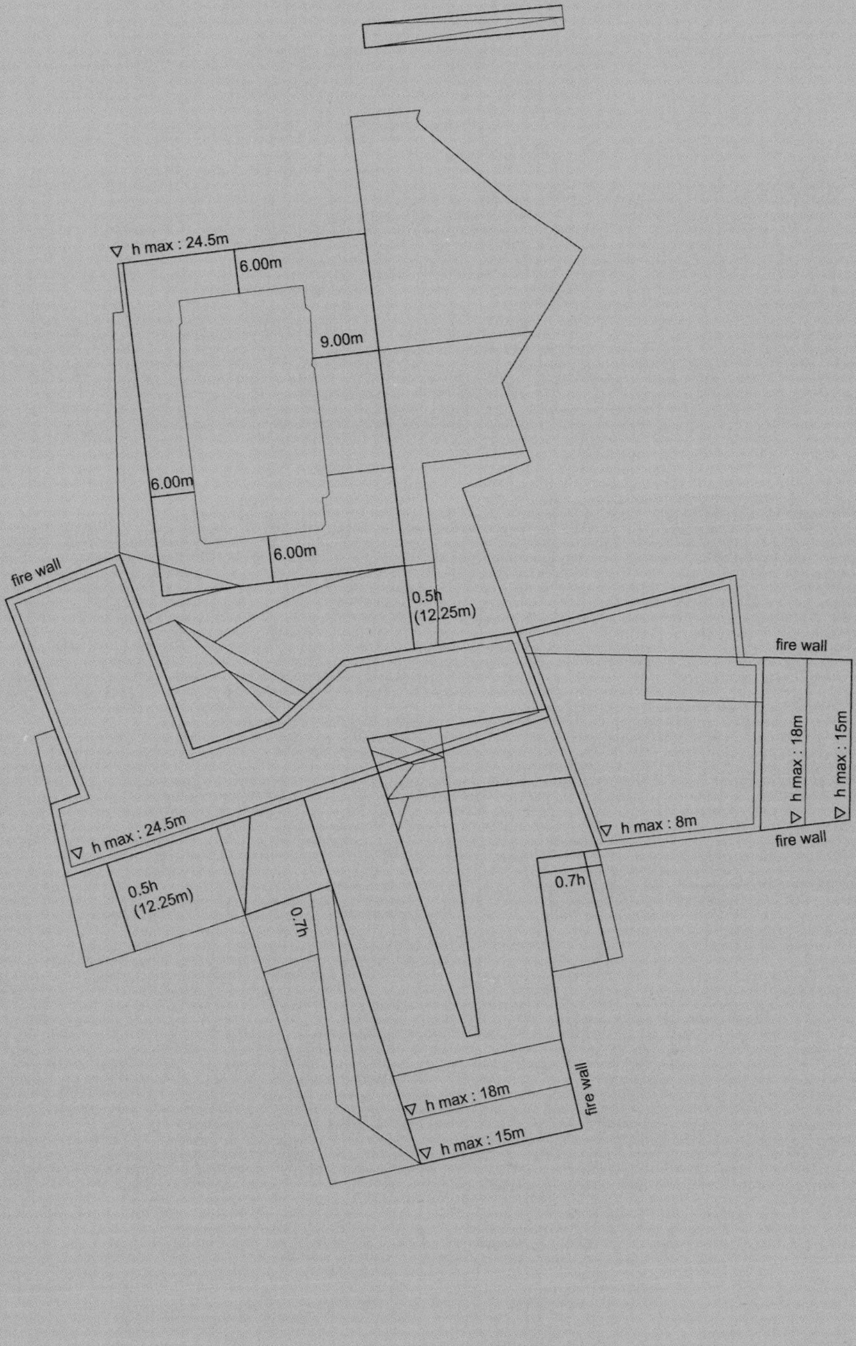

h max : 24.5m
6.00m
9.00m
6.00m
6.00m
fire wall
0.5h
(12.25m)
fire wall
h max : 18m
h max : 15m
h max : 24.5m
h max : 8m
fire wall
0.5h
(12.25m)
0.7h
0.7h
fire wall
h max : 18m
h max : 15m

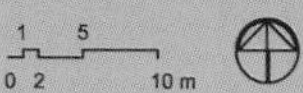

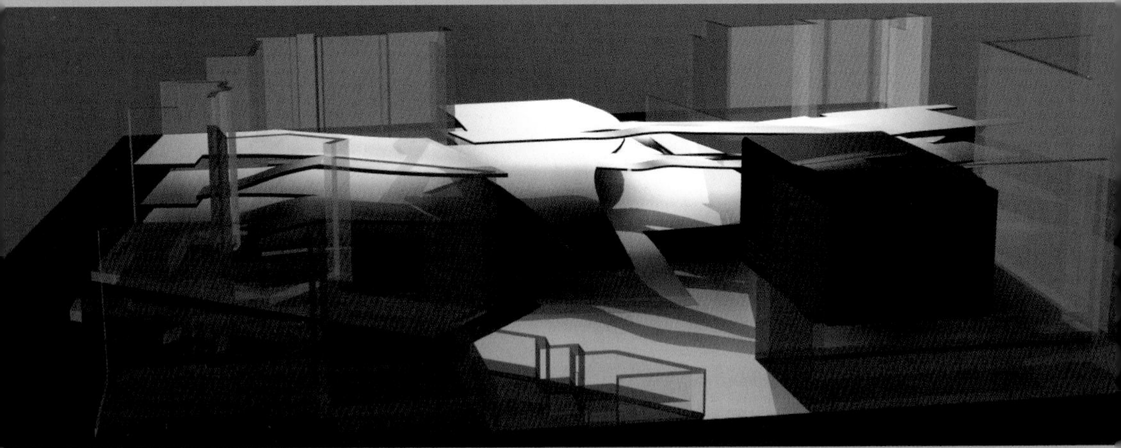

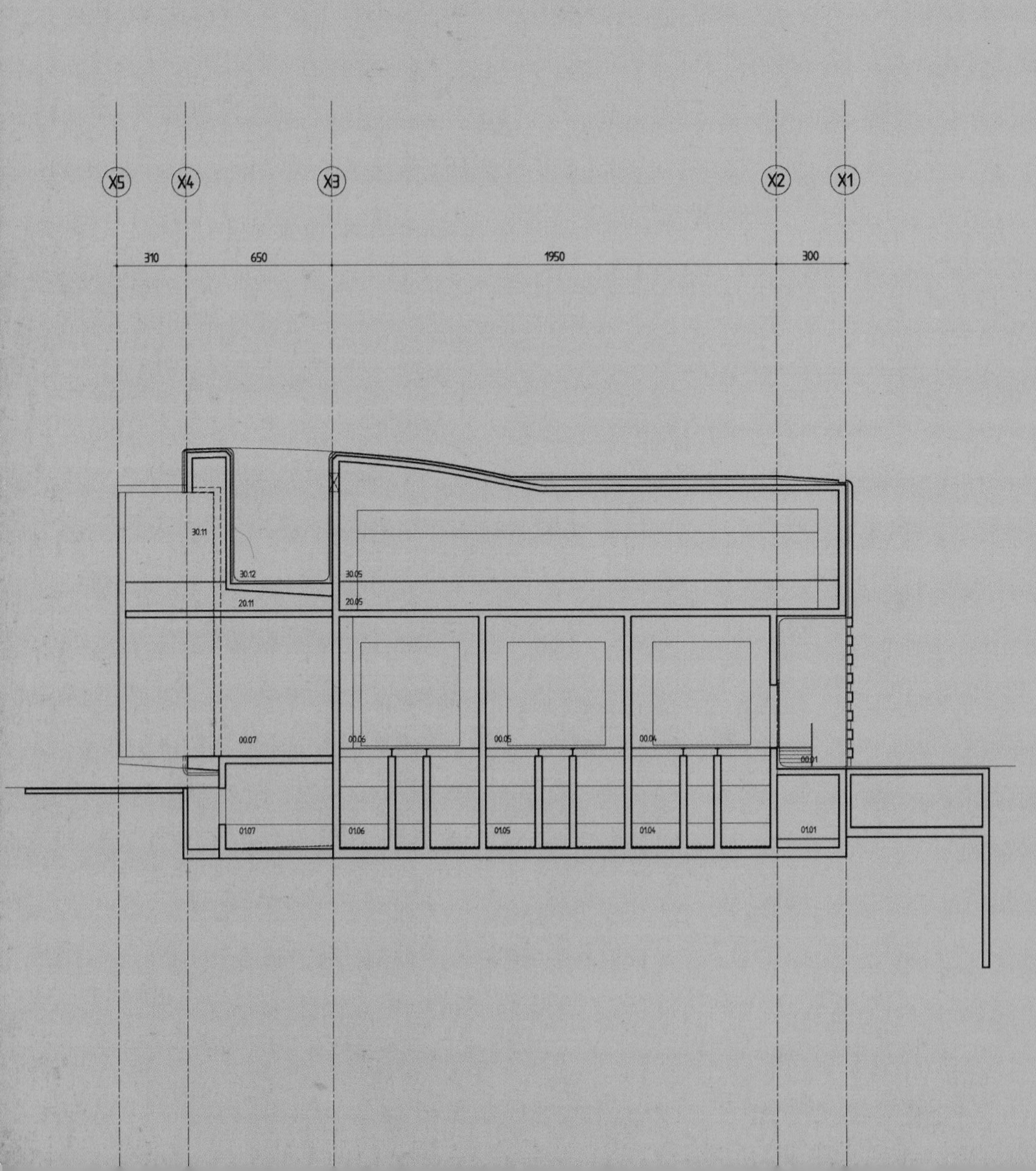

X5
X4
X3
X2
X1
310
650
1950
300
30.11
30.12
30.05
20.11
20.05
00.07
00.06
00.05
00.04
00.01
01.07
01.06
01.05
01.04
01.01

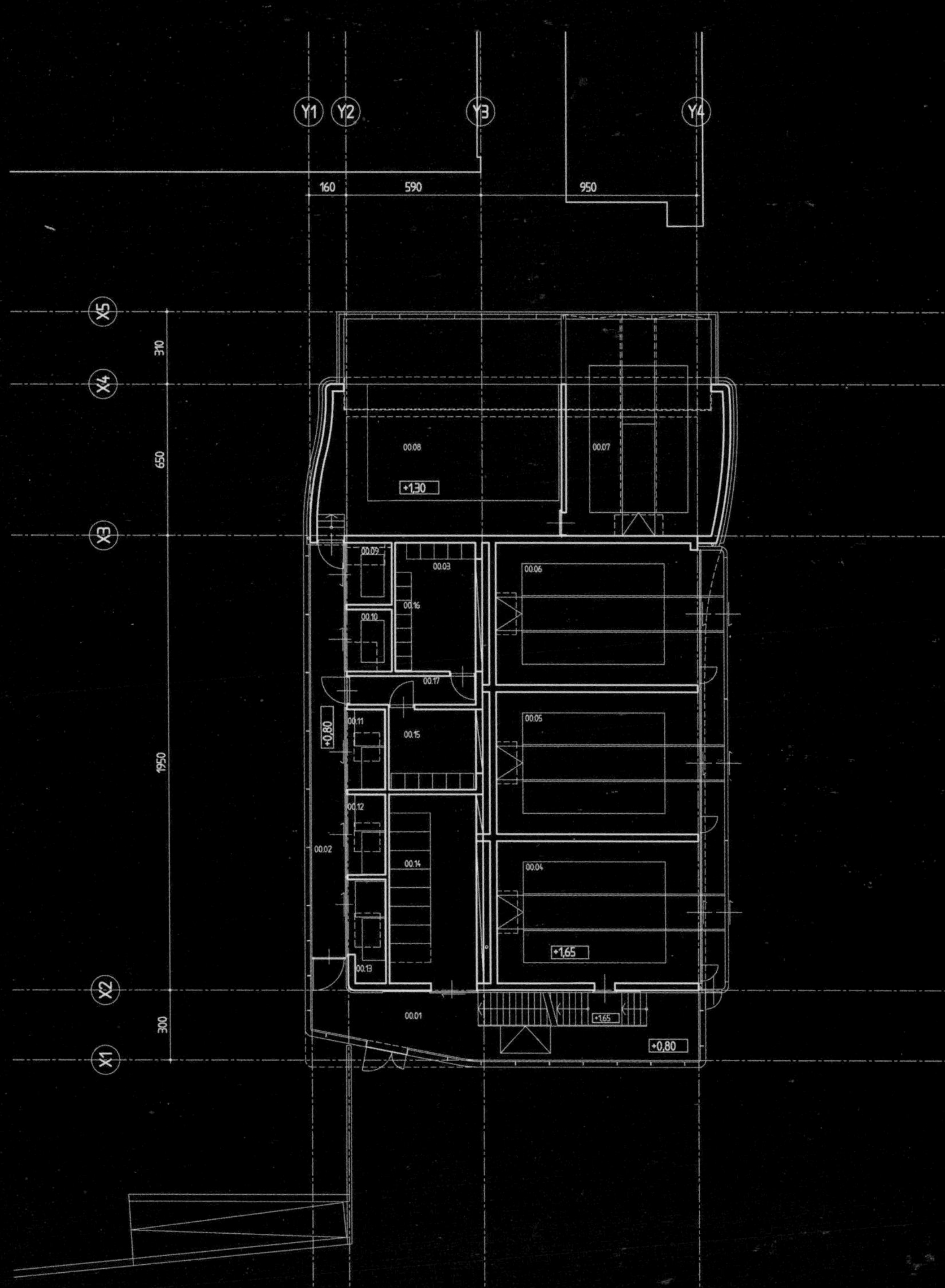
Y1
Y2
Y3
Y4
160
590
950
X5
X4
X3
X2
X1
310
650
1950
300
00.08
+1,30
00.07
00.09
00.03
00.06
00.10
00.16
00.17
00.11
+0,80
00.15
00.05
00.12
00.02
00.14
00.04
+1,65
00.13
00.01
+1,65
+0,80

TRAFO 3
3X500 KVA 3/25 KV

The project combines flexibility, transparency, coherence and diversity through a dynamic, centralised, organisational typology. From a central spiral void, propeller walls project outwards and flap over, acting as structural elements that bind together the four main structural cores and carry the load of the floors. This allows for a flexible, column-free arrangement of programme on the floors.

Systemisation of centrifugality

The Library proposal takes in the four corners of the location by means of its spiral-shaped entrance and centrifugal organisation. All the functions of the building are organised around a virtual core. This central space is infrastructure, construction, landscape and light source.

A continuous, landscaped ground level draws people up from the surroundings. Starting at the ground level, the core becomes manifest as a hollow hill in which an underground theatre is situated. Around the hill runs a spiral ramp giving access to the different parts of the building through wayfinder arms that extend from the core like blades of a propeller. This distribution system runs through the entire building. The wayfinder arms are directional and contain all building services and infrastructure.

LOBBY

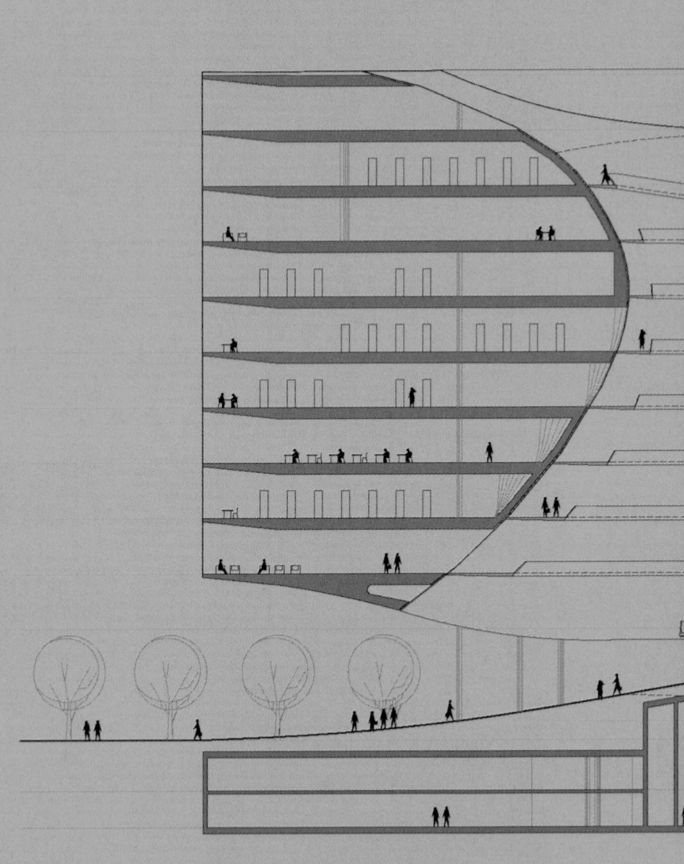

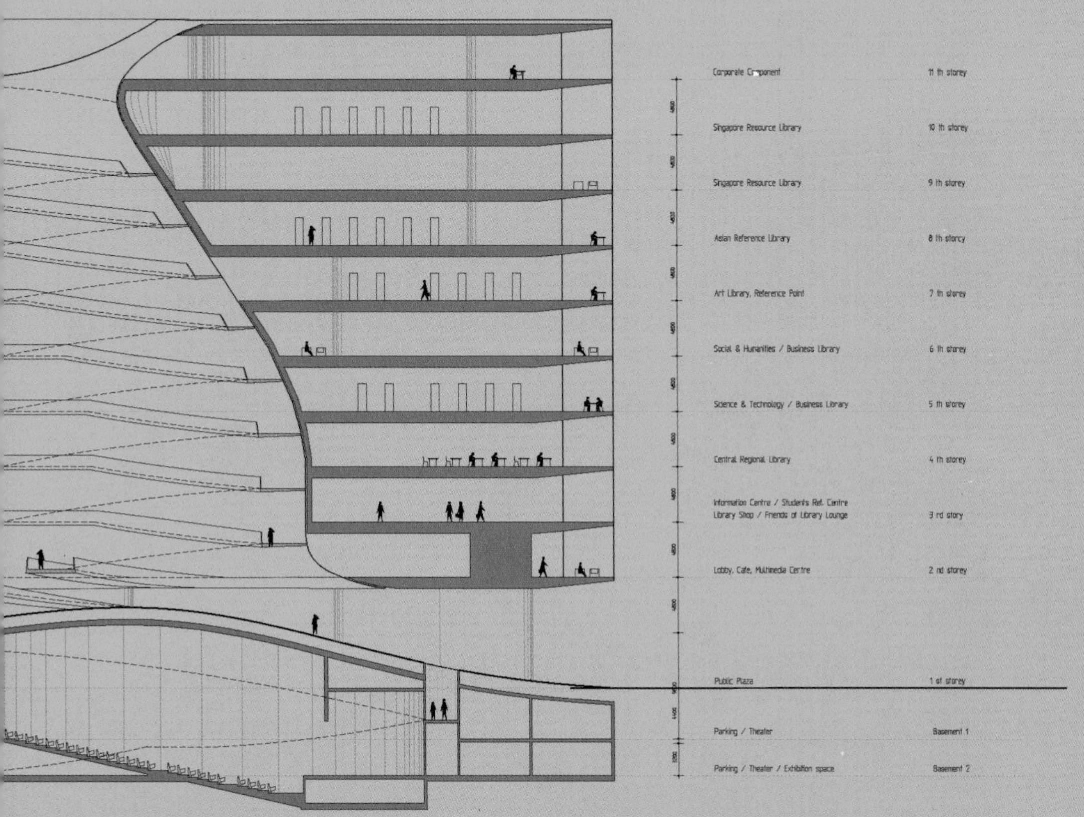
Corporate Component
11 th storey
Singapore Resource Library
10 th storey
Singapore Resource Library
9 th storey
Asian Reference Library
8 th storey
Art Library, Reference Point
7 th storey
Social & Humanities / Business Library
6 th storey
Science & Technology / Business Library
5 th storey
Central Regional Library
4 th storey
Information Centre / Students Ref. Centre
Library Shop / Friends of Library Lounge
3 rd story
Lobby, Cafe, Multimedia Centre
2 nd storey
Public Plaza
1 st storey
Parking / Theater
Basement 1
Parking / Theater / Exhibition space
Basement 2

SECTION A-A

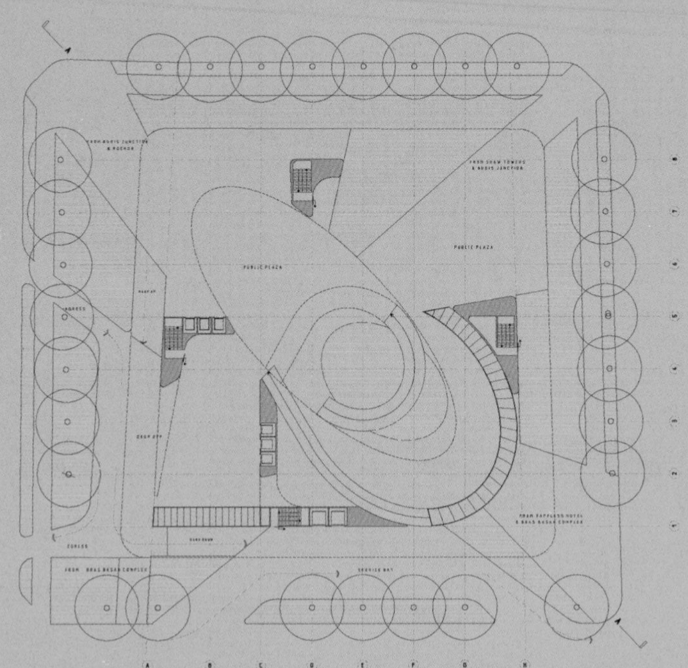

GROUND LEVEL

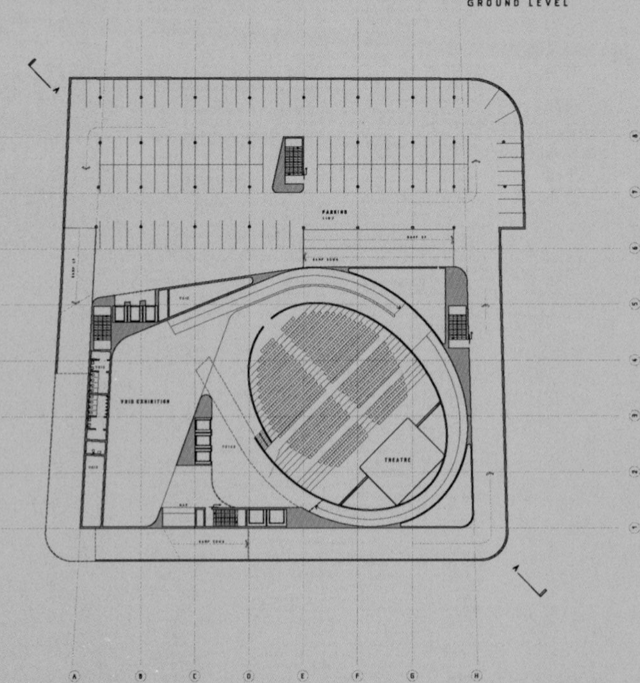

BASEMENT

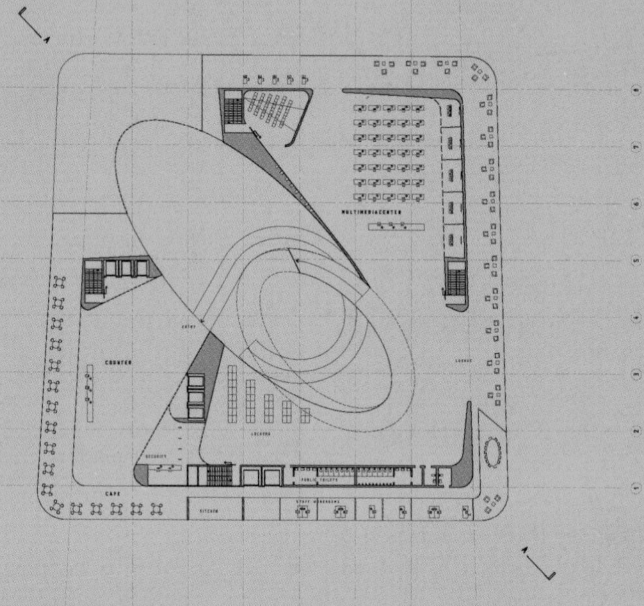

ENTRY LEVEL

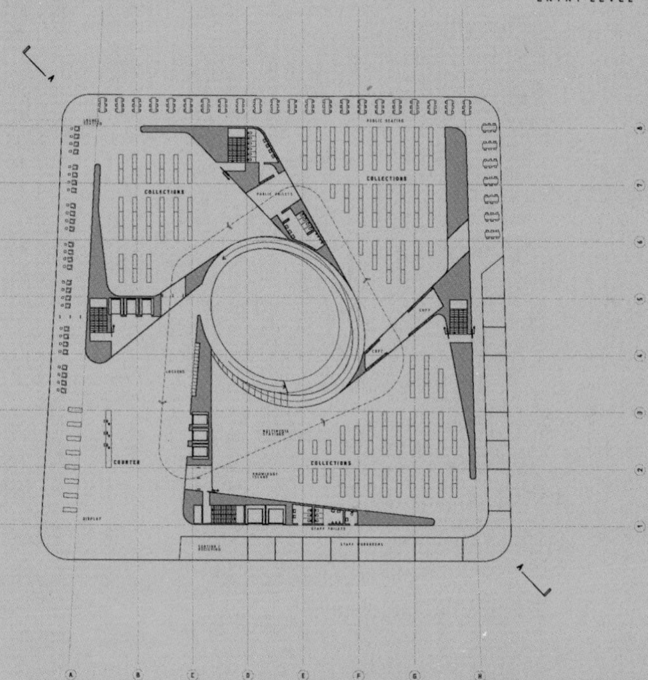

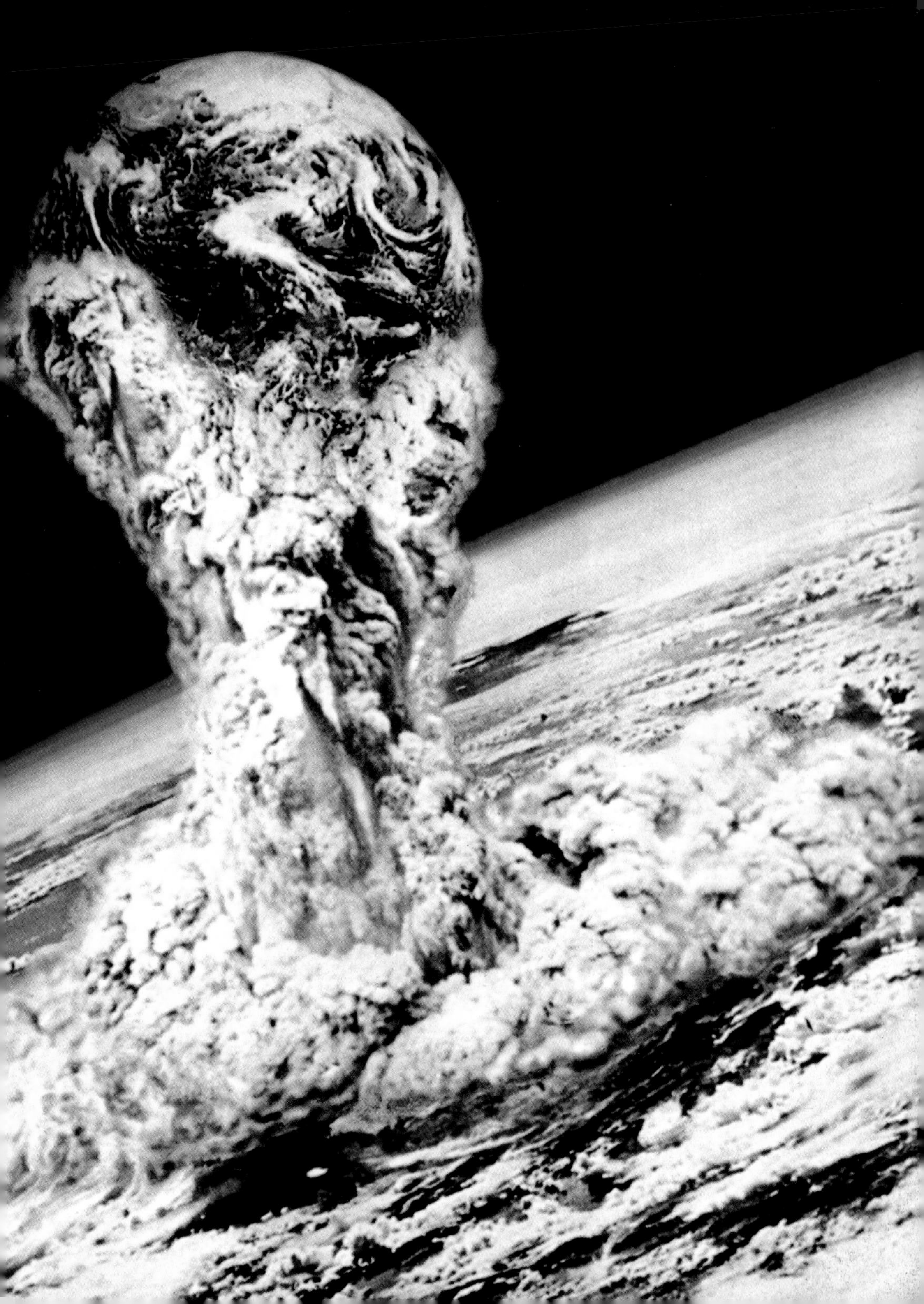

Erasmus Bridge

Rotterdam 1990-1996

Client: *Department of Public Works of the city of Rotterdam, Development Company Rotterdam (OBR)*

Design team: *Ben van Berkel (architect), Freek Loos (project co-ordinator), Hans Cromjongh, Ger Gijzen, Willemijn Lofvers, Sibo de Man, Gerard Nijenhuis, Manon Patinama, John Rebel, Ernst van Rijn, Hugo Schuurman, Caspar Smeets, Paul Toornend, Jan Willem Walraad, Dick Wetzels, Karel Vollers*

Technical consultants: *Department of the city of Rotterdam: Engineering department Concrete and Steel (IBS), Engineering department Harbour Works (IH), Engineering department Road and Water Management (IWG), Project management, Electricity Company Rotterdam - Centrum (ENECO), Lighting Design Partnership Edinburgh*

Building contractors: *Heerema Dock Installations, Vlissingen, Grootint, Dordrecht, Compagnie d'Entreprises CFE, Brussels, Maatschappij voor Bouw- en Grondwerken, Antwerpen, Ravestein-Noell, Deest, Lighting Design Partnership, Edinburgh*

UCP Mainport

Utrecht 1997

Client: *NS Vastgoed, NS Stations, NS Reizigers and Midnet GVU, represented by Ir. F. Koster of NS RailinfraBeheer*

Project Combination: *Holland Railconsult, Utrecht; Van Berkel & Bos Architectuurbureau, Amsterdam*

Design team Van Berkel & Bos: *Ben van Berkel (architect), Freek Loos (project co-ordinator), Thomas Durner, Rajan Ritoe, Andreas Bogenschütz*

Station Balcony

Utrecht 1998

Client: *Winkel Beleggingen Nederland, ING Vastgoed*

Masterplan and supervision: Plein 11, Arnhem

Project combination: *Alsop & Stormer, London; Van Berkel & Bos architectuurbureau, Amsterdam; Neutelings Riedijk, Rotterdam*

Design team Van Berkel & Bos: *Ben van Berkel (architect), Freek Loos (project co-ordinator), Andreas Bogenschütz (project leader) Ludo Grooteman, Armin Hess, Heiner Probst, Paul Vriend*

Double-decker

Randstad 1998

Client: *Bouwdienst Rijkswaterstaat, Afdeling Bruggenbouw, Tilburg*

Design co-ordinator: W. Hartman, Bureau voor Stedenbouw, Amsterdam

Design team: *Ben van Berkel (architect), Andreas Bogenschütz (project leader) Hernando Arrazola, Oliver Bormann, Gianni Cito, Anke Jürdens, Casper le Fèvre (visualisation), Francesca de Châtel (text)*

Pre-plan Study

Nieuwegein 1997 - 1998

Client: *Municipality of Nieuwegein*

Project combination: *Municipality of Nieuwegein: Hans van de Ven (project leader); Van Berkel & Bos Architectuurbureau; Bureau B+B stedenbouw en landschapsarchitectuur: M. van Gessel (project leader)*

Design team Van Berkel & Bos: *Ben van Berkel (architect), Rajan Ritoe (project leader 1), Andreas Bogenschütz (project leader 2), Oliver Bormann, Pedro Campos Costa, KSK Tamura, Armin Hess*

Technical consultants: *Ove Arup & Partners Consulting Engineers, London; Plan- en Adviesburo, Snijder W.B.N.; Kolpron Consultants, Rotterdam; Froger Enkelaar Communication (product & fire experience); Goudappel Coffeng (traffic and transport); Arcadis Heidemij Advies; Companen adviesgroep voor beleid; Triad/Take Five (strategy and creation); Model making consultancy: Frans Parthesius, Rotterdam; Model makers, Made by Mistake, Rotterdam; Deloitte & Touche; Mecanoo Architecten, Delft; Graphic Design, Mijs + van der Wal, Rotterdam*

Two Bridges

Utrecht 1998-2001

Client: *Projectbureau Leidsche Rijn, Utrecht.*

Project combination: Van Berkel & Bos; DHV Milieu en Infrastructuur bv.; Halcrow Group ltd.

Design team Van Berkel & Bos: *Ben van Berkel (architect), Freek Loos (project co-ordinator), Ger Gijzen (project leader), Suzanne Boyer, Henk Bultstra, Ludo Grooteman, Armin Hess, Tobias Wallisser, Jacques van Wijk, Andreas Bogenschütz*

Piet Hein Tunnel

Amsterdam 1990-1996

Client: *Dienst Infrastructuur Verkeer en Vervoer, Projectbureau Piet Heintunnel*

Project combination: *S.A.T Enigeering, The Hague (collaboration between Ingenieursbueau Grabowsky & Poort, Ingenieursbureau Jongen BV, Vlaardingen, Adviesbureau D3BN)*

Design team Van Berkel & Bos: *Ben van Berkel (architect), Harrie Pappot (project co-ordinator), Pieter Koster, Jaap Punt, Onno Reigersberg*

Building contractor: *Combinatie P.H.T. v.o.f, Amsterdam*

Model: *A. J. Bouwman, Rotterdam*

Director's Room NAi

Rotterdam 1993-1994

Client: *Netherlands Architecture institute*

Design team: *Ben van Berkel (architect), René Bouman (project leader), Monika Bauer*

Technical consultants: *Adviesbureau voor Bouwtechniek bv, Velp, Holst Glas bv., Enschede, Charles de Vries Furniture, Amsterdam, Zonwering Westland bv., Vlaardingen*

Aedes East Gallery

Berlin 1994-1995

Client: *Aedes East gallery*

Design team: *Ben van Berkel (architect), Monika Bauer*

Technical drawings and building supervision: *Transform Architekten, Berlin*

De Weiert

Emmen 1994-1996

Client: *Multi Vastgoed bv, Gouda*

Design team: *Ben van Berkel (architect), René Bouman (project co-ordinator) Harrie Pappot (project co-ordinator), Wilbert Swinkels (project leader) Monika Bauer, Henk Smallenburg, Frank van Hierk, Edwin van Namen, Ronald van Nieuwkerk, Sanderijn Amsberg, Hans Kuijpers, Hanna Euro, Tycho Soffree, Marc Dijkman, Jan van Erven Dorens, Fenja Riks*

Technical consultant: *Adviesbureau Maat, Rotterdam*

Constructor: *Ingenieursbureau Molenbroek bv, Rotterdam*

Building contractor: *Thomasson Dura bv, Hengelo; IHN Noord bv, Groningen*

Urban study De Weiert

Emmen 1995

Client: *City of Emmen, sector SOB (R.O.)*

Design team: *Ben van Berkel (architect), Harrie Pappot, Hugo Beschoor Plug, Julia Drücke*

Bascule Bridges

Purmerend 1995-1998

Client: *City of Purmerend*

Design team: *Ben van Berkel (architect), Freek Loos (project co-ordinator), Ger Gijzen, Sibo de Man, John Rebel, Stefan Böwer, Stefan Lungmuss*

Technical consultant: *IBA ingenieursbureau, Amsterdam*

Building contractors: *Bouwcombinatie Vermeer Beton en Waterbouw, Hoofddorp; Genius Klinkenberg, Wormerveer; Hoogovens, Ijmuiden*

National Museum Twente

Enschede 1992-1996

Client: *Rijksgebouwendienst, The Hague*

Design team: *Ben van Berkel (architect), Harrie Pappot (project co-ordinator), Joost Hovenier (project leader), Hugo Beschoor Plug, Pieter Koster, Peter Meier, Martin Visscher, Jan van Erven Doren, Serge Darding, Arjan van Ruyven*

Landscape architect: *Lodewijk Baljon, Amsterdam*

Technical consultants: *Ministry of Housing and Construction, Dept. Design and Technique, The Hague; Engineering and Consultancy A.H. Wiecherinck, Enschede*

Technical installations: *Acoustic consultancy Peutz, Molenhoek*

Building contractor: *Punte, Enschede*

Museum Het Valkhof

Nijmegen 1995 - 1999

Client: *Stichting Museum Het Valkhof, Nijmegen*

Design team: *Ben van Berkel (architect), Henri Snel (project co-ordinator), Remco Bruggink, Rob Hootsmans, Jacco van Wengerden, Hugo Beschoor Plug, Marc Dijkman, Walther Kloet, Florian Fischer, Carsten Kiselowsky, Luc Veeger, Caroline Bos (text)*

Project management: *Berns Projekt Management, Arnhem; Haskoning, Nijmegen*

Technical management: *ABT Bouwkostenservice, Velp*

Technical consultants: *Ketel Raadgevende Ingenieurs, Delft; Adviesbureau voor Bouwtechniek, Arnhem*

Building contractors: *Nelissen van Egteren Bouw, Venray; Blitta BV, Venray; Verwol projectafbouw, Opmeer; electronical installations GTI, Arnhem*

Site management PRC Bouwcentrum: *J.W. Sutmuller*

Diocesan Museum

Cologne 1996

Design team: *Ben van Berkel (architect), Peter Trummer (design co-ordinator), Sibo de Man, Henk Jan Bultstra, Andreas Bogenschütz, Andreas Krause*

Substation

Innsbruck 1996-2000

Client: *Innsbrucker Kommunalbetriebe AG*

Design team: *Ben van Berkel (architect), Henri Snel (project co-ordinator), Hannes Pfau (project leader), Gianni Cito, Ludo Grooteman, Laura Negrini, Hans Sterck, Casper le Fèvre, Jacco van Wengerden, Eli Aschkenasy, Hjalmar Frederiksson*

National Library

Singapore 1998

Client: *Singapore National Board Library*

Design team: *Ben van Berkel (architect), Ludo Grooteman (design co-ordinator), Andreas Bogenschütz, Armin Hess, Hans Kuijpers, Jacco van Wengerden, Sonja Cabalt (graphic design), Caroline Bos*

RSP Singapore: *Christopher Lee*

Photo credits & information

p. 1 Ilhara river, Sonja Cabalt
p. 6 Traffic jam, anonymous; Tokyo 1998, Sonja Cabalt; Mirage 5BR, A. Roels, BAF/VSRP; Virtual Fantasy, Eric Sander, Liason; Olympic Games 1936, anonymous; Dynamic dino G. Steinmetz; Body-altering expedients, Jeffrey Sylvester, FPG; Tunnel, anonymous.

Introduction
p. 14 top: Pattern of orbital pollution, N.L. Johnson, Teledyne Brown Engineering. bottom: Open-air concert in Central Park, New York, Steve Lehmann/Vision.

Imagination
p. 20 Tsunekisa Kimura's visual scandals by photomontage, Kimura Camera.
p. 22-23 from left to right: Pippi Long Stocking; Skinhead in Denver, Colorado, Marc Asnin; Blind Faith, Bob Seidemann Acto Records; A Space Odyssey; Voting Soviet Politicians, Boris Joertsjenko; The Fists, Wladyslaw Bednardczuk; Smearless lip stencil, Kenji Kawakami; Imagination, Sillicon Valley, Jan-Bart van Beek.
p. 25 Rock concert, Hamburg, Glenn A. Baker/Archives Redfans

The new concept of the architect
p. 26 Paris fashion, Remy de la Maviniere /AP Photo
p. 30-31 from left to right: Tokyo, Ben van Berkel; Multi-purpose mittens that keep you ready for anything, Kenji Kawakami; Andy Warhol; Ben van Berkel in swimming pool; Stephen Hawking, David Gamble; The strongest boy in New York, Anonymous; Tokyo, Ben van Berkel; Ben van Berkel, self-portrait; Wind, heat and moisture pattern of El Niño, W. Timothy Liu, NASA.
p. 32 from left to right: Scamozzi design for an ideal city, 1615; Rem Koolhaas, Parc de la Villette, Paris 1982; City plan of Washington D.C., Pierre Charles L'Enfants; Le Corbusier, Plan Voisin, Paris 1925; Rectangular type plan; Richard Kauffmann, Nahal, Israel 1921; Early French town plan; Superstudio, monumento continou, 1969.

Erasmus Bridge, Rotterdam
p. 35 Aeroview, p. 36 Christian Richters, p. 37 Sonja Cabalt, p. 38 Aeroview, p. 42 bottom left: Rob de Witt, p. 42-43 Hans Jürgen Commerell, p. 44 St. Paul's Cathedral at Abidjan, anonymous, p. 47-49 Sonja Cabalt, p. 50 Christian Richters, p. 54-57 Hans Jürgen Commerell, p. 58 Aeroview, p. 60-65 Hans Jürgen Commerell, p. 67-68 Mariette Carstens, p. 69 Hans Jürgen Commerell p. 70 Christian Richters

UCP Mainport, Utrecht
p. 73 Anatomy chart, American map corp., p. 75 flux, p. 84 Flying focus.

Station Balcony, Utrecht
p. 87 Central station Amsterdam, Sonja Cabalt, p. 90 Anatomy chart, American map corp.

Double-decker, Randstad
p. 103 Driving, Sonja Cabalt.

Pre-plan Study, Nieuwegein
p. 113 Collapsing skyscrapers in Chicago, anonymous, p.114-117 Delta Phot, Municipality Nieuwegein, p. 124 Shopping, Sonja Cabalt.

Two Bridges, Utrecht
p. 143 Images of distortion, p. 147 Distortion no. 5, André Kertèsz.

Material organisation

p. 154 Brain scans, anonymous.
p. 156-157 from left to right: Lake of dunes, Chile, Joanna B. Pinneo; Visualisation of heat around a space-shuttle, anonymous; Protective fashion, Dana Menussi; Shawl, Jurgen Lehl; Advertisement Issey Miyake; Highways of Saharan Niger, George Steinmetz; Computer study of the pylon of the Erasmus Bridge; Aspects of nature, Yume Tsuzure.
p. 158 Soapsuds, anonymous.

Piet Hein Tunnel, Amsterdam

p. 161-163 Christian Richters, p. 168 Guido Coolens, p. 170 Tsunekisa Kimura's visual scandals by photomontage, Kimura Camera, p. 172 Christian Richters.

Director's Room NAi, Rotterdam

p. 175-176 Hélène Binet, p. 177 Fetish, Ralph Baiker, p. 178 Zen garden, Sonja Cabalt, p. 180-181 Hélène Binet.

Aedes East Gallery, Berlin

p. 183 Jörg Hempel Photo Design, p. 184 Hans Jürgen Commerell, p. 185 Prison riot Argentina, ABC Press, p. 186-189 Hans Jürgen Commerell.

De Weiert, Emmen

p. 191-192 Christian Richters, p. 193 Cosmetic surgery, anonymous,
p. 194 Japanese cosmetic magazine, p. 197-203 Christian Richters.

Bascule Bridges, Purmerend

p. 205 Christian Richters, p. 207 Transparant faces, Machteld Kors Sonja Cabalt, p. 210 Christian Richters, p. 212 Horsefly, Alain Duran/ANA, ABC Press, p. 214 Christian Richters, p. 217 Ger Gijzen.

Inclusiveness

p. 222-223 from left to right: Stock exchange Tokyo, Internet; Page out of G-shock catalogue; Men's shoes 1986, Pierre Cardin; Medical systems: diagnostic imaging systems, Philips Design; Different digital information layers of bridge deck Erasmus Bridge; Netserver.

National Museum Twente, Enschede

p. 227 Wet/Dry 1981-86, Jeff Koons, p.229 Exhibition spaces, p.228 J. Willebrand, p. 231-235 Christian Richters, p. 236 Jan Derwig, p. 238 J. Willebrand.

Museum Het Valkhof, Nijmegen

p. 243 window cleaners at work in Het Valkhof, Sonja Cabalt, p. 254 Remco Bruggink, p. 256 KNMI, De Bilt, p. 260-263 Remco Bruggink, p. 264 Henri Snel.

Diocesan Museum, Cologne

p. 269 Ruins, Turkey, Sonja Cabalt,
p. 274 Stelarc, Sitting/Swaying 1984.

Substation, Innsbruck

p. 289 Urban camouflage clothing 1986, Adelle Lutz and Annie Leibovitz, p. 298 Powerstation, Spain, Sonja Cabalt.

National Library, Singapore

p. 308 Tsunekisa Kimura's visual scandals by photomontage, Kimura Camera.

p. 318-319 Ilhara river, Sonja Cabalt

First published June 1999
Reprinted December 1999

Text Ben van Berkel & Caroline Bos

Graphic design Sonja Cabalt *(UN Studio)*

Publisher UN Studio & Goose Press
Stadhouderskade 113
1073 AX Amsterdam
The Netherlands
++31(0)20-5702040
info@unstudio.com

Editorial assistants Sonja Cabalt, Machteld Kors, Francesca de Châtel

Translation Kate Simms

Printed by Rosbeek, the Netherlands
ISBN 90-76517-01-0

Trade distribution
Idea Books: world-wide
idea@xs4all.nl fax ++31(0)20-6209299
Architectura & Natura: the Netherlands
kemme@architectura.nl

Colophon

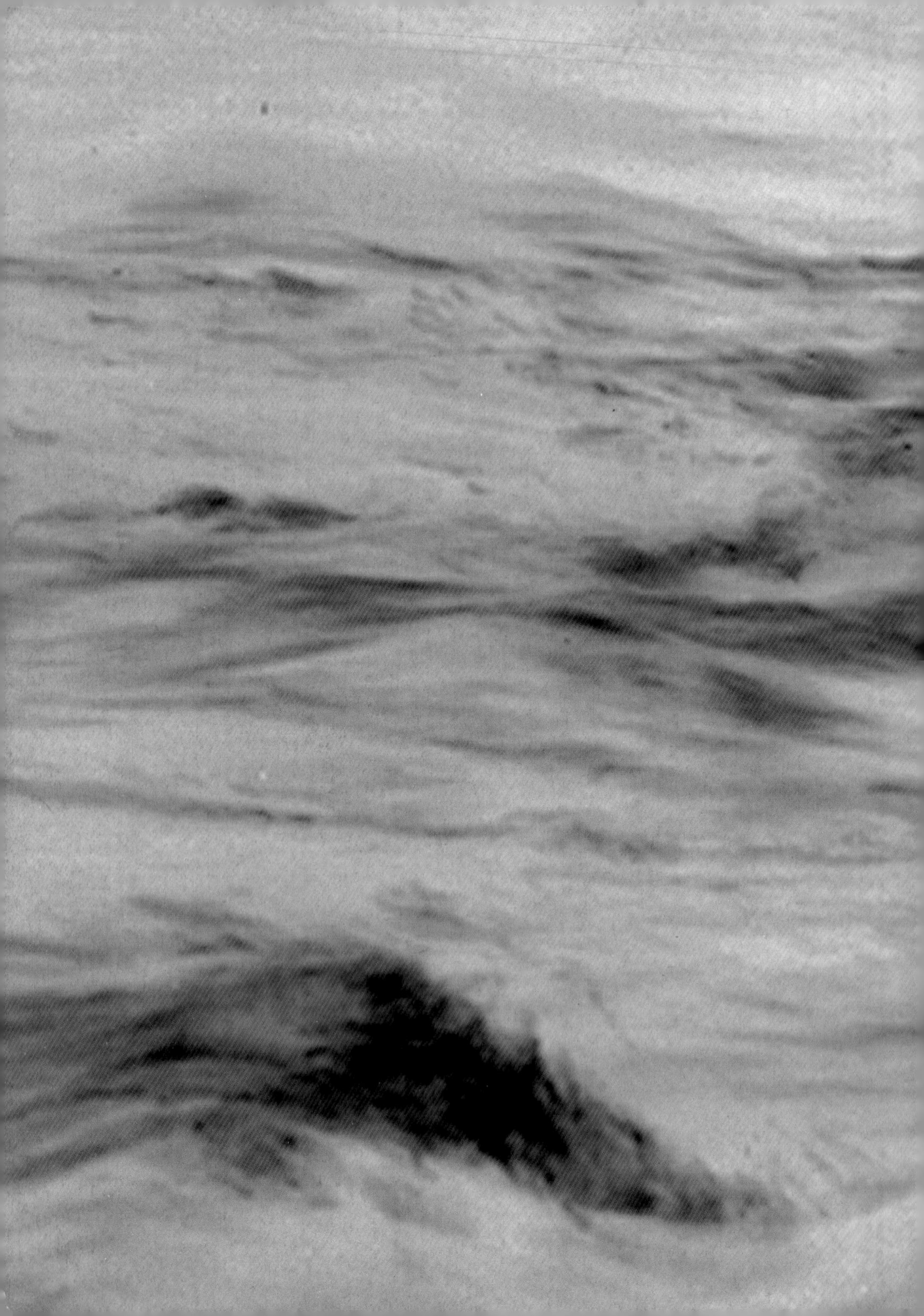

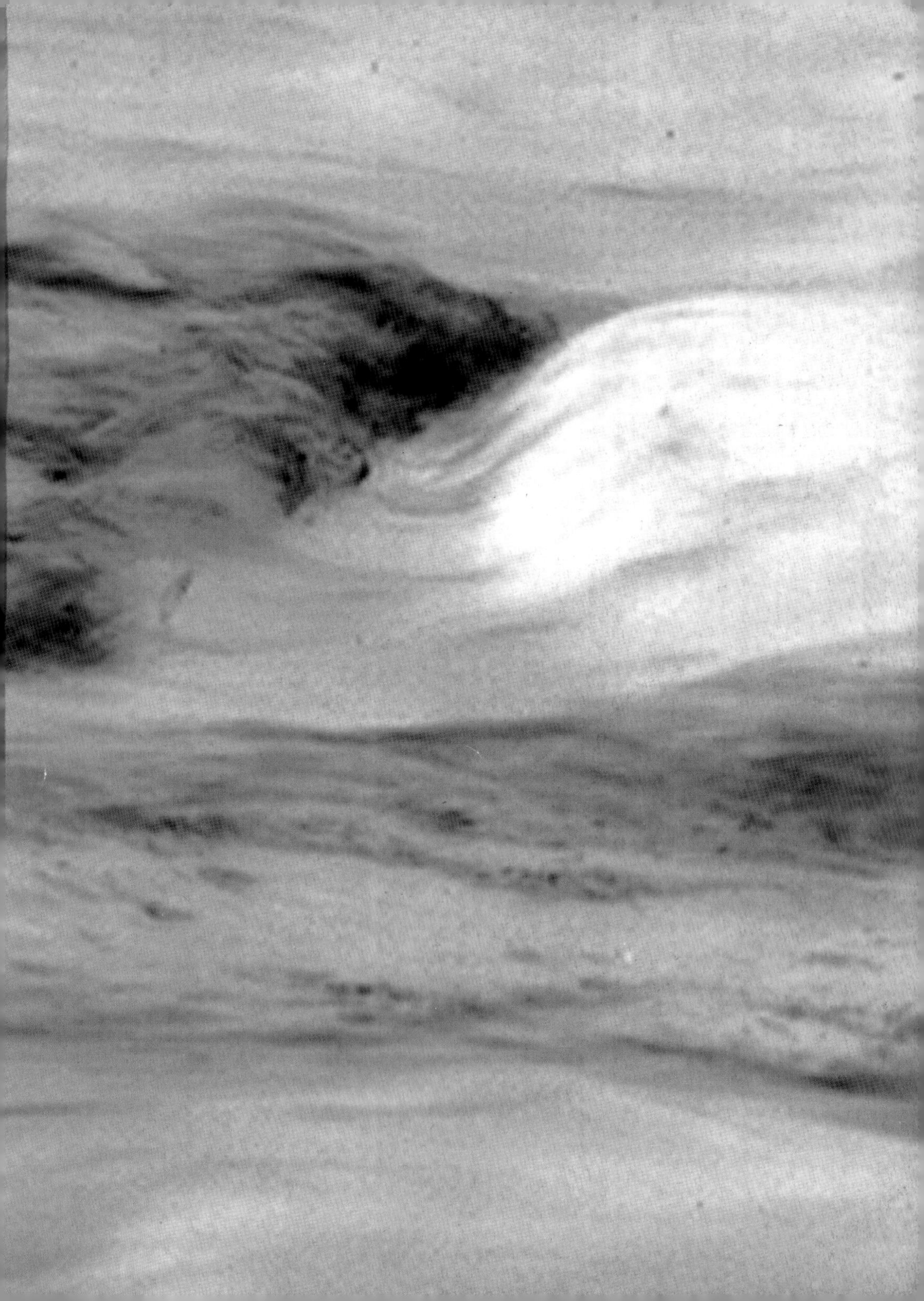

ve

UN S

Ben van Berkel

tudio

Caroline Bos

② Tech

niques

network spin

CT-Scan Montage Plastics
Gamma radiation Frot
tage Mixed media E-mai
Land art Cartoon Statis
tics Cybercash Mass cus
tomisation Aerobics Drip
painting Scuba diving
Video Compact disk Shi
atsu Television Extend
Cloning Mediation Op-Ar
Bungy jumping Graffit
Morphing Car industry
Collage Digital communi
cation Surfing Nano tech

nology Scratching Ultra-
sound Ready-made Holo-
gram Yoga Artificial
intelligence Break dance
Cosmetic surgery Gene
splicing D.J. Marketing
Hybridization Air brush
Mirror Assemblage Ani-
mation Conceptual art
Photocopy S.M. Cloning
Digidesign Acupuncture
Monochrome V.J. Disco
Ready-made Word pro-
cessing Virtual Reality

CONTENTS

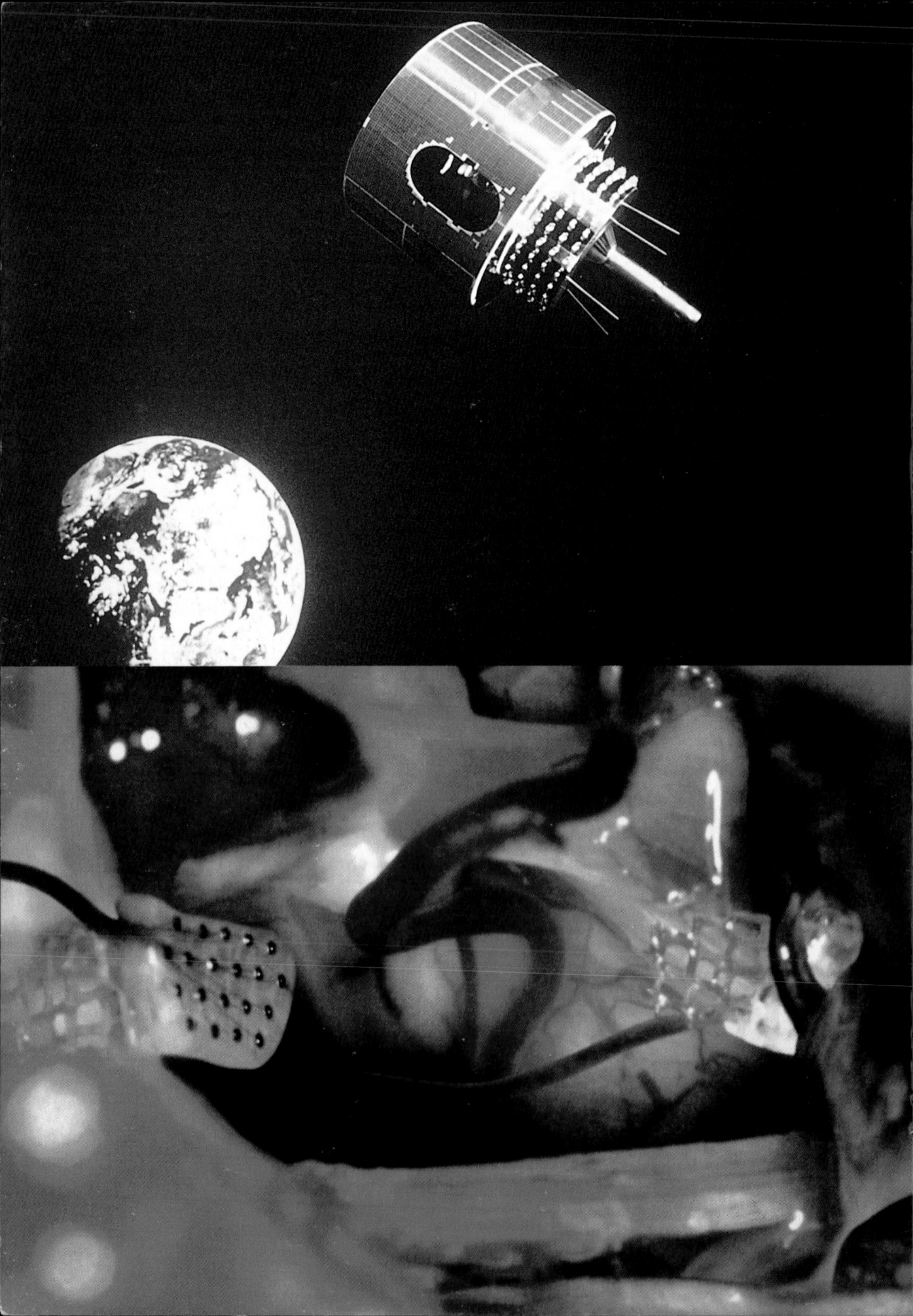

Techniques

Network Spin

Techniques, which are distinct from production methods or style, are the most neglected element of cultural production. Theories are not built around techniques and they are only disseminated in the most direct manner from one practitioner to another in institutions, workplaces, or through handbooks. Techniques are dry - even when there is a narrative attached their significance rests not in that story. Techniques are mostly a thing of the past. The techniques of today, on the other hand, are of interest only to nerds, obsessing over the interior of a computer. Yet techniques form the bridge between abstract thought and concrete production. This is a two-way bridge: techniques also form thought. Technology stimulates mental fabrication by means of the specific potential that it possesses.

Each new technology changes the world. Ontological and technological permutations are interwoven. In the twentieth century, an avalanche of new techniques has coursed through the sciences, industry, the arts and communication, revealing the deep integration in the wider world of all forms of social/cultural production.

The turbulent expansion of the inventory of techniques is interactively related to social, economic and scientific change.
From the practitioner's viewpoint, the advancement of new techniques is an essential part of conceptualising rather than responding to change; the concrete, visual effects generated by the development of new techniques stimulate the imagination. The specific properties of the techniques themselves are instrumental in shaping the concept. You can already see new effects and new models of organisation in a new technology.
Computer and mediation techniques represent the latest development in the twentieth century catalogue of new techniques. They enable the storage, combination, manipulation and display of information. They make time visible and calculable. They breed new words and new procedures - numerous small technologies proceed from the invention of new techniques. Above all,

computer and mediation techniques promote and reveal a world of multiplied communications, in which everything and everyone is connected through technologies that are based on flexible, mobile, operational systems. In the new, mediated world all things spin in an invisible network. All the information that we receive and transmit comes to us through technologies that have reorganised the world. The image of a suddenly small earth encircled by a dense band of revolving satellites is an emblem of our time. Together, earth and satellites form a completely novel organisational typology, a network with a virtual structure, containing solely power points in space. The immaterial nodes in this network are always changing; their instability is as great as their expansiveness. The endless multiplication of communications leads new media to a narcissistic reflection on themselves, resulting in a new type of global success and scandal. Mediation to the present day is what the sublime was to the Romantic era: triumphant, exalted, poignant, massive and uncontrollable. The question is: which

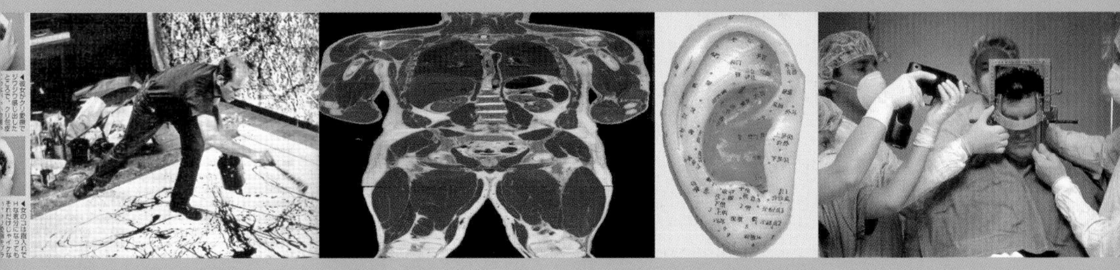

are the appropriate techniques for architecture to use to instrumentalise this new mediated cosmology for its own ends?

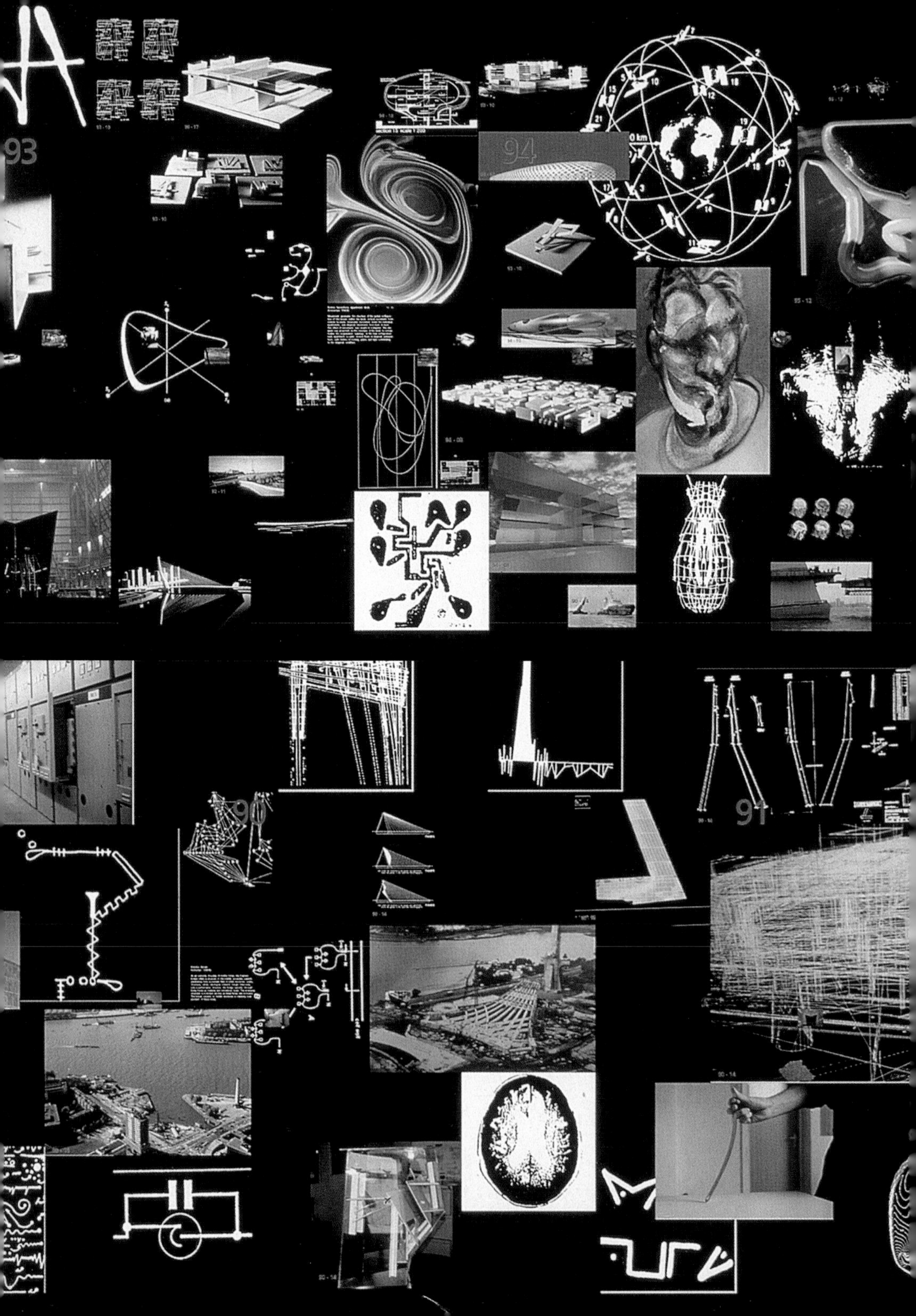

Diagrams

Diagrammatic technique provides a foothold in the fast streams of mediated information. The meaninglessness that repetition and mediation create is overcome by diagrams which generate new, instrumental meanings and steer architecture away from typological fixation.

What is a diagram? In general, diagrams are best known and understood as visual tools used for the compression of information. A specialist diagram, such as a statistics table or a schematic image, can contain as much information in a few lines as would fill pages in writing. In architecture, diagrams have in the last few years been introduced as part of a technique that promotes a proliferating, generating and instrumentalising approach to design. The essence of the diagrammatic technique is that it introduces into a work qualities that are unspoken, disconnected from an ideal or an ideology, random, intuitive, subjective, not bound to a linear logic - qualities that can be physical, structural, spatial or technical.

There are three stages to the diagram: selection, application and operation, enabling the imagination to extend to subjects outside it and draw them inside, changing itself in the process.

Diagrams are packed with information on many levels. A diagram is an assemblage of solidified situations, techniques, tactics and functionings. The arrangement of the eighteenth century Panopticon prison plan is the expression of a number of cultural and political circumstances cumulating in a distinctive manifestation of surveillance. It conveys the spatial organisation of a specific form of State power and discipline. It incorporates several levels of significance and cannot be reduced to a singular reading; like all diagrams, the Panopticon is a manifold. Characteristically, when a diagram breeds new meanings, they are still directly related to its substance - its tangible manifestation. Critical readings of previous interpretations are not diagrammatic. Put in the simplest possible terms, an image is a diagram when it is stronger than its interpretations.

The diagram is not a blueprint. It is not the working drawing of an actual construction, recognisable in all its details and with a proper scale. No situation will let itself be directly translated into a fitting and completely correspondent conceptualisation. There will always be a gap between the two. By the same token concepts can never be directly applied to architecture. There has to be a mediator. The mediating ingredient of the diagram derives not from the strategies that inform the diagram, but from its actual format, its material configuration. The diagram is not a metaphor or paradigm, but an 'abstract machine' that is both content and expression. This distinguishes diagrams from indexes, icons and symbols. The meanings of diagrams are not fixed. The diagrammatic or abstract machine is not representational. It does not represent an existing object or situation, but it is instrumental in the production of new ones. The forward-looking tendency of diagrammatic practice is an indispensable ingredient for understanding its functioning.

Why use diagrams? Diagrammatic practice delays the relentless intrusion of signs, thereby allowing architecture to articulate an alternative to a representational design technique. A representational technique implies that we converge on reality from a conceptual position and in that way fix the relationship between idea and form, between content and structure. When form and content are superimposed in this way, a type emerges. This is the problem with an architecture that is based on a representational concept: it cannot escape existing typologies. In not proceeding from signs, an instrumentalising technique such as the diagram delays typological fixation. Concepts external to architecture are introduced rather than superimposed. Instances of specific interpretation, utilisation, perception, construction and so on unfold and bring forth applications on various levels of abstraction.

How is the diagram chosen and applied? The function of the diagram is to delay typology and advance design by bringing in external concepts in a specific shape: as figure, not as image or sign. But how do we select, insert and interpret diagrams? The selection and application of a diagram involves the insertion of an element that contains within its dense information something that our thoughts can latch onto, something that is suggestive, to distract us from spiralling into cliché. Although the diagram is not selected on the basis of specific representational information, it is not a random image. The finding of the diagram is instigated by specific questions relating to the project at hand: its location, programme and construction.

For us, it becomes interesting to use a diagram from the moment that it starts to relate specifically to

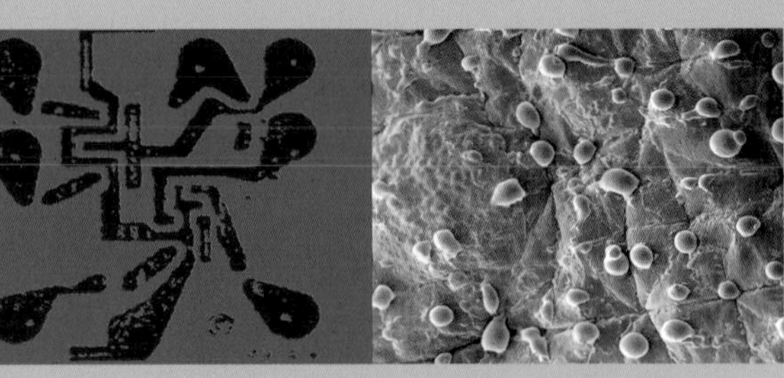

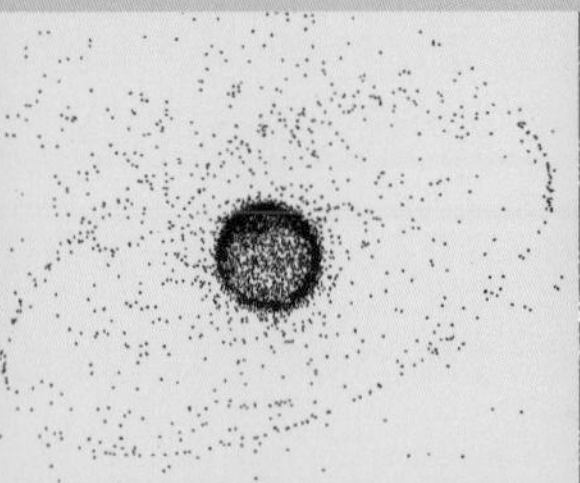

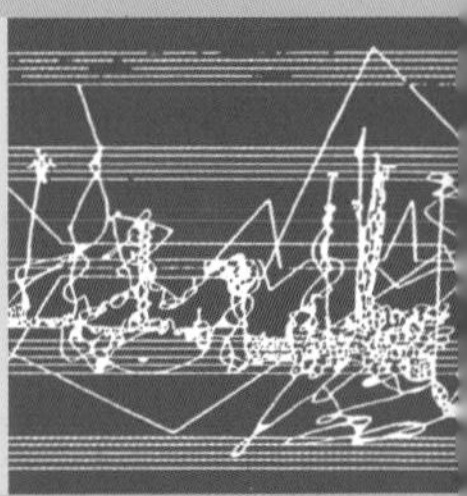

organisational effects. Among our collection of diagrams are flow charts, music notations, schematic drawings of industrial buildings, electrical switch diagrams... all maps of worlds yet to be constructed, if only as a detail. To suggest a possible, virtual organisation, we have used ideograms, line diagrams, image diagrams and finally operational diagrams, found in technical manuals, reproductions of paintings or random images that we collect. These diagrams are essentially infrastructural; they can always be read as maps of movements, irrespective of their origins. They are used as proliferators in a process of unfolding.

How do diagrams become operational? The abstract machine of the diagram needs triggering. It has to be set in motion so that the transformative process can begin, but where does this motion originate? How is the machine triggered? What exactly is the principle that effectuates change and transformation? Furthermore, how can we isolate this principle and give it the dimensions that make it possible to grasp and use it at will? The insertion of the diagram into the work

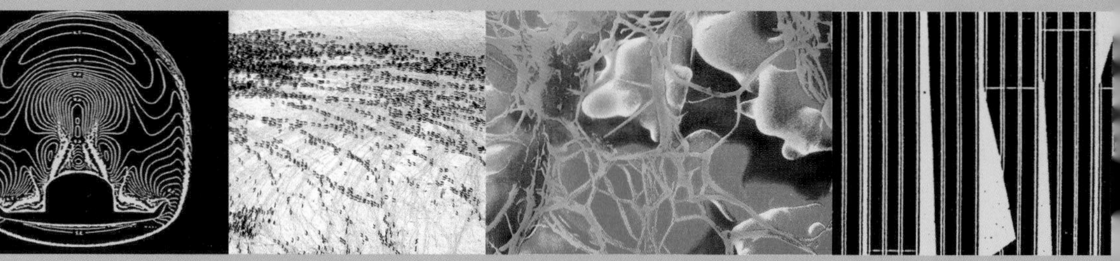

ultimately points to the role of time and action in the process of design. Interweaving time and action makes transformation possible, as in novels where long narrative

lines coil around black holes within the story. If there were no black holes for the story's protagonist to fall into, the landscape of the narrative would be a smooth and timeless plane, in which the hero, whose character and adventures are formed by this landscape, cannot evolve. The story is an intrinsic combination of character, place, event and duration. The landscape of the story, the black holes and the character become one. Together they trigger the abstract machine. In architecture, it goes something like this: the project is set on its course. Before the work diverts into typology a diagram, rich in meaning, full of potential movement and loaded with structure, which connects to some important aspect of the project, is found. The specific properties of this diagram throw a new light onto the work. As a result, the work becomes un-fixed; new directions and new meanings are triggered. The diagram operates like a black hole, which radically changes the course of the project, transforming and liberating architecture.

The diagram of the bunker demonstrates how the posture of defensiveness can produce a gesture of unexpected roundness, an efficient lining up of inside spaces and a simple and tidy circulation pattern. The solidity and the protection afforded by a bunker with its structure based on a position of radical, dug-in defensiveness have been instrumental in developing the organisational principle of this modest family home in an average Dutch suburb.

1-Family lifestyle 1: the bunker

The search for this particular diagram was instigated by the question posed in relation to the suburban house, in which the inhabitants seek seclusion, privacy and, above all, the recognition of their individuality within a dense housing area in which everything and everyone is hopelessly the same. Simultaneously with the posing of this question, a book on bunkers circulated in our studio. There is always something in the studio on which the collective fascination greedily focuses - music CD's, El Croquis magazines, exhibition catalogues, samples from the building industry. In 1992 it was bunkers.

The diagram of the bunker provides the first step in the process of unfolding the introverted

house. While the massive construction of the bunker protects against external force, its organisation is based on the central position of the occupants. The defensiveness of the house is most strongly expressed in its absence of an elevation. Seen from the street, the house does not exist. Only planes of shingle and smooth, rising grey walls are visible. A narrow path placed in between the sloping side wall leads to the hidden entrance at the heart of the house. Particular aspects of a diagram can be isolated for use in the construction, or as a detail, or to introduce a technique. In the Villa Wilbrink, the idea of strong, heavy, fluent walls has resulted in gluing the sand-stone bricks on to form smooth, uninterrupted surfaces.

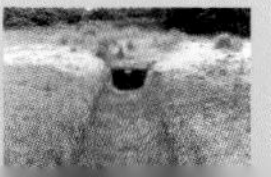

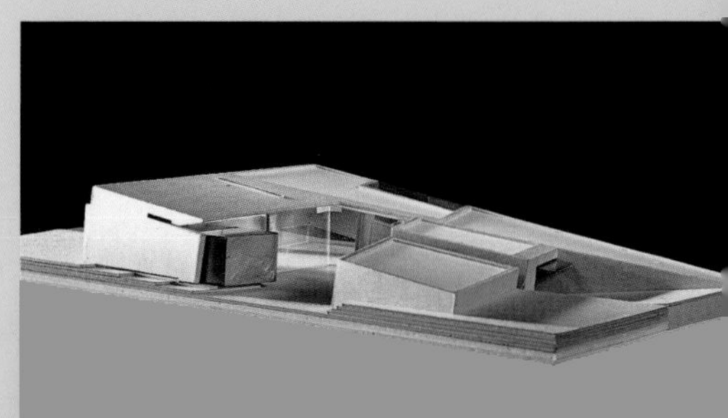

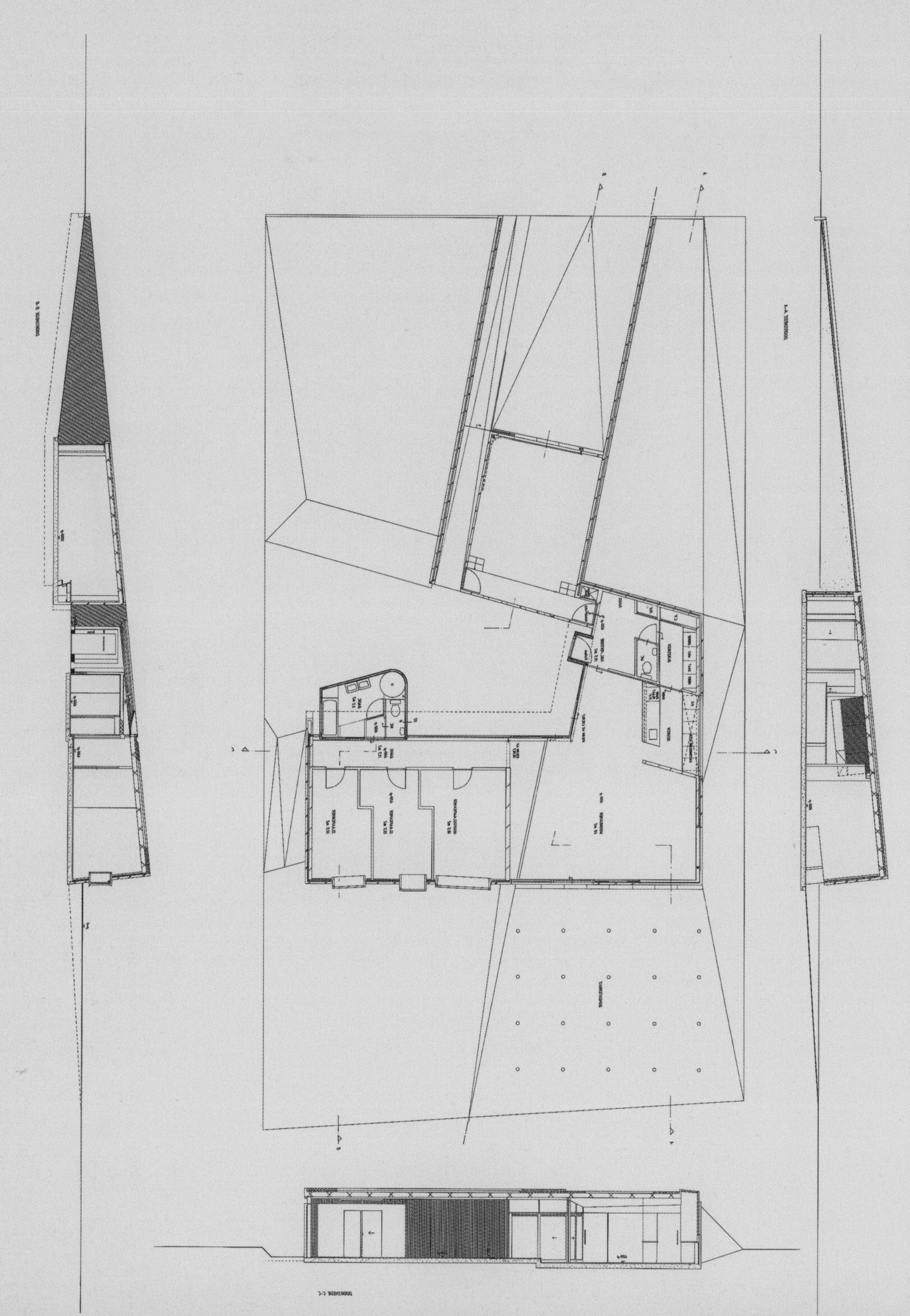
DOORSNEDE B-B
DOORSNEDE A-A
DOORSNEDE C-C

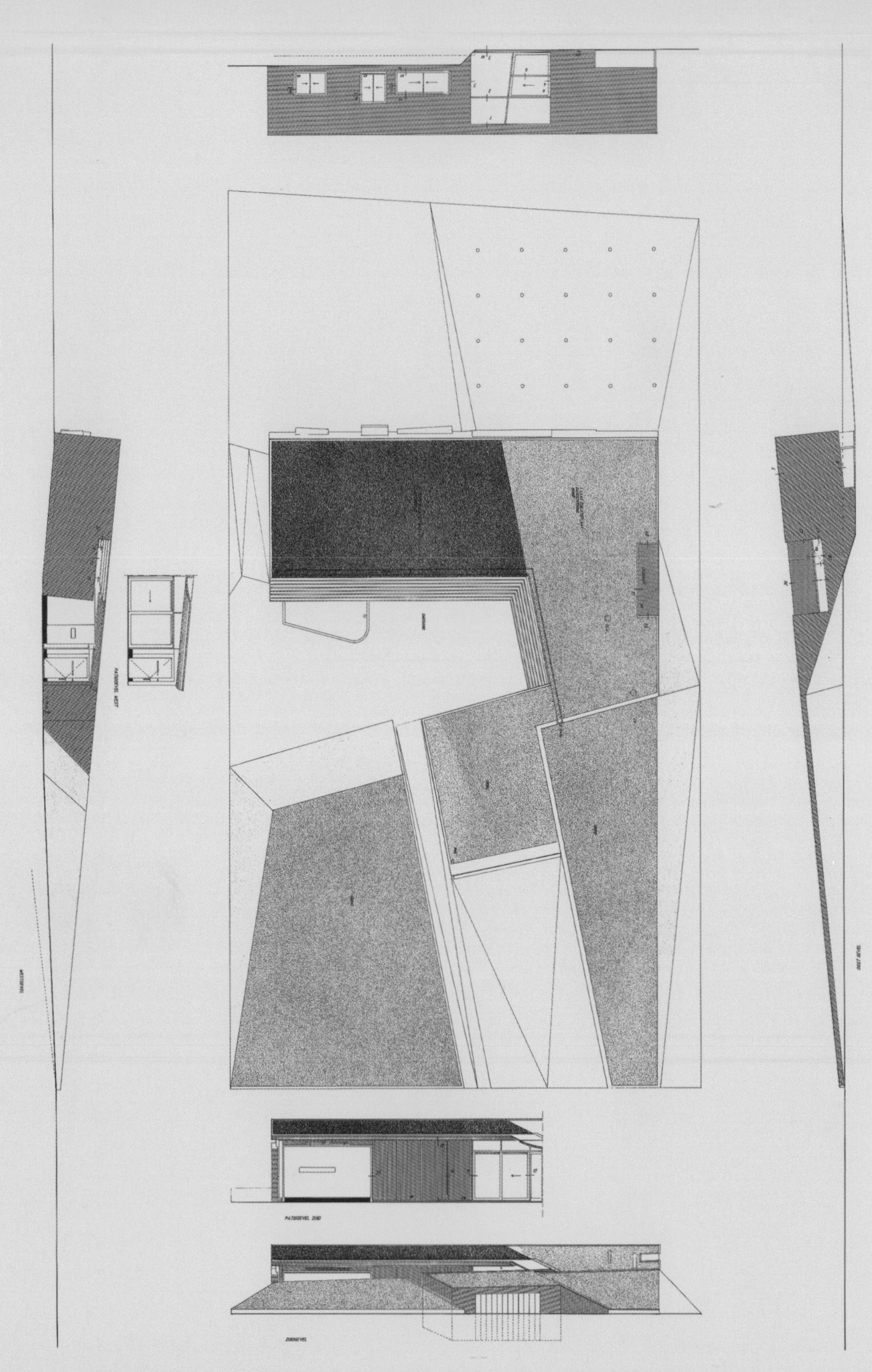
WESTGEVEL
PATIOGEVEL WEST
OOST GEVEL
PATIOGEVEL ZUID
ZIJGEVEL

The diagram of the double-locked torus conveys the organisation of two intertwining paths, which trace how two people can live together, yet apart, meeting at certain points, which become shared spaces. The idea of two entities running their own trajectories but sharing certain moments, possibly also reversing roles at certain points, is extended to include the materialisation of the building and its construction.

1-Family lifestyle 2: ***the walk in the wood***

The Möbius house integrates programme, circulation and structure seamlessly. The house interweaves the various states that accompany the condensation of differentiating activities into one structure: work, social life, family life and individual time alone all find their places in the loop structure. Movement through this loop follows the pattern of an active day. The structure of movement is transposed to the organisation of the two main materials used for the house; glass and concrete move in front of each other and switch places. Concrete construction becomes furniture and glass facades turn into inside partition walls.

As a graphic representation of 24 hours of family life, the diagram acquires a time-space dimen-

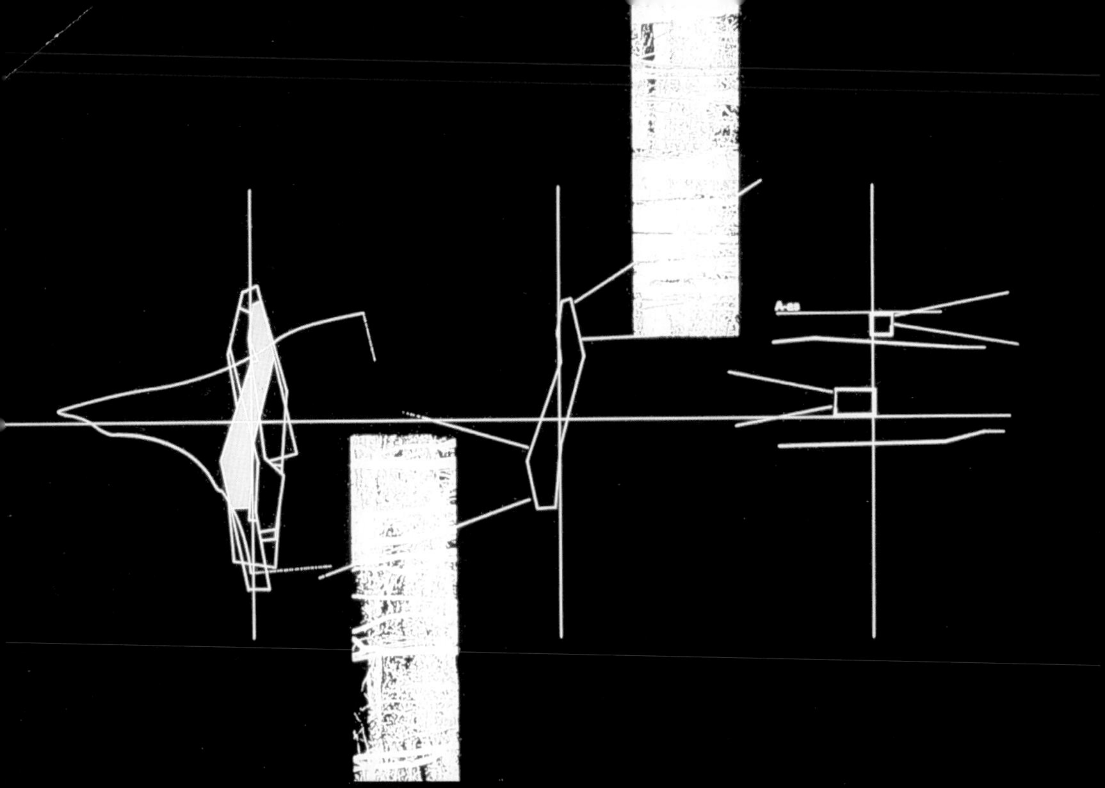

positioning in landscape

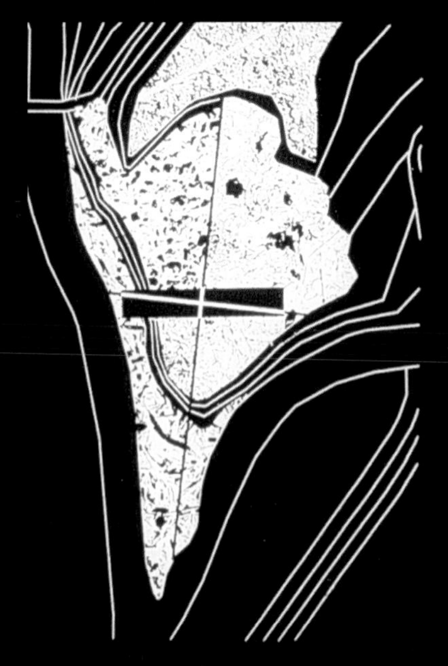

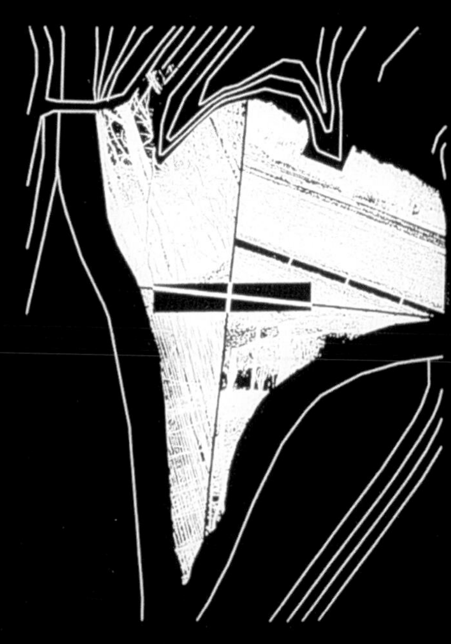

sion, which leads to the implementation of the Möbius band. Equally the site and its relationship to the building are important for the design. The site covers two hectares, which are divided into four areas distinct in character. Linking these with the internal organisation of the Möbius band transforms living in the house into a walk in the landscape.
The mathematical model of the Möbius is not literally transferred to the building, but is conceptualised or thematised and can be found in architectural ingredients, such as the light, the staircases and the way in which people move through the house. So, while the Möbius diagram introduces aspects of duration and trajectory, the diagram is worked into the building in a mutated way.
The instrumentalisation of this simple, borrowed drawing is the key. The two interlocking lines are suggestive of the formal organisation of the building, but that is only the beginning; diagrammatic architecture is a process of unfolding and ultimately of liberation. The diagram liberates architecture from language, interpretation and signification.

Staking the plot

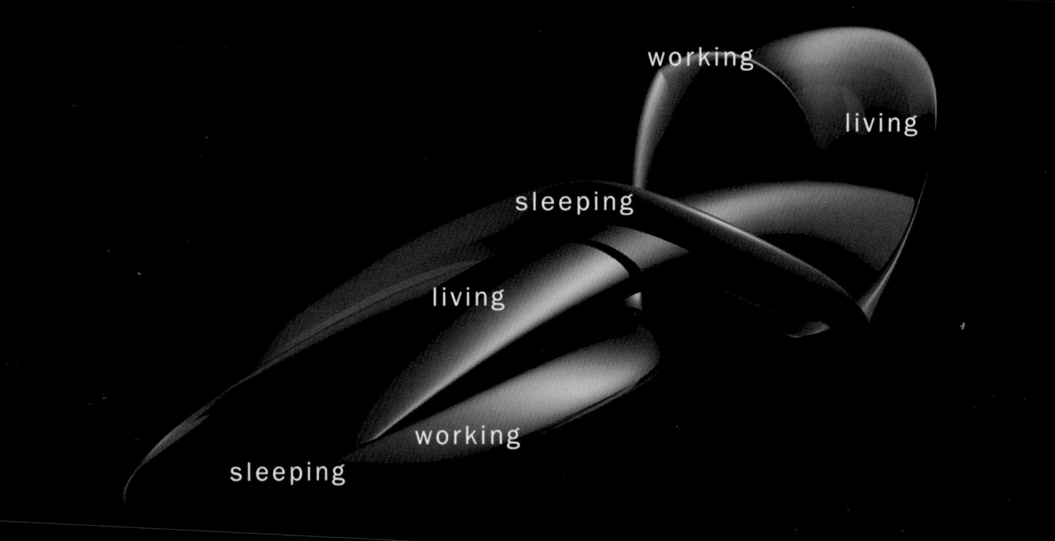

orientable surface diagram

24 hours of family li

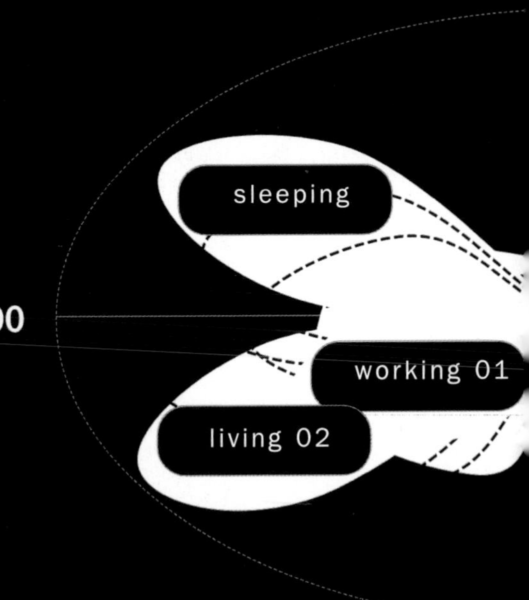

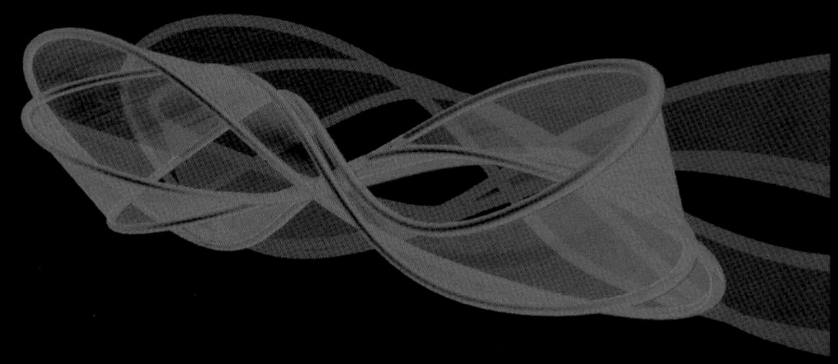

constructive diagram, trajectories of time, movement and construction generating column-free surface

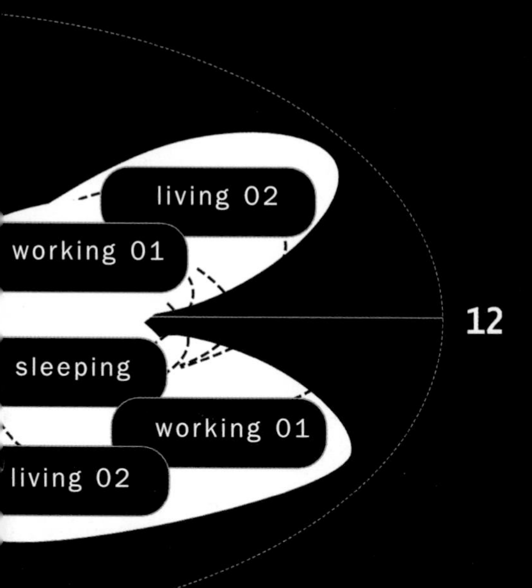

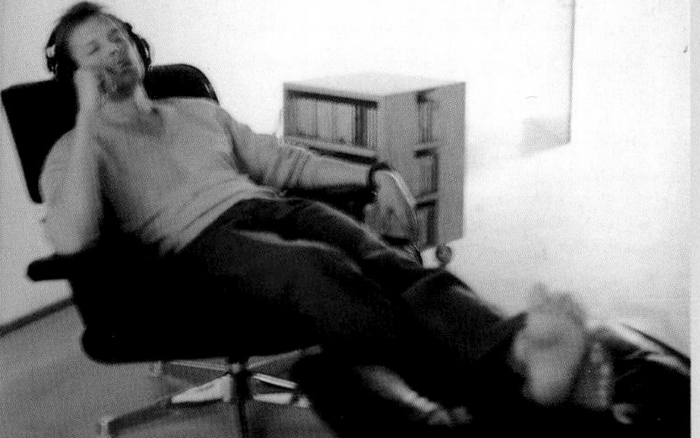

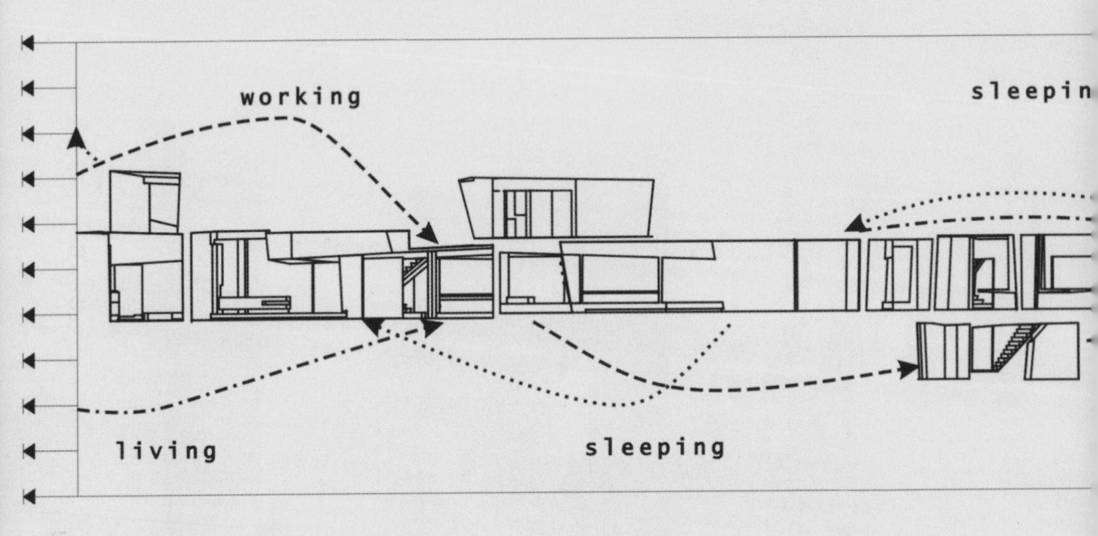

Unfolded concrete structure wit

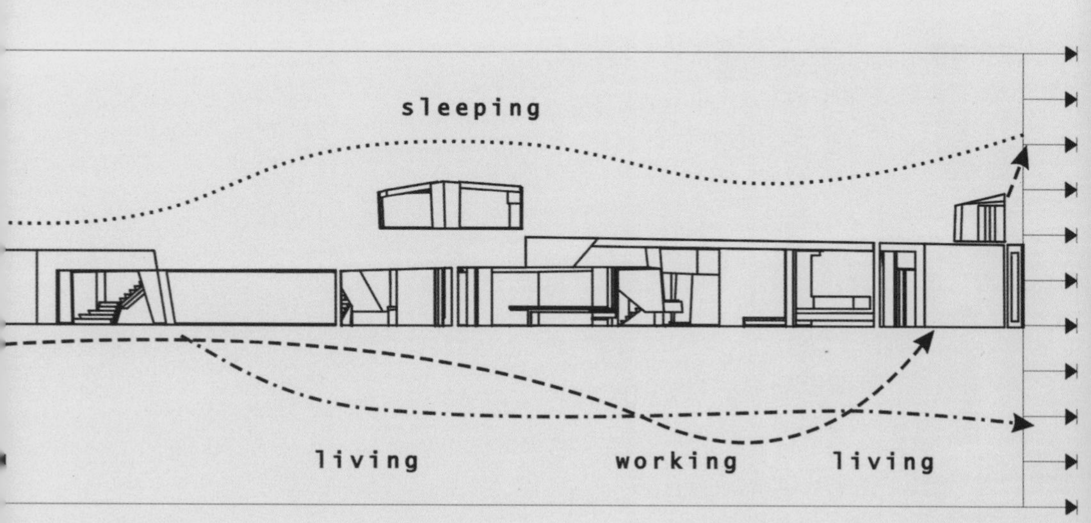
sleeping
living
working
living

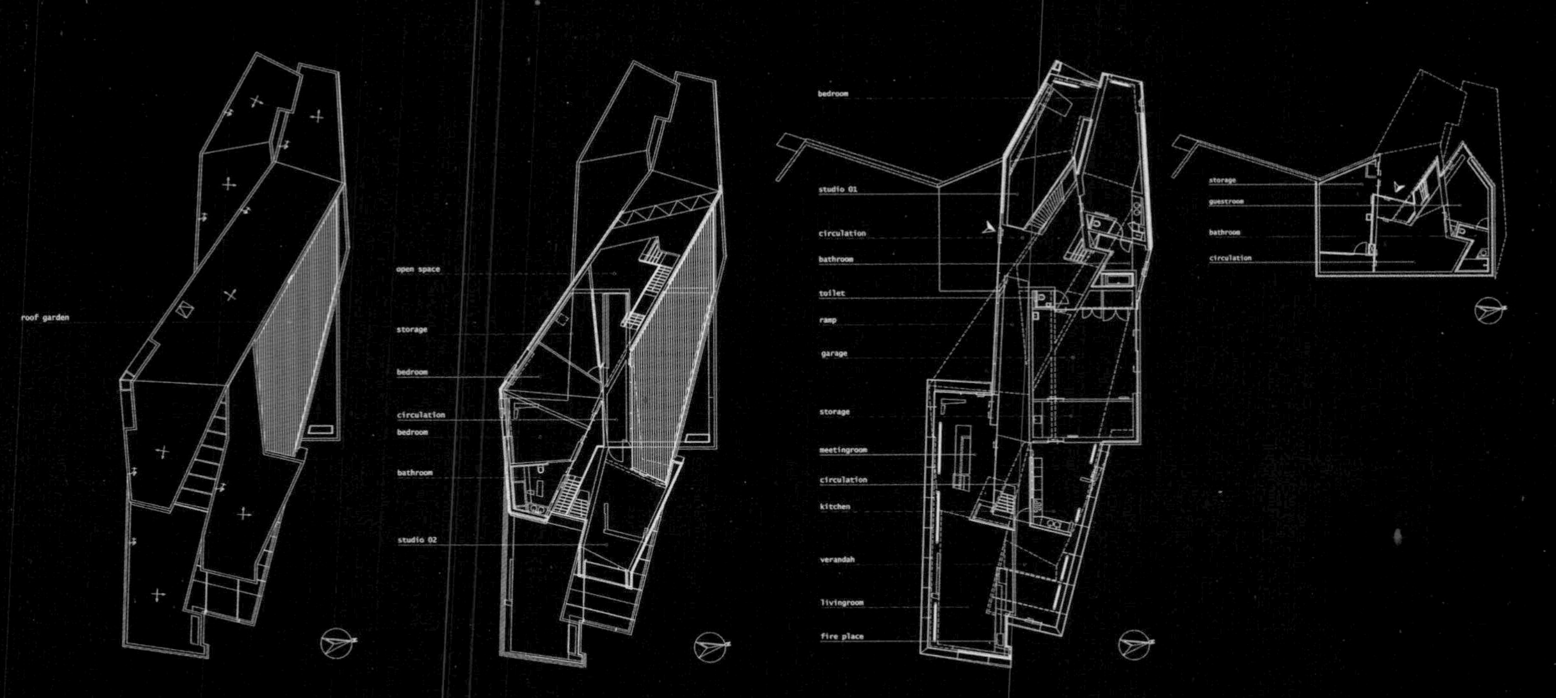
roof garden
open space
storage
bedroom
circulation
bedroom
bathroom
studio 02
bedroom
studio 01
circulation
bathroom
toilet
ramp
garage
storage
meetingroom
circulation
kitchen
verandah
livingroom
fire place
storage
guestroom
bathroom
circulation

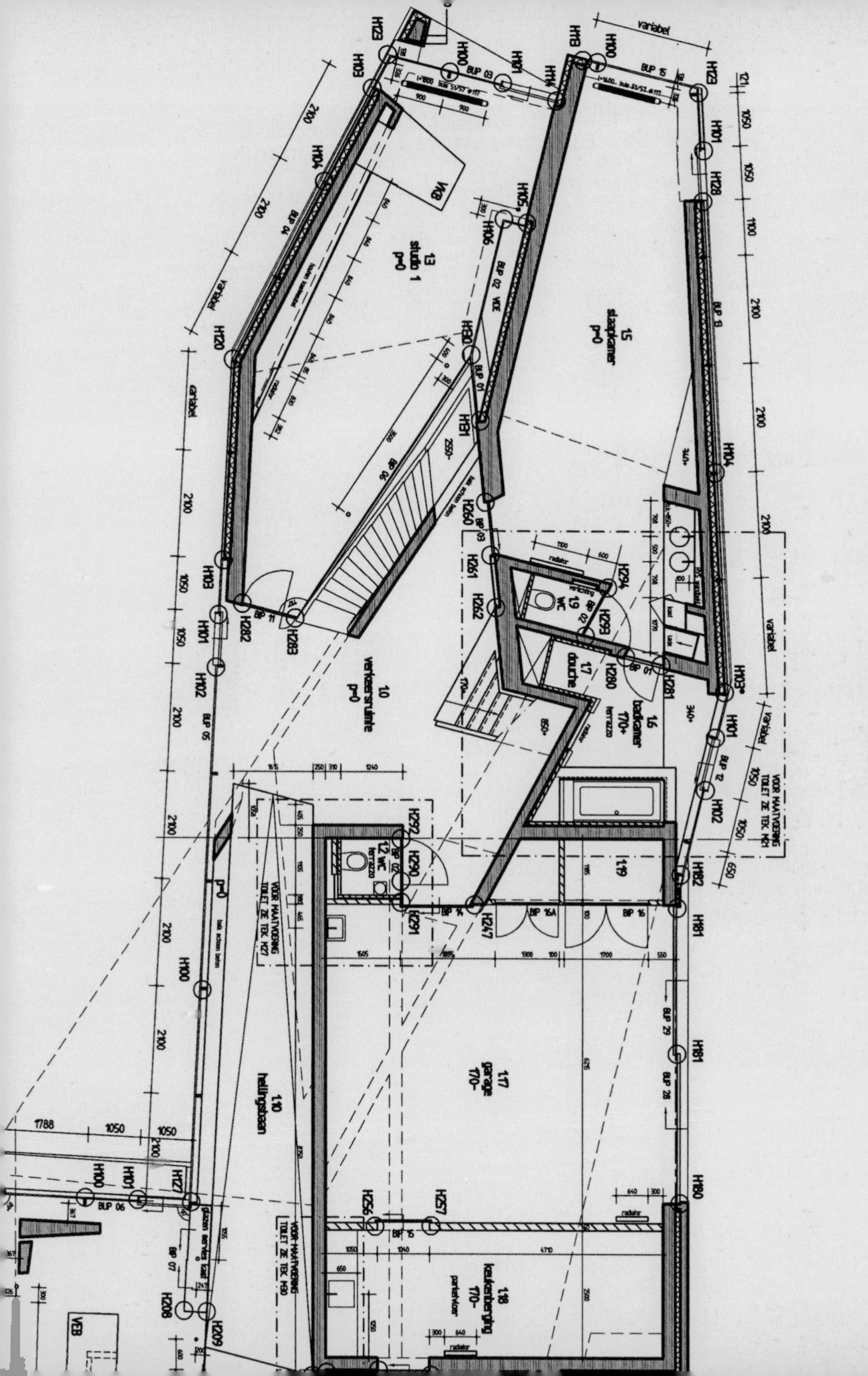

Diagrammatic practices relate to time and duration in two ways; diagrammatic time is understood as a structure informing the design and as an internal measurement punctuating the design process. In the first sense, the diagram maps solidified time in the form of movement traces. In this project, the diagram presents itself as a trajectory, which is the sediment of the simultaneous duration of movement and time, being run within a rigid structural situation. In the second sense, the timing of the introduction of the diagram within the evolution of the project itself is traced.

Multi-family lifestyle: **individuated apartment building**

The project for a three-storey housing block at the end of the former industrial island of Sporenburg uses diagonal movement as the element that structures its spatial configuration. The block is one of densely built up arrangement of almost identical housing blocks. They all use the same prescribed constructional outlines and materials. Inside the block, the expected movements of future inhabitants have been mapped with the aim of creating a secondary structure to establish differentiation within the rigid sameness. The movement is three-fold: movement from outside to inside, movement inside the six indi-

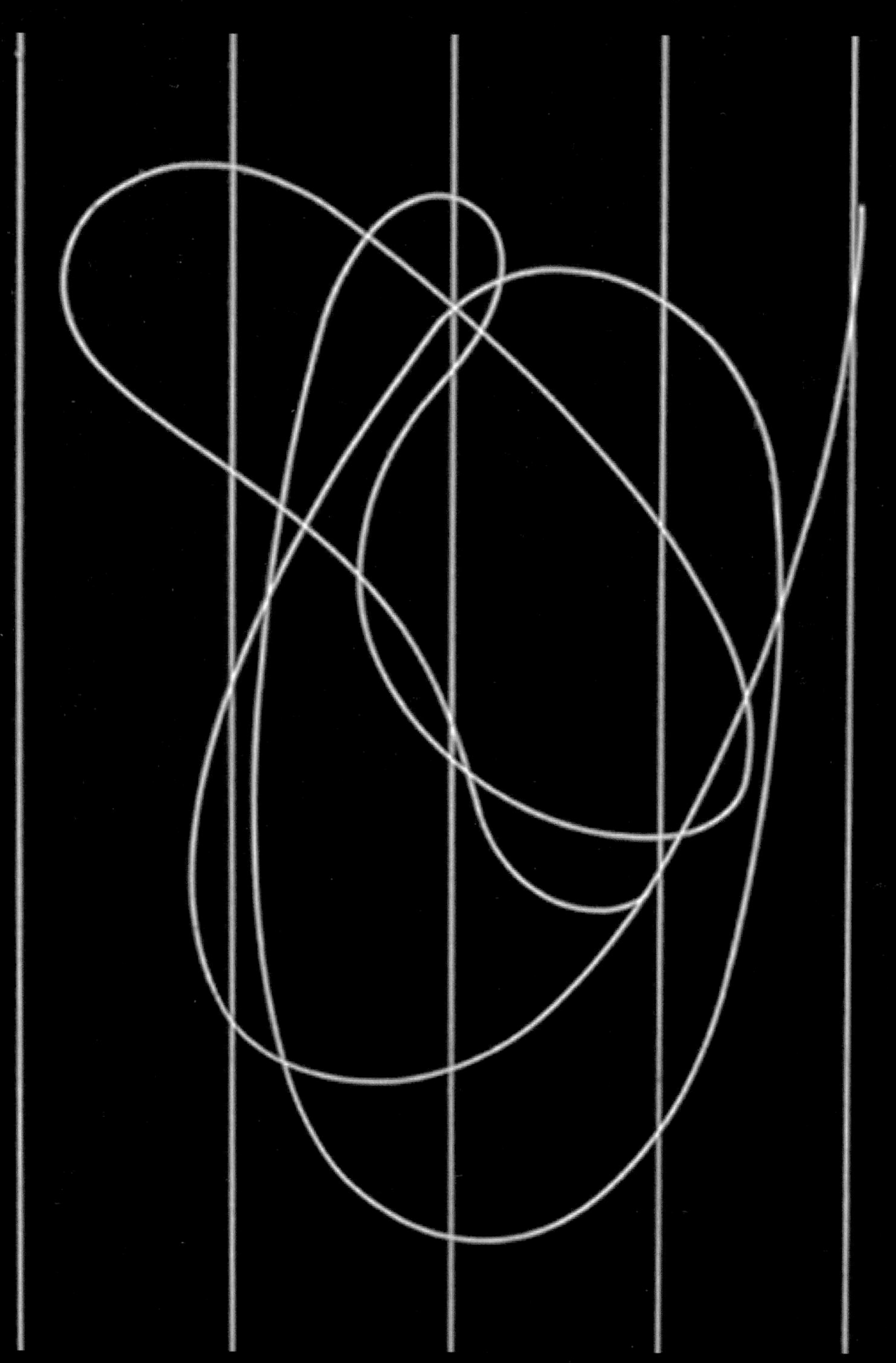

vidual apartments and movement from layer to layer. After the initial design phase, in which sketch models were used to test out different spatial configurations prior to the final design, the effect of movement was summed up in a diagram of free, circulating, walking patterns within a striated system. This diagram was projected on the structure of the block to instrumentalise the organisational typology.

The inhabitants burrow their way through the oblong block like moles. Each apartment is situated on three floors. Thus, all apartments are juxtaposed diagonally and relate to each other in various ways. Being situated in different sections of three floors, each apartment also possesses several orientations within the block, which has practical advantages regarding daylight and views out.

Simply placing two of the six sectional walls of the block at a tangent actualises this diagonal arrangement.

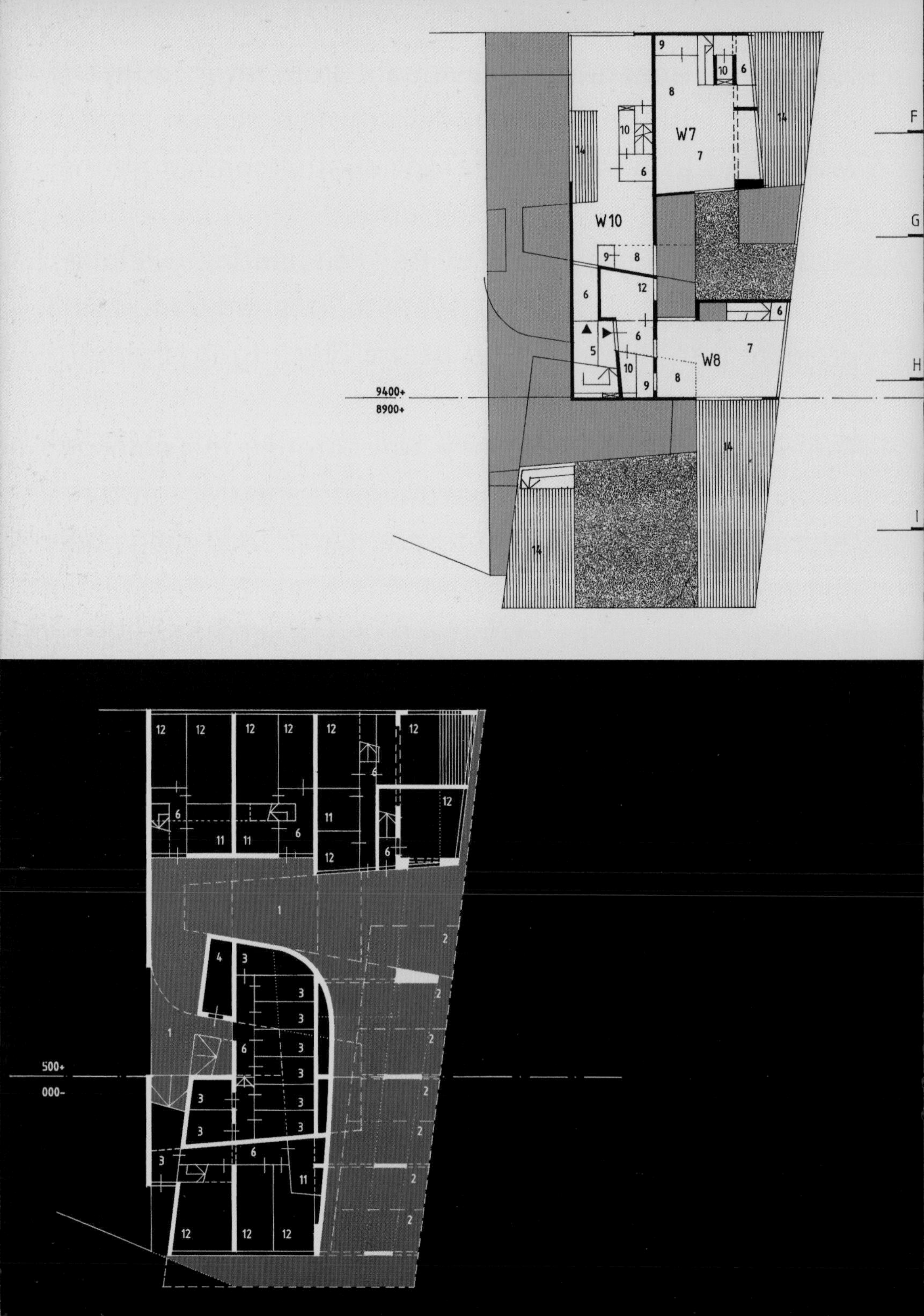

W7
W8
W10
F
G
H
I
9400+
8900+
500+
000-

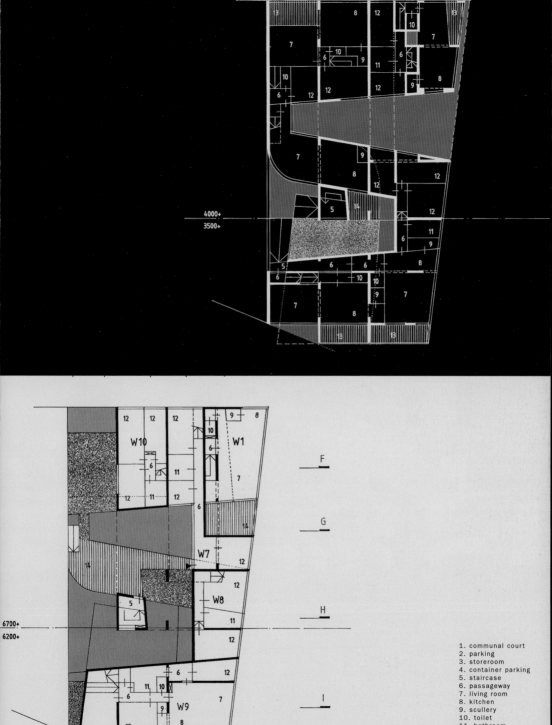

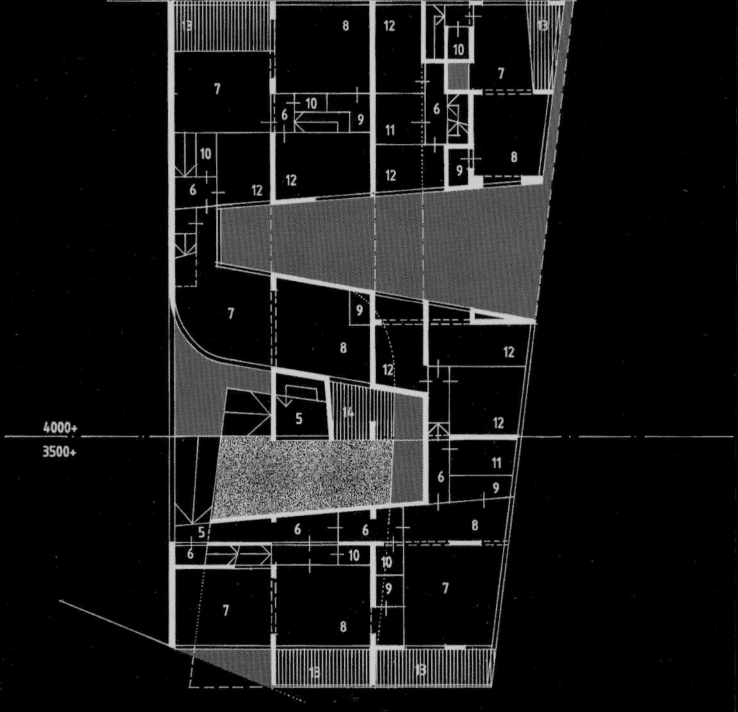

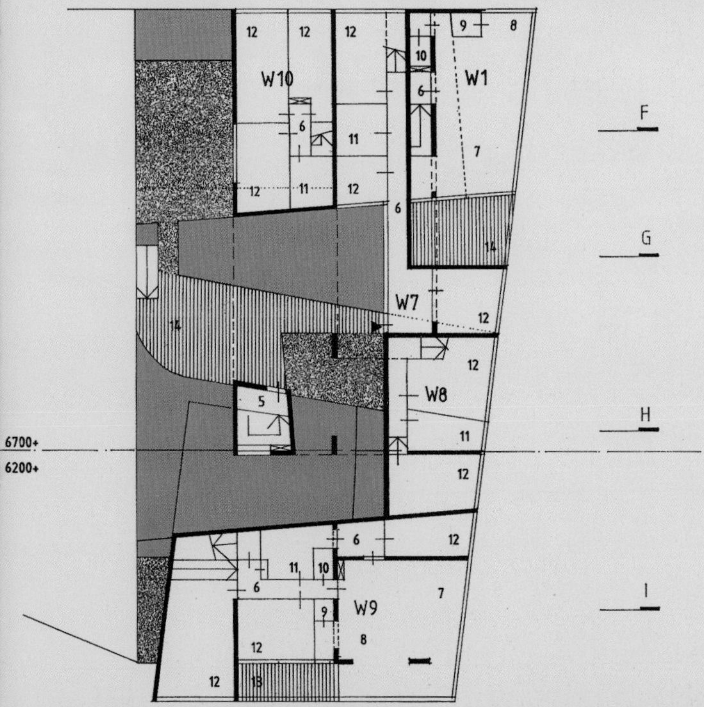

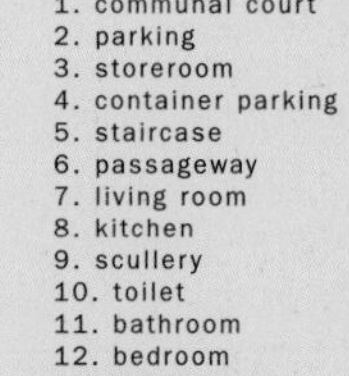
1. communal court
2. parking
3. storeroom
4. container parking
5. staircase
6. passageway
7. living room
8. kitchen
9. scullery
10. toilet
11. bathroom
12. bedroom
13. balcony
14. terrace

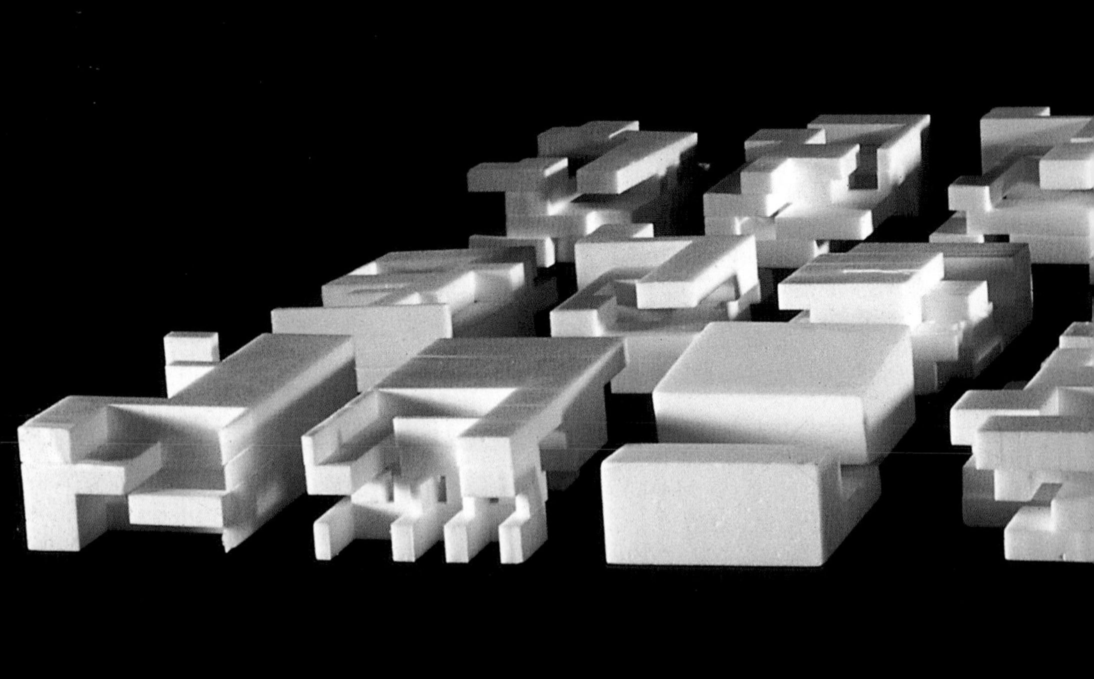

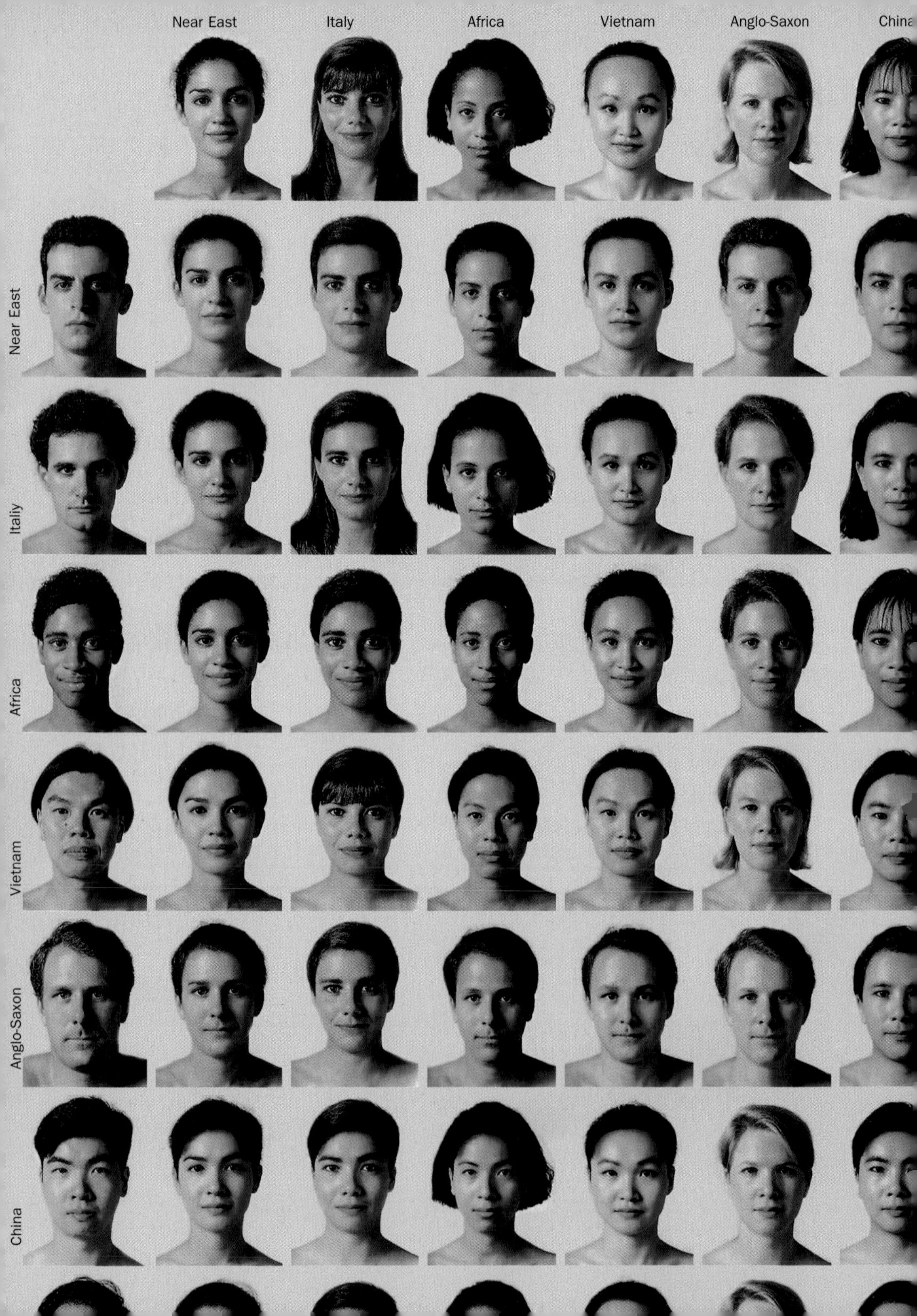

Near East
Italy
Africa
Vietnam
Anglo-Saxon
China
Near East
Italiy
Africa
Vietnam
Anglo-Saxon
China

Hybridization

Architectural constructions that were pure fantasy a few years ago can now be built thanks to new design and construction techniques. Fluorescent, fluid structures that began life by weightlessly warping on computer screens are beginning to make the transition into a haptic, gravitational existence. Apart from their shiny artifice and wavy contours, these technological fantasies are also characterised by a sense of alienation. This specific type of alienation bears little relation to the anxiety and persecution accompanying early twentieth century urban disentitlement, but pertains to a denationalised, genetically manipulated state of dis-authenticity. An intense fusion of construction, materials, circulation and programme spaces creates uncertainty as to the exact properties of the components from which these structures are assembled; they are hybrids which don't know their history. Architectural works like that result from a holistic merger of disparate elements, bringing about vagueness with respect to the scale and proportion of structures. The amalgamation generates a new notion of identity. The different features of the work are blurred and exist in layers which do not necessarily relate to each other or to the scale and structure of the shapes and substances from which they originate. Hybrid structures have no authentic, recognisable scale, their organisation is geared towards allowing function-related expansion and shrinkage and this results in overlaps and non-determinate spaces that flow into each other. The two icons for the hybrid building are the Manimal and Frederick Kiesler. The Manimal is a computer-generated image of the hybridization of a lion, a snake and a human. The Manimal does not divulge any concrete information about its complex parentage. All traces of the previous identities have been seamlessly absorbed within the portrait; they exist simultaneously and integrally within one, cohesive organisation. While the Manimal projects its own strong identity, it is one of questions and indeterminacy, not of direct reference. The technique that generates the image is as interesting as its effect and more interesting than the imagination that has engendered it. As an effect, the image makes you wonder how something like this would translate spatially. As a technique, it excites because it has been produced in a manner radically different from all pictorial techniques that have been previously employed by artists. The three main aspects that make the hybridizing technique of the Manimal architecturally interesting concern the relation of technique to

author, the relation to time and the relation of component part to whole. The Manimal was produced by one artist, but looks like the product of a group, which in a way it is, since the anonymous software programmers who created Photoshop also have a large hand in the portrait. Architecture too must get used to ambiguous authorship issues, entering a dialogue within design processes that have many, sometimes invisible, participants, yet trying to retain the active position needed for the origination of new works.

The Manimal derives its effect from mutation over accelerated time. It is the product of animation, of which duration forms a central part; the morphed picture is just one still frame in a sequence that could, in principle, run indefinitely. This calls up questions that apply equally to architecture: when to stop, when is it finished? What is the 'right' solution? Capitalism and photography have conspired to make architects more

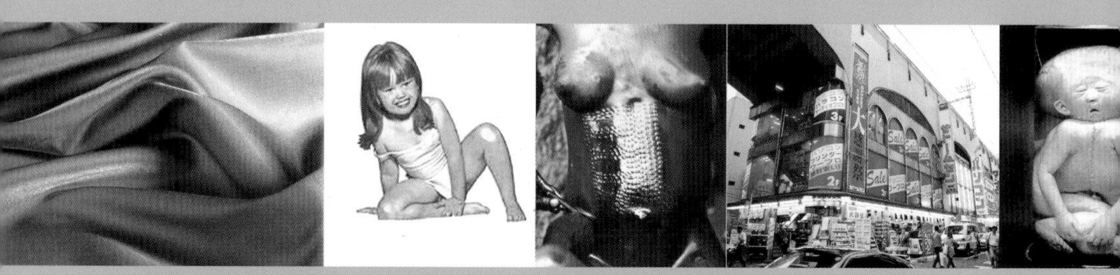

anxious than ever to freeze architecture in time and suppress the reality that 'all buildings are the mothers of ruins', that only change exists.

Thirdly, the fact that the unity of the image is not disrupted by the diversity of its ingredients is what distinguishes this hybridizing technique most from traditional collage. This is the most radical choice for architecture to face. The totalising, decontextualising, dehistoricising combination of discordant systems of information can be instrumentalised architecturally into one gesture. An extreme blurring of architectural properties into cohesive oneness implies an extension of the single surface organisation from a primarily horizontal structure to a three-dimensional organisation encompassing the vertical and the diagonal as well, allowing a totally column-free structure. Enriched by light, sound and movement, a situation emerges in which the unified organisation is permeated with changeable substances.

The convergence of sameness and difference into one coherent structure is already found in the works of

Kiesler, the second icon of hybridization. Kiesler attributes the unified organisation with endlessness. This allows the structure to assume different identities.

Even more strongly than in his projects, Kiesler's capacity for endlessness is conveyed in the series of photographs of him: Kiesler as a Surrealist, as a minotaur, as Willem de Kooning, as a chess player, as Mies van der Rohe, are just some of his incarnations. The message that can be read in those photographs is: imagine, invent, expand and pretend. With this variety of poses, the contemporary reading of Kiesler is that multiplicity can constitute a cohesive identity. The whole Kiesler is found in this wide-ranging series of Kieslers. Kiesler-as-Kiesler is a manifold - generating, proliferating and projecting an infinite measure of possible identities.

The two icons of hybridization, Kiesler and the Manimal, demonstrate the proliferating forces of disauthentication and non-determination within a unified organisation. The architecture of hybridization, the fluent merging of constituent parts into an endlessly variable whole, amounts to the organisation of continuous difference, resulting in structures that are scale-less, subject to evolution, expansion, inversion and other contortions and manipulations. Free to assume different identities, architecture becomes endless.

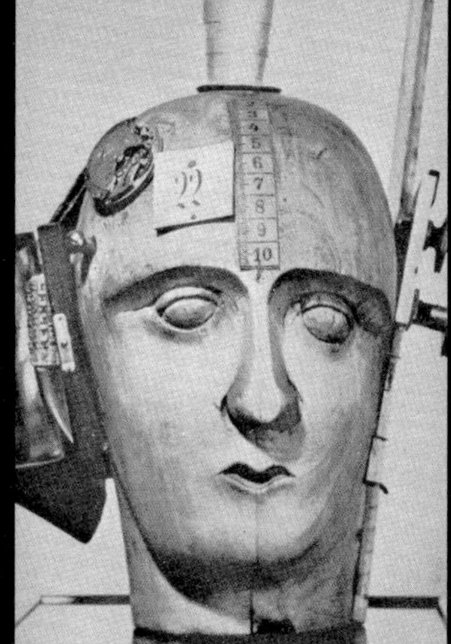
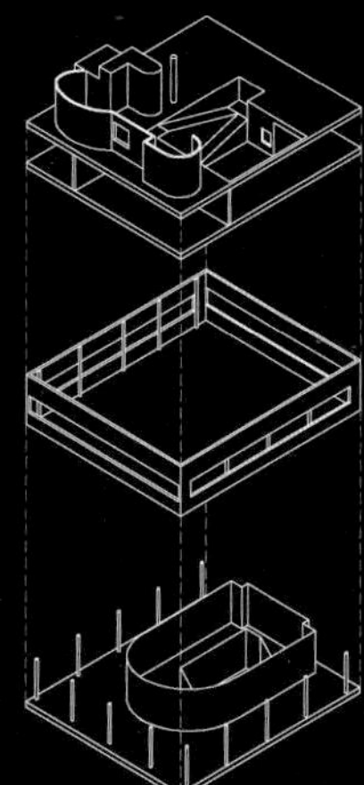

fragmented organisation of disconnected parts

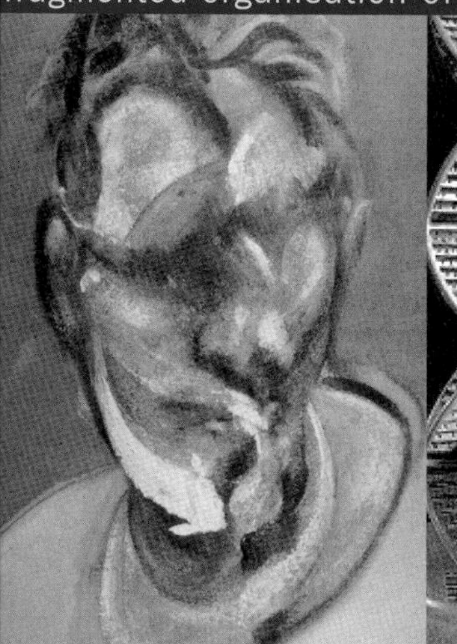

displaced organisation of connected parts

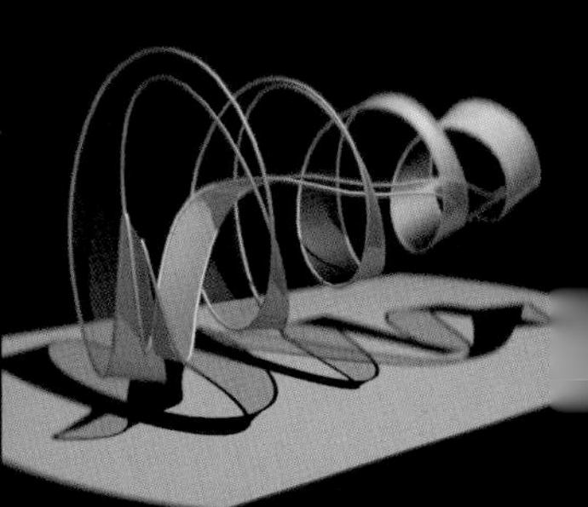

seamless organisation of disconnected parts

This design-by-section represents one of our first, incomplete, experiments with 4-D architecture. The building itself was never designed, but 30 sections were worked out, after which 3-D Studio was used to fill in what was left. The point of the project was not to make the small and large components, which constitute the puzzle pieces, watertight and sound-proof. It was to organise the whole. For this is not a building design - it is a design of the relations between structure, circulation systems, programmatic spaces and surfaces.

Exploration of diving, swooping, zooming, slicing, folding space

The organising principle of the terminal is the structural association of architecture to infrastructure and landscape; garden-like voids are absorbed into the architecture and then proceed to transform it. The three thematic voids - microscope garden, telescope garden and kaleidoscope garden - are suspended in a mesh of circulation and construction principles. Analogous to the way in which the urban plan of Yokohama with its grid structure is interrupted by the space bubbles of parks and gardens, this project merges the codes of architectural structure and fluidity.

横浜新港倉庫
港湾合同庁舎
水上警察署
産業貿易センター

The public events, voids and gardens of the building are organised as a long, meandering walk in which the horizon opens up and shrivels; enclosed spaces alternate with wide open areas. The various circulation systems of the terminal wind their different paths through the structure. This free arrangement is made possible by the solidity of the structural cross, the main structuring element, punctured and encircled in various ways by the different infrastructure routes and their satellite programmes.

This interweaving of various structuring principles - the gardens, infrastructure and construction - makes up the organisation of the project. Finally a photoshopped skin was wrapped around the resulting composition in order to simulate the appearance of a building.

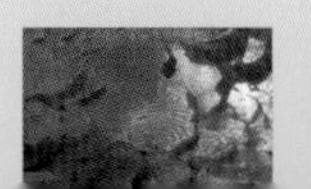      

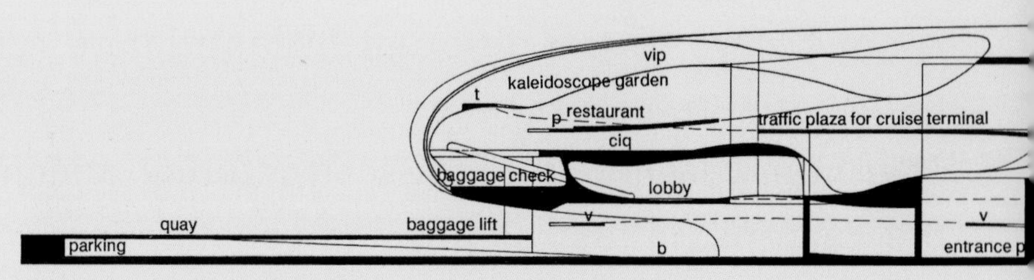
vip
kaleidoscope garden
t
p
restaurant
traffic plaza for cruise terminal
ciq
baggage check
lobby
quay
baggage lift
v
v
parking
b
entrance p

kaleidoscope garc

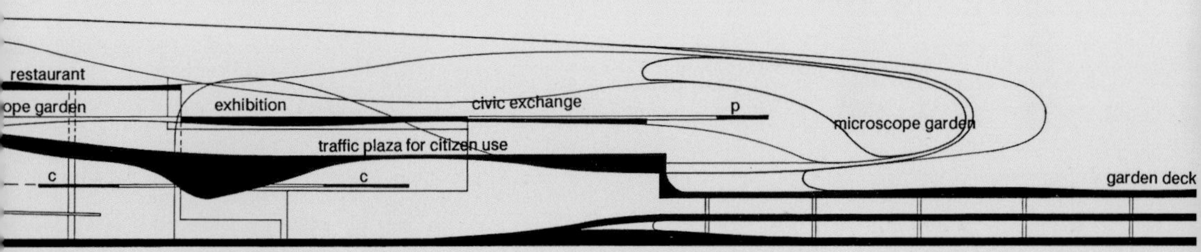
restaurant
ope garden
exhibition
civic exchange
p
microscope garden
traffic plaza for citizen use
c
c
garden deck

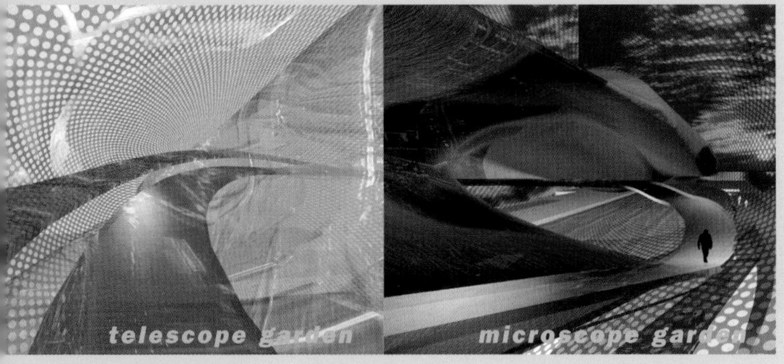
telescope garden
microscope garden

Infrastructure
combinatior

gardens
cladded

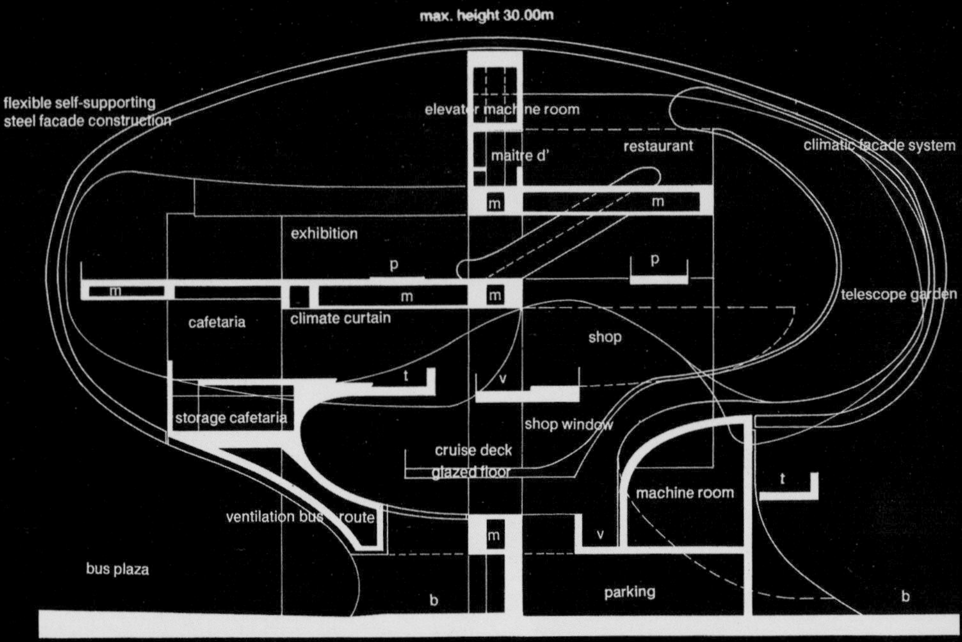

max. height 30.00m
flexible self-supporting
steel facade construction
elevator machine room
maitre d'
restaurant
climatic facade system
m
m
exhibition
p
p
m
m
m
telescope garden
cafetaria
climate curtain
shop
t
v
storage cafetaria
shop window
cruise deck
glazed floor
machine room
t
ventilation bus route
m
v
bus plaza
b
parking
b

9
12
15
18
20
23
25
restaurant
kaleidoscope garden
31
microscope garden
e
e
e
m
e
cafetaria
administration
restaurant
vip
telescope garden

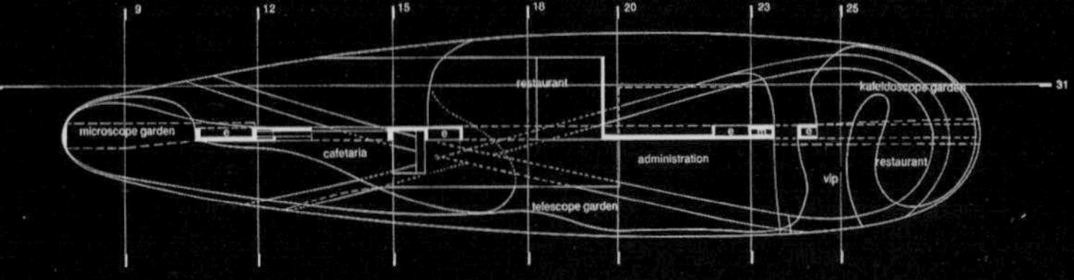

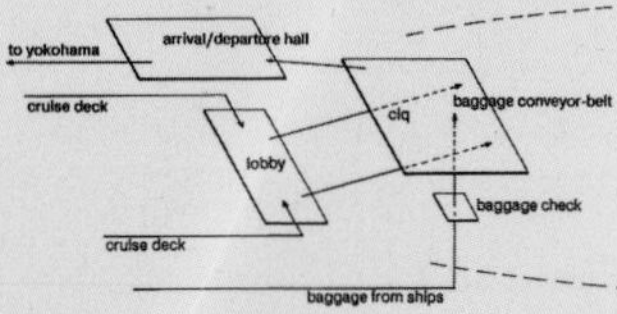

to yokohama
arrival/departure hall
cruise deck
lobby
ciq
baggage conveyor-belt
baggage check
cruise deck
baggage from ships

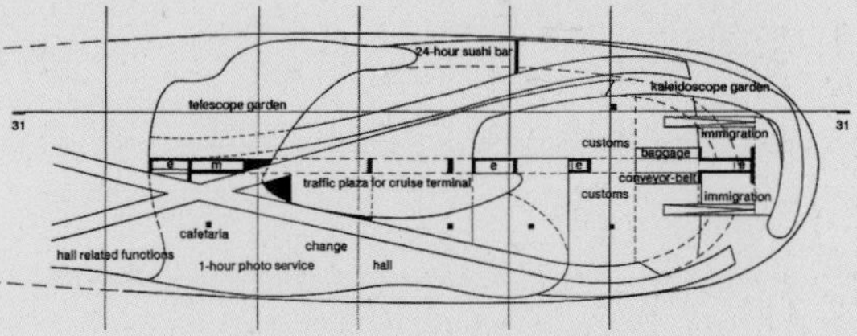

24-hour sushi bar
kaleidoscope garden
telescope garden
31
31
immigration
customs
baggage
conveyor-belt
customs
immigration
traffic plaza for cruise terminal
cafetaria
change
hall related functions
1-hour photo service
hall

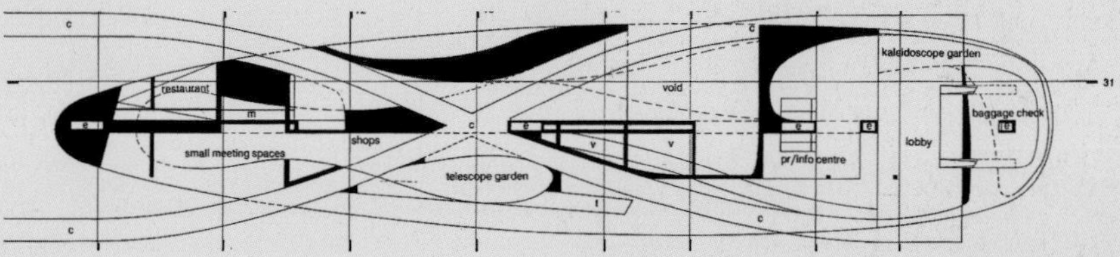

kaleidoscope garden
restaurant
void
31
baggage check
shops
lobby
small meeting spaces
pr/info centre
telescope garden

storage
machine room
service zone
machine room
bus stop seabus
void
void
24-hour gambling hall

bus plaza
entrance plaza to hall
toll-exit
entrance hall
machine room
parking 61 cars
storage
bus stop seabus
to seabus
parking 144 cars
machine room

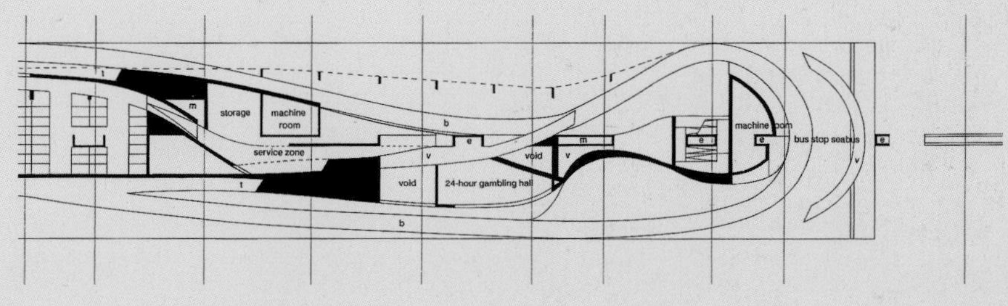

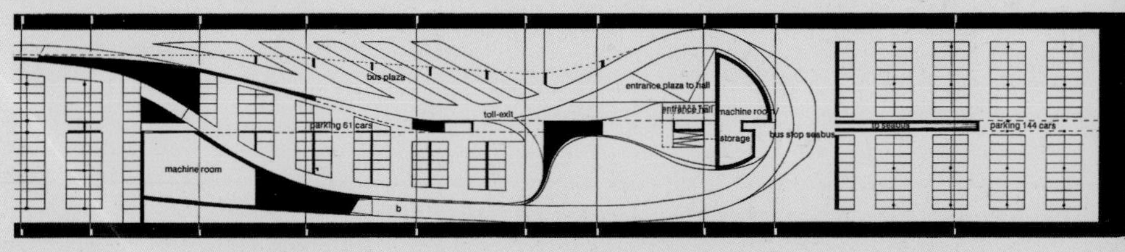

visiting Yokohama's newest event:
osanbashi pier

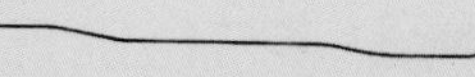

bus route to seabus

embarking a cruiseship

cruising on a sunday afternoon

This is one of our first experiments with infrastructuralism. Floors, walls and ceiling become one continuous element that forms the construction, spatial arrangement and circulation.

Concert Hall Dusseldorf 1995

***Columnlessness:** circulation turns into programme space and construction*

The study involves extending and refurbishing a Victorian Concert Hall with its intricate and, for our time, unusual organisation. The rigid structure and complex internal circulation system of the 19th century building segregate its different users: artists, male and female members of the public all have individual entrances and circulation systems within the building.

This organisational system is taken up and transformed in the proposed new design for the Concert Hall. The existing structure is analysed, laid bare and subsequently liberated. The interior spaces have been rationalised, while the circulation routes have been externalised and draped around the structure like an ascending ledge. The integration of circulation, construction and distribution of the programme has resulted in a column-free internal space.

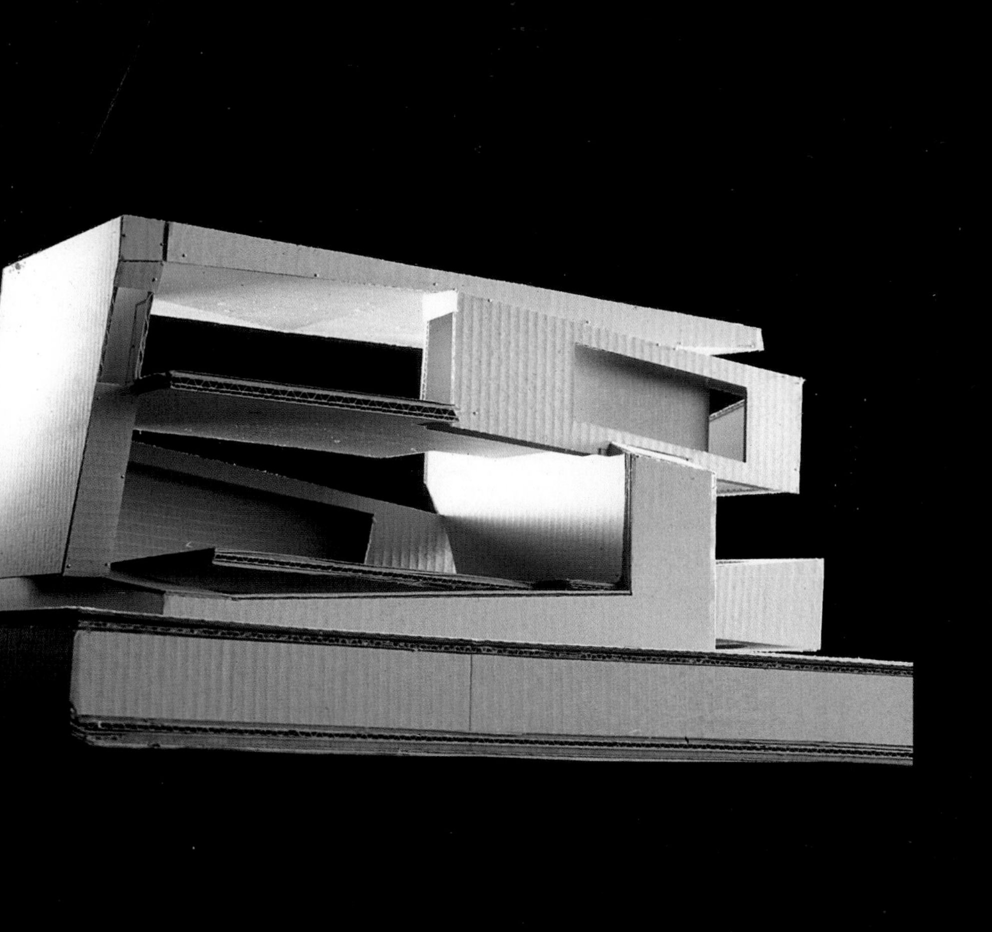

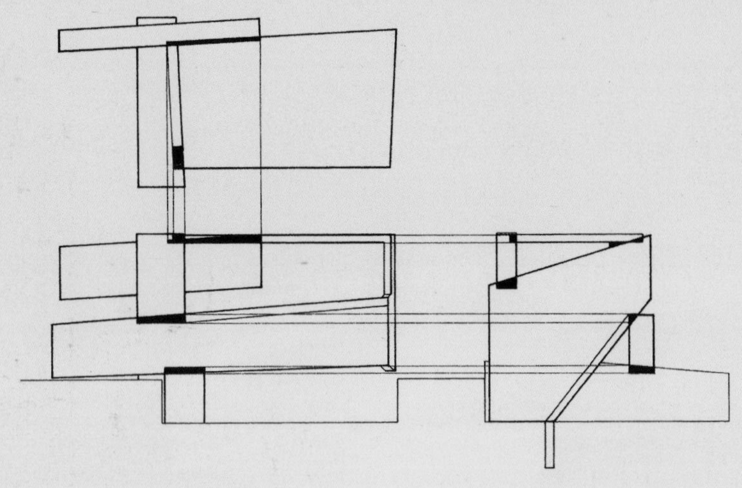

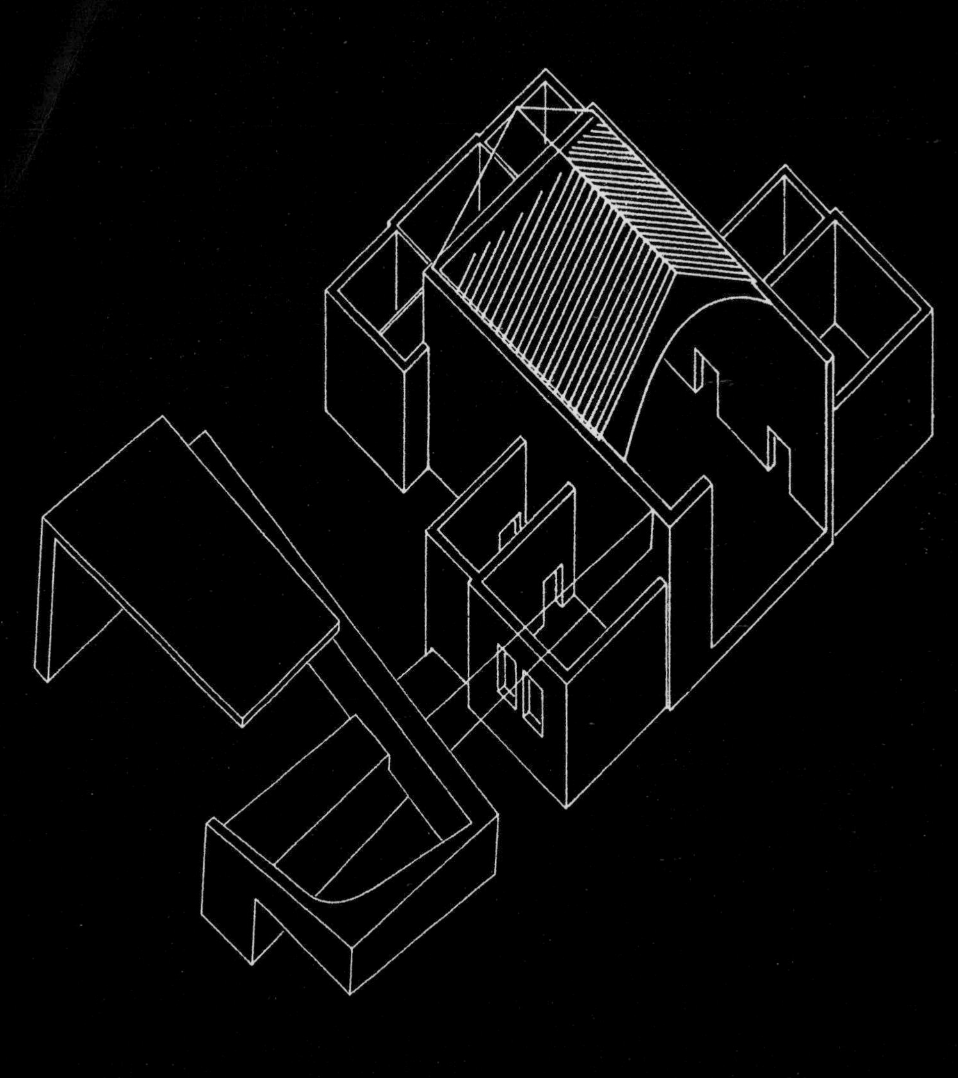

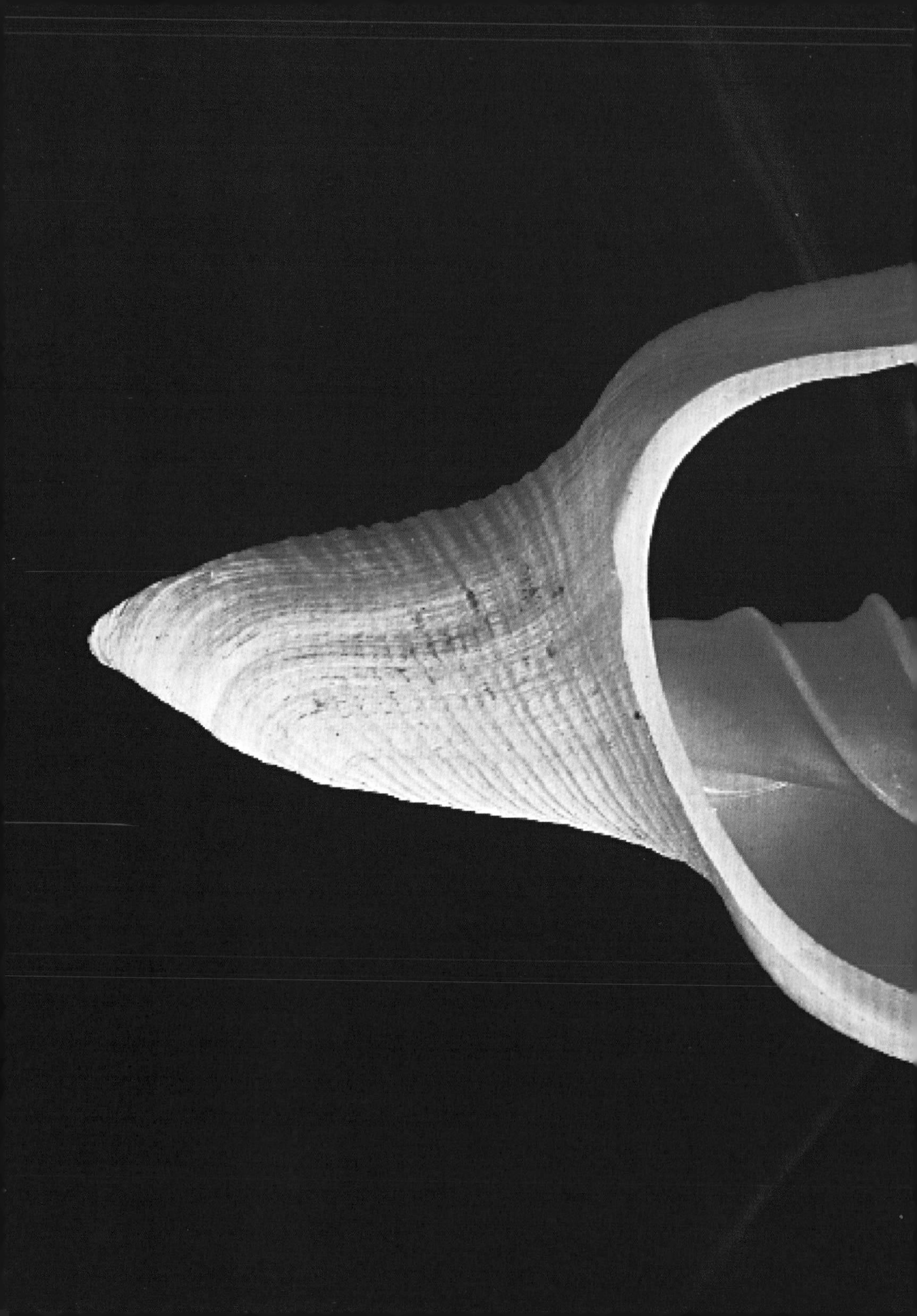

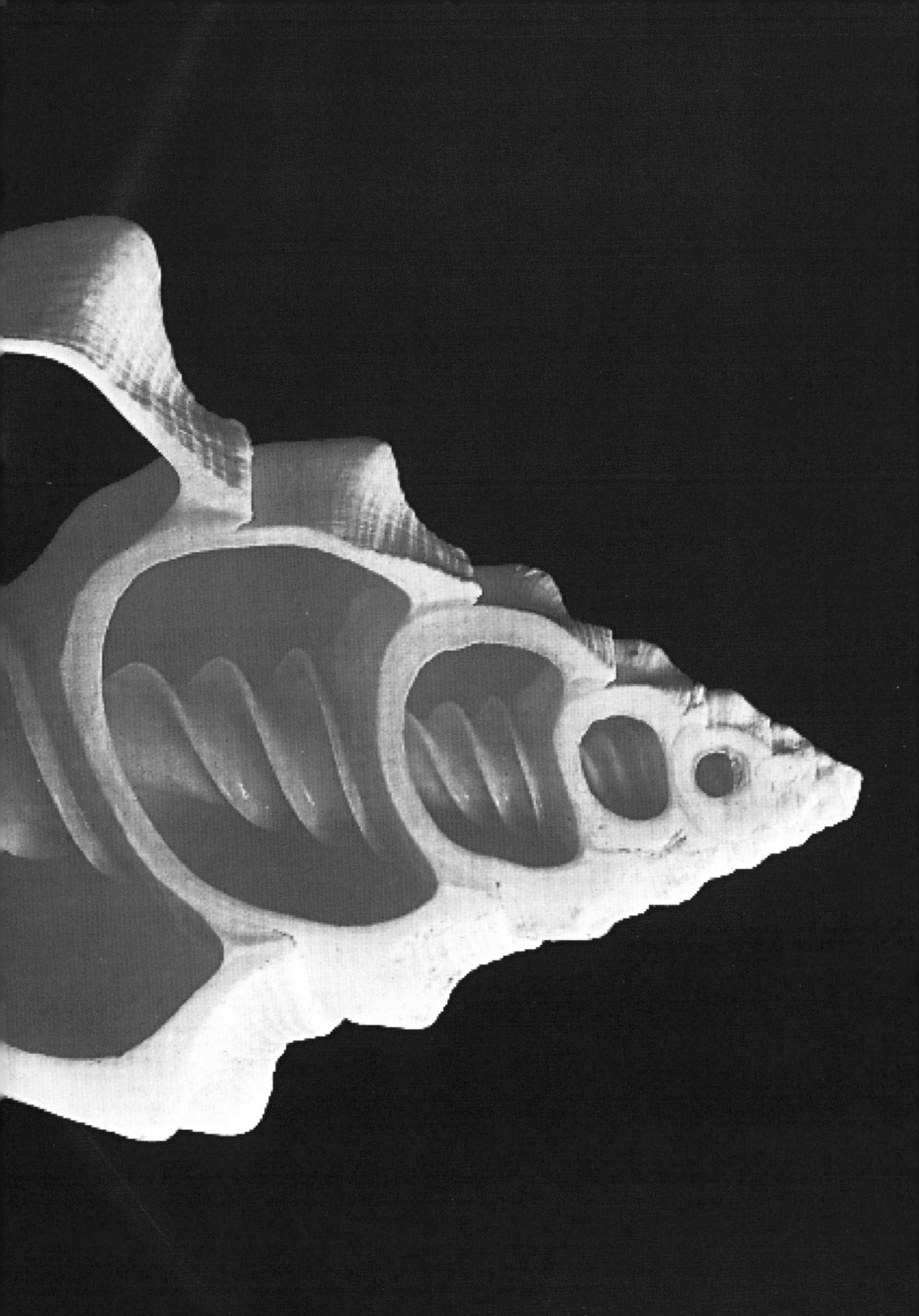

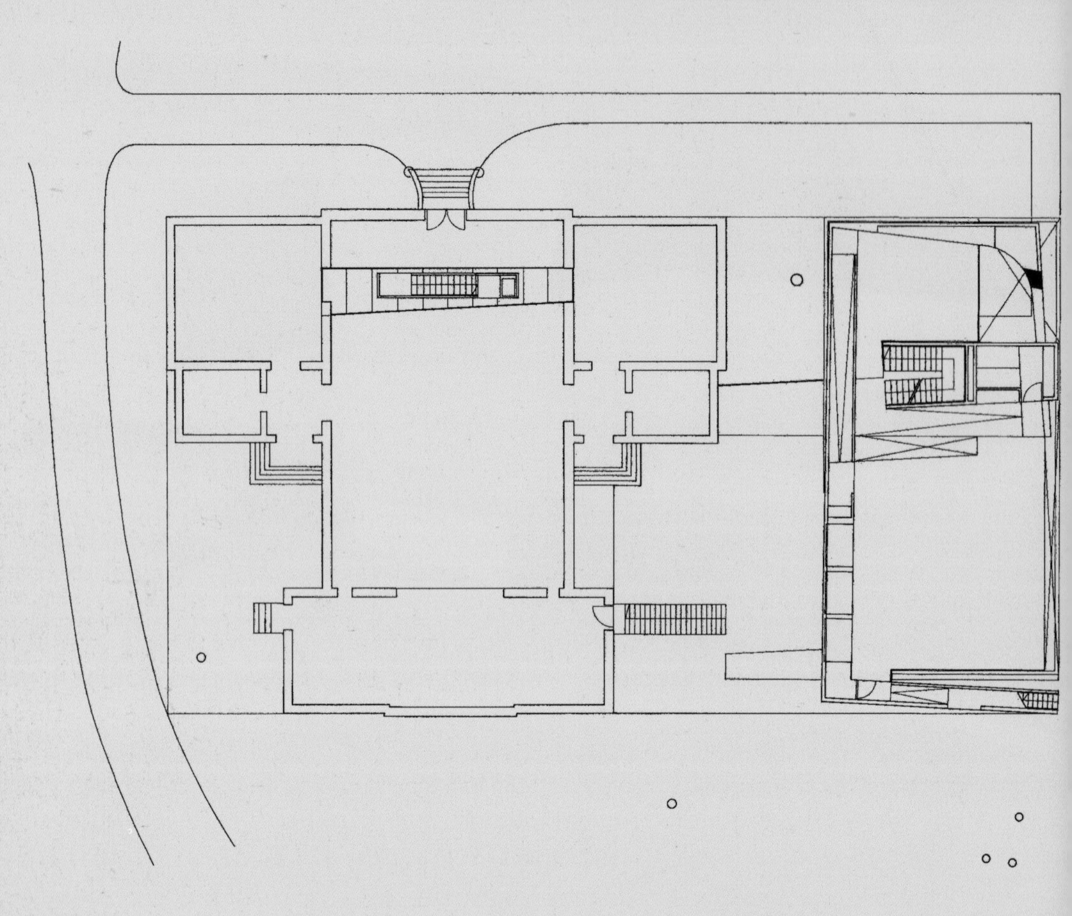

In the artificial world of the computer rendering unwavering light shaves as sharp as a razor over planes so smooth that not a single molecule is out of line. Slowly, the planes curl over and contort. Next, the computer-generated fantasy is being transformed into reality. The rendering becomes real; it is being reproduced in the constructed realm. Now that techniques have been found to enable the imagination to project these images on a computer screen they can also be built.

Virtual-actual: *fusing time, event, construction, circulation and display into one surface*

The Dutch pavilion for the 19th Milan Triennial was intended as a virtual pavilion, a new-media presentation to make the spectator directly experience the impact of computer technology on architecture and the building industry. Research both with computational techniques and with traditional models led to the integrating shape of the pavilion, in which the structure forms both the carrier and the content of the exhibition. Construction, circulation and contents have been integrated to create a virtual walk through the pavilion. The plywood structure incorporates an analogous and a virtual space; the disembodying effect of the computer is manifested as outside

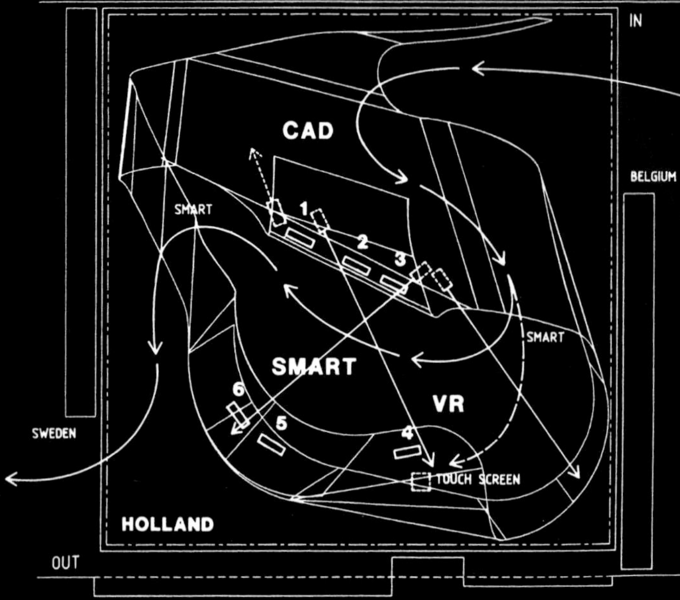

IN

CAD

BELGIUM

SMART

1

2

3

SMART

SMART

VR

6

5

4

SWEDEN

TOUCH SCREEN

HOLLAND

OUT

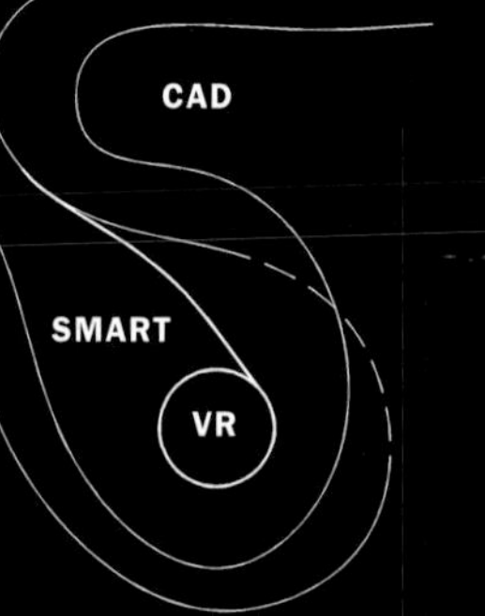

and inside become one. Projections dissolve the solidity of the plywood walls and organise the circulation for the spectator. The surface of the confined room, measuring nine by nine metres, is expanded as the amorphous, shell-like structure winds around the space.

The logistic effects of computer technology are reflected in the actual construction of the pavilion. The plywood construction was cut out with the aid of a computer-controlled mill. The elements were subsequently transported to Milan and assembled at the exhibition site.

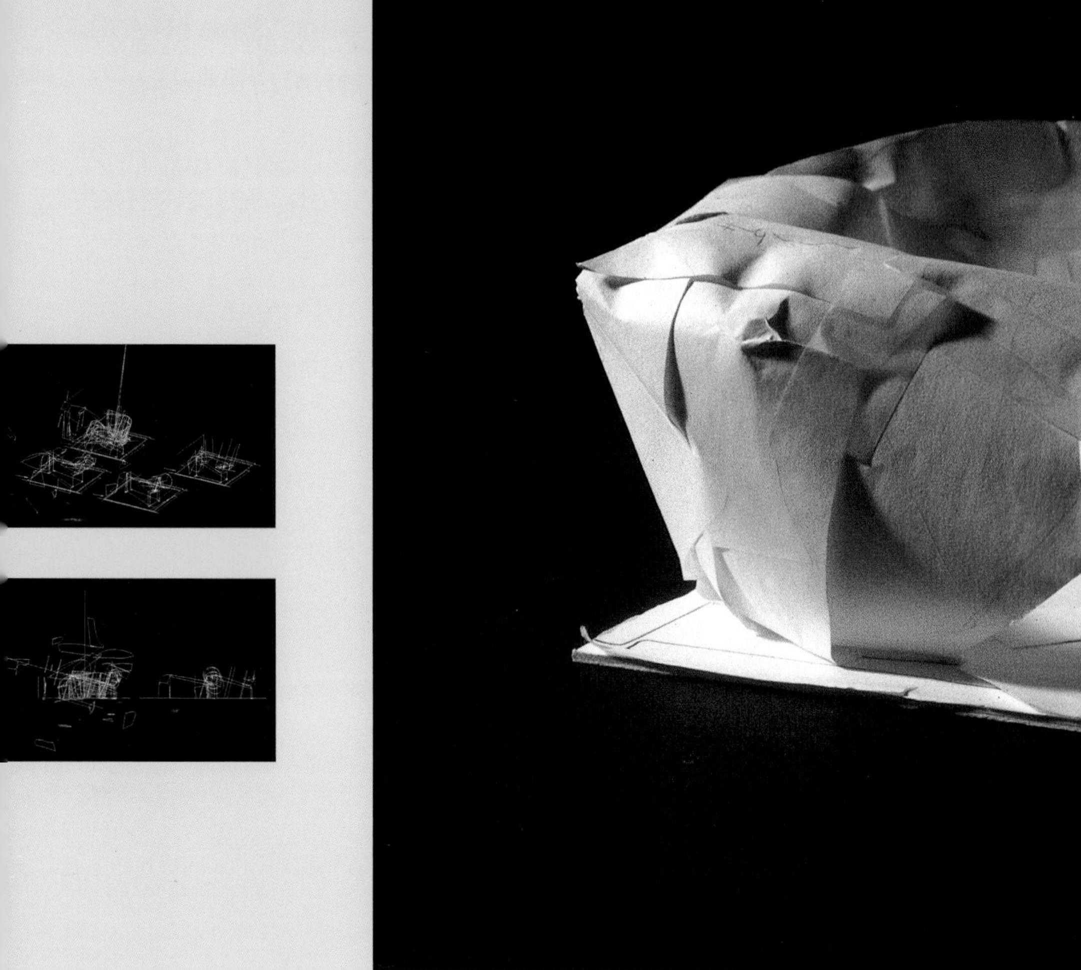

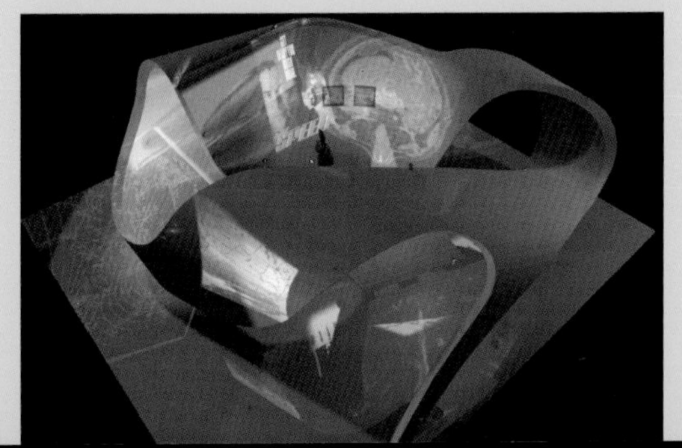

SPEED

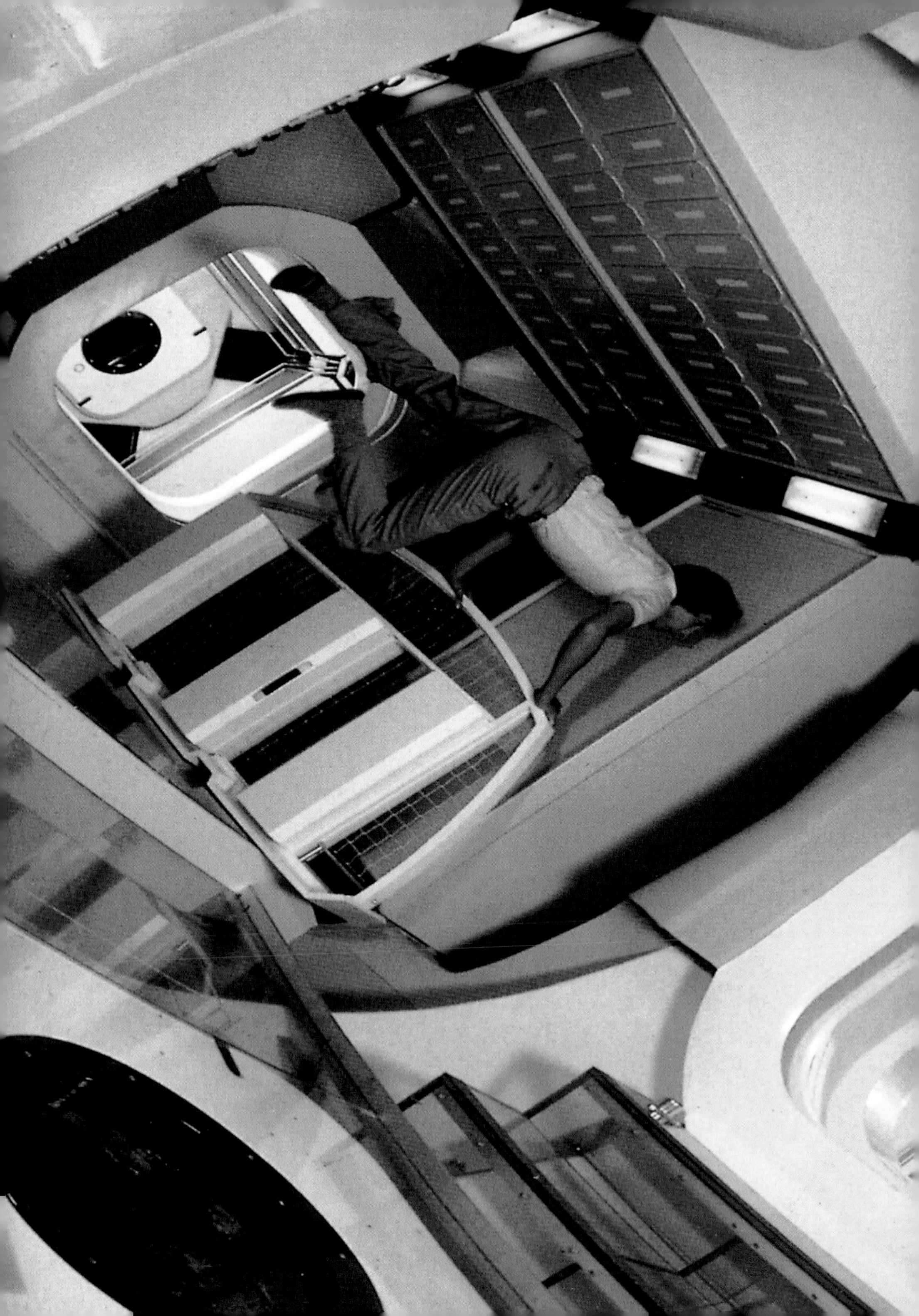

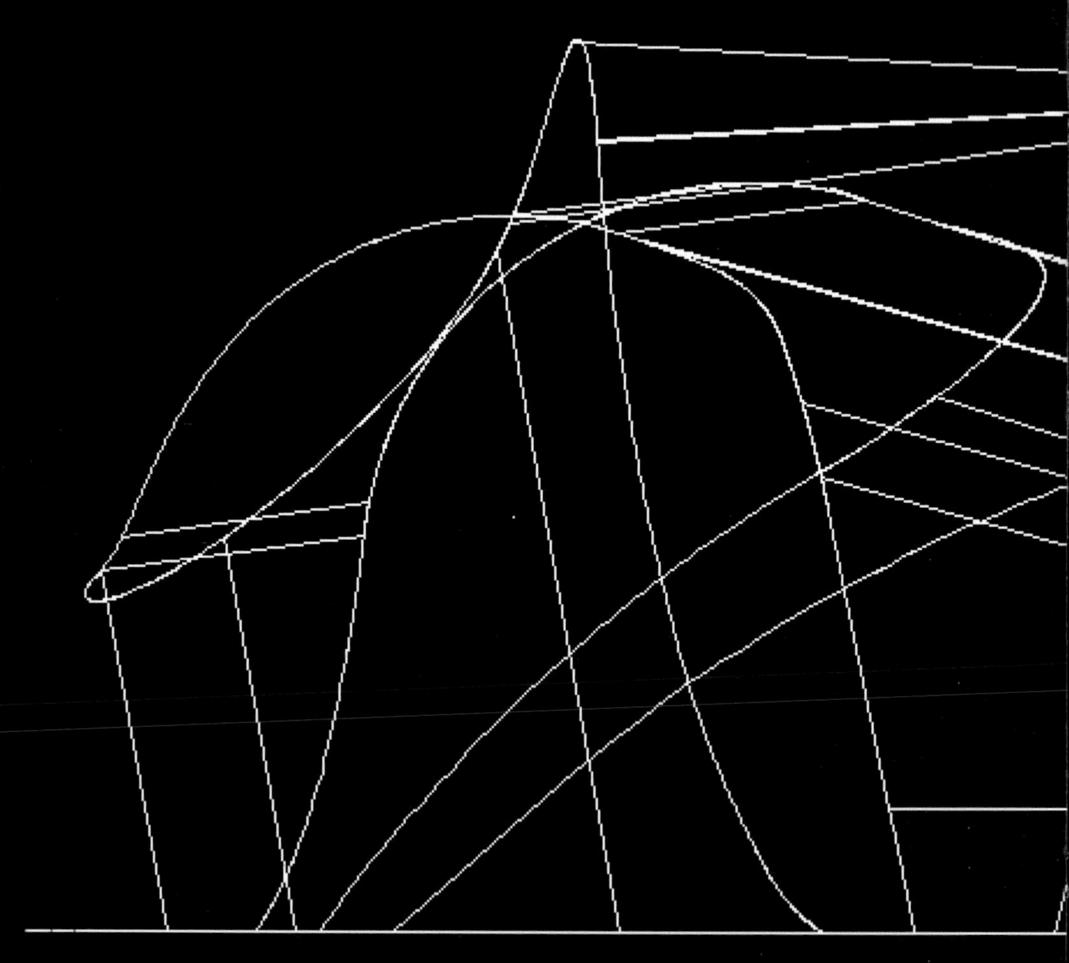

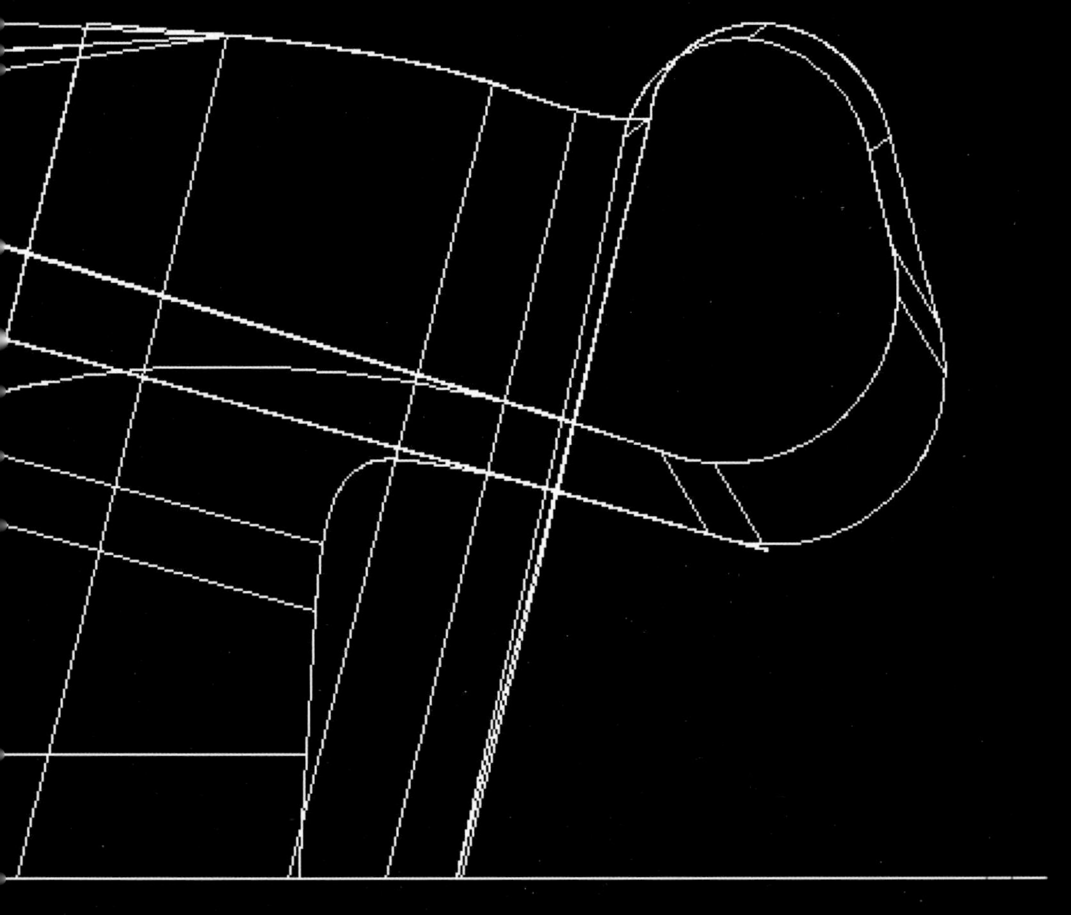

It is a dream house because two people intended to live their perfect lives there, after having made their fortunes and found each other. All houses are to some extent portraits of their occupants. At the same time, the private house is still a laboratory for architecture, in which new ideas can be tested out relatively quickly and inexpensively. The dream house shows an ideal client caught in an experiment: pragmatism is being bred to utopia in the hope that a painless merger between the two can be brought about.

Towards a new endlessness

The house consists of a series of interconnected platforms suspended from a wide and hollow core. Domestic activities are loosely grouped in areas devoted to sleeping, cooking, parking, playing and sitting around. These large programme groups are divided over two-and-a-half undulating layers, consolidated in a compact volume. This arrangement makes it possible to use the rooms flexibly. The majority of spaces are non-determinate in character. The yielding horizontal planes have large cut-outs at their centres, as the core of the house is an oval void. The concave interior walls around this void form the central support structure, resulting

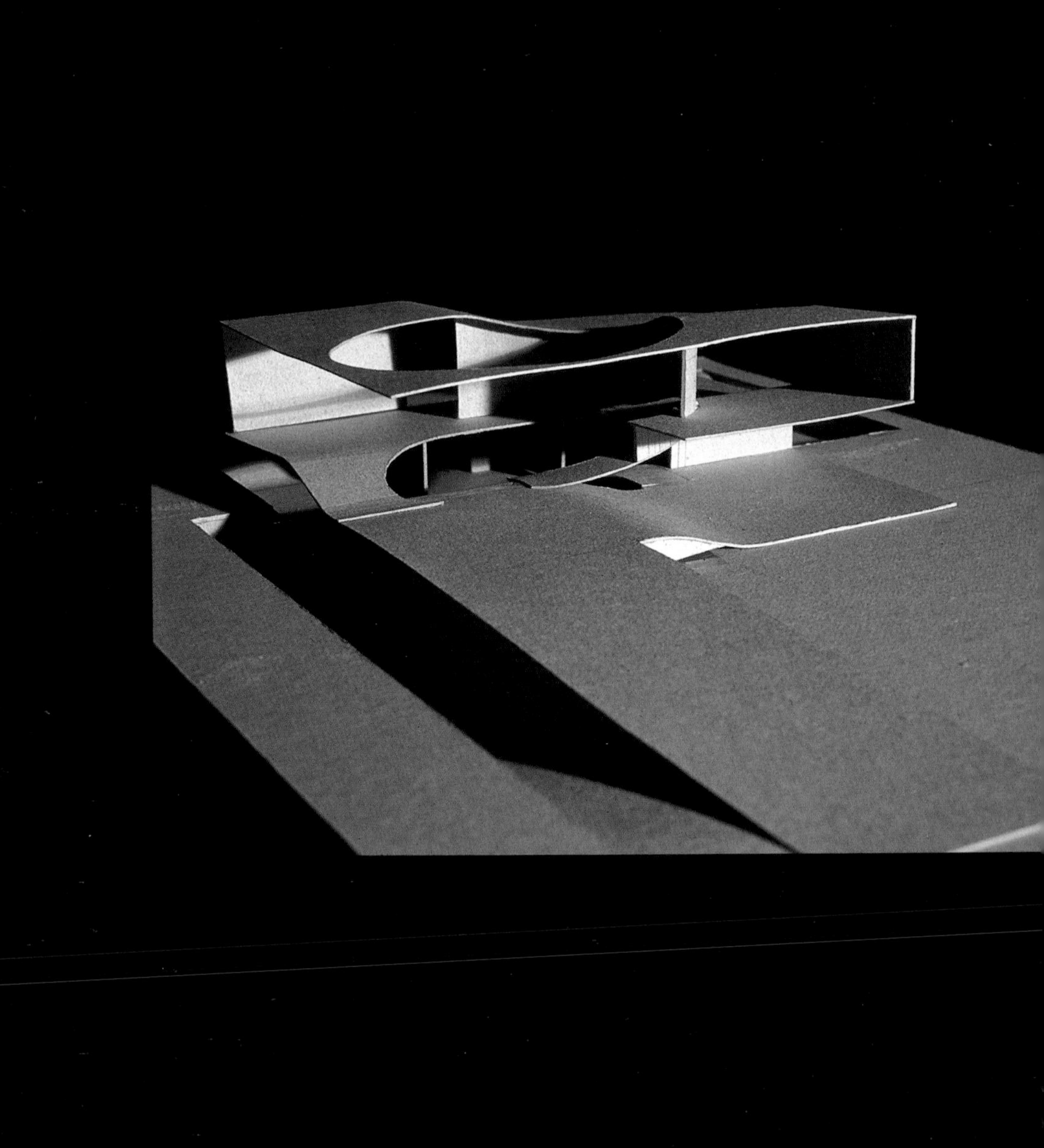

in a mushroom-like principle.
The interior spaces are gathered around the void, letting daylight penetrate deep into the house. With their orthogonal external borders, these rooms appear boxy in plan, but are diagonally connected to each other and to the outside by ramps and short flights of stairs, resulting in fluent transitions between the rooms.
This house was not built - but the organisation of rooms flowing in and out of each other on several levels, centrally connected by a framed void, has recurred in our dreams.

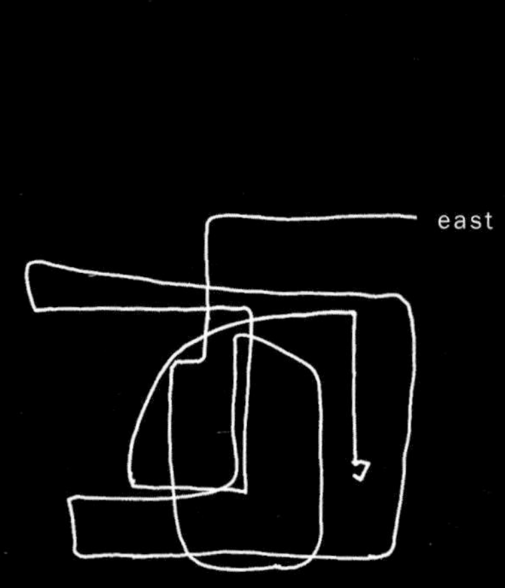
east

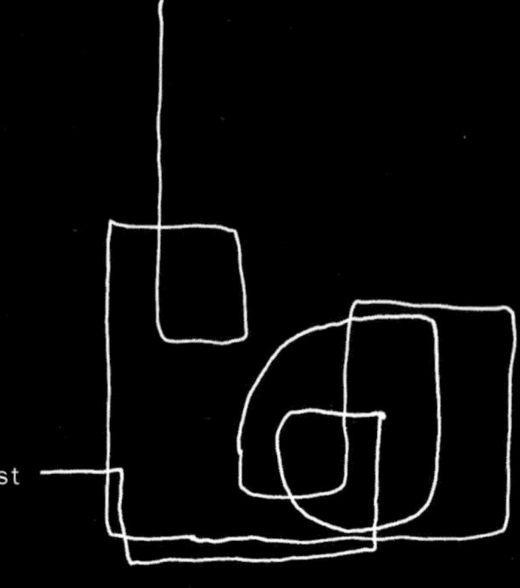
west

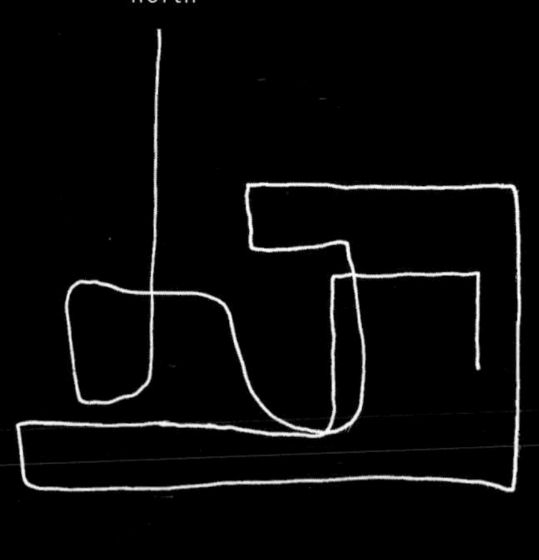
north

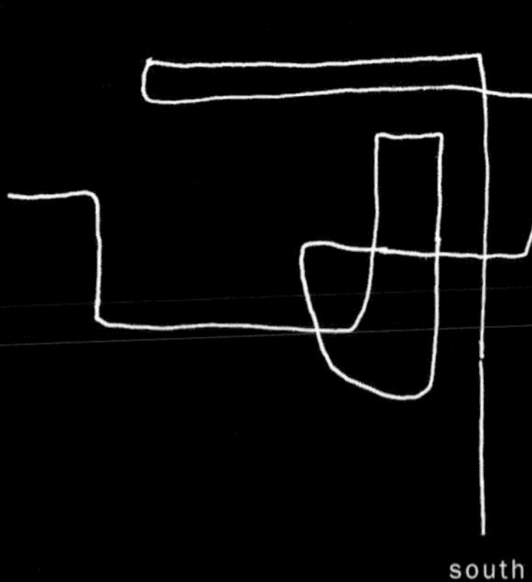
south

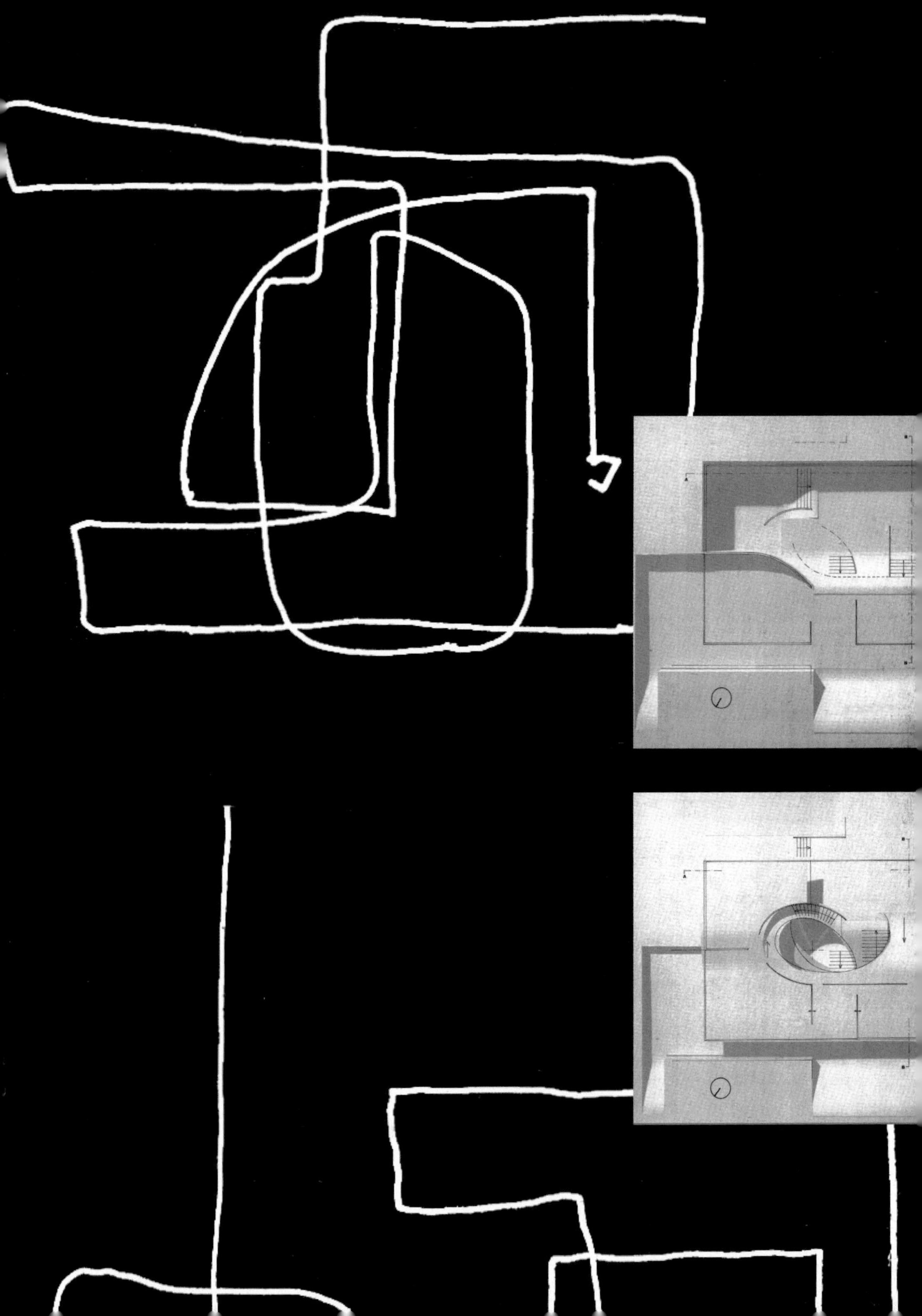

Regardless of the result, the effort involved in taking part in open competitions is not wasted. Late-night, pizza-fuelled quests for the perfect project form the pumping heart of the studio. Competitions supply the spark for real innovation: instances of specific interpretation, utilisation, perception, construction and so on, unfold and proliferate, leading to applications on various levels of abstraction. Like musicians following a jam session, the bleary-eyed collective of design assistants and trainees disbands afterwards, but components from competition entries turn up, enlivening other projects for years to come.

Pyramidal organisation: *shafts extrude from the ground plane to become hybrid structure*

The structure of the museum confronts the visitor with an integrated environment; this fuses with the rich differentiation that characterises an ethnographic collection. The museum revolves around seven deep light wells, which integrate the construction, programmes, infrastructure and lighting of the building. The concrete shafts, massive in appearance, extend from the ground plane like pyramids emerging from the desert, but their insides are hollow, accommodating the museum spaces. The structure generates rooms

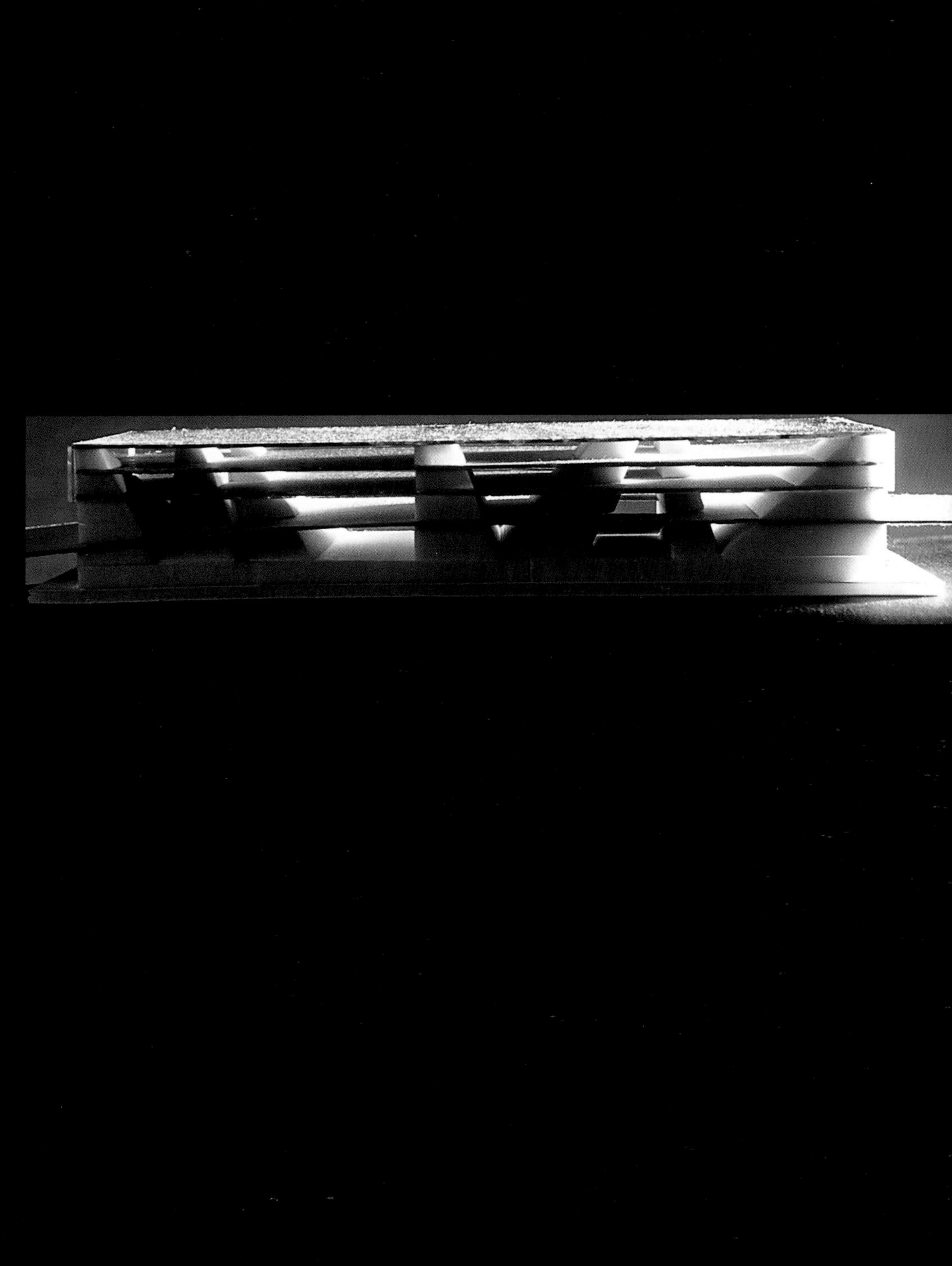

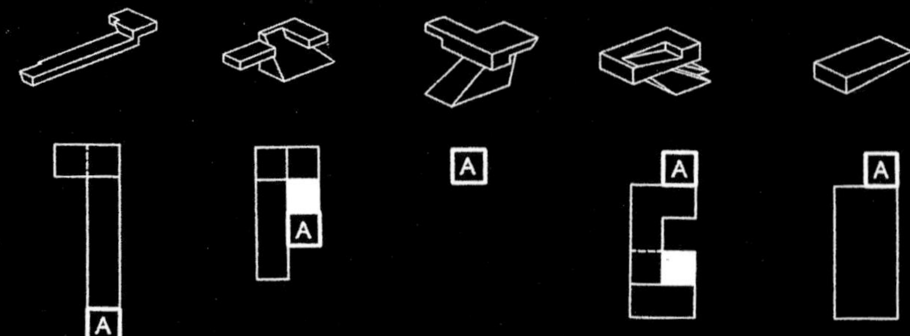

A public entrance

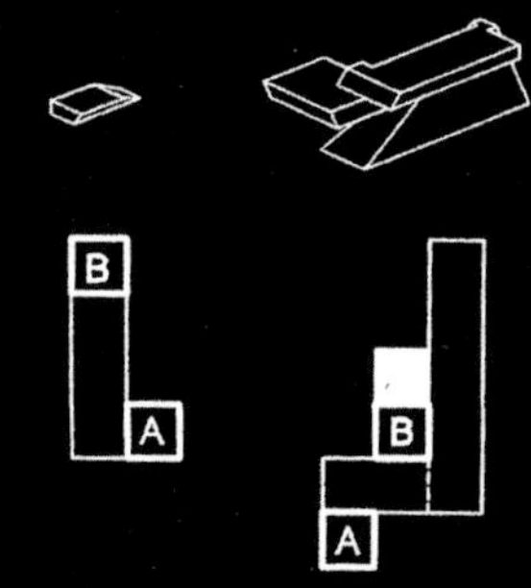

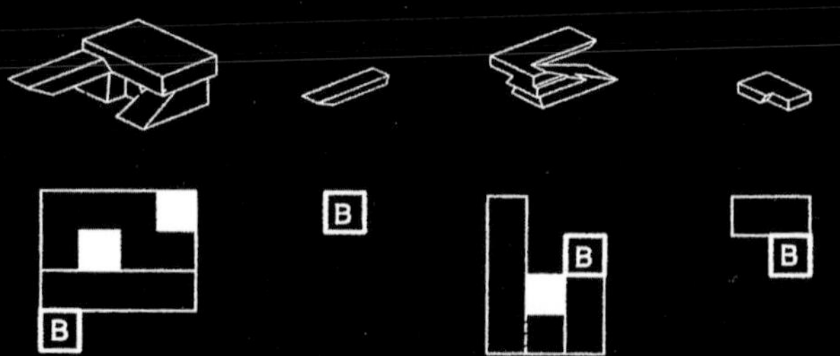

B staff entrance

having no ceilings and sloping walls; routes are located between the shafts.
The distribution of the programme follows the structure of the wells; it winds its way along the sloping walls of the shafts over three floor levels. The three lower levels of the building are dedicated to distant cultures and museology; the upper two to contemporary culture and research. Storage spaces are situated on the lower level. The visitor entering the museum at ground level descends to the central zone of the museum, which leads to the museum rooms and to the research section.

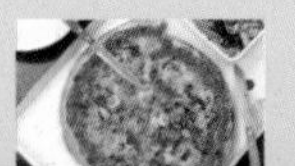    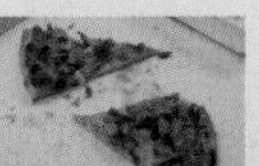  

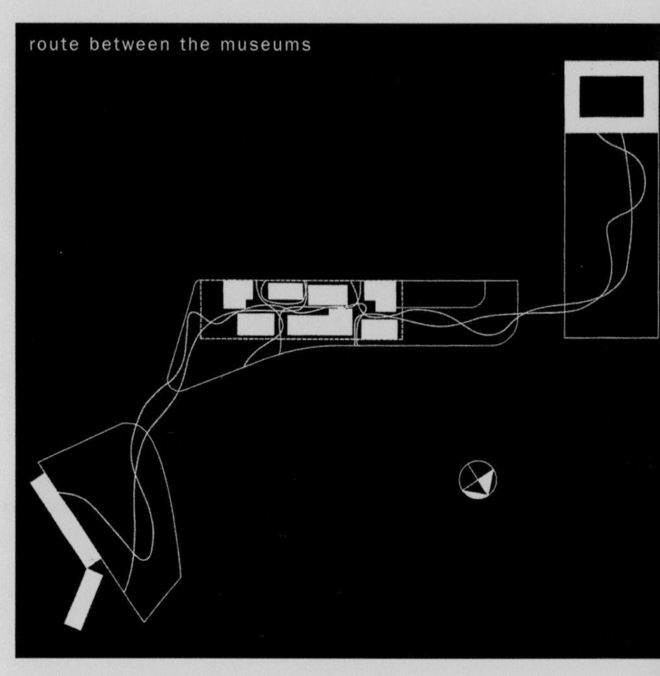
route between the museums

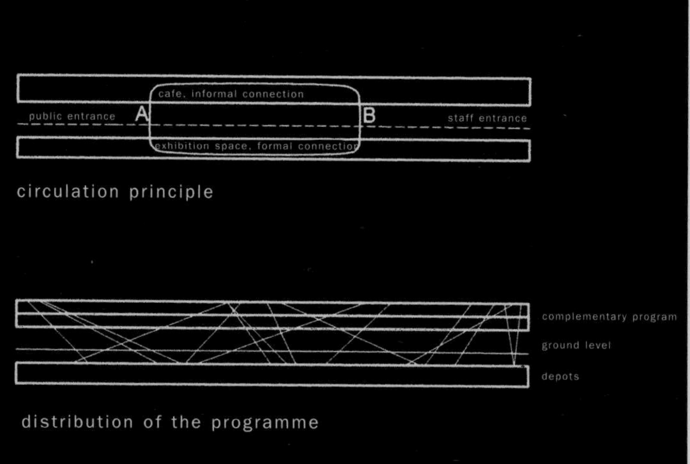
cafe, informal connection
public entrance
A
B
staff entrance
exhibition space, formal connectio
circulation principle
complementary program
ground level
depots
distribution of the programme

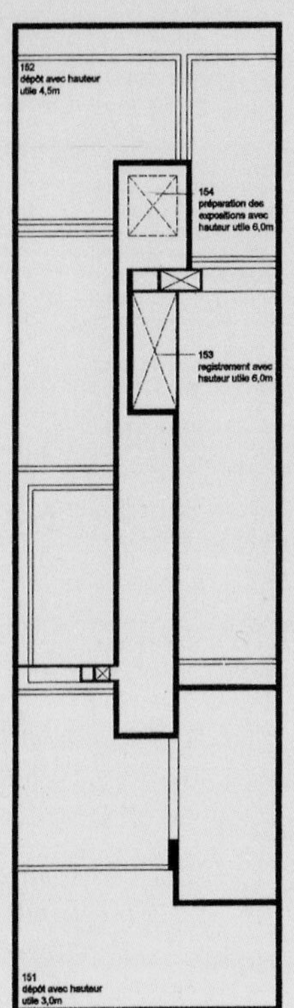
152
dépôt avec hauteur utile 4,5m
154
préparation des expositions avec hauteur utile 6,0m
153
registrement avec hauteur utile 6,0m
151
dépôt avec hauteur utile 3,0m

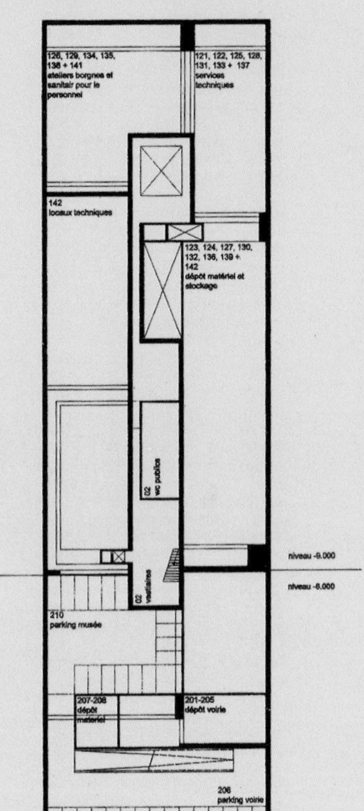
126, 129, 134, 135, 138 + 141
ateliers borgnes et sanitair pour le personnel
121, 122, 125, 128, 131, 133 + 137
services techniques
142
locaux techniques
123, 124, 127, 130, 132, 136, 139 + 142
dépôt matériel et stockage
02
wc publics
niveau -9.000
niveau -6.000
02
vestiaires
210
parking musée
207-208
dépôt materiel
201-205
dépôt voirie
206
parking voirie

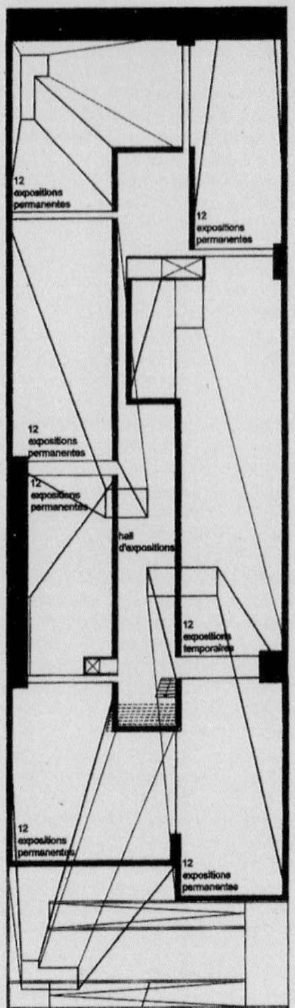
12
expositions permanentes
12
expositions permanentes
12
expositions permanentes
12
expositions permanentes
hall d'expositions
12
expositions temporaires
12
expositions permanentes
12
expositions permanentes

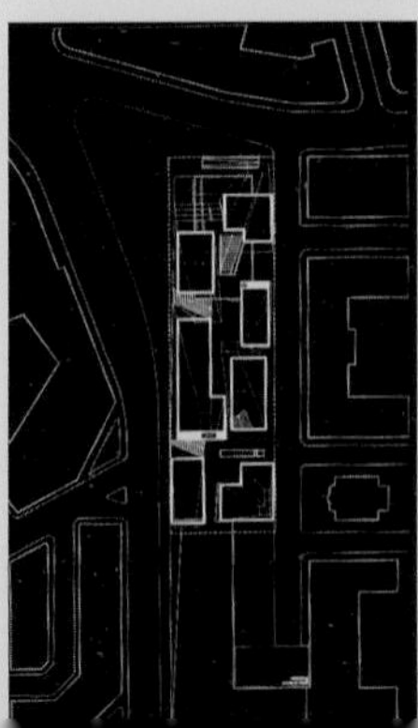

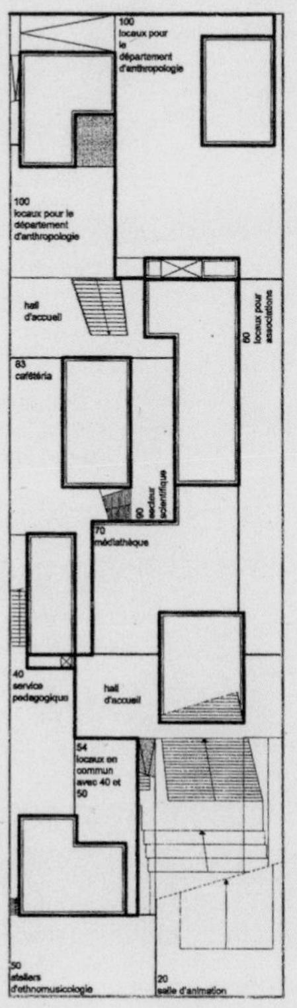

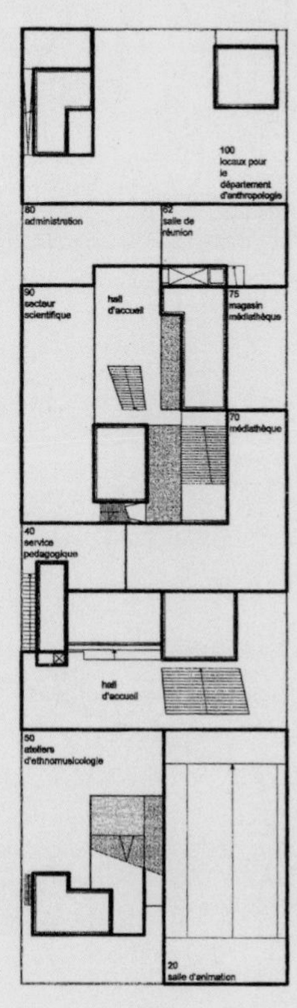

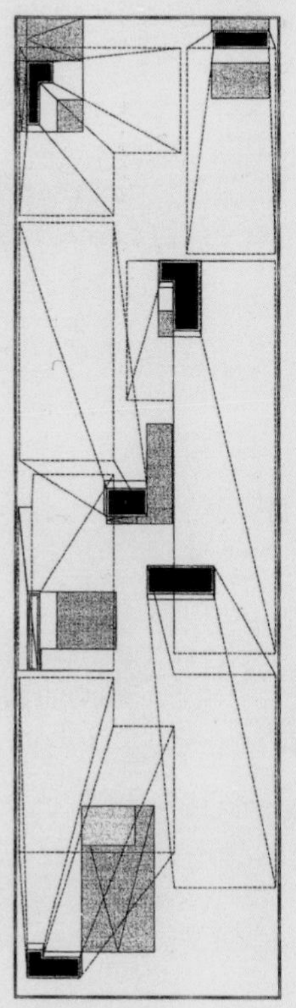

00 public entrance
10 exhibitions
11 temporary exhibitions
20 assembly room
30 cafe
40 lecture room
50 studio for ethnomusicology
60 education room
70 multimedia centre
80 administration
90 scientific sector
100 anthropology room
120 technical services
150 collection depot

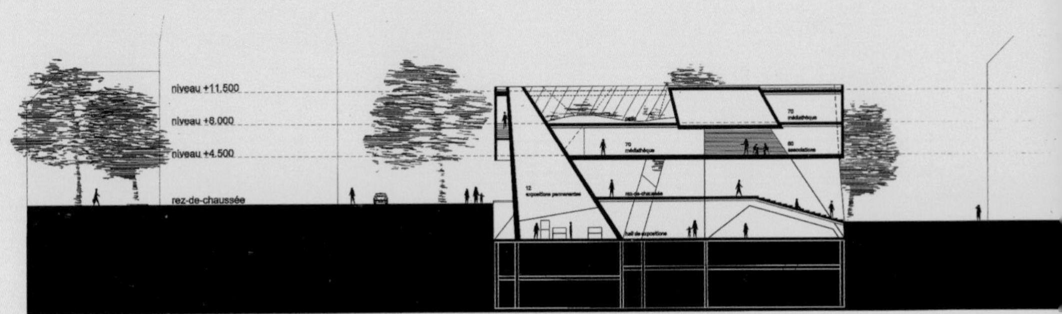

cross-section

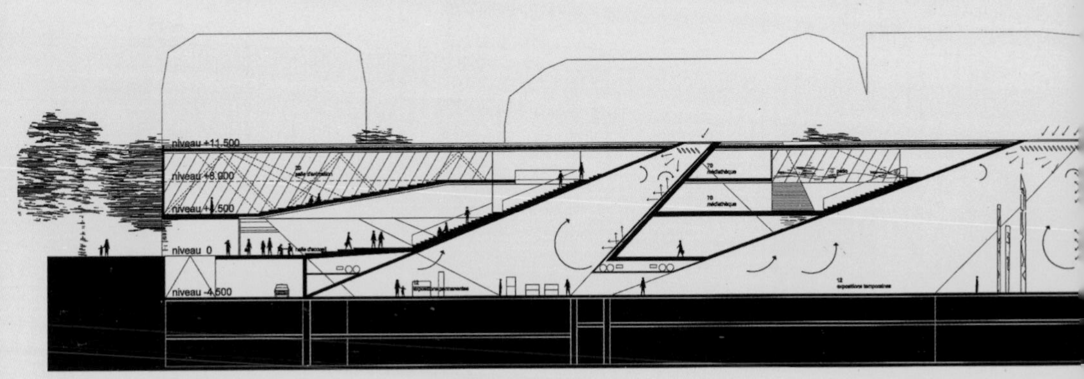

longitudinal section

11.500

8.000

4.500

4.500

.000

12.500

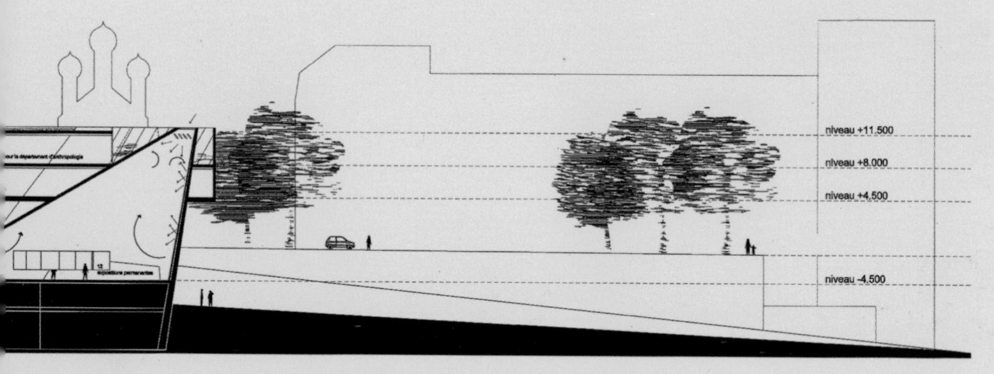

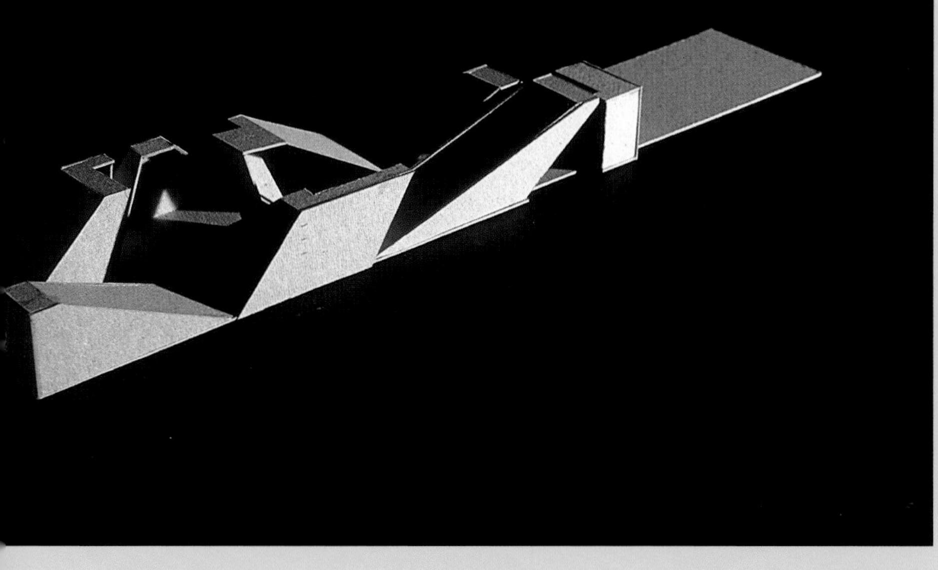

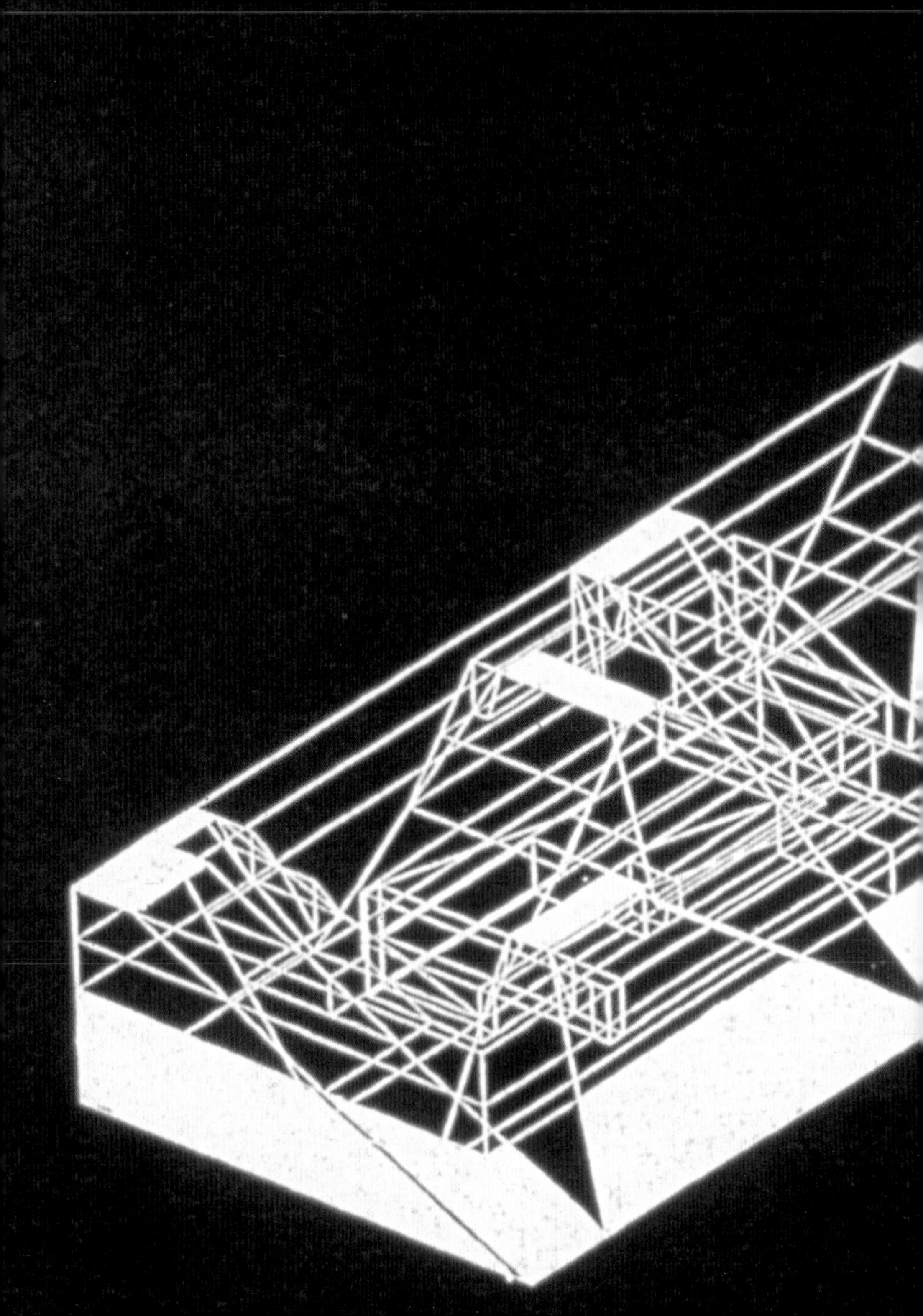

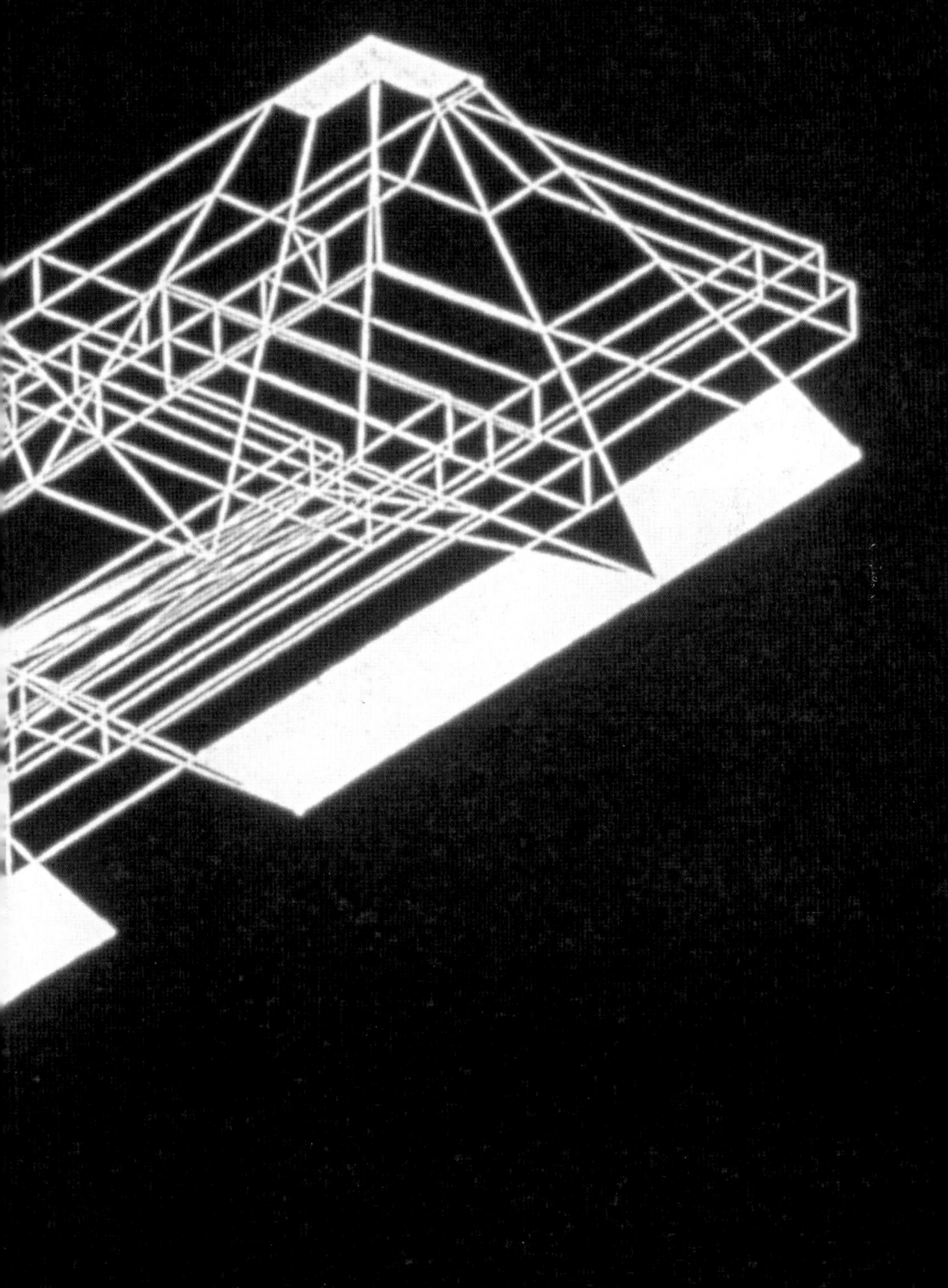

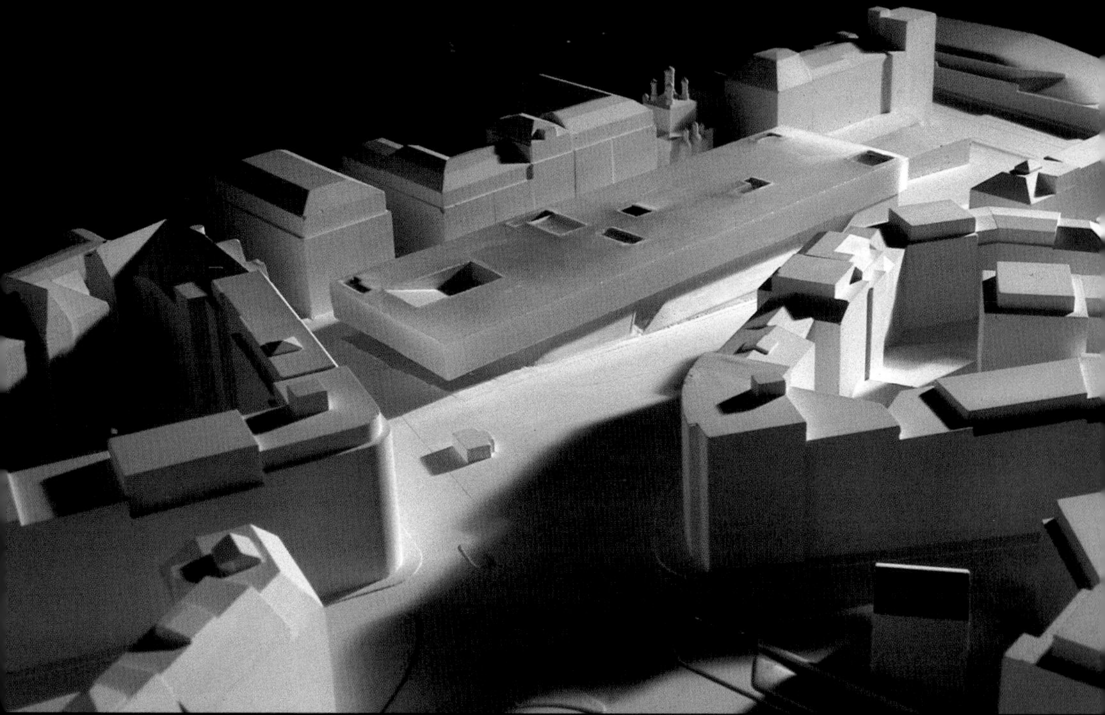

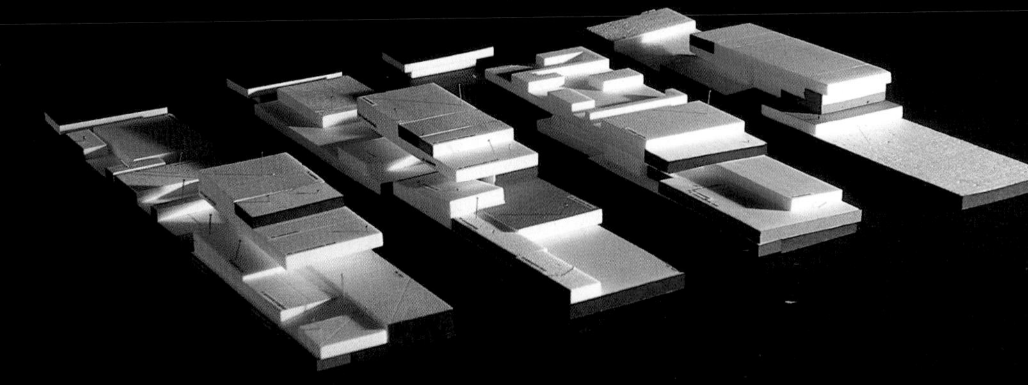

operational matrix

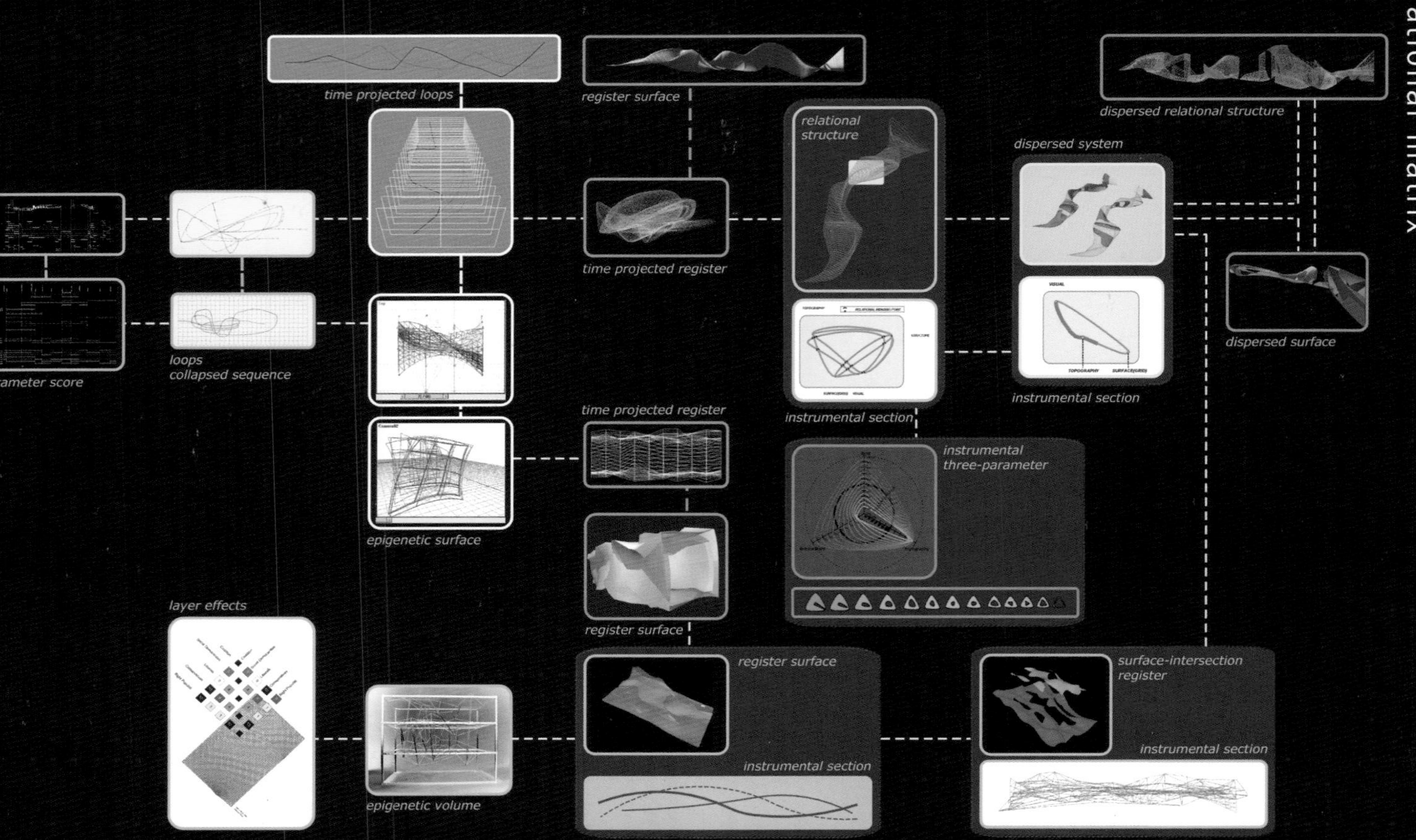

Mediation

New media have been successfully taken up in music, films, car design, fashion, magazine and book publishing, the sex industry and education. Only architecture and urban design are slow to incorporate new media technologies. To some extent, architecture and mediation are locked into a conflicting, for the most part mutually excluding relationship. At first sight this looks logical; architecture is a place, a real, once-only place, which you experience by visiting it. You do not experience architecture through dissolving a building and electronically replicating it a billion times in the air. But architecture is also a public science and a product of its time. It is deeply rooted in the larger world and in the issues that originate from the introduction of new techniques. As architects we are obliged to look for relevance in contemporary practices, events and technologies - or disappear. 'All technology is social before it becomes a technique' means in this case that the technology of mediation needs to be more deeply incorporated within the practice of architecture and to be more widely understood and supported before it can be fully exploited as a tool. This process is just beginning; as yet there is no fully evolved ideological scope that incorporates the new mediated position as an essential part of architecture. New mediation technologies have taken over some of the functions of buildings, such as security, surveillance and communication with the outside, but these are not the most relevant aspects for the practice of architecture itself. The three most important architectural potentials of the new mediation techniques are: the expansion of the spatial imagination, the radical break with a hierarchical design approach and the introduction of different disciplines into the design process, relating the design immediately to its realisation. To begin with the first: the new spatial modes displayed on computer screens result in a general familiarity with the potential of a multi-dimensional spatial experience. Computer-generated special effects express a delight in explorative spatial situations, leading to a rapid increase in the capacity for spatial conceptualisation. The digitalisatio[n] of architectural practice takes various forms. The choice of computer software is an important factor in the procedure of the technique as different application[s] contain their own rules and instrumentalising qualities. All mediation techniques have in common that they abandon the hierarchical way of building up the architectural body, which starts with the ground plan. Not the object itself, but the sets of relationships between

the component parts are articulated and defined.
At the moment, there are four dominant approaches to computational and mediation techniques: the first sees the new techniques as a way to realise a virtual reality, which is related to the radical physiological interventions, disenfranchising social, political and economic powers and inanimate environment of cyberspace. This thinking relates to a tradition of visionary architecture. Fantasies of imaginary cities and buildings are connected to cybernetics, the science of communication and automatic control systems. As with all fantasies, it is to a large extent the current reality that directs these visions. The mediated world implies that new media have massively overshadowed the communicative powers of architecture. Accelerators such as motorways and airports have destabilised the public domain in which the architectural body is embedded. In this world of potentially limitless freedom of movement through geographical, social, economic and cultural strata, the old dream of transcending materiality begins to approach realisation. A substantial virtual control of human bodies and urban and architectural spaces already exists.

For now, architecture cannot be fully virtual and at the same time be a real, solid place that can be physically entered. It is only possible to extend and enrich architecture with virtual means. This entails a specific use of mediation techniques, to some extent overlapping with the process of hybridization. The most important consequence of this interpretation of computer architecture is that it explores the inventive and utopian potential of the new media techniques and expands boundaries.

A second application of the introduction of computational techniques centres on the intensification of the connectivity between the partners in the architectural process. The line between design phase and construction has shortened and has unravelled into different, non-simultaneous strands. The traditional order of the design stages has broken down, with reality checks on money and feasibility being worked into the process at the earliest moment. Traditionally, the period of preliminary design would be a quiet, concentrated stage, during which architects would prepare their designs in

relative isolation. After this, a series of cutbacks would proceed to frustrate everyone and kill the project. Now, the architectural process may be organised in

many different ways, with widely used new methods such as 'design & construct' and 'definitive design plus'. Designing with computational techniques involves abandoning the traditional hierarchy of a design approach that begins with the plan. Today, we begin with a point. A point in three-dimensional space. The architectural drawing, a scaled-down, two-dimensional representation of an aspect of a building, is obsolete. A project is built up in three dimensions and with its real measurements in the infinite mediation space. Having captured this space within a personal computer station, that is, having confined it to proportions which enable us to manipulate, divide and layer this space it goes ahead to generate its own small technologies like extrusions and rotating sections - little tricks which simply let us see more than before.
While the software programmes compatible for engineers and contractors have not been written for archi-

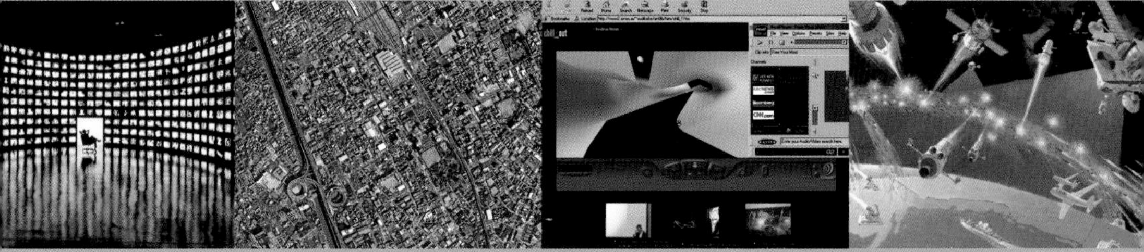

tects and are far from user-friendly, the up side of connectivity is that more can be achieved. Complex projects, assembled from components of many different shapes and sizes, are realised thanks to computationa techniques. Constructions that deviate from the mainstream are becoming accessible to architects, because along with everything else, the knowledge that belonged exclusively to engineers is also being injected into the design process at an earlier stage. Digital calculating enables more complex geometrical structuring Meanwhile, production methods have also changed under the influence of the development of new mediation technologies. Computerised laser-cutting mills execute complex shapes with the same ease as rectangular ones, so that non-standardised profiles and details become cheaper.

This, in combination with the changing and in some ways diminishing role of the architect informs the third approach to computer architecture. This third adaptation revolves around the objective, pragmatic properties of techniques. The techniques offer an opportunity to hang on to a belief in reason - in there being a righ choice to make. Otherwise, it has become difficult to rationalise design choices. If any form is possible and all are equally functional in an economic sense, the pragmatic, standardised language of Modernism has lost its imperative. A simple, self-evident reasoning no longer justifies any specific form. With the criteria for functionalism changing and the co-operative design process rendering uncertain the position of the architect, new digital techniques are exploited to shake off traditional architectural pretensions. New models of organisation are developed in order to proportion and structure digital information. Parameters are formulated, once again expressing architectural values in rational, functional and objective terms. An extremist interpretation of this technique would lead to a deterministic view of architecture. As the evolution of the chosen parameters is traced over time, the project emerges as if of its own accord. In reality, the number of parameters is always too large for this to happen. The techniques are used as a direct and transparent medium to uncover the neutral values forming the basis of the project. This approach has some similarities to the rationalist and structuralist architecture of the 1960-s. Both share a conviction that a neutral, business-like architecture can emanate out of underlying data, less dependent on the personality of the architect or on aesthetic conventions than before.

While this approach already begins to incorporate moveable criteria, parameter design is primarily a static summing up. Only when the data begin to interact, do the elements of time and movement enter the process. At that point, the fourth important adaptation of new media techniques enters the equation: animation.

This approach entails a different choice of software, focusing on time-based animation software environments, which are no more designed for architects than CAD systems, but which take the design process in a new direction. Three-dimensional modelling already dispenses with the idea of the designed object as the construction of outlines and instead begins with a point; animation abandons even the network of points and works with the interrelations of parameters and forces. The object is formed as the result of this process; it is the solidification of energies acting on each other, as in a chemical experiment. The animation technique involves setting up a design path. The end result is subject to change as long as the project follows its course.

In a controlled experiment the choice of ingredients is vital to the outcome. Therefore, it would be an exaggeration to see the project as the passive product of a self-organising process, but this technique still involves greater openness with reference to the end product than any other technique. The fact that objects are modelled by means of a dynamic process implies that changes in the organisational patterns taking place during the process are also evaluated, enabling a complete acknowledgement of complexity.

Animation as a technique could not have been developed

without virtual architecture and parameter-based strategies; in a way animation hybridizes the two and optimises potentials inherent in both. There is a tendency for architects, probably because of the large investments of time and money required to become digital, to concentrate almost exclusively on one specific usage and heavily integrate it into their design approach. This total identification of practices with specific techniques is now the factor that most inhibits the successful integration of mediation technology in architecture. Let's put an end to digital sectarianism. The potentials of mediation, the expansion of the imagination, the break with a hierarchical design approach and the introduction of different disciplines into the design process, go beyond the small technologies. Architecture needs the varied and free use of new mediation techniques in order to keep its relevance as a public science with tentacles in areas such as design, art, film, computer technology, engineering and infrastructure.

The computerised organisational model of the Rubber Mat avoids architecture; it projects four urban situations as four layers, or mats, on a specific site. With its value-free urbanism and flexible layers, the Rubber Mat constitutes an early version of an aesthetically neutral, futurological instrument.

First experimental moving matrix of interacting parameters

As a way of wrapping up and celebrating fifty years of post-war reconstruction, Rotterdam commissioned a group of architects to produce speculative schemes for various parts of the town for the next fifty years. But there is no way to realistically answer the question of how Rotterdam will be in 2045 in architectural terms. For our allocated area, the site of the first Dutch margarine factory, we chose therefore to develop a model without architecture.

The Rubber Mat consists of four conditions, living, work, fun and landscape, which are plotted on a horizontal time line in a 3-D model which follows the physical shape of the location. A vertical line charts the parameters structuring change in the layers. These parameters are land value, rent level, building density, occupational

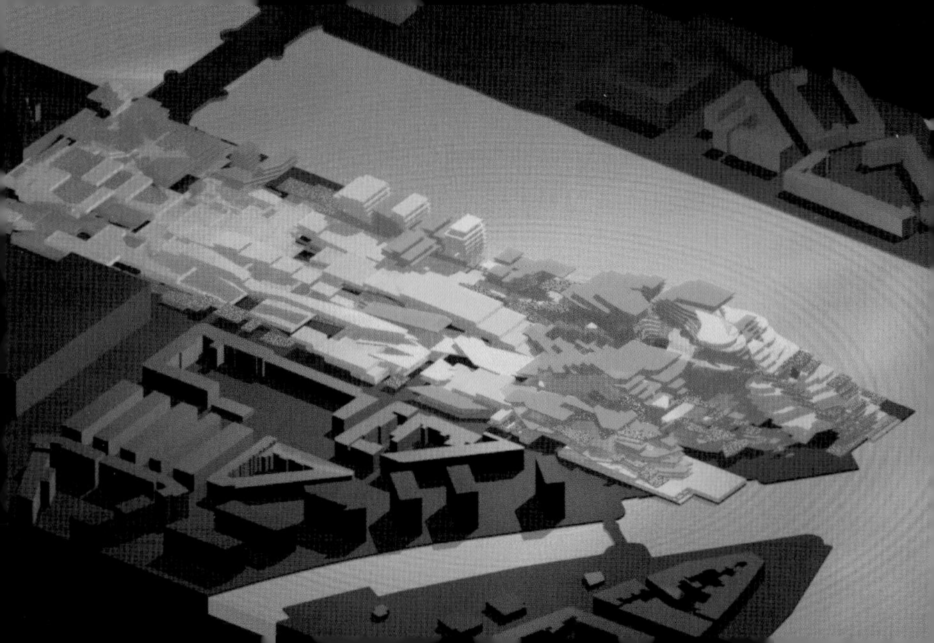

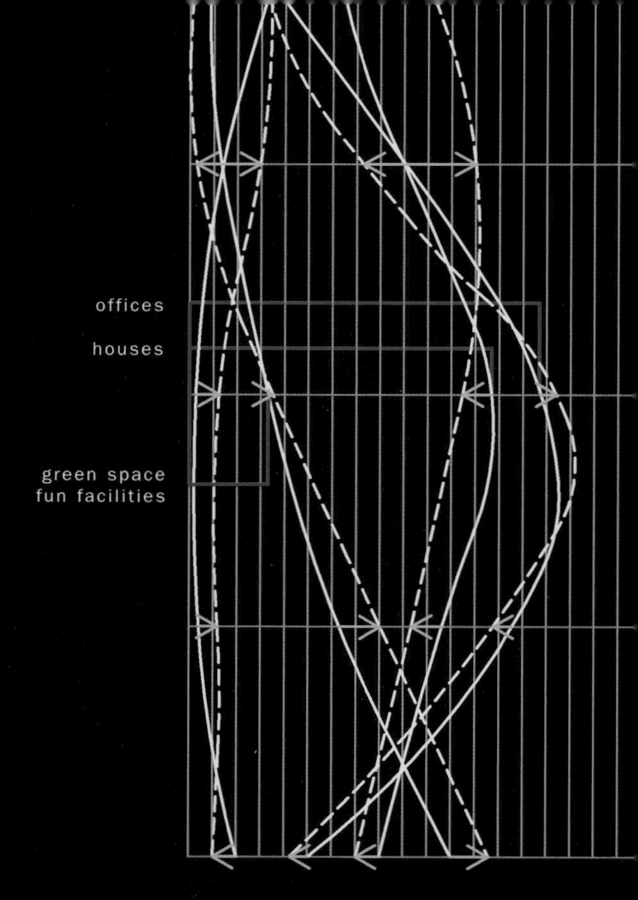
offices
houses
green space
fun facilities

density, increase in business activities, in services and in landscape quality. Changes in one parameter would resonate in each of the four layers of the mat, like applying pressure to a point on a waterbed. The extrusion of changes already taking place on the river-bound Unilever terrain allows certain predictions to be made as to possible land use in the future; the margarine factory will shrink and ultimately disappear, to be replaced by representative office functions and housing. On the basis of this pattern of change,the 3-D model is animated and shows a moveable organisational principle of function allocation, changing with time.

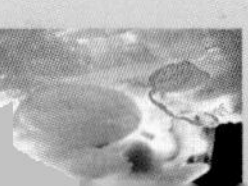
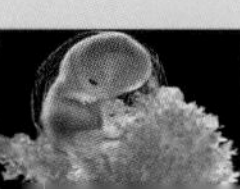
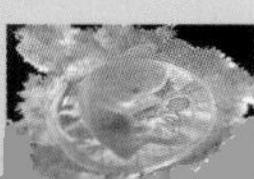
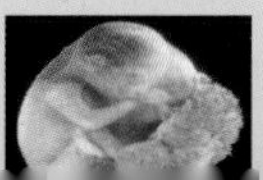

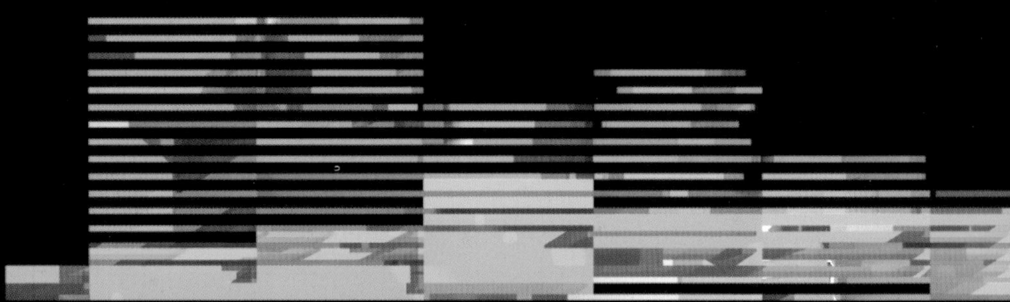

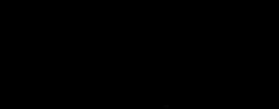

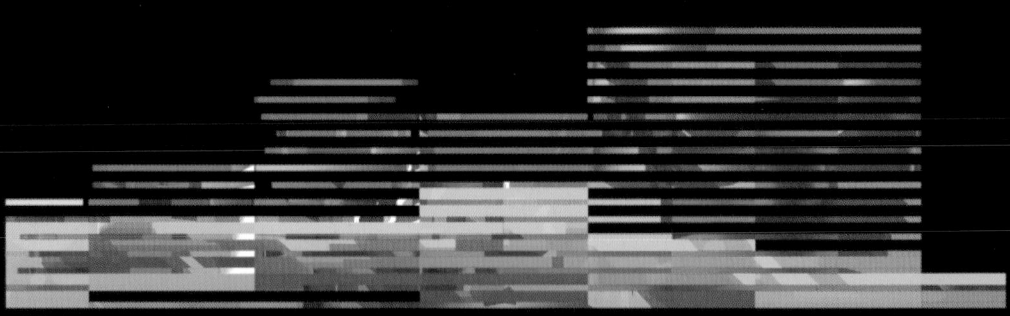

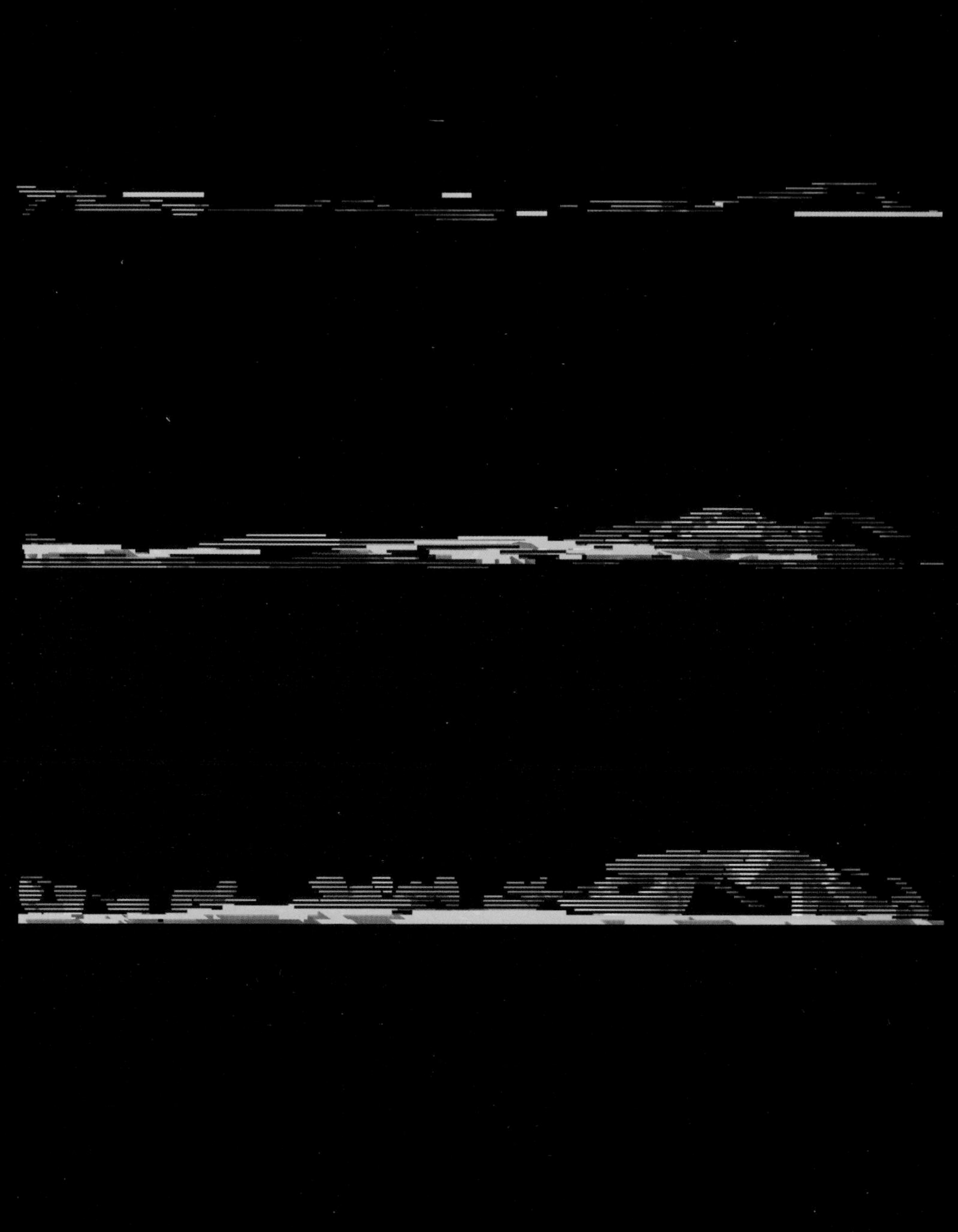

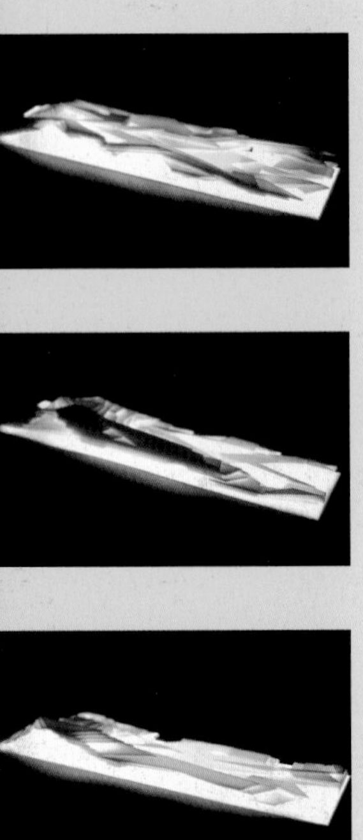

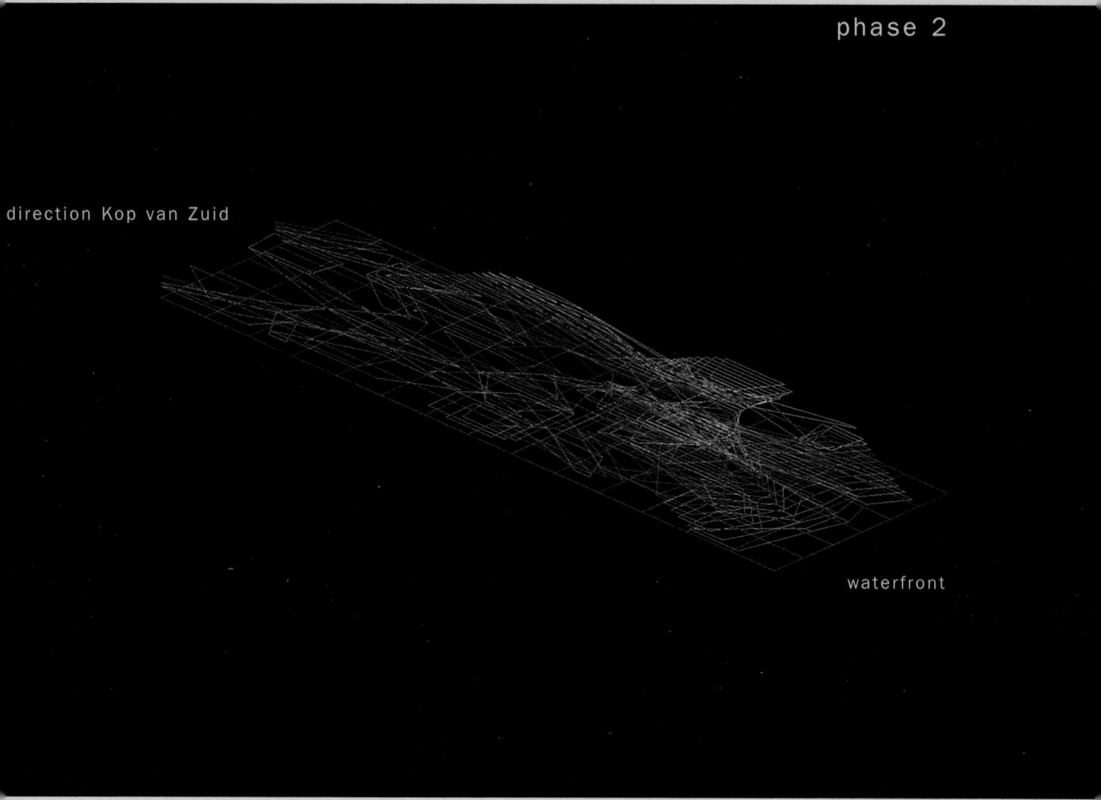

phase 2

direction Kop van Zuid

waterfront

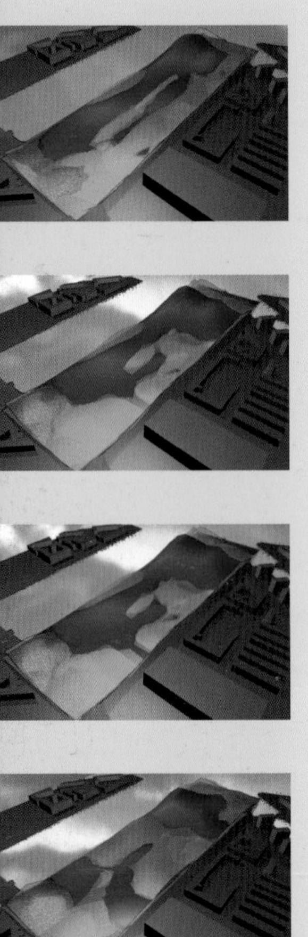

sections phase 1

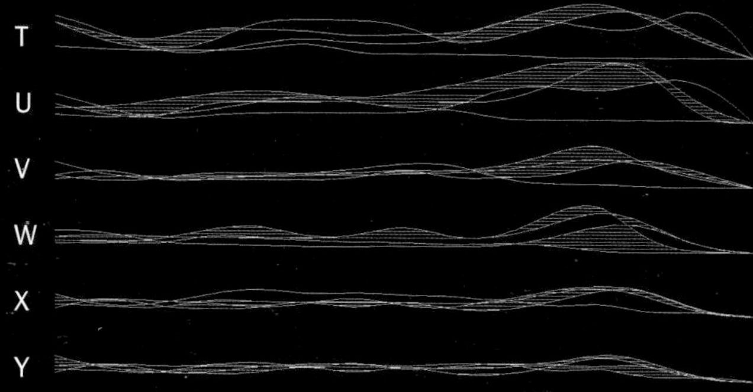

sections phase 2

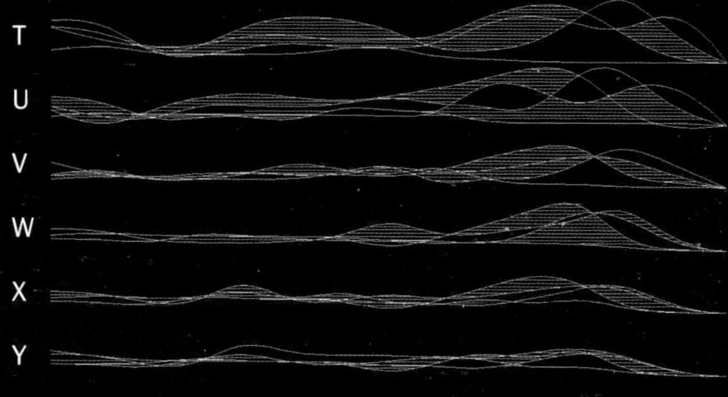

sections phase 3

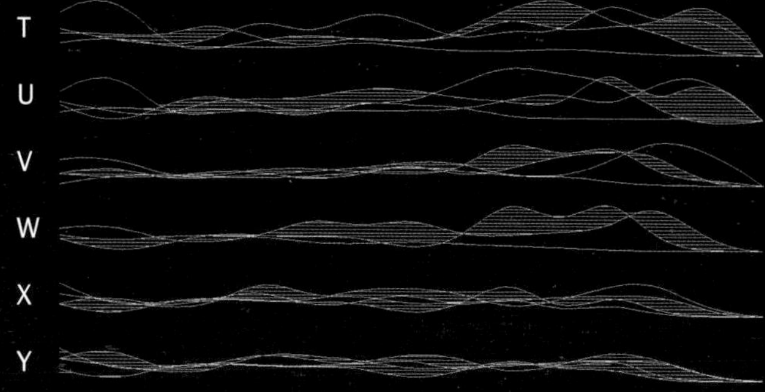

The building can be seen as celebrating the material produced by the principal client, the Hoogovens Steel Plant. But it is not solely the end product that is taken into account, but more particularly the process by which steel is manufactured and manipulated.

Virtual-material: ***streamlining steel parameters***

This proposal for a building as a new gate to the Hoogovens came about through the introduction of compact, high-tech installations into the industrial process. This resulted in surplus space, some of which will be developed as Business Park Ymond. In urban terms, the Business Park can be compared to an Expo terrain; four individual buildings are scattered like separate pavilions. These are physically connected by a trajectory following the length of location. They are also linked by a shared theme - the historic and ongoing relation to Hoogovens.

Architecturally, the buildings express their relation to Hoogovens in their materialisation. When steel is liquefied during the industrial process, the material reaches its optimum potential and is most productive and flexible. The fluid, column-free architecture of the main building is a reminder of this change of state and is organ-

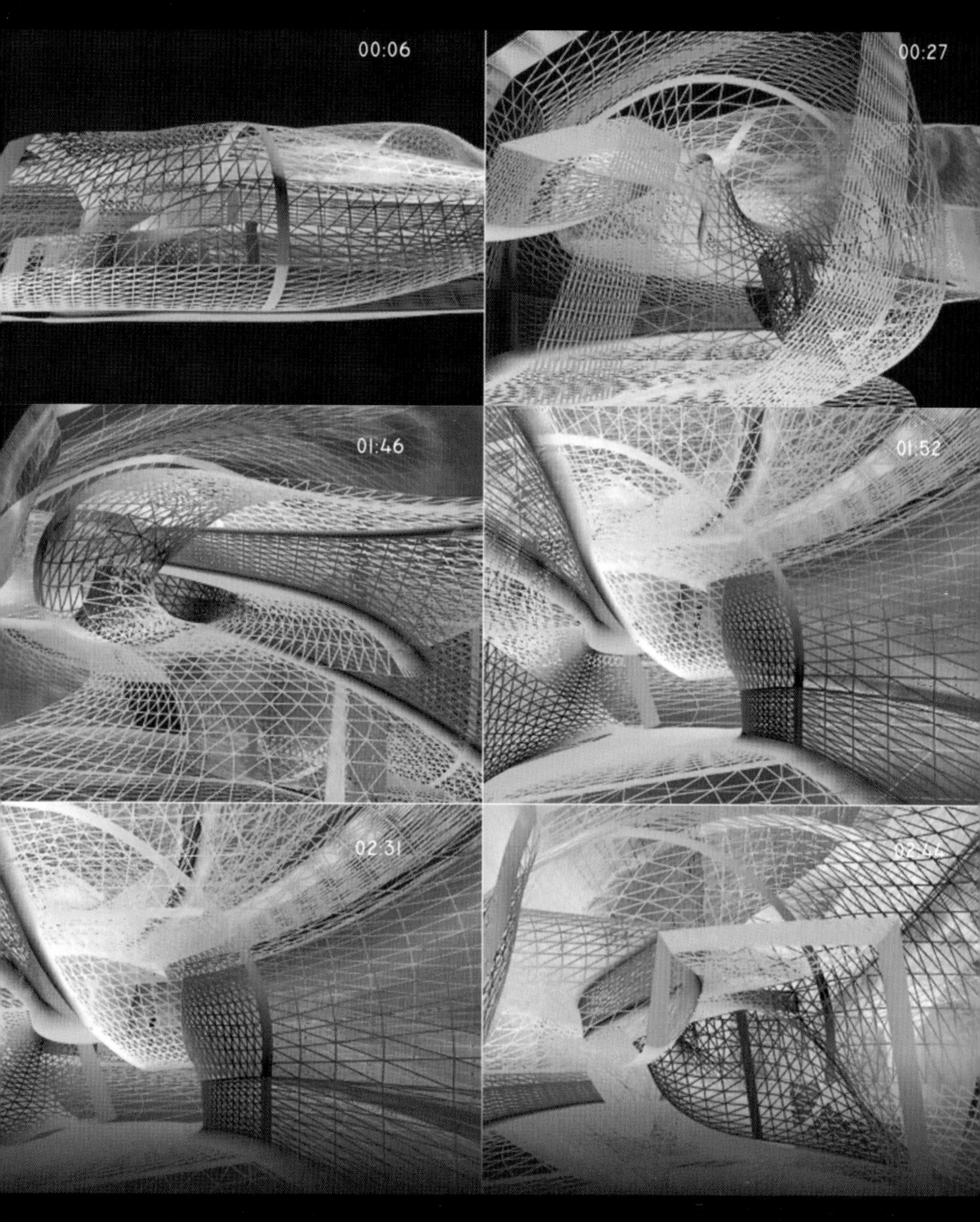
00:06
00:27
01:46
01:52
02:31

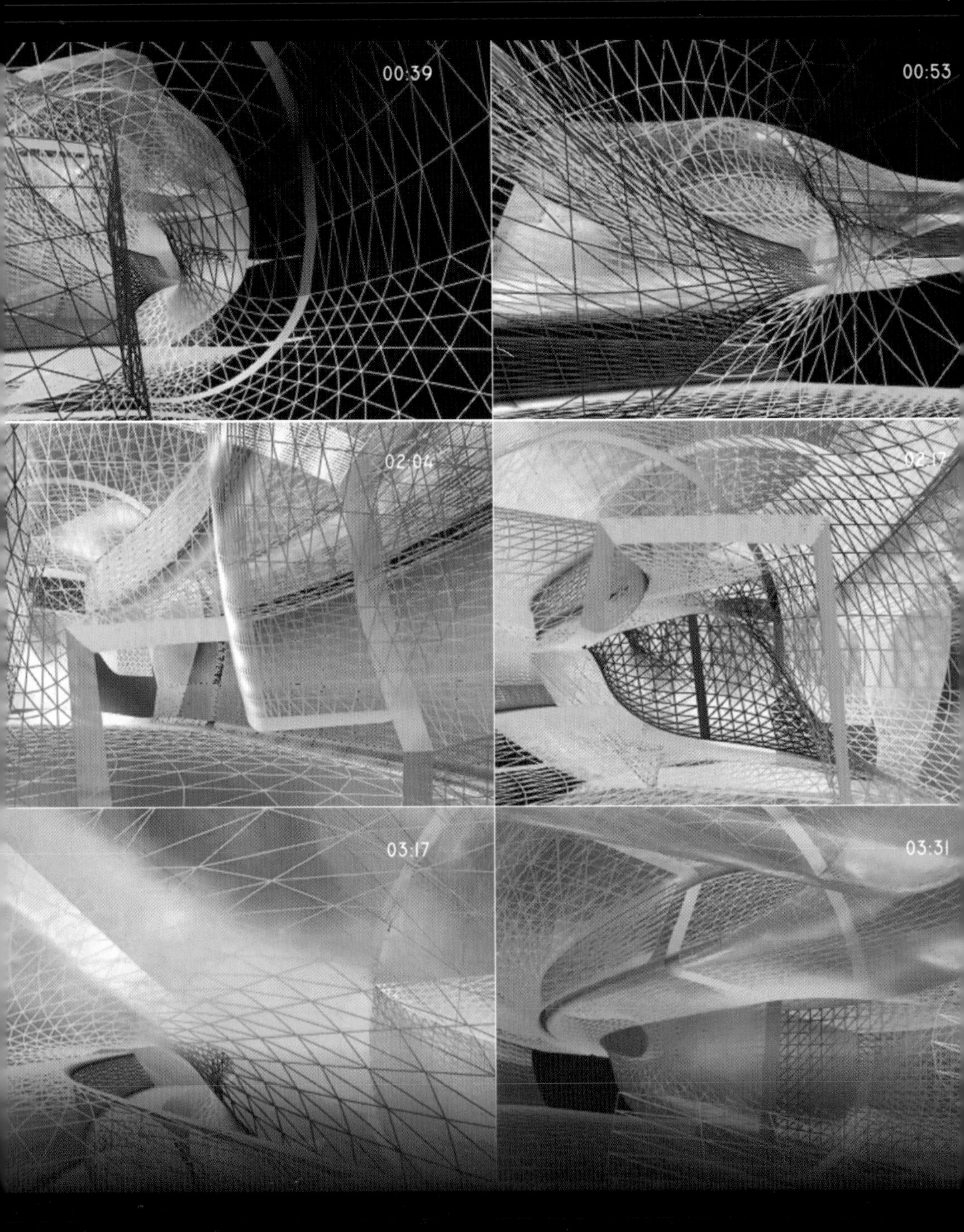
00:39
00:53
02:04
02:17
03:17
03:31

ised to ensure a similar, intense productivity.
This building has a threefold function as visitor centre, office and workshop. The construction consists of a smooth, steel envelope in which the exterior surface morphs into the interior and programmatic areas merge. The interaction of the urban lay-out of the trajectory, the surface contours of the terrain and the programmatic dimension requirements generates the material organisation.
Current thinking about maximising the use of office space has played a role in the proposal for the three smaller units. Notions of time-sharing have been researched. One of the suggestions is that, of the three buildings, the middle one will provide facilities to be used by the other two as well.

location study

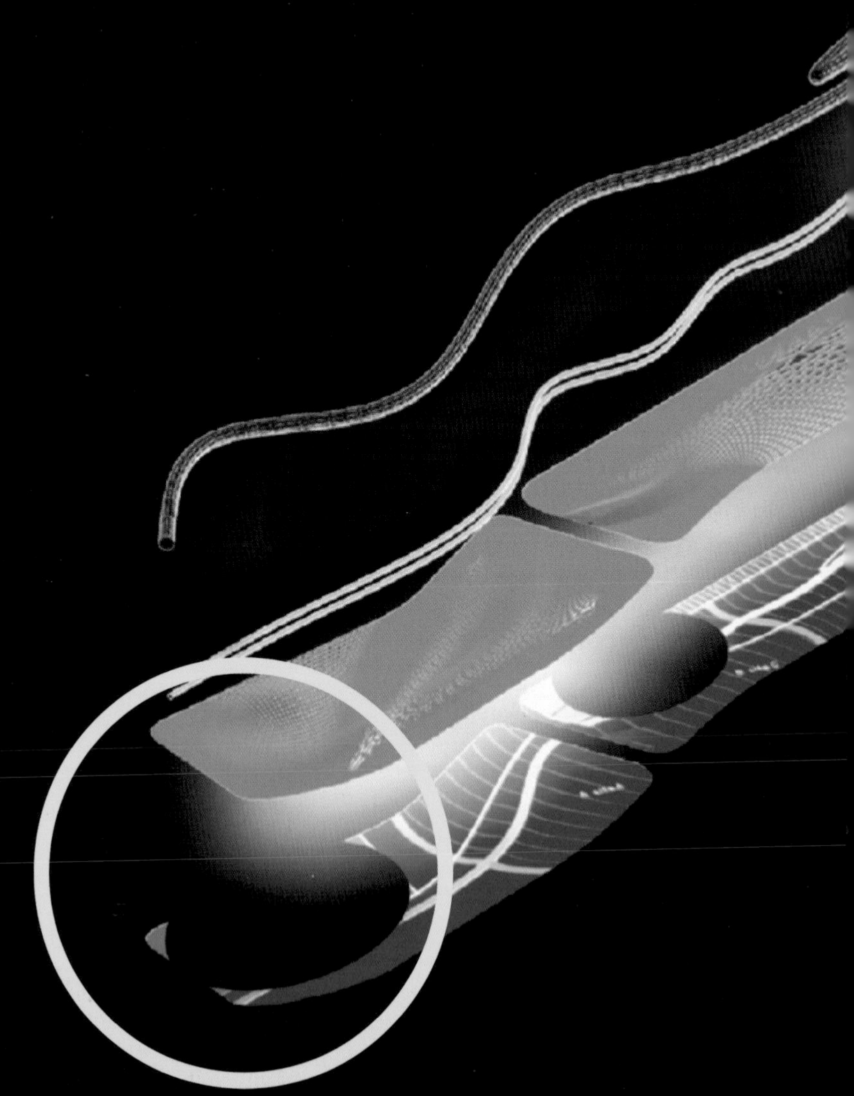

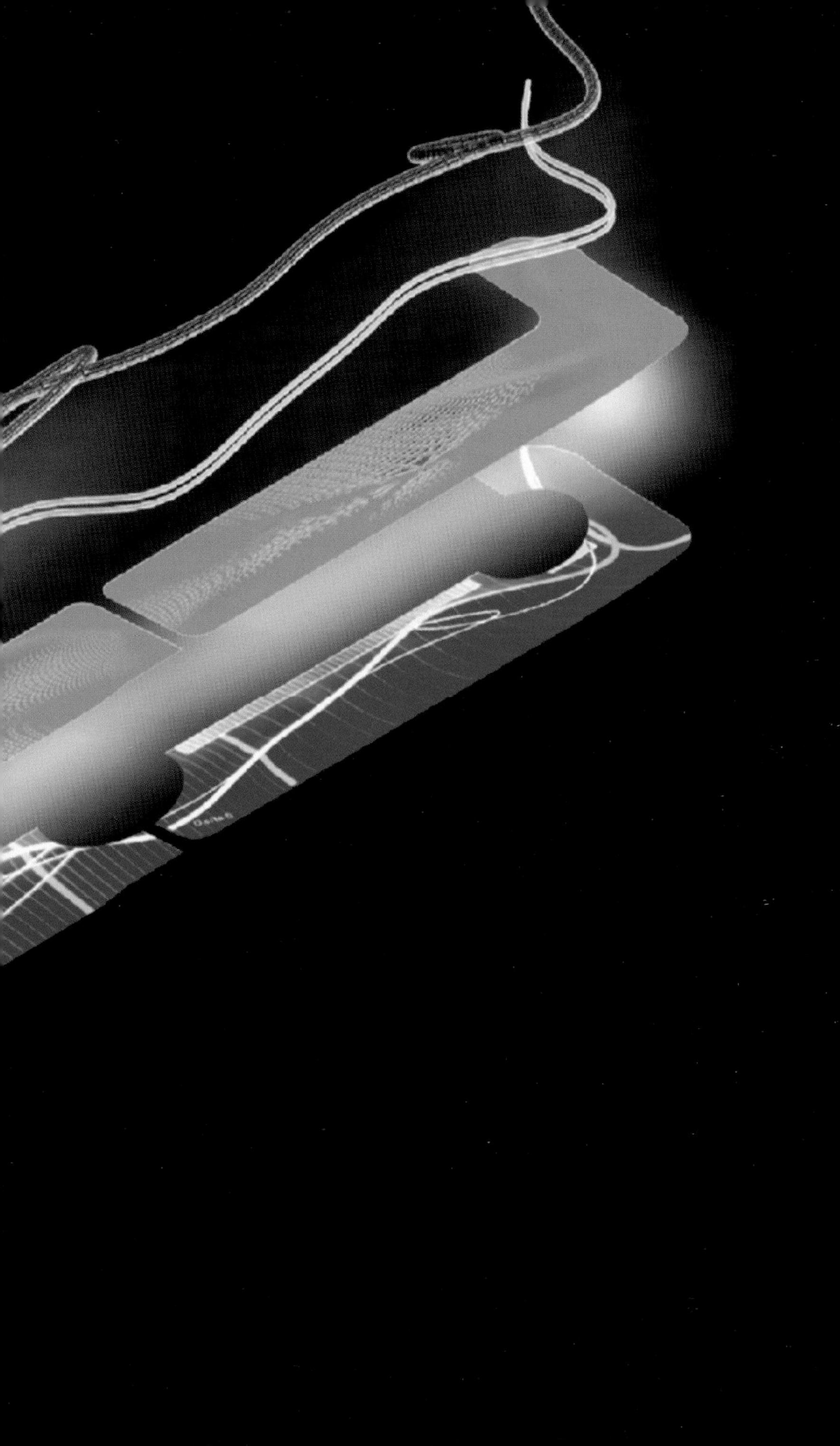

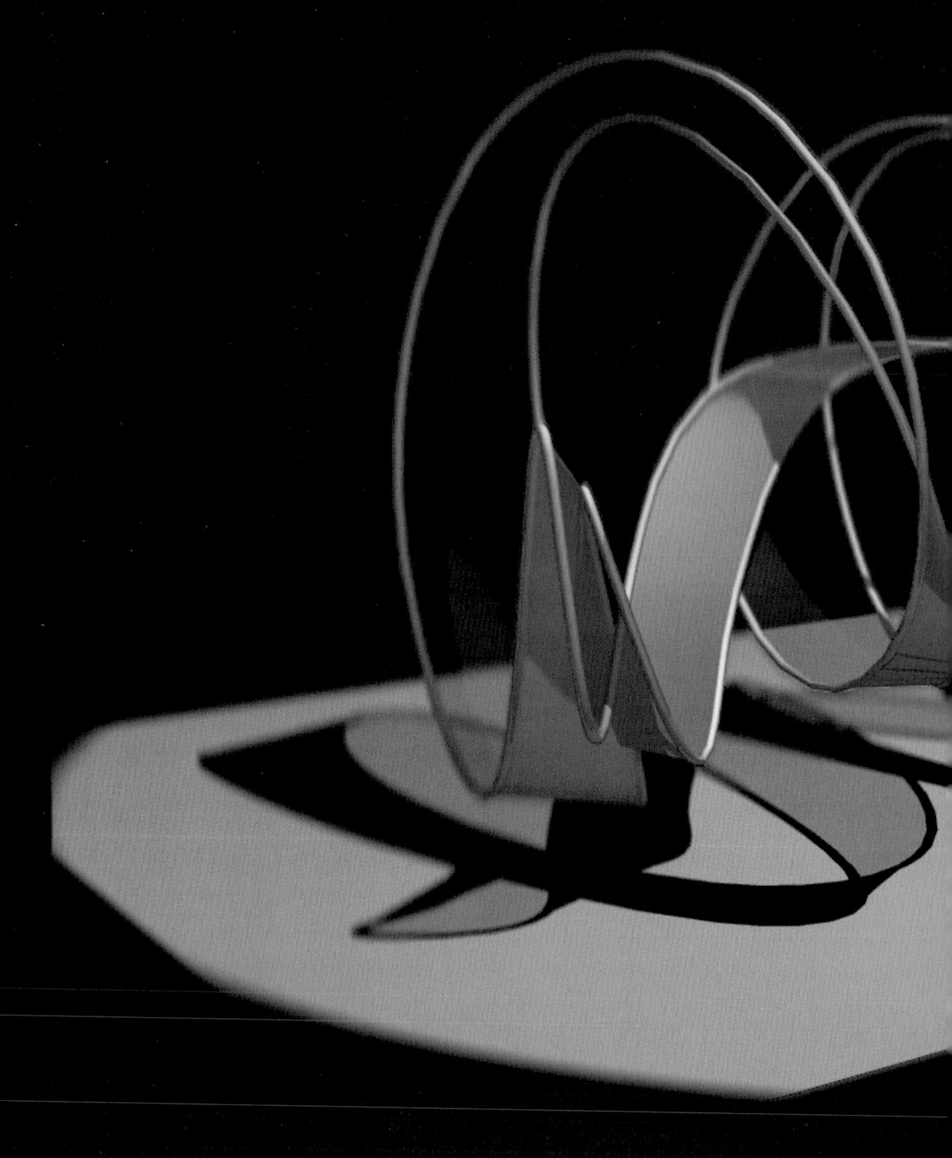

diagram investigating inclusive, infrastuctu

programmatic and constructive connectivity

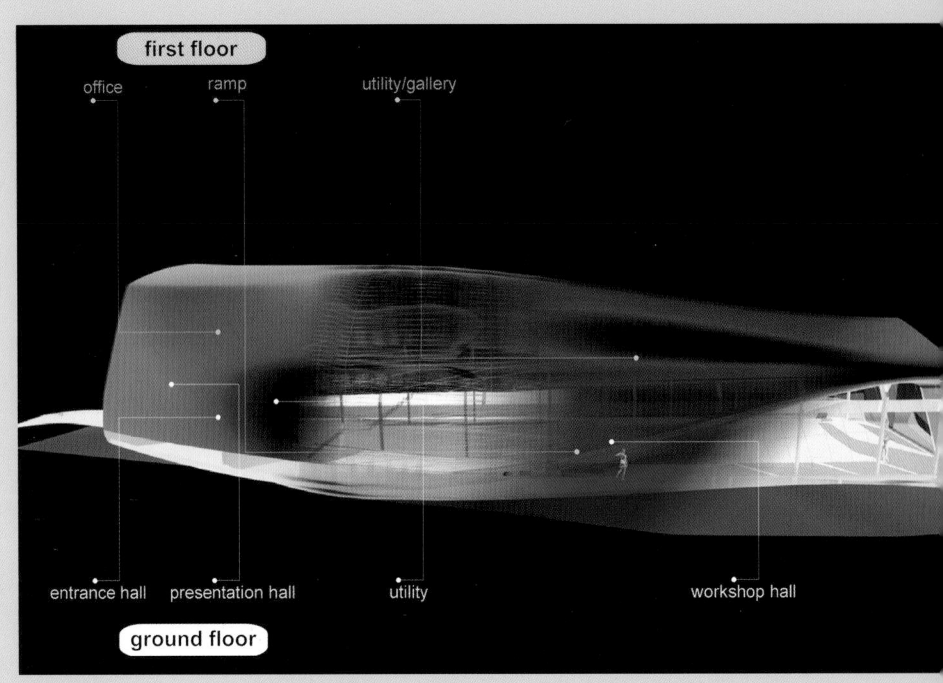
first floor
office
ramp
utility/gallery
entrance hall
presentation hall
utility
workshop hall
ground floor

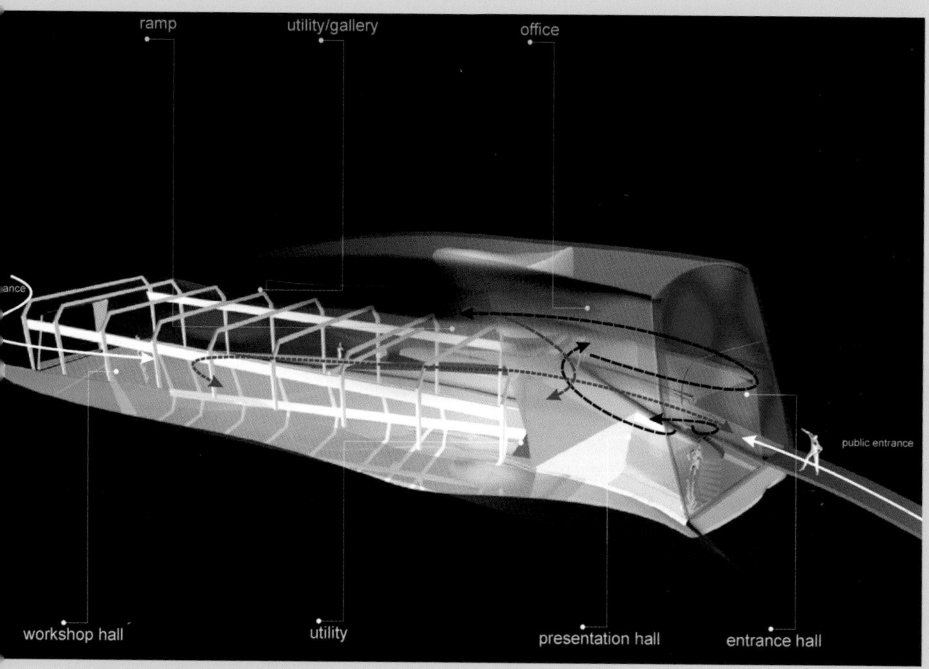
ramp
utility/gallery
office
ance
public entrance
workshop hall
utility
presentation hall
entrance hall

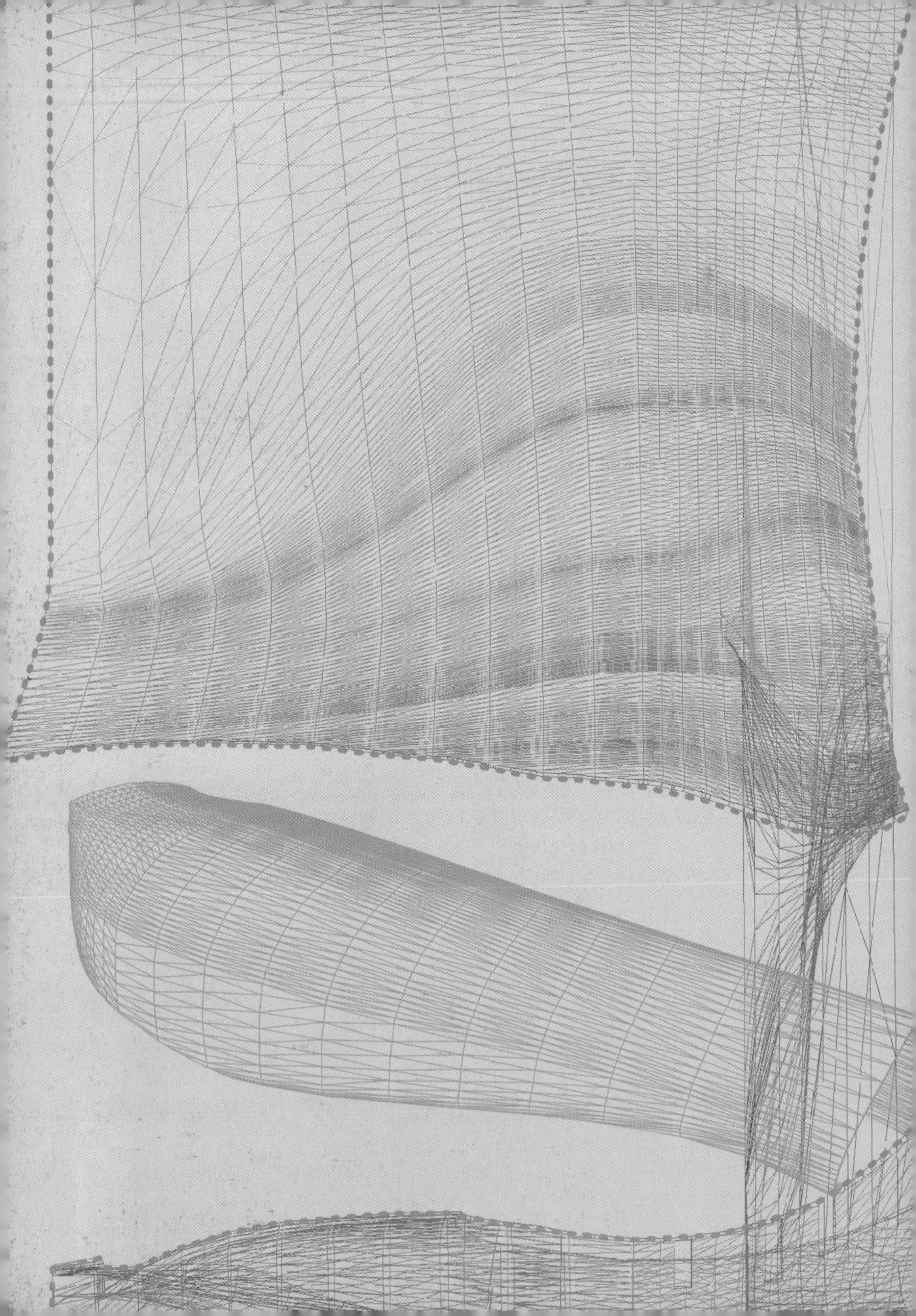

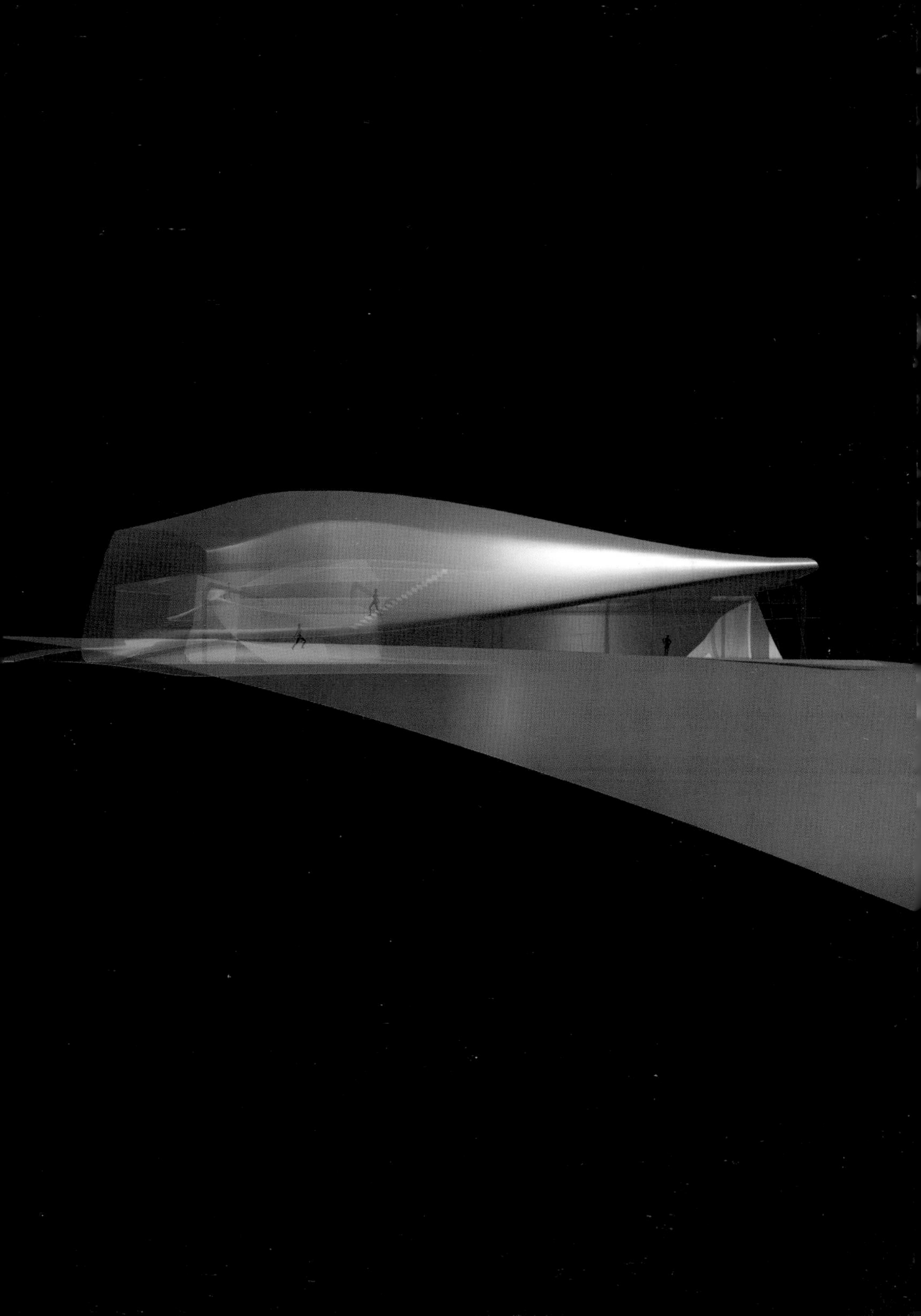

A new type of event structure is sought, based on a reinterpretation of the idea of event. Events are seen as hard, soft, or undefined. A hard event has a specific location and duration; its visitor curve is one of steep peaks and dales. A soft event shows a less cyclical structure; its location is visited by a more or less continuous flow. The undefined event is proportionally the largest of all and functionally breaks down into waiting, circulation, distribution and logistics. The project takes this last type of event as its main structure and, within this soft structure, establishes strata incorporating the hard events.

Event structure: **hard unit and soft unit**

A multidisciplinary design team executed the competition entry for the Swiss National Exposition of the summer of 2001. The project calls for a proposal for an 'Art beach', an integral, waterside construction incorporating all Expo facilities and providing a philosophical landscape in which the visitor will encounter various, thematic works o art, performances and events. The theme given by the Expo organisers for the Arteplage Yverdon is 'Me and the Universe'; questions of philosophical sensual, organic and ontological nature are posed The programme area of the project consists of the

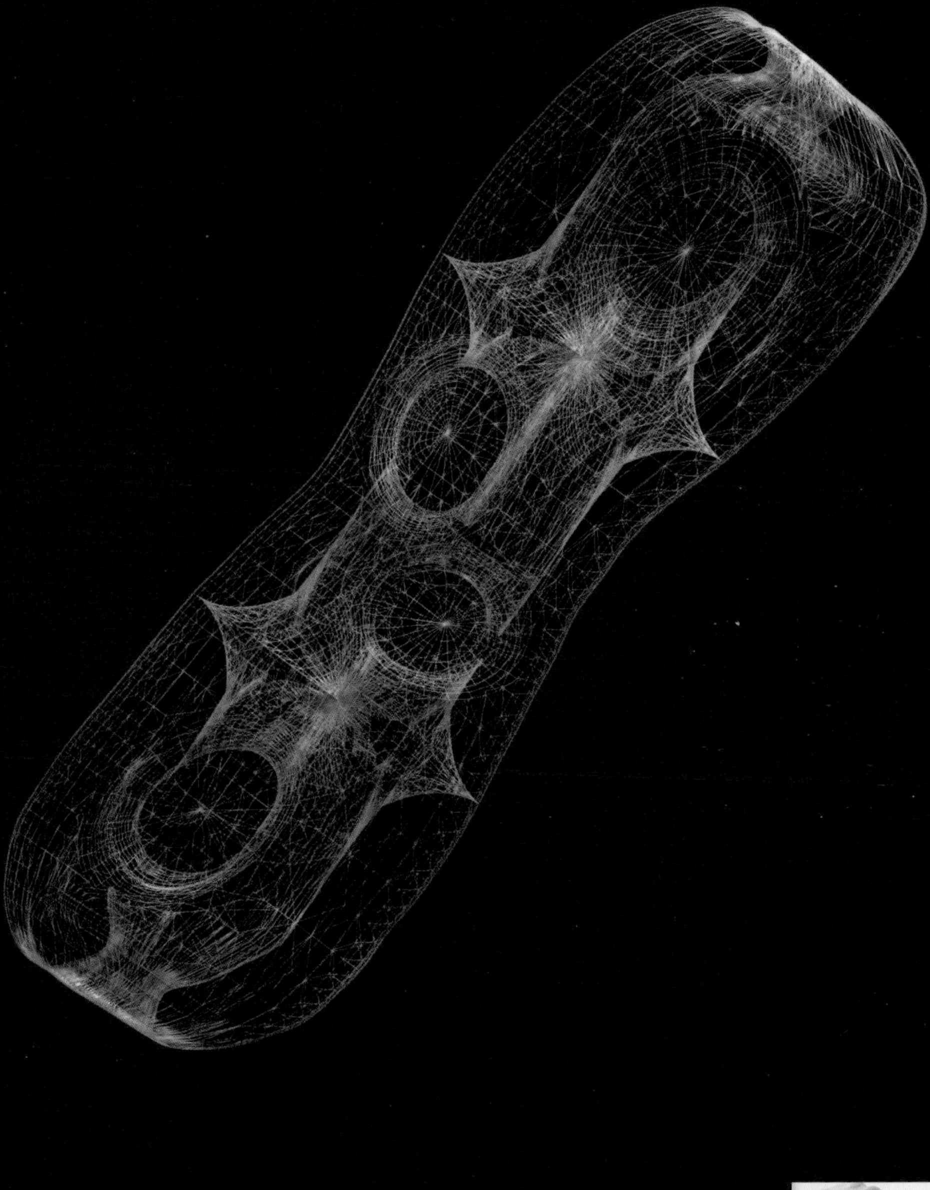

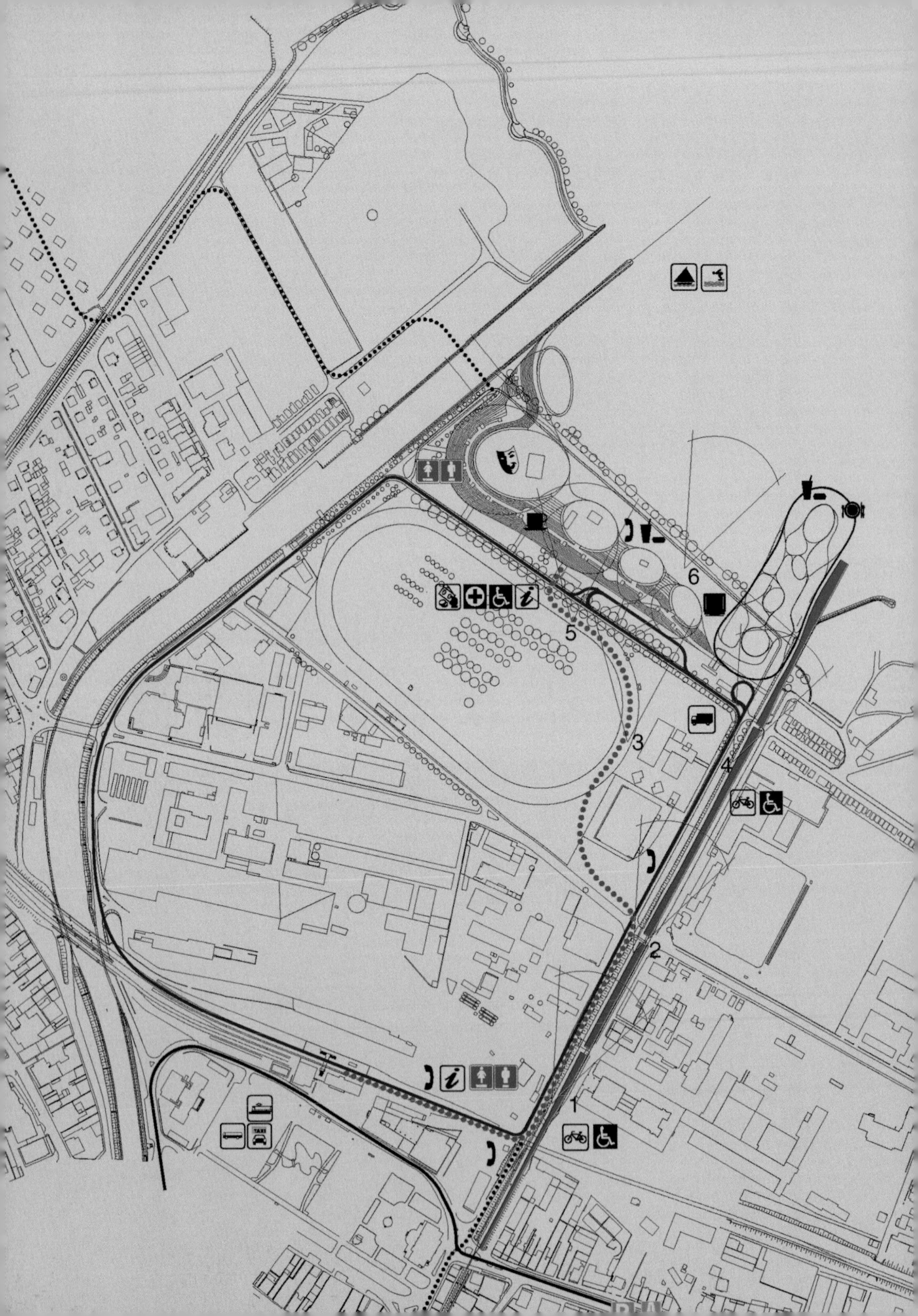
6
5
3
4
2
1

Expoparc with existing sports facilities and the Forum with its temporary construction. The Expoparc is conceived as an enlarged arena, with a continuous platform as a woven superstructure, which is only interrupted by the bubbles of specific events. The partially roofed platform of the Expoparc supports and facilities all activities. Variable circulations based on visitor duration are possible. The covered Forum proposes a double loop, spaced by event bubbles. Its constructional principle is that of the heleoid as a knot between three spheres.

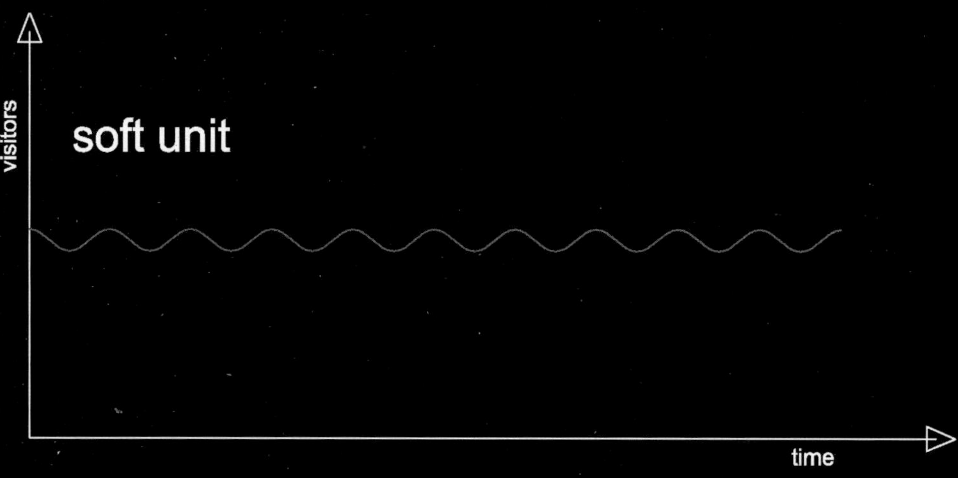

medium flow, flowing through, not controlled

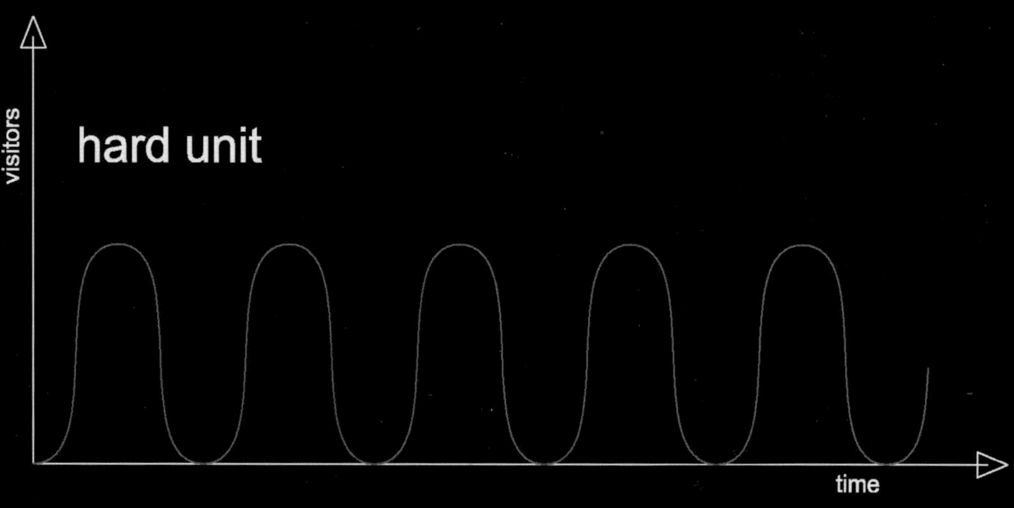

peak flow, pumping, controlled exits and entrances

the forum as many-body

Body, spirit and sexuality

Health

Switzerland, Europe and the Universe

Personal relations

Tourism, leisure and sports

time organisation by events

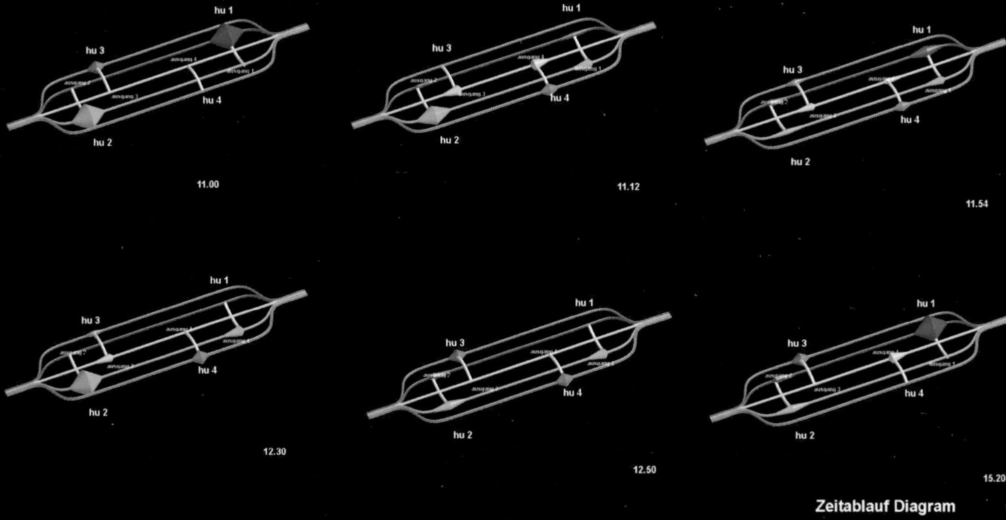

Zeitablauf Diagram

programme engineere

andscape

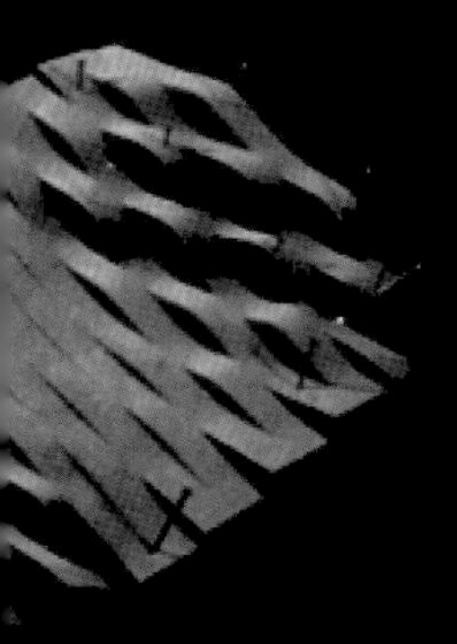

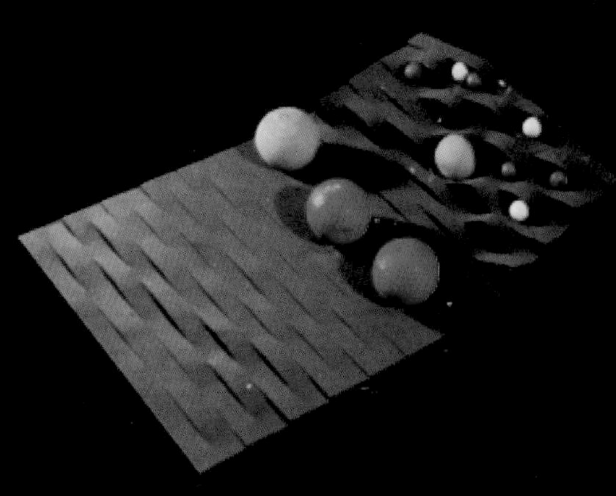

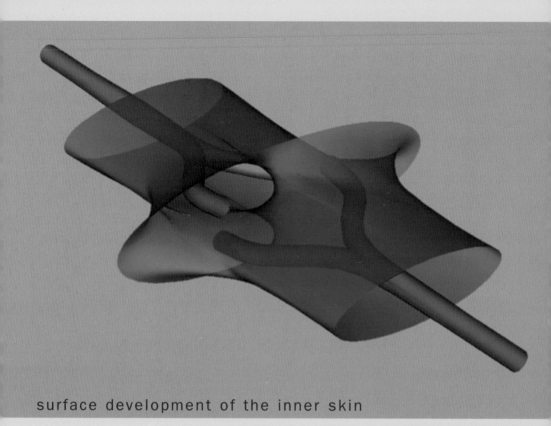

surface development of the inner skin

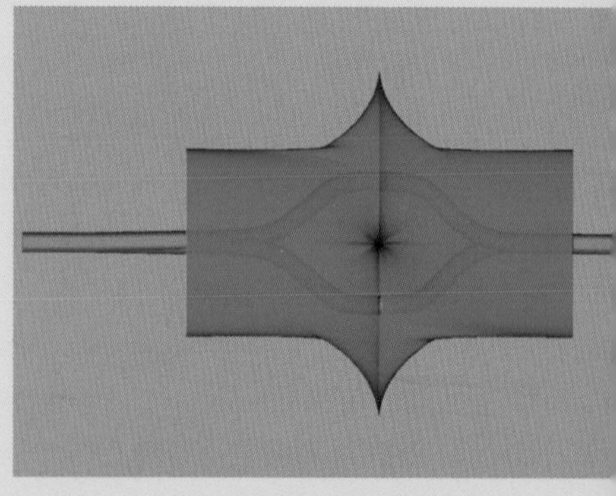

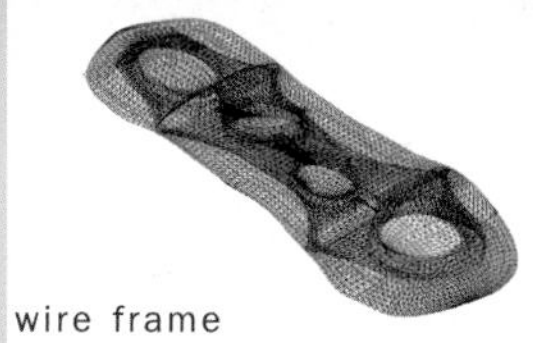
wire frame

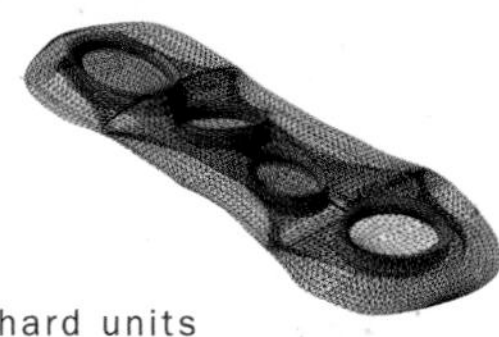
hard units

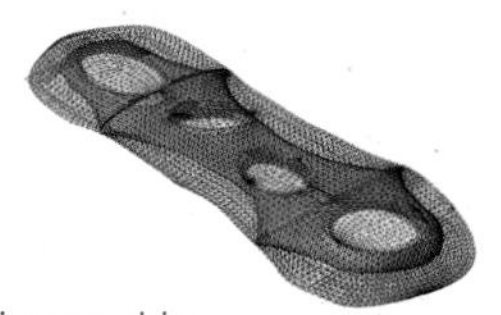
inner skin

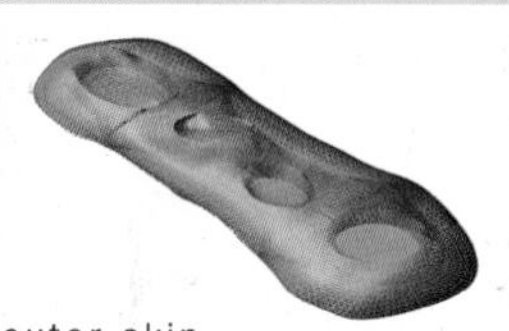
outer skin

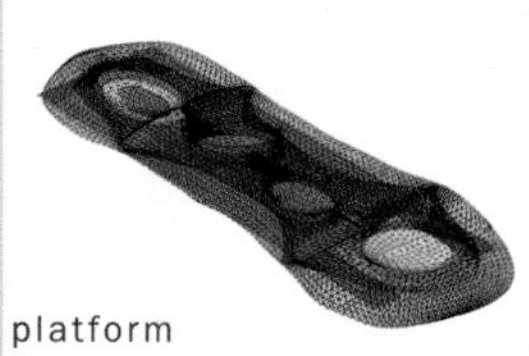
platform

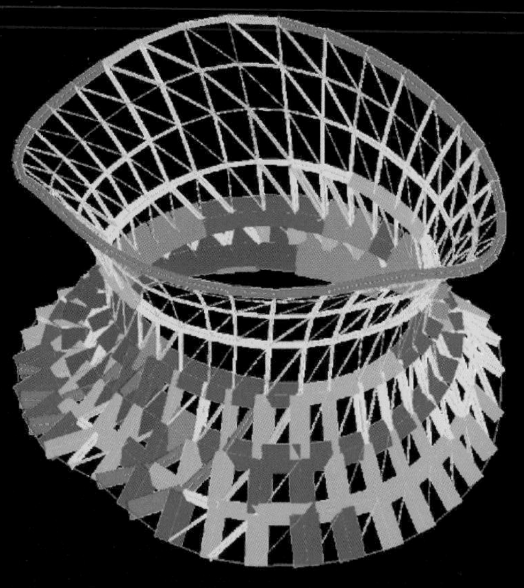

visualising forces

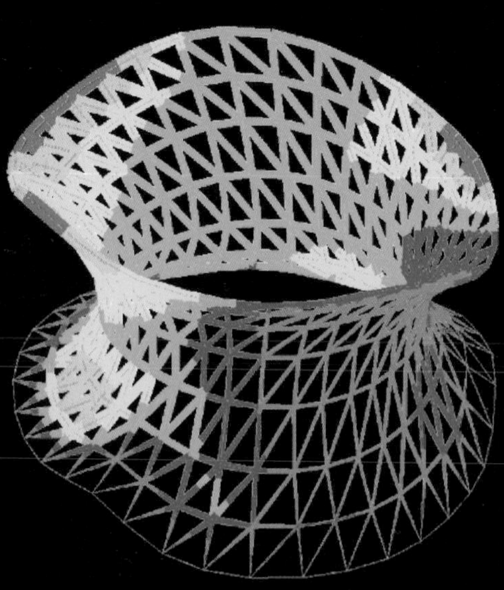

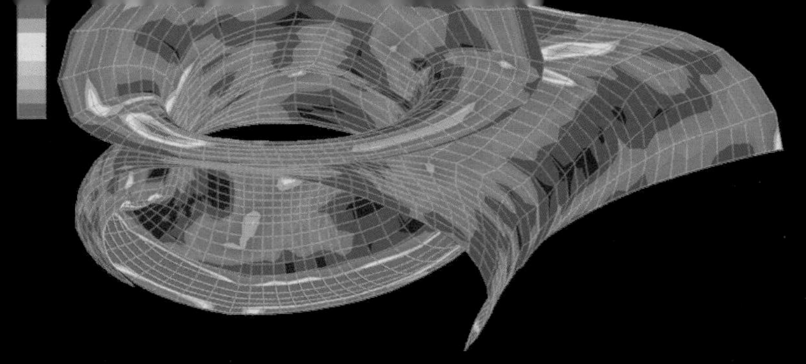

s t r u c t u r a l   w i r e f r a m e   a n d   s h e l l   m o d e l s

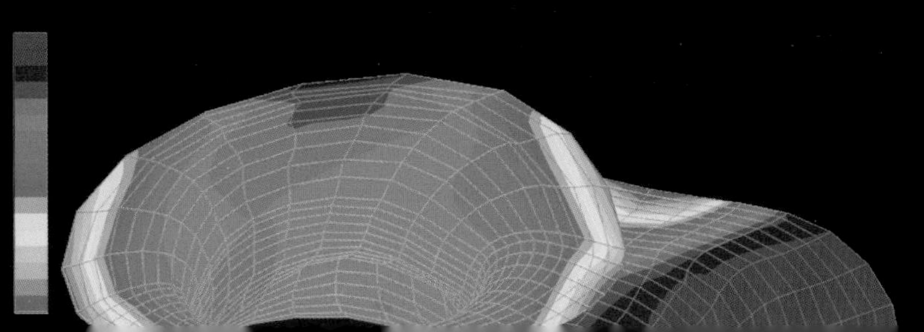

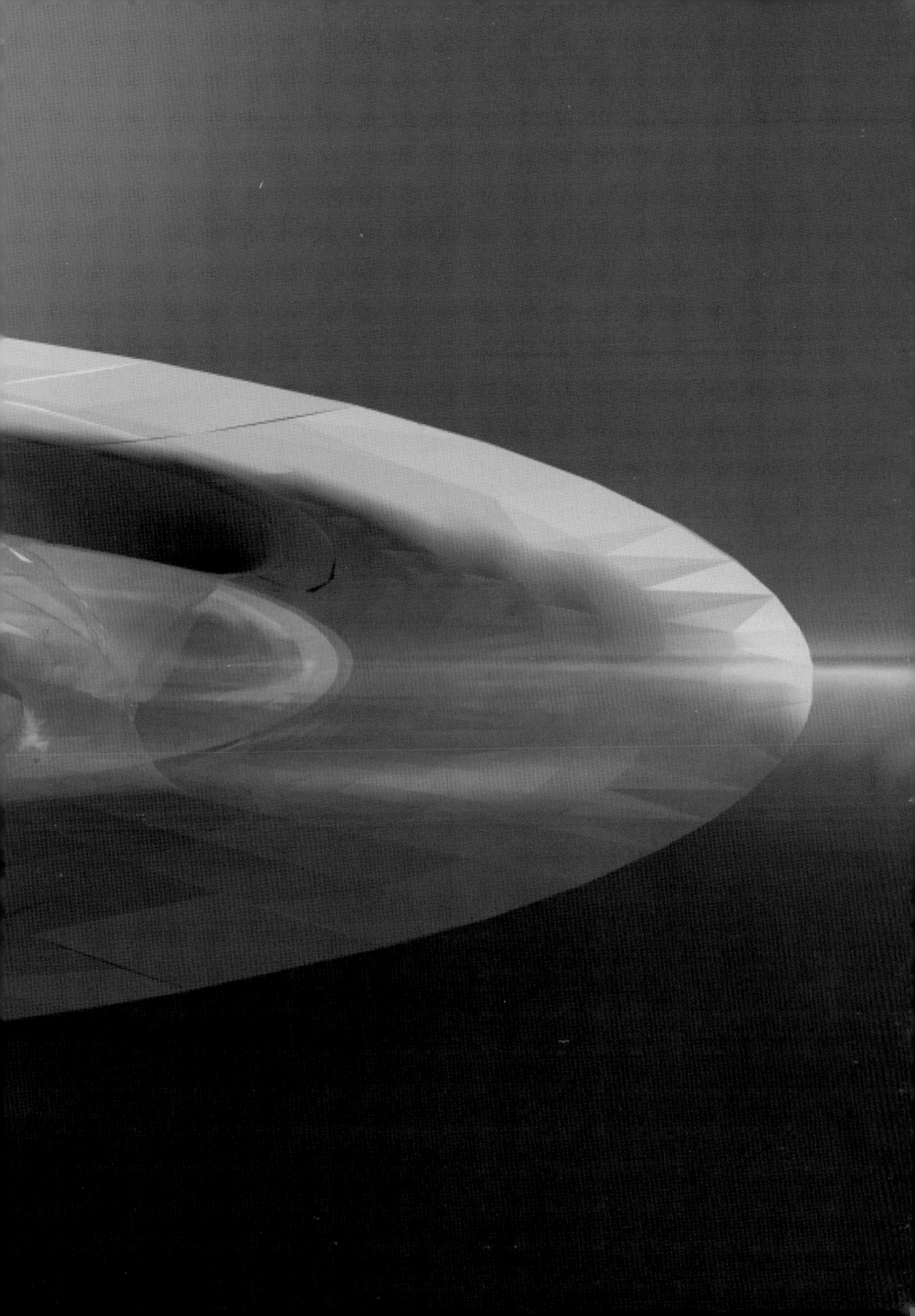

Project credits

Villa Wilbrink

Amersfoort 1992 - 1994

Client: *Mr. and Mrs. Wilbrink-Van den Berg*

Design team: *Ben van Berkel (architect), Aad Krom (project management), Paul van der Erve, Branimir Medic*

Building contractor: *Aannemersmaatschappij ABM, Amersfoort*

Constructor: *Bureau Bouwpartners, Hilversum*

Möbius House

Het Gooi 1993 - 1998

Client: *Anonymous*

Design team: *Ben van Berkel (architect), Aad Krom (project management), Jen Alkema, Matthias Blass, Caroline Bos, Remco Bruggink, Marc Dijkman, Casper le Fèvre, Rob Hootsmans, Tycho Soffree, Giovanni Tedesco, Harm Wassink*

Interior Design: *Ben van Berkel, Hans Kuyvenhoven, Jen Alkema, Matthias Blass*

Garden Design: *Adriaan Geuze, West 8 Landscape architects, Rotterdam*

Technical consultants: *ABT, Velp, Heijckmann Bouwadviesbureau, Huissen*

Building contractor: *Kemmeren Bouw, Aalsmeer*

Interior contractor: *Meubel & Interierbouw Wageningen BV*

Borneo Sporenburg

Amsterdam 1994 - 1998

Cient: *New Deal Projectontwikkeling, Amsterdam*

Design team: *Ben van Berkel (architect), Walther Kloet, Rob Hootsmans (project co-ordinators), Matthias Blass, Henri Snel, Jacco van Wengerden*

Building contractor: *V.o.f. De Realisatie, Almere*

Constructor: *Pieters Bouwtechniek, Amsterdam*

Technical consultants: *Adviesbureau T&H, Nieuwegein*

Port Terminal

Yokohama 1995

Design team: *Ben van Berkel (architect), Rob Hootsmans (project co-ordinator), Sanderijn Amsberg, Hugo Beschoor Plug, Henri Borduin, Caroline Bos, Hanna Euro, Casper le Fèvre, Cees van Giessen, Moriko Kira*

Concert Hall

Düsseldorf 1995 - 1996

Client: *Pan Bautrager GmbH*

Design team: *Ben van Berkel (architect), Rob Hootsmans (project co-ordinator), Florian Fischer*

Pavilion Triennial

Milan 1995 - 1996

Curator: *Ole Bouman*

Client: *Netherlands Architecture Institute, Rotterdam*

Design team: *Ben van Berkel (architect), Caspar Smeets (project co-ordinator), Caroline Bos, Remco Bruggink, Rob Hootsmans, Ger Gijzen, Freek Loos*
Structural engineering: *Ingenieursbureau Zonneveld, Rotterdam*
Technical realisation: *HBG, Amsterdam, Vandie Interieurbouw, Maarssen*
Art direction: *BRS Premsela Vonk, Amsterdam, René van Raalten*
Computer 3-D Modelling: *Cees van Giessen*

Dream House
Berlin 1996
Client: *Mr. and Mrs. Graalfs*
Design team: *Ben van Berkel (architect), Gianni Cito, Thomas Dürner, Astrid Schmeing*

Ethnological Museum
Geneva 1996
Design team: *Ben van Berkel (architect), Rob Hootsmans (project co-ordinator), Henri Borduin, Remco Bruggink, Gianni Cito, Roelof Krijgsman, Casper le Fèvre, Robert van Sprang, Hans Sterck*

Rubber Mat
Rotterdam 1995
Client: *Dienst Stedenbouw en Volkshuisvesting, Gemeente Rotterdam*
Design team: *Ben van Berkel (architect), Caroline Bos, Henk Jan Bultstra, Casper le Fèvre, Moriko Kira*

Hoogovens Triport
Beverwijk 1998
Client: *Project team Business Park Ymond*
Design team: *Ben van Berkel (architect), Aad Krom (project management), Igor Kebel, Ger Gijzen, Remko van Heummen, Walther Kloet, Jeroen Kreijne, Tobias Walisser*

Expo 2001
Yverdon-les-Bains 1998
Client: *Expo 0.1*
Design: *Ben van Berkel (UN Studio) in collaboration with Ove Arup & Partners*
Design team UN Studio: *Ben van Berkel (architect),Peter Trummer (design co-ordinator), Susanne Boyer, Olaf Gipser*
Contributors UN Studio: *Ludo Grooteman, Freek Loos, Laura Negrini, Mark Westerhuis*
Design Team Ove Arup: *Cecil Balmond, Charles Walker, Patrick Teuffel, Finola Reid (acoustics), Steve Jolly (installations), David Johnston (infrastructure)*
Contributors: *Rudi Fuchs (Stedelijk Museum Amsterdam), Claudia Gould (Artist Space, New York), Gerard-Jan Rijnders, Paul Gallis (Toneelgroep Amsterdam), Mark Cousins, Herbert Klimke*

Photo credits & information

p. 1 Weather movement, KNMI, De Bilt
p. 6 Move UN Studio, Sonja Cabalt; cheerleaders (1939); Tokyo by night, Sonja Cabalt.

Techniques

p. 14 Satellite, KNMI, De Bilt; Revolutionary neurological ear chip sending signals to the brain, M. Smith.
p. 16-17 from left to right: space technology, astronauts floating in space; medical technology, instrument that penetrates into veins to prevent arteriosclerosis; egg cell injected with sperm; CERN research centre (ALEPH), particle hunter catches collision debris, Patrick Landmann; demonstration of masturbation techniques with a piece of fruit, Japanese magazine; action painting, Jackson Pollock; Visual Human Project, computer animated model of a sliced human body, Internet; pressure points for acupuncture delineated on an ear; brain surgery using gamma radiation techniques, Presbyterian Academic Hospital in Pittsburgh, W. Mcnamee.

Diagrams

p. 18 exhibition in gallery Artists Space, New York 1996
p. 22-23 from left to right: computer chip; drops of sweat on skin, magnification x 40, R. Wehr; pattern of orbital pollution, N.L. Johnson, Teledyne Brown Engineering; music notation, S. Bussotti; flow around space shuttle; runaway herd, Photo researchers Inc.; blood clot trapped behind a web of fibrin, magnification x 4750, David Philips; SWOZ-project, section of facade, UN Studio
p. 24 Paradise files, Lars Spuybroek

Villa Wilbrink, Amersfoort

p. 26 bunker, type 98, p. 28 Klaus Kinhold, p. 29 various bunker types, p. 30 Sonja Cabalt, p. 32(left) Klaus Kinhold, p. 32 Hélène Binet, p. 32 (right) Jan Derwig, p. 34-36-39 Hélène Binet.

Möbius House, Het Gooi

p. 40 the fold in the soul, G. Deleuze, p. 43 lifestyle in the 50's, p. 50-51 Christian Richters, Ingmar Swalue, p. 52-53 Cristian Richters, Ingmar Swalue, p. 56 Christian Richters, p. 60 Christian Richters, Ingmar Swalue, p. 62 Ingmar Swalue, p. 64 Christian Richters, p. 66 Christian Richters, Ingmar Swalue, p. 68 Ingmar Swalue.

Borneo Sporenburg, Amsterdam

p. 73 construction site Borneo Sporenburg, Sonja Cabalt

Hybridization

p. 78 hybridization of world population, Kim Wah.
p. 81 Manimal, original art work by Daniel Lee.
p. 82-83 from left to right: iridescent satin, K. Yoshimura; Dirty Wendy, Inez van Lamsweerde; electric passage, railway bridge and shopping arcade, Momoyo Kaijma; siamese twin embryo preserved in nitric acid, D. Michener; hybridized broccoli; Michael Jackson, a major work in progress; Kiesler as Mies van der Rohe; Kiesler and Willem de Kooning; genetically manipulated mouse in laboratory, Inter topics.

p. 85 from left to right: Mechanical head 1920, Raoul Hausmann; Villa Savoye 1930, Le Corbusier; Self-portrait Bacon, Francis Bacon; Helix city 1961, Kisho Kurokawa; Manimal 1996, David Lee; diagram Hoogovens project 1998, UN Studio.

Port terminal, Yokohama

p. 87 inquiry into the behaviour of coloured streams in salt water, J. v. Heijst, University of Utrecht, p. 89 various garden structures.

Concert Hall, Düsseldorf

p. 100 Jan Derwig, p. 104 Mitra Linneaus shell, biologic columnless architecture.

Pavilion Triennial, Milan

p. 115 computer games, p. 116 computer 3-D Modelling: Cees van Giessen, p. 118 NASA training, R. Reyesmeier/Corbis, p. 124 BRS Premsela Vonk.

Dream House, Berlin

p. 129 'dream castles', p. 132 spiral Jetty, Robert Smithson, p. 127-136 Thomas Dürner.

Ethnological Museum, Geneva

p. 141 late-night pizza, Sonja Cabalt, p. 152 pyramids in Giza, Sonja Cabalt.

Mediation

p. 158 Architectural Association Diploma Unit 4, Operational design matrix, Ben van Berkel, Michael Hensel, Ludo Grooteman, Chris Dondorp (student), Danilo Dangubic (student).
p. 162-163 from left to right: aeroplane flying over Simpson Bay, L. Aubert; mobile telephones; capital of Mauritania, planned and unplanned structures, G. Gerster; satellites serving earth; media, 500 television channels shown at once; anti-Dialectic Library Competition proposal for ACADIA 1998 International Design Competition - Library for the Information Age, Mika Cimolini and Igor Kebel.

Rubber Mat, Rotterdam

p. 171 development of embryo, L. Nilsson, p. 174 Tsunehisa Kimura.

Hoogovens Triport, Beverwijk

p. 183 Hoogovens Business Park, Sonja Cabalt, p. 184 Engine of aeroplane, Sonja Cabalt.

Expo 2001, Yverdon-Les Bains

p. 197 mouse pad stuffed with silicon material
p. 199 from left to right: women on the beach; arrival of the Beatles, Ira Rosenberg; president Daniel Ortega, Nicaragua; empty dream, Mariko Mori; audience tennis match; Tai Chi, Luchinni; people flux in the rain, G. Gerster.
p. 200 foam party, N. Luhmann; Piano Americano, Vanessa Beercroft.

p. 222-223 Weather movement, KNMI, de Bilt

Colophon

First published June 1999
Reprinted December 1999

Text Ben van Berkel & Caroline Bos

Graphic design Sonja Cabalt (UN Studio)

Publisher UN Studio & Goose Press
Stadhouderskade 113
1073 AX Amsterdam
the Netherlands
++31(0)20-25702040
info@unstudio.com

Editorial assistants Sonja Cabalt, Machteld Kors, Francesca de Châtel

Translation Kate Simms

Printed by Rosbeek, the Netherlands
ISBN 90-76517-01-0

Trade distribution
Idea Books: world-wide
idea@xs4all.nl fax ++31(0)20-6209299
Architectura & Natura: the Netherlands

The article on Mediation is based on research which was made possible by a grant from the Stimuleringsfonds voor Architectuur, Rotterdam